Wellington's
CHARGE

Wellington's Charge

A PORTRAIT OF THE DUKE'S ENGLAND

—⚬—

BERWICK COATES

ROBSON BOOKS

This revised paperback edition first published in 2003 by Robson Books, The Chrysalis Building, Bramley Road, London W10 6SP
First published in Great Britain in 2002 by Robson Books, 64 Brewery Road, London N7 9NT

A member of **Chrysalis** Books plc

British Library Cataloguing in Publication Data
A catalogue record for this title is available from the British Library.

ISBN 1 86105 653 2

Maps by Stephen Dew
The illustrations on pages 1–6 of the picture section are courtesy of Chrysalis; those on pages 7–8 are courtesy of the Mary Evans Picture Library.

Typeset in Times by FiSH Books, London WC1
Printed in Great Britain by Creative Print and Design, Ebbw Vale, Wales

Contents

Bibliographical Note

This book does not push forward the boundaries of original research, but I like to think it might push forward the boundaries of understanding and enjoyment. It is the result of many years of reading, teaching, discussing, and pondering the subject. Rather like James Whistler with the painting of his mother, I have been working at it for a good part of my life. It is a picture, an impression. So every brush-stroke represents some nugget of information dug out from I don't know where over the years – documents, previous authors, conversations, lectures, conferences, radio programmes, students' classes, examination papers, examiners' comments, book reviews, and so on.

I have tried to check my facts, and I hope I have not said anything that is too outrageous or silly. I have also made clear, where possible or practicable, who said, or is supposed to have said, whatever small quotation I have used. I have repeated the occasional good story, a sequence or coincidence of events which I have come across somewhere, but I do not know whether the author in question discovered it for himself, or whether he in turn took it from somebody else. So I hope I can not be accused of stealing anybody's thunder. If something is worth passing on, it is worth passing on – as long as the writer does not try to claim the original discovery for himself.

So the paint and the canvas are not mine. What is mine is the pattern of brushstrokes with which I have built the portrait – which only I could have done, and for which I must take the responsibility.

Introduction

There were several royal dukes in England after 1815, but, when people mentioned 'the Duke', everyone knew who was being talked about. It was Arthur Wellesley, first Duke of Wellington. This instant recognition was a measure of his enormous stature.

In order to understand this rare man, it is necessary to understand the country he served. England was his cause, his love, his master, and his responsibility, and he served it unswervingly for the whole of his long active life. Hence the parameters of the book – from the 1780s, when young Arthur first entered the Army, to 1851, when, as 'the Duke', he attended the opening of the Great Exhibition, on his 82nd birthday, sixteen months before he died. In between, he became his country's greatest soldier (with the possible exception of the Duke of Marlborough) and one of its most authoritative person-alities. He was the only professional soldier to serve also as Prime Minister. He enjoyed (and deserved) a unique level of deference and respect from people, politicians, and royalty. They may not always have liked him, or savoured his advice, but they trusted him.

In his sixty-odd years of service, he saw enormous changes – most of which he deplored – revolution, industrialisation, the reform of Parliament, the beginnings of welfare legislation, concession in Ireland, the rise of free trade. Having survived the cannons of Waterloo, he lived to see a Cabinet colleague run over by a railway train. Throughout those years, regardless of fad or fashion, crisis or doldrum, invasion threat or party split, he saw himself as a servant of the Crown – at a time when scandal and ridicule threatened to engulf it.

In order explain how and why he reacted to the events which faced him, I think it is necessary to set out the main features of the country's history during that time, and to offer some background material as well. I try to answer some of the questions that are not often explicitly addressed. How did this tiny island beat the giant of Napoleonic France? Why did we have, and need, the biggest navy in the world? How did we lose one empire and gain another? Why did we have an industrial revolution? And why did we have it first? What is foreign policy, and how did we get ours? What was the Eastern Question? Why has Ireland been such a problem for so long?

In this analysis will be found themes that echo today: Ireland, of course, a war in Afghanistan, the powers of the House of Lords, odd treatment of British subjects by the Greek Government. A constant motif is England's role *vis-à-vis* Europe – do we really belong or don't we? How do we clean up our cities? How do we fight crime? How do we protect people from disease? What do we do about our Royal Family? If you think today's Royal Family is the butt of gossip and insult, you should read what they thought of George III, George IV, and William IV – a periodic idiot, a roll-fat hedonist, and an uncouth dullard with a string of bastards. Yet royalty survived. And it survived partly because men like the Duke of Wellington served it without question. Not without grumbling – true – but certainly without question.

The format of the book is primarily narrative, with each chapter based on half a decade. I pause only to explain a complicated problem, to highlight an individual character, or to tell a good story. I maintain that anybody is potentially interested in history; we all want to know where we come from. I maintain too that readers will appreciate the care of an author who takes the trouble to go right back to square one, and that they relish the meat of an explanation that goes beyond square two. A seasoning of humour helps as well. I maintain – I am constantly surprised at the number of things I maintain – that there is no end to what people will tackle if they feel that the author is on their side, and, above all, has a smile on his face.

Finally – for those who do not need much explanation, for those who have been here before, for those who know better – let me make clear at the outset that this is, as it says in the title, a portrait: a view, an impression. Almost an invitation. I do not claim to 'do' England between 1782 and 1851. I do not claim to 'do' the Duke either, if it comes to that. Rather I hope that a reading of this book will be an enjoyable experience, and that it will stimulate further enquiry. If this further enquiry turns out to show that the book is wrong, at least it will prove that the book provoked the effort to do so, and thereby deepened interest and understanding – to say nothing of the pleasure to be derived from catching out an author in error.

CHAPTER ONE

The Schoolboy Prime Minister
1782–88

On 20 March, 1782, London had a freak late snowstorm. On that day too the King's chief minister, Lord North, announced his resignation. England had lost her American colonies; Lord North and his Government were held responsible. They had bungled the war. They had caused professional armies to be defeated by ill-equipped gangs of undisciplined backwoodsmen. The Americans had committed treason: they had raised arms against their sovereign lord King George III – and they had got away with it.

North might point out that it was difficult to conduct a war three thousand miles away with communications as slow as a sailing ship battling against westerly gales in the Atlantic. He might complain that France, then Spain, then Holland had joined the Americans, and thereby given even the mighty Navy too much to cope with. He could try to blame his difficulties on the refusal of Denmark, Sweden, and Russia to trade with England in vital shipping supplies. Excuses were not enough. Thirteen valuable colonies had been lost, whole armies had been forced to surrender, generals had been disgraced, all before the eyes of the world. The situation was intolerable. England *lose* a war? It was unheard of. It was almost unfair.

Lord North's ministry shook, cracked, and finally crumbled before the tidal wave of criticism and outrage. Nor was His Majesty left untouched; it was darkly suggested that part of the trouble had been caused by George's interference in the running of government. The King's power was becoming too great. This was a sensitive topic to a ruling class proud of its parliamentary freedom. In the last 140 years England had already executed one king, expelled another, and compelled a third to sign a contract with her elected representatives before she gave him the crown. (This interpretation may not be in line with that of modern historians, but it was what many Englishmen at the time firmly believed, and it was contemporary Englishmen, not historians, who bemoaned the King's 'interference' and howled for North's dismissal.)

George had clung stubbornly to North for twelve years. He had paid North's debts on the understanding that North would serve as his chief minister. Despite North's frequent requests to be released, George held him to his bargain. North after all was a likeable man, and a good handler of the House of Commons. (Although North was a 'lord', it was only a courtesy title; his father was still alive and held the earldom of Guilford in the House of Lords. North sat in the Commons.)

The alternative was awful. George did not like Whigs. Indeed, when he was finally forced to accept the fact that North really would have to go, he considered abdication rather than appoint as one of his ministers the hated, the unspeakable Charles James Fox. The strain on him was such that some observers feared another disturbance of His Majesty's mind.

In the event George did not go mad; losing the American colonies turned out not to be the end of the world; the French were at least put in their rightful place of defeat by Admiral Rodney's late victory in the West Indies at the Battle of the Saints. Moreover, the alleged villain of the piece, the amiable Lord North, had the last laugh. He had always kept his sense of humour, and was able to indulge it on the very day of his downfall. His announcement that His Majesty had at last accepted his resignation took the House of Commons by surprise, and brought the sitting to an unexpectedly early end.

As the honourable members huddled and stamped outside in the snow, waiting for drivers to be dug out of taverns and coaches to be brought up, Lord North strolled through them straight to his own coach, which was standing ready. He put his foot on the step and turned to smile at his shivering opponents. 'You see what it is, gentlemen,' he said, 'to be in the secret.'

The Opposition leaders now had their best opportunity for years, yet within twenty-one months most of them were back in opposition, some in disgrace. The King's power had triumphed. The new Prime Minister, his own choice, was a newcomer of twenty-four, who was to remain in office for the next seventeen years, during which time the Whig following in the Commons was to shrink to a mere fifty or so. How had it happened? What had gone wrong?

To begin with, it is a mistake to think of a Parliamentary Opposition in the eighteenth century in terms of a Parliamentary Opposition in the twenty-first. Nowadays it means a large group of MPs, usually one of the two big parties, highly organised and highly disciplined, the members of which behave, speak, and vote according to strict policies and instructions laid down by their party leaders. As WS Gilbert put it cheekily a hundred-odd years ago, they 'always voted at [their] party's call, and never thought of thinking for [themselves] at all'. An eighteenth-century Opposition could be made up of any number of groups, both large and small, with no overall organisation whatever. There was no leader, no discipline, no policy. It was very rare for them all to be in disagreement with the Government at the same time. Indeed one of the reasons why governments in the eighteenth century never lost an election was that their opponents were often in far greater dispute with each other than they were with the ministry of the day. In short, a modern Parliamentary Opposition means everyone who is *opposed* to the Government; two hundred years ago it meant simply everyone was *not in* the Government.

The Government itself would be made up of various groups, or factions, as they are often called. Each faction usually had a leader in the House of Lords, and he could call on the support of so many members of the House of Commons. If a leader of a particular faction died, or left the Government through disagreement with his colleagues, or was dismissed by the King, the Government then offered a Cabinet post and other offices to a faction that commanded enough seats in the Commons to enable the Government to maintain a working majority. A huge majority was not usually necessary; it did not pay to have too many factions on the Government side, because there were not enough Cabinet posts and jobs and pensions to go round.

So North took his personal following with him into opposition, and the great game of political checks and balances began. One by one the Whig Opposition factions failed when they at last gained office. The leader of the biggest one, the Marquis of Rockingham, died (of influenza, in July!), leaving his group weakened and divided. Fox ruined another chance by quarrelling with Shelburne. Shelburne in turn could not command enough confidence among his colleagues. Fox lowered his reputation further by joining forces with, of all people, Lord North, whom he had spent years criticising in the most bitter manner. All might have been well if they had only enjoyed the support of the King. George, however, merely tolerated them, and did that only with difficulty. They annoyed him still more by attempting to challenge his rights over the selection of ministers, and the Fox–North coalition committed a bigger error by trying to increase the income of the Prince of Wales to an outrageous £100,000 per year. George had always been convinced that Fox was to a large extent responsible for helping to turn his eldest son into a rake and a wastrel.

George, then, watched and waited, and allowed the Whigs to make one mistake after another. In the meantime, he cast about for someone to fill the gap left in his plans by the 'desertion', as he viewed it, of North. He found his man at the end of 1783. He found his opportunity too, for the Fox–North coalition brought in a new India Bill. The bill proposed to take control of British possessions in India out of the hands of the East India Company and place them with seven commissioners appointed by the Government. By a suspicious coincidence, all seven commissioners just happened to be followers of Fox and North. George could not prevent the bill passing the Commons, but he could, and did, bring pressure to bear on the Lords. Through Lord Temple, he informed their lordships, unofficially but unmistakably, that anyone who voted for Mr Fox's India Bill would no longer be his 'friend'. It was breaking the rules, or at least bending them, for a monarch to interfere as directly as this in the workings of Parliamentary power, but then Fox had broken, or bent, them as well by his attempts to interfere in the workings of Royal power, so he could hardly complain. Whatever the rights and wrongs, enough peers in North's group took the hint, and the bill was defeated.

George now turned to his new man, who took office on 18 December, 1783. However, the struggle was not yet over. Fox's supporters could still outvote the new Ministry in the Commons, and taunted it with jibes about mince pies and being swallowed up and gone by the end of Christmas. The Prime Minister was an unbelievable twenty-four years old, a mere schoolboy by political standards.

But the new Prime Minister had a magical name – William Pitt. His father, the Elder Pitt – later the Earl of Chatham – had been England's greatest war minister. In one of the country's dark hours, when the current war against France was going badly, he had announced, 'I know that I can save this country, and that no one else can.' It was not conceit, or vain boasting; he meant it as a cold statement of fact. Appointed Secretary of State in 1757, he had proceeded to do exactly what he had promised. Under his dynamic leadership, English soldiers and sailors, and their allies in Germany, had defeated the French all over the world, and snatched glittering colonial prizes in Canada, India, Africa, and the West Indies. By 1761, he was out of office again. The new young King, George III, did not find him easy to get on with. Neither, for that matter, did most other politicians. He was proud, moody, impatient, and scalding in his criticism. Indeed the violent extremes of his bursting enthusiasm and bleak depression often pushed him to the borders of insanity. By any standards he was difficult. But his record of achievement between 1757 and 1761 had been matched by no other minister, nor as a public speaker did he have an equal. On his day, that hawklike figure could make his audience believe that his was the voice of Destiny. One eyewitness after another declared that the effect of reading his speeches afterwards in cold print was worlds apart from the pin-drop spell he could cast upon the House of Commons when he was in full spate.

This, then, was the extraordinary man who had fathered another prodigy, it seemed, in 1759, when young William, his second son, was born. Even allowing for the oddities of a private education in the eighteenth century, it must have been an unusual boy who could write regular letters to his father at the age of seven, in Latin. He was at Cambridge before he was fifteen, and an MP at 21. He had already held office as Chancellor of the Exchequer before George offered him the premiership at the end of 1783. It says a great deal for his self-confidence, if nothing else, that he considered it, never mind accepted.

He soon showed that he was a good deal more than a cocky young man with a famous name. Intellectually, he had no superior. As a debater he was quick and clever, and skilful at knocking the bottom out of false arguments. Without the theatrical magic of his father, perhaps, but he possessed the family knack of making members listen to him. He had a poise and judgment beyond his years. His self-control became legendary, at a time when public behaviour could be more flamboyant and outspoken than would be acceptable now. Stiff, shy, and aloof, Pitt and his poker face puzzled friends and baffled opponents.

Oddly, his very youth and 'newness' were in themselves a recommendation. Many people now felt that the loss of the American colonies had shown up not only Lord North, but the whole system of government, the whole generation of politicians. There was a sudden fit of disgust about the entire atmosphere of faction squabbles, backstairs intrigue, seedy bargains, pension-grubbing, jobs for the boys, bribery, corruption, and self-seeking. Pitt was too young to be a part of this. He was the new broom who would sweep everything clean. All kinds of reformers and crusaders were attracted to his side. Those who hoped to change the corrupt system of 'pocket boroughs', whereby whole parliamentary constituencies could be bought and sold like furniture, looked to him for support. Religious reformers who wished to relax the unfair laws against Nonconformists hoped to gain his sympathy. Critics of the British rule in India sought his attention. William Wilberforce, the champion of all slaves, was his best friend. The possibilities were endless. Good heavens! He might even get around to doing something for Ireland.

Pitt already enjoyed the support of the City of London, with its huge mercantile interests, partly because his father had brought them so much profitable imperial trade, partly because Fox's India Bill had offended them.

His biggest ally was, understandably, the King. Fox might outvote Pitt in the Commons and clamour for his resignation, but Pitt could afford to hang on because he knew he had royal power, influence, and favour behind him. Nevertheless, with constant Parliamentary defeat, it was an unhappy time, and brought out of him yet one more quality which he was to show in full measure in the years to come – his courage.

Luckily, too, Fox blundered from one mistake to another. He refused Pitt's generous offer to join him in office. Then his supporters were involved in some jostling of Pitt's coach. He at once disclaimed all knowledge of it, but public opinion set the incident against him. His regular defeats of Pitt in the Commons made it clear that he was intent merely on causing trouble, and public opinion swung further. Fox seemed to be casting all judgment to the winds. As the weeks and months of early 1784 passed, his majority steadily fell. The Opposition, rarely united and never for long, began to splinter as more and more waverers realised that Pitt was going to stay. Career politicians and promotion-hunters saw that there was no future with Fox, however charming his friendship and exciting his oratory.

When the Whig majority was down to one, Pitt and the King felt that the time was ripe to test the opinion of the country.

The general election of April, 1784 was a traditional eighteenth-century-type election. Barely one in twenty of the male population voted. There was no secret ballot; voters could therefore be bribed or frightened. Those who were servants or tenants of the man who owned the constituency did as they were told if they valued their job or their house. Many constituencies had no contest, because there was only one candidate. Most of the new industrial towns had no candidate at all, because there was no seat for them. Many old constituencies with only a handful of voters returned two MPs. Polling was spread over several days, and was the occasion, or the excuse, for celebrating, eating, drinking, brawling, and carrying on generally. Leading politicians regularly poured fortunes into this stew of jobbery, graft, and intrigue, until despairing reformers wondered how any honesty or sincerity could possibly survive untainted.

However, in the 1784 election, for once, it did. Public opinion at last had its chance to express itself about the loss of America and the bungling of second-rate politicians. Pitt moreover was a name they knew and respected. The glamorous Duchess of Devonshire, who toured Fox's constituency in Westminster selling kisses for votes, traded her favours in vain. Fox's Whigs were resoundingly defeated. It is also arguable that the declared interest of the King, the hard work of Mr John Robinson (at the Treasury) drawing up detailed lists of possible supporters *before* taking the risk of an election, and £193,000 of Treasury money probably had something to do with it. Whatever the reasons, the Whigs were out, and the Tories were in.

Another era, albeit a less notorious one, also came to an end early in 1784. Arthur Wesley, the third surviving son of the late Lord Mornington, was taken away from Eton, aged only fifteen. His widowed mother had to find money for the education of his two younger brothers, and Arthur had not dazzled anyone with his Latin scholarship, least of all herself; she was wont to refer to him as 'my blockhead of a son'.

So it seemed a happy release, at least for the time being – though he continued to treasure Eton stories, like the one about the maids' dormitory, which was customarily described by the boys as 'the Virgins' bower'.

The years from 1784 to 1789 can be misleading, because of the tendency we have to be wise after the event. Because England now entered upon a period when her economy improved, her government stabilised, and her reputation rose, we tend to take it for granted that this was almost bound to happen. By the same token, because France had a revolution in 1789, we are inclined to think of all events in France in the 1780s as either causing or foreshadowing revolution. This is not necessarily true. Because certain events in history took place, it does not follow that they ought to have taken place, or that men at the time expected them to take place.

On the face of it, for example, France was the last country where a contemporary observer might have expected revolution. She had just won a war. Her economy, though it had its weaknesses, was stronger than that of Spain, Prussia, Austria, or Russia. Paris was the cultural centre of Europe, the home of high fashion, good taste, wit, and talent. True, there were some things seriously wrong, and a few sharp critics were beginning to comment on them; but even when the Bastille was stormed in July, 1789, no one could have foreseen the world-shattering changes that were to follow in the next few years – the abolition of feudalism, the nationalisation of the Church, the deposition and execution of the King and Queen; the new systems of legal procedure and of local government; the over-zealous reform of the calendar; the Declaration of the Rights of Man; the opening of any rank in any career to pure talent rather than to birth and family; the Reign of Terror, and the carrying of war into almost every country in Europe.

Conversely, it was England which had the reputation in the early 1780s for instability. In June 1780 the Gordon Riots had occurred, when for four days a wild anti-Catholic mob terrorised London. Chapels and houses were pillaged and burned; Newgate jail was demolished; Parliament itself was briefly besieged. Order was not restored until the crowd broke into a distillery and drank itself to a standstill. When burst casks spewed their contents into the gutters, crazed wretches flung themselves down to lap raw spirits from between the cobbles. The Government was forced to call out soldiers, and the capital was treated to the rare sight of cavalry charging up Downing Street.

Then came the shameful loss of the American colonies, and the undignified shufflings of factions for power in Parliament. India was being misgoverned, and ministers always dreaded news from Ireland because it was so often bad.

The most optimistic observer could hardly have foreseen that England would remain the one permanent bastion of resistance to French revolution, French war, and French conquest for more than twenty years. Nor could anyone have imagined the growth of empire, the expansion of industry, the explosion of population, the hugely increased volume of trade, the advance to an unchallengeable position as a first-rank power in international affairs.

It would have needed imagination indeed. An English chief minister in 1784 could not move for problems. There was the obvious one of money, or rather the lack of it. The war in America had cost about £100,000,000. Control of profitable American markets had been lost. Huge sums were paid out every year to holders of Government pensions, and sinecures ('jobs' that brought fat salaries for little work to men who were prepared in return to present themselves at the House of Commons, whenever required, in order to vote as the Government directed them). A large navy had to be maintained to protect the coasts, the empire (what was left of it), and the trade routes. There was the day-to-day running of Government departments, the diplomatic service, and the Army. Customs and Excise costs were high; smuggling was a thriving business. The Royal Household's bills had to be met. The Royal Family was not extravagant by the standards of the time, but it was certainly numerous – nine sons and six daughters. The Prince of Wales, moreover – the one exception to the family's thrift – ran up gambling debts that became a public scandal.

The Empire was in a bad way. American was gone; could Canada be next? They were very close, and the disease of revolution could be highly infectious. The germ, it was feared, might also contrive to cross the Atlantic and cause open war in Ireland, and rebellion could not come much closer to home than that. Any sane, patriotic Englishman could tell you that the average Irish peasant was a shiftless, uncouth, lying Papist who regarded violence as natural as breathing. India badly needed reform; the Governor-General, Warren Hastings, was the centre of a storm of criticism and controversy. Finally, there was the odd little problem of convicts. Now that they could not be transported to the American colonies, where on earth (quite literally) were they to go?

The foreign situation was just as depressing. The old enemy, France, was elated with her recent victory. The other two great naval and colonial powers in Europe, Spain and Holland, had been her allies. In the not-so-distant Seven Years' War, Austria had been England's enemy, and was still unofficially allied to France. Indeed it had not been long since an Austrian princess had made her way to Paris to become the wife of the new young King, Louis XVI. (The world was to hear more of Marie Antoinette.) England had once possessed an ally in Frederick the Great of Prussia, but he had bitterly resented her decision to withdraw from the war in 1762, leaving him to deal alone with the combined might of Austria, France, and Russia. Frederick, now crabbed and ageing, saw no reason to change his mind; England had a bad reputation in Europe for backing out of alliances when it suited her. In distant, chilly St. Petersburg, the wily Empress Catherine disliked the English Navy's annoying habit in time of war of searching neutral ships for 'contraband', and had formed the Armed Neutrality with Denmark and Sweden to try to stop it. She knew too that England would never agree to her ambitious designs to conquer Greece and put Russian warships in the Mediterranean.

To the crowned heads of Europe, the English in 1784 were an impossible people whose pride had just been dealt a blow they richly deserved. Their government was rickety, which was no more than you could expect with their stupid idea of parliamentary democracy. It served them right for having elections and allowing every ignorant oaf to interfere in politics. Their chief minister was a highly-strung youth, and their King was rumoured to be a periodic lunatic.

Within ten years the situation had been changed out of all recognition, and the man chiefly responsible was Pitt. His gifts, though different from his father's, were just as great. Fellow-MPs freely acknowledged that he was not merely a chip off the old block, but 'the old block itself'. For sheer brain power, no colleague or rival could touch him. He worked long hours. He never minded the drudgery of office routine. He actually enjoyed subjects like political economy, taxation, and finance. In an age of universal political racketeering, he was totally incorruptible. It was customary, for instance, for the chief minister to accept a sinecure known as the Clerkship of the Pells, worth £3,000 per year. Nobody would have raised an eyebrow if Pitt had done so. (Pells were skins, parchments. The Government office of 'the Pells' was the place where two rolls of parchment were kept, one recording Exchequer receipts, the other recording disbursements. All very ancient and traditional. So the Clerkship of the Pells – the guardianship of these venerable documents – was not exactly onerous.) Pitt turned it down. He could not be pushed, bribed, bought, or frightened. He was completely dedicated to his work. He had no interests outside politics; he never married, and he had no known love affairs. His only weakness was a fondness for port, but that was common to most 'gentlemen' of the day. All his life he remained above, or at least outside, petty party squabbles. He was a Tory, and admitted as much; but before that he saw himself as the King's chief minister. His job, quite simply, was to make the country run as cheaply and as efficiently as possible.

He had no fancy theories, and no blind beliefs; he treated each problem just as it came.

Take his handling of tea smuggling. A lesser man might have enlarged the Customs Service, or imposed stiffer penalties on those who were caught. Pitt simply lowered the tea import duty from 112 per cent to 25 per cent. At one stroke he cut his costs and put many smugglers straight out of business. To make up for the loss in customs revenue he revived, and extended the tax on, of all things, windows. It was childishly simple; you could not hide windows, and those with the most windows – that is, with the biggest houses – were just the ones who could most afford to pay. He was also one jump ahead of the tax-dodgers, those who craftily had several of their windows bricked up; he put a tax on bricks too.

He took advantage of the simple and obvious fact that the most profitable people to tax were the rich. (A rich man today could argue, with a certain amount of justification, that a modern government made considerable inroads into his bank balance – unearned income tax, supertax, capital gains tax, death duties. In the eighteenth century this did not apply. The rich had a freedom to enjoy their wealth beyond a modern tax exile's wildest dreams.) Pitt decided to make use of luxuries; in the course of the next few years, he imposed taxes on dogs, horses, hackney carriages, servants, clocks, watches, hats, ribbons, and hairpowder. He also tried taxes on 'everyday' things like candles, tiles, paper, and shops.

Or again, instead of trying to improve the nation's morals by preaching against the national passion for gambling, he attempted to make money out of it by running a national lottery. It was not particularly profitable as it turned out, but it did have the useful advantage of bringing in money some time before it was necessary to pay out on prizes, and so provided him with convenient funds to tide the Government over awkward moments.

Pitt was skilful, too, at doing things so quietly and so gradually that you hardly noticed that anything was happening until it was nearly all over. If, for example, he had publicised a campaign against corruption, he would have brought into being a solid wall of opposition. Instead, he simply waited; and, as each holder of a Government sinecure or pension died, he made it a practice not to appoint another one, and took the spare money back into the Treasury. Slowly, inch by inch, pound by pound, he cut wastage. He trimmed an expense here; he did away with a luxury there; he sorted out a costly tangle somewhere else. Each single incident might be boringly insignificant, but the cumulative, long-term effect of scores of such instances produced something little short of an unseen administrative revolution.

Like Disraeli much later, Pitt was a believer in the idea that politics was the art of what is possible. If he set out to make any change, and found that the opposition was tougher than he had bargained for, he would rarely turn the issue into a major trial of strength. In 1785, he proposed to disfranchise – that is, remove the MPs from – thirty-six 'rotten' boroughs where the number of voters had fallen scandalously low, but gave up in the face of loud criticism. The same year, he made some suggestions for improving Irish trade in the hope that it might ease the tense political situation there, but was surprised by the bitterness of Whig opposition, and gave way again. He spoke on the same side as Fox in a debate to try to secure greater religious freedom for Nonconformists, but Anglican prejudice was too entrenched, and the bill to repeal the Test and Corporation Acts failed. In deference to his friend Wilberforce, he spoke against the slave trade, but West Indian plantation interests were too well represented in the House, and the gruesome market in black ivory continued.

Pitt returned to his daily routine, where he could pursue his passion for economy without having to justify every decision to a noisy group of contentious Foxites.

He did, however, take two steps into the unknown, which were to have far greater effects than he could have foreseen at the time, and both came in 1786. In that year the answer was found to the question of where to send convicts now that America was no longer available. After listening to suggestions about north-western Canada, Tristan da Cunha, the Gold Coast, and Newfoundland, the Government made up its mind. Accordingly, in May, 1787, eleven ships left Portsmouth, and nine months later dumped 736 convicts in Botany Bay – the first of 160,000 over the next seventy years – prisoners of His Majesty. The initials on the back of their convict garb – 'POHM' – were to give rise to the first piece of Australian slang about England.

In that year too Pitt, or rather his representative, William Eden, signed a trade treaty with the French. It says a lot for Pitt's broadmindedness that he was prepared, less than three years after a war, to sign an agreement that allowed freedom of movement in both countries without passports. There were many noblemen in England who still regarded France as the 'natural enemy', and to most ordinary folk the French were little more a dirty lot of downtrodden Papist frog-eaters. Pitt had no time for such threadbare prejudices. He wanted to improve British commerce, especially the growing textile trade, and one of the ways to do that was to open up new markets. A French market was as good as any other. Sales both ways were to be encouraged by a lowering of customs duties, or tariffs. French wines would become cheaper here, and English cloth would sell more cheaply there.

In the event Pitt proved his point. Exports to France shot up, so much so that thousands of workers in Normandy and elsewhere in France were laid off. Indeed, the treaty proved so successful for British trade, at the expense of French industry, that one of the other aims of the treaty – the improvement of Anglo-French political relations – was frustrated. Too many French unemployed workers came to regard it as yet another devious trick by the treacherous English.

The Eden Treaty was, however, a landmark in a long process that was to extend right through the nineteenth century – the free-trade movement. Pitt did not introduce free trade, but he was impressed by the arguments for it, as set out, for instance, in *The Wealth of Nations*, published in 1776 by a Glasgow professor called Adam Smith, who virtually founded a new subject for academic study – political science.

Any country, like any commercial firm or any family, tries to make ends meet, to balance its books, to make sure that it has more coming in than it has going out. A country does this usually by means of trade; the aim is to sell more than it buys. Exports must equal, or if possible exceed, imports. If there is a danger of foreign goods flooding the home market because of their cheapness, the government will 'protect' the home market, and home industry, by imposing tariffs, or customs duties, on these imports. This will have the effect of making the imports dearer to the customer. Either people will not then buy foreign goods so much, or, if they do, the government will get a steady income from it. Or, thirdly, they will prefer to buy products of their own country which will keep their own industry healthy. The eighteenth century believed firmly in this 'regulating' of trade, as it was called.

This belief was particularly strong in countries with colonial empires, of which Britain was a prime example. Colonial trade had to be 'regulated', not only to ensure that foreign goods did not upset colonial economies, but also to channel all colonial produce through English ports. The argument was that, as Britain had founded, financed, governed, and protected the colonies, she deserved to get whatever profits from them that accrued. The theory worked satisfactorily until colonies began developing their own industry and trade, and naturally wanted to sell their goods where they could get the best price – France, Spain, Holland, or wherever. When the British Government tried to stop this happening, often by imposing stiffer rules, the colonists proceeded to break the rules.

The Americans not only broke the rules; they declared war in order to be able to go on breaking the rules. They took the supreme risk of going it alone, three thousand miles away from the 'civilised' world. To everyone's surprise, including possibly their own, they made it. The effects were shattering. Their success in winning their war of independence, besides causing the downfall of North, and the discredit of the whole political system, also caused men to consider that it might be time for a change too in the economic system which had brought the war about. Adam Smith argued that the trouble with trade was that governments interfered with it too much. If they left it alone, individual businessmen and industrialists would have ample scope to use their own ability and initiative to develop their own branch of trade as fully as possible. Industry would therefore become healthier and stronger, production would rise, sales would be greater, and more money would be available to buy more foreign goods. The absence of any customs duties would bring prices down. The workers in that healthy industry would have more money to buy all these goods. Higher sales profits would in turn provide confidence for further investment, greater output, and so on. The general result would be a vast increase in trade, prosperity, in fact in 'the wealth of nations'.

That was the theory: leave things alone. The French phrase for it – *'laissez-faire'* – was the one that caught on. The idea became increasingly popular as the nineteenth century advanced, especially as the Industrial Revolution was to provide Britain with far more manufactures to sell than anyone else.

For the time being, however, men were wary of it, and Pitt did no more than lower some tariffs. He did not go the whole hog, and abolish them altogether. In short, he believed not so much in free trade as in free*er* trade.

Still, by his tariff cuts, his encouragement of foreign trade, his numerous new taxes, his humdrum economies in daily administration (and also by some unpopular cuts in expenditure on the Navy), Pitt achieved the near-impossible; he balanced the accounts. Indeed, he did more. To prove how healthy the finances were, he announced that he intended to start a scheme to pay off the National Debt, no less. This was the combined total of all the money the Government had ever borrowed from its own people, and not paid back. It still of course paid annual interest. This alone amounted to about £9,000,000 a year, nearly half the Government's total income. To pay off the actual capital of the Debt itself was ambitious, some said, to the point of romantic daydreaming. How could he hope to pay off £250,000,000 out of an annual national income of barely £20,000,000?

His answer went like this. He proposed each year to put £1,000,000 aside, into a Sinking Fund. He appointed commissioners of this fund, who would use the money to buy Government stock – that is, part of the National Debt. Interest would be paid on this in the usual way, just as if the commissioners were normal stockholders. So, at the end of the year, assuming an interest of, say, 3 per cent, the Sinking Fund would be enjoying an income of 3 per cent on £1,000,000 – £30,000. The following year, this £30,000 would be used to buy more Government stock, along with another £1,000,000 set aside for the same purpose. (Pitt estimated that he could afford a million out of his budget surplus every year for this.) At the end of the second year, interest would now be paid on the original million, on the £30,000, and on the second million. The Sinking Fund would now stand at £2,090,900. In the third year, this entire sum would earn interest, and so would the third million set aside out of budget surplus, and so it would go on. If this plan were to be followed rigidly, the amount of Government stock that could be bought up would increase each year, and at an increasing rate – until, in theory, the whole £250,000,000 worth had been absorbed into the Sinking Fund, and the National Debt would have cancelled itself out. It would take about twenty-eight years, thought Pitt.

Unfortunately, the theory, as is the case with most theories, did not work out so magically in practice. It relied upon a long period of peace, and upon the £1,000,000 surplus being available every year. It was hardly Pitt's fault that within a short time of his starting the Sinking Fund England entered a period of almost continuous war for twenty-two years. Pitt struggled bravely to keep his Fund going, to the extent of borrowing the million each year in order to do so. But it soon became pointless to pay off one debt at a lower rate of interest by borrowing more money at a higher rate, and the Sinking Fund, sadly, sank.

That, however, was in the future. In the summer of 1788, most English gentlemen were more than pleased with the country's recovery from the American disgrace, and cheerfully allowed Billy Pitt most of the credit for it. The Empire's trade was picking up again; India was being reorganised; the finances had not been so healthy for years; England had now re-entered the European circle by signing a Triple Alliance with Prussia and Holland; and a host of centenary celebrations were going on, in which English 'lovers of liberty' passed the port and patted each other on the back in memory of 1688, the 'Glorious Revolution', when noble patriots had expelled the hated Stuart tyrant, James II, and forced his successor, William of Orange, to agree to the terms laid down by Parliament before he was allowed on the throne. It was smugly agreed that what the English didn't know about freedom and government wasn't worth knowing, and one or two glances of lazy curiosity were cast across the Channel, where the French, it appeared, were actually going to have a parliament, their first in 175 years. It was going to be interesting to see what the Frogs made of it.

The air of cosy comfort was soon upset, by the coldest winter in living memory, by a Government crisis that threatened Pitt himself, and by a following summer which proved hot in more than one sense of the word.

CHAPTER TWO

The Rights of Man
1788–1804

In November, 1788, while driving in Windsor Park, His Majesty stopped the coach, got down, walked across to a nearby oak tree, and spoke to it as if it were the King of Prussia. George III had gone mad again.

At least, that was the story put out by the Prince of Wales and his friend Fox, for obvious reasons. If the King really was off his head, he could not govern, and his place would have to be taken by his eldest son, the Prince of Wales. The Prince would rule as Regent, he would naturally dismiss his father's minister, Pitt, and he would give rewards and high office to his cronies from the racecourse and the gaming tables – the Foxites.

The truth about the King's illness was rather more complicated. Modern medical research, based on the official records of many Court doctors, has now shown that George was suffering from a rare disease called porphyria. The disease could be transmitted from one generation to the next, and has been traced as far back as the sixteenth century. What made George's case special was that he suffered from it more seriously than earlier members of the Hanoverian family. Among other unpleasant things, the disease caused pains and agonising cramps, and made the water turn purple. (The name 'porphyria' comes from the Greek word '*porphura*', which means 'purple'. And, now that the two words appear together, it becomes obvious that our word 'purple' comes from the same source.) Worse still, it upset the whole nervous system, which could make the patient uncontrollably excited, perhaps liable to violence. In short, there is a *physical* explanation; George was not suffering from a disorder of the brain. The trouble was that his behaviour made it look as if he was. Doctors in 1788 had not heard of porphyria, and they knew little of psychiatry. All they saw was a man who was obviously very ill, and unable to explain his illness; he was either doubled up in pain, attacking people, or talking nonstop for hours on end. Their work was not made any easier by the constrictions of court etiquette, which forbade anyone to speak to His Majesty unless His Majesty addressed him first.

One gleam of hope, however, was that His Majesty had had similar attacks before, and had recovered. His general health was both usually good and unusually good. It was this which helped Pitt to fight Fox; it might give him time. Pitt knew that, if the Prince of Wales became Regent, there was going to be a change of Prime Minister. What nobody knew at the time was how long the Prince of Wales would remain Regent. That depended on how long it would take His Majesty's robust constitution to see him back to full vigour, and on whether that robust constitution was helped or hindered.

The Prince produced a doctor, Warren, who declared that the King was incurably insane. Pitt listened to another doctor, a Dr Willis, who said he thought the King would recover. If the Prince had his way, it looked as if his father would not even be *allowed* to recover. Luckily for the patient, the Queen stepped in to protect her husband. Dr Willis was given a free hand, and the corrective regime began – a terrifying business of straitjackets, bleedings, and hot poultices on the bare scalp. It says a lot for George's patience, bravery, and strength that he survived the treatment, never mind the disease.

While he fretted and sweated at Windsor, another battle was going on in Westminster, where Pitt was trying to delay matters; the longer he held up business, the more time the King had to recover, and so make a formal Regency unnecessary. The Foxites forced him to accept that the Prince of Wales should be Regent; there was no question about that. What Pitt wanted to avoid was this: if the Prince used full royal powers as Regent, he could promote Foxites to high offices, and give them peerages, so that, even if his father did recover, and reinstate Pitt, they would be faced with Fox's supporters in all the key positions, and a Whig majority in the House of Lords. (This fear of the Lords being 'swamped' with new peers from one particular party was to cause concern in later government crises, in 1832 and 1911.)

The atmosphere of uncertainty produced two startling results. Firstly, Pitt, who had always represented royal power, claimed that Parliament had a right to keep a check on the Regent's actions. Secondly, Fox, who for years had championed the rights of Parliament against an over-mighty Crown, now argued that there should be no limits to the Regent's powers at all. Pitt proclaimed, in one of his rare public jokes, that he had 'un-Whigged' Fox.

In the end, there was no final decision; George recovered. Pitt could relax, and Fox and the Prince flounced back to the card tables. In the spring of 1789, His Majesty drove once more round his estates at Windsor, and his tenants knelt weeping at the roadside as he passed. George was a popular king nearly all his life.

It was well for England that he returned to his full powers when he did, and that Pitt was able to remain in office. The spring and summer of 1789 produced some of the most shattering news since Saratoga and Yorktown, the two worst defeats of the American War. The French had a revolution.

It was a very odd revolution. It was not easy to pinpoint a single event in France as the precise start of it. Louis XVI was not deposed overnight, nor were thousands marched off to execution – not yet, anyway. No single death or battle or riot turned French politics upside down. Nevertheless, so many things happened so quickly, one after the other, that the general impression given was one of tremendous movement and excitement. Between May and November, 1789, the French elected their first parliamentary body for 175 years; that body, the Estates-General, later reorganised itself against the King's wishes, called itself the National Assembly, and swore that it would not disband until it had set up a new and democratic system of government; freedom of religious thought was proclaimed; so was the right of every adult male to exercise the vote; feudal taxes were stopped; torture was abolished; thousands of nobles ran away from angry peasants; the biggest jail in Paris was a smoking ruin, and Louis was a virtual prisoner in his own palace.

By any standards something extremely unusual was happening

across the Channel. And still the dramatic news flowed thick and fast. Refugee nobles had their land confiscated; local government was overhauled; courts were reorganiscd; France had a new national flag, the tricolour; the Church was nationalised; ranks in society were done away with, and everybody started calling everybody else 'citizen'.

Communications being what they were, and France being in such a disturbed state, news was scrappy, and often unreliable. Englishmen therefore reacted to the revolution according to the information they could collect, and according to their own prejudices.

To begin with, some admired the revolution. Any country, they felt, which, after so many centuries of royal tyranny, religious persecution, and government corruption, was trying to set up an honest democracy for all free men deserved to be admired. It was only twelve months since Englishmen had been celebrating the centenary of 1688, their own 'Glorious Revolution', and the coincidence was too obvious to miss. They made the mistake of thinking that the French were having the same sort of revolution. Fox allowed himself to be quite carried away with this excitement, and he continued to champion the French Revolution long after most of his Whig friends had changed their minds.

There were others, including some Whigs, who were suspicious of it from the outset. Insults had been hurled at the King and Queen; property had been attacked; the Church had been robbed of its land and money (never mind that it had been a Papist Church – what was relevant was that it had been an *established* church); wild mobs had pulled down buildings and committed murder; there had been much loud talk of carrying the 'revolution' into other countries – whatever that meant. It looked sinister, even dangerous. Fox's great friend, Edmund Burke, put these fears into print in his *Reflections on the Revolution in France*, and the book was a bestseller.

It was very fine, he said, to try and set up freedom and equality for all. The trouble was that it was being done too fast, and by the wrong people, and too much was being destroyed in the process. Royalty, religion, good manners, rank, property, experience, tradition, honour, law, order – everything was being overturned. Was nothing sacred to this revolution?

To borrow an image from the 1940s, it was as if the French

Revolution were a huge political atom bomb. Burke and his friends gazed in horror across the Channel. They knew that colossal forces had been let loose upon the world, many of them possibly evil. They did not know how widely those forces would stretch, they did not know what dreadful chain reactions could be set off by the explosion, and they did not know when, if ever, those reactions would cease. (The proletarian atom had been split.) Burke did realise clearly, however, that the French Revolution was special, that it was unlike any other revolution, and he said so. It was not an upset that would remain confined to a single country; it would affect others.

There was a third view. It was a narrow one, but it was a sincere one, and it was held by the King, among other people. This idea started from the point that France was the enemy of England. There was some good reason for this, since there had been wars between the two countries on and off since – well, since the Norman Conquest. Indeed there had been so many wars packed into the seventeenth and eighteenth centuries that it was commonplace to speak of France as the 'natural enemy'. George was not a great brain, but he was a hearty hater of frog-eaters, and he easily grasped (and clung to) the idea that the revolution was keeping France in confusion, and anything that confused the enemy was fine by him. It served them right for poking their noses into the American War.

Finally, there was Pitt. He was Prime Minister, and he had to maintain a sensible attitude. He could not afford to get excited like the Foxites, and he could not agree in public with the violent opposition of Burke. Nor did he go along with the King in saying that the French could stew in their own juice. It was his job to keep the peace in Europe, and to maintain friendly relations with the official government of France, whatever sort of government that might be. As long as the French kept their treaties, respected boundaries, and did not cause trouble in other countries, it was no business of his what they did in their own.

Pitt's view was no doubt the correct one, but it was the other three that proved right. Fox was justified because the French Revolution stated great truths about the rights of man – the right to vote, the right to freedom of religious thought, the right to freedom from wrongful arrest, the right to a fair trial, freedom of speech, freedom of the press, and so on. No honest, civilised person can deny these. Burke's argument was vindicated because the French Revolution, as he prophesied, did cause disorder, bloodshed, dictatorship, tyranny, and war. The King was right too, in a way. He had known all along that France was the enemy. It did not matter whether the revolutionaries called themselves citizens or democrats or patriots or anything else; Frenchmen started to fight Englishmen again in 1793, and continued to do so for the next twenty-two years.

Pitt did not want a war, and did everything he could to avoid it. He had taken office in order to repair the damage caused by the American War, and all his new financial schemes depended on peace for their success – especially his precious Sinking Fund. As late as the spring of 1792, he was predicting fifteen years of peace ahead. But events and opinions were against him, in both France and England.

In France, the Revolution did what Burke said it would do – it went sour. Moderate leaders were elbowed out by extremists. The King suffered insult after insult, until he was finally stripped of all authority, and put on trial for his life. Rival groups plotted and fought to gain supreme power. Wicked men, who had seen what city mobs could do, now began to use crowds deliberately as a weapon of terror. Street-corner speakers whipped up jealousies and hatreds; newspapers peddled propaganda; greedy politicians followed any fad or fashion in order to keep office. Any honest man who suggested that perhaps something had gone wrong would be accused of the worst of all crimes – 'betraying the Revolution'. Hypocrites, rogues, and bullies were in high office. The French Revolution had left the ordinary man miles behind. It had gone way past the early, sincere Declaration of the Rights of Man, and it had careered off on a wild orbit of its own, which was in the end to bring it on to a collision course with the whole of Europe.

For not only were the revolutionaries convinced that they were right; they said, publicly and often, that they would not rest until they had carried the ideals of the Revolution into every country in Europe. Kings and queens everywhere were outraged, not least George III. If he had had his way, he would have started a war long before Pitt let him. Pitt himself was annoyed when a French minister, Lebrun, told him that he (Pitt) did not have his own people behind him, and that it was only a matter of time before Englishmen rose and turned George off his throne.

Lebrun was wrong. Too many violent events in France were putting most men off the Revolution. Everyone knew that Louis and his Queen were helpless prisoners. In August, 1792, a mob had attacked his palace, the Tuileries, and massacred his Swiss bodyguard. In September, an invasion panic seized Paris, and over a thousand people were arrested or dragged from prisons, and executed – in only a few days. A new and hideous device for mass-produced sudden death, the guillotine, made its appearance in the big cities of France. In December, 1792, the King was put on trial, and on 21 January, 1793 he was beheaded. Most Englishmen were sickened (even though the English had done the same thing 144 years before; most had been sickened then).

They were wary too, for France had gone to war. In April, 1792 the French Government had decided to carry the spirit of the Revolution into Austria, and in June they gaily added Prussia to their enemies. In September they actually defeated the Prussians, at Valmy, in Flanders. (It was difficult to know who were more surprised – the French or the Prussians.) By the autumn French troops were invading Belgium. In November, Paris issued a decree opening the River Scheldt and the port of Antwerp. As the river had been declared closed by every European treaty since 1713, it would have been hard to find a bigger breach of international law. The French had in effect stuck their thumbs to their noses at all the European powers, and asked them what they were going to do about it. The Revolution in one sense had ceased to matter. It was the old story of France trying to conquer Western Europe, chasing the dream of the Rhine frontier; it was Richelieu and Louis XIV all over again.

Pitt was forced to take action. The French had issued another decree in November, the Fraternity Decree, in which they promised to go to the help of any nation that wanted its 'liberty'. Pitt regarded it as a public advertisement for high treason, and laid his security plans accordingly. But it was the opening of Antwerp that really decided him. It was too big a threat to British and Dutch trade; that was why they had closed it in the first place. (Whether it *should* have been closed was, in 1792, irrelevant; Pitt's point was that the closure, right or wrong, was part of international law.) Perhaps more important,

England had never allowed any hostile power to control Belgium or Holland. It was far too easy to strangle Channel trade, and to mount an invasion from these places. This fear of an enemy in the Low Countries remained a central feature of British foreign policy right into the twentieth century. As long as England relied on the Channel for defence and trade, her reaction was bound to be the same.

The September Massacres and Louis' execution disgusted the people of England, but it was the invasion of Belgium and the opening of the River Scheldt that settled the Government's decision. Pitt sent the French ambassador packing, and made arrangements to increase the armed forces. The French beat him to it; it was they who actually declared war, on 1 February, 1793.

The war would not last long. How could it? France was in confusion; assemblies and committees seemed to come and go almost from month to month. The newspapers were full of news about the execution of generals and political leaders. Most of the French nobility were by now dead, in prison, or in exile, and that meant that the entire officer class of the armed forces was gone. Paper money was sending prices to inflationary levels. There were Royalist rebellions in various parts of the countryside. It would have looked foolish if France had declared war on only one country; in 1793, she was fighting England, Austria, Prussia, Spain, Holland, Sardinia, and Naples.

Understandably, Pitt laid plans for a short war, and he used the advantages that appeared at the time to be available to him. Almost the whole country was behind him, from the King downwards. Whatever may have needed reforming in England, men were prepared to forget about it for the time being in order to concentrate on beating the French. (At the height of disorder during the Fleet mutiny, the mutineers made it clear that they would suspend their complaints – and they certainly had enough of them – if the French war squadrons put to sea.) Fox's Whigs changed their minds. Fox had continued to defend the French Revolution, but his followers had felt increasing doubts. Burke had split publicly from him in 1791, to his great personal grief. Despite the coming of war, however, Fox stayed loyal to his declared support for the Revolution's ideals, but he lost the allegiance of most of his party in doing so. By 1794, they had left him to join Pitt, who rewarded them with a timely batch of Government posts. The Whig faithful shrank to fewer than fifty – a pitiful, sheepish remnant of the pack that had bayed for Pitt's resignation in 1784.

England was prosperous, she had a powerful navy, and she had allies. She was concerned to keep her trade routes open, to keep France out of the Low Countries, and to prevent her from dominating Europe. Pitt, therefore, used his money to pay for the allied armies; he used the Navy to strangle French overseas trade, and to steal colonies; and he planned that the allies should fight France on land while he defeated her at sea. Such methods had worked before, and he saw no reason why they should not work again.

Unfortunately, there was a reason; France had changed. That massive political detonation which Burke had watched with such concern let loose a blast of energy which knocked Europe right off its feet. The French may have executed weak ministers, but those who had the strength to survive pulled France together by the scruff of the neck to meet her invaders. The organising genius of Carnot put hundreds of thousands of soldiers into the field with unheard-of speed. The guillotine may have been a harsh punishment for unsuccessful generals, but it made the others put their backs into the war effort. The absence of an officer class forced the authorities to promote men from the ranks, only this time men became officers not because their father was a duke, but because they were good at their job. A young gunner called Buonaparte was to become a brigadier at twenty-six; his friend Marmont later reached field-marshal at thirty-five (a young English officer, Arthur Wesley, went from ensign at eighteen to lieutenant-colonel at twenty-four). Almost overnight, it seemed, French armies dwarfed their opponents, and they were officered by men of blazing talent at the height of their powers. Another rarity was that the French soldiers actually understood, and believed in, what they were fighting for – the Revolution. They were the disciples of a new creed – the Rights of Man. They were not bemused by complicated squabbles over border towns in Flanders, and they did not march under officers who made them more afraid of the lash than of the enemy. That does not mean that they were angels; indeed they were still like any other soldiers on campaign – rogues. The difference now was that they were rogues with proper leadership and solid purpose; they had other things on their minds besides the usual loot and women.

It did not matter that they made mistakes; there were so many of them, they were so quick, so keen, and so good, that they made their own luck. They broke all the rules for the simple reason that they did not even know them. The invaders, expecting a normal leisurely war, were baffled. Rumbling armies and bumbling generals were swept aside one after the other.

Pitt too felt the same frustration. His expeditions captured French colonies, especially in the West Indies. His admirals ruled the Channel and the Atlantic, and, later, the Mediterranean. It did not seem to affect France at all. He sent the Duke of York to help defend Holland; the small British force (which included Colonel Wesley and his Thirty-Third of Foot) was soon bundled out. He sent soldiers and ships to assist the Royalist risings in Brittany and Toulon; they failed too. The money he poured into allied pockets turned out to be money down the drain.

The alliance was not a real alliance. The armies were slow, and there was no supreme military commander. The allies distrusted each other, and they all distrusted England. To them, it seemed that England was doing what she had always done – pay them to do the hard fighting while she used her navy to pick up valuable colonies, which could be used as bargaining counters before the signing of the peace treaty. Austria and Prussia did not give the war their full attention, because they had their eyes constantly drawn to the east, in particular to Poland. They had already carved out three sections of Poland between themselves and Russia in 1772, and they were afraid that the Empress Catherine would help herself to another slice while their backs were turned. Not one of France's enemies grasped the fact that this was a different sort of war; this was not part of the old game of parade-ground battles in summer time and haggling over border towns at the conference table when the armies got tired.

France was fighting for her life, and for her new beliefs – 'Liberty, Equality, Fraternity'. When she had saved them, she was not content. She then wanted to make everybody else accept those beliefs, if it meant conquering the whole of Europe, and destroying the political system of an entire continent. Each country fighting France had more mundane priorities; each decided to back out when it seemed an opportune moment to bargain for a few places, steal a few quick moves under the old system. What none of them saw was that the system itself was crumbling.

In April, 1795, Prussia made peace. In May, so did Holland. In July, the Spaniards dropped out. In 1796, a lightning war by a long-haired, sawn-off young general with a shocking Corsican accent bullied Sardinia, Naples, and Austria into a peace treaty. By 1797 England was on her own.

1797 was a bad year; in fact the middle nineties were a bad time generally for the British Government. Everything seemed to go wrong. There was not enough money to pay for the war, and raising the 'luxury' taxes – on servants, windows, carriages, and so on – did not solve the problem. There was a lot of Government borrowing, which added to the size of the National Debt (on which annual interest had to be paid). Pitt struggled for a while to keep his Sinking Fund going, but he found himself trying to pay off one loan by raising another at a higher rate of interest. The old land tax was not producing enough, so in 1798 Pitt was forced to introduce something new – an income tax. Incomes below £60 per year were exempt; between £60 and £200 there was a graduated scale; above £200 it was two shillings in the pound, or 10 per cent. It was intrusive on a gentleman's privacy, and it was deplored, but, as a war measure, it was grumpily accepted.

As is often the case, bad times seemed to bring bad harvests, and bad harvests certainly brought bad times. The crops were poor in 1792, 1794, and 1795, just when England's regular supplies from Eastern Europe – Poland and Prussia – were interrupted by the war. England no longer grew enough to feed her growing population (ten million according to the first census in 1801). The result was a sharp rise in bread prices. Indeed, the war brought a rise in the whole cost of living. Riots and demonstrations, especially in the growing industrial towns, became commonplace. A crowd booed and hissed the King's coach at the state opening of Parliament in 1795.

The Government's first duty (besides fighting the war) was to keep order. Moreover, it had to do this without a telegraph system, without any reliable statistics, and without a police force, when the fastest means of travel was a man on a horse. Agricultural workers were bitter about losing their land through enclosures; industrial workers hated the new machines that took away their jobs; prices were rising faster than wages; the growing cities and the factories made it easier to gather large crowds; and France was busy urging the 'people' everywhere to strike for their 'liberty' against their wicked masters. Small wonder that the Government took harsh measures; it could not afford to do otherwise. It came down hard on those who disturbed the peace; it was equally hard on those whom it suspected of inciting such disturbance.

Ever since Edmund Burke had published his *Reflections* in November, 1790, there had been no shortage of replies. The most famous of them was *The Rights of Man*, by Thomas Paine, a self-educated Quaker, who had written some pamphlets for the Americans during their War of Independence. (He is credited with coining the phrase 'The United States of America'.) Paine spent half his book attacking Burke, and the other half claiming that man was basically a reasonable chap, and that if you left men alone to think and work things out for themselves they would always get them right. The trouble was that governments always got in the way, and the only means of settling the problem was for all men to choose and set up their own government, which they could change again any time it misbehaved.

The Rights of Man did well; children sold cheap verse editions for sixpence on street corners. The French made a great fuss of Paine; they invited him to Paris as an honoured guest; they elected him as a member for three constituencies in their new governing body, the Convention, in September, 1792. He left England just in time, for Pitt prosecuted him for seditious libel, and he was, in his absence, declared an outlaw.

There had been writers before who criticised the government of the day, and there had been reform clubs. What worried Pitt was the fact that there were now so many of them – the Society for Constitutional Information, the Friends of the People, the Friends of Universal Peace and the Rights of Man, and a host of Revolution Societies (celebrating, incidentally, 1688, not 1789). Worse still, he did not know how closely they were connected with the French revolutionaries. Many of them were respectable, middle-class affairs, doing little more than run debates and circulate pamphlets, but Pitt could not be sure.

The London Corresponding Society was different. It was highly organised; it attracted working men with its cheap subscription (only a penny a week); it set up branches in the industrial north, and corresponded regularly with them – hence the title. It talked loudly of reforms of the legal system, of a universal vote, of annual parliaments – not violent changes, but important ones, getting to the roots of the problems. The Latin word for 'root' is *radix*. These men – Hardy, Tooke, Thelwall, and others – were the Radicals. (The term was applied to any group that wanted drastic or rapid changes.) They called each other 'citizen', and they really did write to various groups in France, even after the war broke out. There were Radical elements in Scotland too, and in December, 1792 a Convention of the Friends of the People was held in Edinburgh.

It is most unlikely that any of these groups, radical or moderate, wanted to overturn Parliament or murder the King. Many of the working-class members were more worried about day-to-day things like the price of bread, or enclosures, or unemployment. Many of the intellectuals were carried away by excitement with *The Rights of Man*, and did not know what dreadful things were now being done in France. Almost all of them were on England's side when the war came.

But Pitt and the authorities could take no chances. The words 'revolution', 'convention', 'citizen' were now being used too often for their liking. The clubs' activities were making the French more convinced than ever that English society was split from top to bottom. The country was busy fighting a war; there had to be security measures. For all Pitt knew, French spies by the hundred might be circulating among these societies.

So the great repression began, in the courts and in Parliament. In Scotland, Chief Justice Braxfield sentenced a young lawyer, Muir, to fourteen years' transportation, and a Unitarian minister, Palmer, to five. The Scottish Radicals bravely tried a second convention in Edinburgh at the end of 1793. Their leaders – Gerrald, Margarot, and Skirving – were charged with attending meetings 'of a dangerous and destructive tendency', and were sent to the colonies for fourteen years each.

The English Radicals replied by calling for an English national convention. This was an open challenge to Parliament, which was the only body that could represent the people. In May, 1794, Hardy, Tooke, and Thelwall were arrested, charged with treason – and acquitted. The Government had overplayed its hand, and could not back up its charge. Hardy was acquitted by a London jury (Braxfield had packed the Scottish ones). Tooke added a touch of near-comedy; he conducted his own defence, and put Pitt himself in the witness box, forcing the Prime Minister to admit that he had once attended a meeting outside Parliament for the purpose of discussing reform.

Pitt gave up the attack in the courts, but he made his point with ferocious new laws in Parliament. Already in 1793 there had been the Aliens Act, which had attempted to keep French agents out of the country. In 1794, Pitt suspended *Habeas Corpus*, the Act of Parliament which had always guaranteed a citizen's freedom from wrongful arrest. Now anyone could be arrested and held without trial. The Treasonable Practices Act in 1795 widened the meaning of the word 'treason': a man who dared merely to criticise the constitution could now be transported for seven years. In the same year the Seditious Meetings Act required all meetings of more than 50 persons to have a licence from a magistrate. In 1798, Pitt attacked the Press; his Newspaper Publication Act put publishers under close supervision by magistrates. In 1799, he closed down the London Corresponding Society.

He also went for trade unions. He went for any combination of workmen (or employers) who were trying to improve their wages, their trade, or their conditions of work. Such unions were hardly likely to be plotting treason, but they were criticising authority, and that was good enough for Pitt. The Combination Acts of 1799 and 1800 banned them.

Army barracks appeared. For the first time soldiers were kept separate from the civilian population. Instead of billeting them in private houses, the Government began to build barracks in trouble areas such as the North of England. It would keep the soldiers away from discontented people, and have them conveniently concentrated in moments of sudden unrest.

Such a policy was harsh and unfair. Its critics, the Foxites, said it was a sign of panic. Pitt was interested not in criticism, but in results.

The policy worked; England did not have a revolution. She had hardly
any Radical activity at all until after the war. Fox's Whigs grew smaller
still in number. Fox may have been right; perhaps Pitt was over-
reacting. But nobody knew, at the time, for sure. The Radicals had
always seemed more numerous because they made so much noise. The
fact was that in the mid-nineties the main body of public opinion was
on Pitt's side. They may not have liked his new Acts, but they accepted
them, because the possible alternative – revolution – was worse. The
Gordon Riots were still fresh in men's minds. Respectable shopkeepers
and craftsmen who might have been attracted to Radicalism
remembered the raging mobs, and backed the Tories instead. The
violence of the French Revolution brought them even more firmly
behind the Government. 'Church and King' clubs were founded to rival
all the 'reform' societies. In July, 1791, the house of a famous Radical
scientist, Dr. Priestley, was sacked by a Birmingham mob. In
November, 1792, instead of Guy Fawkes, they burnt effigies of Tom
Paine. As the war went on, the hatred of the 'natural enemy', France,
became stronger than Radical propaganda.

Pitt, poker-faced and tight-lipped, soldiered on. He endured the jibes
of Fox; he survived the embarrassment of the treason trials; he put up
with having his windows smashed in Downing Street; he bore up
courageously every time he heard the news that yet another of his
schemes to defeat France had come unstuck. It was said that his pulse
rate went up from 80 to 120 whenever one of the green dispatch boxes
was brought into the room.

There was, however, one good thing to be said for having no allies;
there was nobody left to let you down. It did simplify matters. Money
need not be wasted in Europe, and Britain could use her precious Navy
to suit herself. It was back to blockade and empire-protection and
colony-stealing, and no European voice now to say it was wrong.

One of the regiments posted to protect British interests in India from
the French was commanded by young Colonel Arthur Wesley – later
Wellesley. (The name had been originally spelt 'Wellesley', but the
family had begun to spell it 'Wesley' in the seventeenth century. When
Arthur's eldest brother Richard was created Marquess in the peerage of
Ireland in 1798, he changed it back to 'Wellesley', and Arthur followed

suit.) Arthur had hitherto been overshadowed by the brilliant Richard. He had been put into the Army by a distraught family because they did not think he was capable of much more. 'Food for powder' was his mother's terse verdict. And he had been put into the infantry at that; they did not think he was up to the technical details of the artillery either – unlike another young soldier, who in the same year (1787) was posted to his first regiment, in France. A scruffy little Corsican gunner called Buonaparte.

From 1787 to 1794, Wesley cooled his heels as staff officer at Dublin Castle, then saw a brief spell of active, if inglorious, service in Flanders in 1794 and 1795. Withdrawn home, and deprived of active command, he seriously considered leaving the service. (At about the same time, Buonaparte, blocked in promotion, was applying to be transferred to the Turkish Army.) Later in 1795, helped partly by his brother's influence, he was posted, with his regiment, to the West Indies, but a seven-week winter gale drove the ships back to port. Then in 1796 came the posting to India, where brother Richard was soon to be appointed Governor-General.

In the next few years, Colonel Wesley learned his trade as soldier and commander, including the invaluable lesson that successful campaigning was a matter not of jingling spurs and unleashing cavalry charges, but of drawing good maps and building sound bridges and collecting enough bullock carts to carry the rations. The lesson was to serve him well for the rest of his career.

As Colonel Wesley's ship crossed the South Atlantic *en route* to the Cape and India, news arrived at Downing Street that Britain's late allies, the Spaniards, had signed an alliance with France. Orders were promptly issued to find the Spanish Fleet and defeat it. This was duly done, on St Valentine's Day, 1797, when Sir John Jervis caught up with them at Cape St Vincent, just off the south-western coast of Spain. The vigilance, nerve, and brilliant timing of one of his senior captains, Commodore Horatio Nelson, helped to turn a profitable skirmish into an outright victory. It brought Jervis his peerage, and it brought Nelson much-desired glory and publicity.

Then came another disaster, worse than anything so far. In April, the British Fleet mutinied. Every politician and errand-boy knew what that meant; without the Navy, Britain simply was not a going concern. At all costs the ships must be got back to sea. The French Fleet was undefeated, apart from an early battle in 1794; there had already been an attempt to invade Ireland; and the Dutch Fleet was now under French direction. Someone would have to listen to the mutineers.

They certainly had enough to complain about – low pay (unchanged since Stuart times), poor medical services, swindling by corrupt pursers, and practically no shore leave. Curiously, they did not make a fuss about poor food or the notorious flogging. Most of them could not have expected much better ashore in the way of meals (the diet aboard, if poor, was at least regular); and most of them accepted the necessity of maintaining discipline. Indeed, the leaders of the mutiny at Spithead, near Portsmouth, behaved with great courtesy and restraint. There was no violence, no disrespect to officers, no damage; Jack Tar simply went on strike. They would put to sea, they said, if the enemy appeared; otherwise they intended to stay on strike until their demands were met, and guaranteed by an Act of Parliament. Within a week the Cabinet agreed. The mutineers still feared reprisals. Mutiny was the most serious crime in the book, punishable by death. The only two men they trusted were the King himself and Admiral Howe, the victor of the Battle of the Glorious First of June, 1794. Before they would submit again to normal discipline, Howe had to be rowed round the Fleet from ship to ship with George III's pardon in his hand.

Just as the Channel Fleet put out from Spithead, a second mutiny broke out, this time in the North Sea Fleet, stationed at the Nore, on the Thames Estuary. This was not so peaceable, and there was talk of blockading the Thames to secure their demands. The Government used force, and the leader, Richard Parker, and twenty-nine others, were hanged. The North Sea Fleet put back to sea, and only just in time.

The Dutch had been preparing a fleet to invade Ireland, but had been unable to sail owing to a blockade by Admiral Duncan. When the Nore mutiny came, Duncan found himself left with only two ships at sea against the Dutch sixteen. If they came out, he was finished. He kept them in by making regular signals to a non-existent fleet over the horizon. In the end the Dutch realised he was bluffing, and decided to come out to call his bluff. By that time the mutiny was over, the sailors had returned to work, and he really did have a fleet over the horizon. At the Battle of Camperdown, in October, 1797, he destroyed the Dutch Fleet, and ended the invasion scare, at any rate for the time being.

By the end of the year the Navy was in control; the French, and their Dutch and Spanish subordinates, were bottled up by the British blockade in every port on the west European coast. The longer the blockade lasted, the less seagoing practice the enemy ships could get, and so the more likely they were to be defeated if and when they ever did get to sea. Moreover, British expeditions had captured a string of French and Dutch colonies all over the world. It did not seem to make any difference to the French, who were so sure of themselves in Europe that they turned down some generous peace terms (by no means the first) offered by a tired Pitt.

The position was very nearly stalemate. The Navy could stop England being defeated, but it could not win the war by itself. Something would have to be done on the mainland of Europe, and that meant that Pitt had to start collecting allies again. He persuaded Austria and Naples to try a second time, and the new Tsar, Paul, agreed to send his most famous general, Suvorov, at the head of a Russian army. The allies almost took it for granted that England would pay them, and they also demanded that England should show more willing. They expected Pitt's war effort this time to be rather more than sending a few bags of gold and picking up some West Indian islands.

Pitt accepted their criticism, and ordered Admiral Jervis, now Earl St Vincent, to spare a squadron of ships under Nelson to police the Mediterranean. For once Pitt had some good fortune. At that very time, the French Government, the Directory, had decided to allow General Bonaparte to attempt the conquest of Egypt (he had vague designs on India too). Bonaparte – he had dropped the 'u' in his name because it sounded too Italian – was France's most successful general, and far too popular for the Directors' liking. They were only too glad to let him go; with any luck he might be defeated. He duly left Toulon with a huge convoy of troopships and men-of-war commanded by Admiral Brueys.

Nelson knew the invasion convoy had left Toulon, but he did not know where it was going. England? Ireland? Portugal? Naples? It could be anywhere. And the prize was so tantalising. If he could catch that convoy at sea, he could destroy a whole army and France's most dashing general without the cost of single soldier's life. In his frantic search he twice missed it by hours. When he heard that the French had captured Malta on their way, he guessed, rightly, Egypt. Unfortunately he chased them so fast that he got to Alexandria before they did. Finding the harbour empty, and thinking he had been mistaken, he dashed off again – Syria, Crete, Sicily, Greece. By the time he realised that his first guess had been right, the French had landed, and Bonaparte had won the Battle of the Pyramids. Nelson had missed destroying the French army, but at Aboukir Bay, on the night of 1–2 August, 1798, he made up for it by annihilating the French fleet. The French commander Brueys was killed, cut in half by a cannonball. Only two ships escaped.

At one stroke Nelson had mastered the Mediterranean and stranded France's idol, a hungry tiger with nothing to rage at but the sand. He had made Russia and Austria feel that the Second Coalition was worthwhile, and had become a national hero. At St Vincent in '97 he had attracted notice, but Jervis was his superior officer. At the Battle of the Nile he was in sole command, and so collected all the honour and glory, for which his appetite was insatiable.

1799, then, looked promising. British troops were sent to Holland. A Russian army under the legendary Suvorov threatened France through Italy and Switzerland. The Austrians had troops in Italy and on the Rhine, and nobody knew where Bonaparte was, least of all his own government.

They found out soon enough. After trying, and failing, to conquer the Turkish Empire, Bonaparte deserted his own army, sailed secretly to France, and began plotting in Paris. In November, 1799 he overthrew the Directory and made himself head of state. (In theory he was First Consul, one of three, but nobody really had any doubt what 'First' meant.) To gain time he offered peace terms, but it was the Allies' turn to refuse; they were beginning to realise that there was no hope of true peace with France in its present fever of revolution and aggression. They thought too that they were going to win.

They were wrong. Suvorov was halted in Switzerland by Masséna, a wily French general (once a smuggler) second in ability only to Bonaparte. Tsar Paul quarrelled with his allies and left the Coalition in a huff. (Gossip alleged that he was mentally unstable.) The English in Holland fought the French, and the mud, and were beaten by both. Pitt and his War Secretary, Dundas, persisted in wasting soldiers in tuppeny-ha'penny expeditions to help various Royalist revolts in France – all of which failed. Bonaparte swept into Northern Italy and smashed an Austrian army at Marengo; his colleague Moreau broke another at Hohenlinden in Germany. That accounted for the Austrians. By the end of 1800, England was on her own again.

Not only had she lost her allies; she had gained an enemy – the Armed Neutrality. As in the American War, the northern powers resented British captains capturing their ships which traded with France. Tsar Paul, still angry with England, and egged on by France, formed a union with Sweden, Denmark, and Prussia, to exclude all British ships from the Baltic. England drew many of her timber and other naval supplies from the Baltic, and relied on imports of wheat from Prussia and Poland through the Baltic. There could be only one reply. Eighteen ships of the line were sent to deal with the Danish Fleet, the core of the Armed Neutrality.

On 2 April, 1801, after terrible slaughter, the Danish Fleet was virtually wiped out. The commander of the British squadron was Admiral Sir Hyde Parker, but the hero of the battle was, again, Nelson, his second-in-command. Nelson chose to ignore Parker's order to withdraw when the decision looked doubtful. At the time Parker hoisted his signal, he could be forgiven for thinking that Nelson was in danger, but Nelson, from his own position in the thick of the fighting, was better placed to judge. One of his many gifts was his ability to 'read' a battle as if it were an open book; all his professional experience and instincts told him that if he hung on a little longer, the day would be his. Ignoring a senior officer's signals in action was a risky business; only a Nelson would dare to do it. But then only a Nelson would have Nelson's reasons for doing so. He won the battle, the nation cheered, and everyone forgot about the admiral's signal – except the writers of history books. The Armed Neutrality broke up, the Baltic was reopened, and somebody conveniently murdered the Tsar.

Less than a month before the Battle of Copenhagen, the unbelievable happened in England, Pitt was out of office. After seventeen continuous years of service, Pitt had tendered his resignation, and the King had accepted it. The odd thing was that it had nothing to do with the war – at any rate nothing directly connected with it. Pitt was not hounded from Downing Street by mobs yelling about bread prices and *Habeas Corpus*, nor by angry MPs complaining about his failure to defeat Bonaparte.

It was Ireland. Through the nineteenth century, Ireland was a British prime minister's cross in life. Time and time again prime ministers – whole governments – staggered, broke, and fell because of Ireland. They could no more shake off Ireland than Christ could the original cross. The events of the 1790s set the pattern for this, and provide a perfect illustration.

Ireland was – is – an island. That made it separate, distant, unfamiliar. (Wales and Scotland might be outlandish, but at least one could get there easily.) On the other hand Ireland was unquestionably part of the British Isles. British cabinets would no more consider making Ireland fully independent than they would giving home rule to the Isle of Wight. It would be like cutting off a limb. Yet Ireland was never regarded as wholly British. Nor was it a colony in the normal sense of the word. It was Britain's back yard ruled like a conquered foreign country.

To begin with, Ireland *was* a conquered country; the Normans had begun conquering it in the twelfth century. As early as that the Irish had a reputation for being quarrelsome; tribal 'kings' were regularly engaged in wars among themselves. There was a High King at Tara, near Dublin, but the four main provinces – Ulster, Leinster, Munster, and Connaught – were usually in rivalry over which of them should hold this title. The province of Ulster was already regarded by the other three as something of an odd man out – cut off from the others by natural boundaries of hills and lakes and rivers.

All the Normans did was complicate the situation. They were foreigners, they were conquerors, they took some of the best land, and they lived apart from the native Irish. They only gave the provincial leaders one more enemy to fight. As the years went on, the descendants of the early Norman conquerors became a sort of second Irish nobility. The longer they stayed there, and the more they extended their estates, the more they identified themselves with

Ireland, until they came to resent interference from England even more than the original Irish had done.

So the native Irish society of squabbling provinces was overlaid with a new class of landlords from England who looked down on them, and who also proved very awkward for English kings to govern from London. As the centuries advanced the pattern was repeated. The sixteenth century saw a fresh wave of land-hungry adventurers, who were met by hostility from two quarters – the original Irish, and the Anglo-Norman families (who were now entrenched behind four hundred years of tradition and semi-independence). The Reformation complicated matters further by creating the split between Catholic and Protestant. Not all newcomers were Protestant; not all Anglo-Normans remained Catholic.

In the seventeenth century more colonisers arrived in Ulster, many of them Presbyterians from Scotland. So they met prejudice from old Irish *and* Anglo-Normans, from Catholics *and* Anglicans. It also gave the other three provinces more reason for disliking Ulster.

From time to time English armies descended upon Ireland to put down a rebellion or besiege a mutinous town. Armies putting down rebellions or capturing cities after sieges rarely behave well, but something about Ireland seemed to bring out more evil in soldiers – and their commanders – than usual. Whatever the reason, the Irish Catholics had good cause to hate the names of Cromwell and William III. By the same token William III (of Orange) is a great hero to many Irish Protestants – the Orangemen.

If it can be put any more simply, the problem of Ireland went something like this. The Irish, who were not united among themselves, did not like England, because England tried to conquer them. As each wave of invaders (or colonists or adventurers or whatever) came to Ireland, they usually took the best land still available, and either turned the native Irish into poor tenants or drove them into the poorer areas. As each wave settled and put down roots into the soil, they came to regard Ireland as their own; they felt contempt for the native Irish, and annoyance at English governments' 'interference' in the running of 'their' country. English ministers were enraged by the baffling fact that whoever settled in Ireland became difficult to handle.

So each of the three main parties involved had no affection, respect, or understanding for the other two. The Irish were sullen, devious, and hostile; the landlords were haughty, clannish, and contentious; governments in London were ill-informed, baffled, and exasperated.

If that had been the only trouble, man might in the end have seen reason, but Ireland has a knack of imposing one layer of crises on top of another. In this case religion as the tool of politics turned dislikes into prejudices, and then into paranoid hatreds. Accepting that over-simplification is the unavoidable result of generalisation in the interests of speed and clarity, it is reasonably fair to claim that most native Irish tenants remained Catholic, and many landlords turned Protestant. And, after the Glorious Revolution of 1688 and the expulsion of James II, the cause of Catholic kingship was dead; Protestants were to rule at Westminster hereafter.

The parliaments of William III, Anne, and the first two Georges wanted therefore to make it clear that the respectable religion, the safe religion, the correct religion to follow henceforth, was to be their brand of Protestantism: that of the Church of England – Anglicanism. They wished to convey the message that obedience to a distant pope could get you into trouble, that showing support, even feeling sympathy, for a Roman Catholic claimant to the throne was extremely ill-advised.

They conveyed the message with steam-roller thoroughness. By the time they had finished with the statute book, Catholics could do hardly anything that was not illegal. They could not vote; they could not sit in Parliament. They could not enter any establishment for higher education; they could not hold commissions in the armed forces. They could not be judges or jurymen; they could not hold any public office whatsoever. No Irish Catholic chapel was allowed a bell, the English apparently hoping that if the Irish did not hear the ringing they would forget to go to Mass. No Irishman was permitted to own a horse worth more than five pounds. If he did, he was compelled by law to sell it to the first Protestant who offered him the price for it. (A horse – a good one – was a potential mount for rebel cavalry.) If any member of an Irish Catholic family turned Protestant, all the land of that family was to pass to him on the death of the father.

This vicious code of law, remember, was approved of not only by the

English Parliament, but by the Protestant landlords in Ireland. They were the magistrates who enforced it (though, to be fair, there was a certain amount of blind-eye-turning; after all, they did all have to live together). There existed an Irish Parliament, but it was entirely Protestant. Half its House of Lords were Anglican bishops. Two-thirds of its House of Commons were simply the nominees of the landlords – there were very few contested elections.

So the Irish tenant had a terrible time. He had lost his ancient rights over the land of Ireland. He was forced on to the poorer soil, or he paid rent to a Protestant landlord who sat on a magistrate's bench, and could make his life unbearable simply because the tenant believed in the Church of Rome. If he broke the law he was pursued by Protestant constables, and if he joined a civil riot he was beaten and arrested (or worse) by soldiers under the command of Protestant officers. He was then held in a Protestant jail, tried in a Protestant court, found guilty by a Protestant jury, and sentenced by a Protestant judge.

It is worth noting that Catholics were not the only sufferers. Many of the Presbyterians in Ulster were not much better off either; there were similar Anglican laws against them. Perhaps not quite so many, and perhaps not quite so savage, but Nonconformists of any persuasion, in both Ireland and England, were regarded by the Establishment as, at best, suspect citizens. It was an overhang of the old idea, stemming from the sixteenth century and before, that, if you were not totally loyal to the official church, you were potentially disloyal to the official government.

This situation in Ireland might well have continued unchanged had it not been for the French Revolution and the war. Each one of the three main groups involved – the 'home-grown' Irish, the landlords of the Irish Parliament, and the Government at Westminster – reacted. Each produced a policy to solve the problem, each was split as a result, and each failed.

To begin with, the French Revolution, as might be expected, stimulated a lot of radical feeling in Ireland. Before long a new society had been formed, the United Irishmen, which aimed at expelling English influence – landlords, monarchy and all. Its leaders were Lord Edward Fitzgerald, a member of one of the old Irish-Norman families, and Wolfe Tone, a young Belfast lawyer. They hoped to appeal to all who suffered from the vicious Anglican laws, that is to Catholics in the south, and to Presbyterians in Ulster. They corresponded with the French revolutionaries. Tone went on a tour of the two new republics – France and the USA – to drum up some support. France sent an expedition to Ireland in 1796. The invasion fleet reached Bantry Bay, but a storm broke it up before it could land.

The 'United Irishmen' idea did not work. Presbyterians and Catholics would not work together. Ulster had always feared being swamped by the three southern provinces, and Presbyterians knew that the southern Catholics were much more numerous than they were. They did not want to throw off the tyranny of London only to fall under the tyranny of Rome. They preferred to go it alone. The result was that the Viceroy of Ireland (the King's representative) had two possible rebellions on his hands, not one.

He moved on Ulster early to nip it in the bud. Soldiers and militia (part-timers) descended, and pillaged, robbed, and killed on the excuse that they were punishing treason. In the south the United Irishmen decided to strike first before they were arrested in their beds. In the spring of 1798 they came out in open rebellion. General Lake's army was not up to much, but it coped easily with the wild, untrained Irish, who were broken at Vinegar Hill on 21 June, 1798. Semi-outlaw gangs continued the fight for a few months afterwards, and the French sent some more troops. They landed too late to do any real good, and were soon rounded up by the new Viceroy, Lord Cornwallis. Fitzgerald died of his wounds received in the fighting. Tone came back in a French ship, was captured, condemned to death for treason, and cut his own throat in prison.

The first move, then, to remedy the situation had failed. A crusade to unite all Irishmen who suffered religious persecution had resulted in a savage minor war, in which Protestants and Catholics killed each other for their religion.

The second solution was tried by a member of the Irish governing class, Henry Grattan. He believed that two things were wrong: the Irish Parliament was not free enough from London's interference; and the Irish Parliament itself did not represent enough Irishmen. How could it, when it was all Protestant, and three-quarters of the population were Catholic? He wished, therefore, to win greater freedom for the Irish Parliament, to abolish some of the corruption in Irish elections, and to give full civil rights (emancipation) to the Roman Catholics. He tried to make his fellow-landlords see that their first loyalty was not to their property, but to Ireland.

He failed. Protestants were afraid of being outnumbered in Parliament by Catholics. Landlords feared that if tenants were given political power they would attack property. If they, the landlords, separated themselves too much from England, there would be nobody to defend them when the attack came. The threat of a French invasion backed by a Catholic revolution only confirmed their opposition to Grattan. So the Irish Parliament, divided, could do nothing.

Finally, then, it was Pitt's turn. His chief concern was not land, or religion; it was security. England was clearly responsible for Ireland. It was up to its Prime Minister to see that Ireland was governed as peaceably as possible. But in time of war, Pitt had a duty above and beyond that – to defend the British Isles. As the 1790s advanced, it became increasingly clear that he needed a single policy with which to rule both countries. A war had to have unified direction, and he would get that not with two parliaments, but with one. The United Irishmen rebellion had demonstrated too how much the Dublin Government depended upon English troops. There had already been three attempts to invade Ireland. Pitt felt that he had to have direct control, and that he had to give the Irish Catholics a good reason for *not* joining the French if they should try again.

His plan was twofold. One part was to remove the Irish Parliament; the second was to bring about religious peace by granting full civil rights to Roman Catholics. (He had already given them the vote in 1793, on the same terms as Protestants – about one man in twenty.) Pitt, Viceroy Cornwallis, and Castlereagh, the Secretary for Ireland, were all convinced that without Catholic Emancipation Ireland would never be safe.

In order to make the Bill of Union legal, it had to pass both English and Irish Parliaments. That is, the Irish Parliament had to be persuaded to abolish itself. Grattan and his moderates were promised that full emancipation for Catholics (one of his dreams) would follow. The die-hard landlords were won over by the argument that if Catholics were let in, their (the landlords') property would be safer with the English Parliament directly behind them. Castlereagh also handed out bribes wholesale. In 1800, the Dublin Parliament, by 158 votes to 115, voted itself out of existence.

Pitt, however, was not through the wood yet. The second bill, for Catholic Emancipation, ran into Anglican opposition in his own cabinet. When he had talked it round, Pitt met a stiffer obstacle – the King's conscience. George had his limitations, but he was a devout Anglican, and he felt, quite sincerely, that Catholic Emancipation was a blow at the Church of England, which he had sworn to defend and uphold in his coronation oath. Pitt saw that the cards were stacked against him. The King was stubborn, and too much nagging might produce another nervous attack. The Cabinet were dragging their feet, and there was a lot of opposition in Parliament. He could not make too big an issue out of it – there was a war to be fought.

But the Prime Minister had given his word to the Irish that the Act of Union would be followed by Catholic Emancipation. Now he could not keep that promise. All he could do therefore was offer to resign. George, who had been looking for a replacement, found a suitable one in Henry Addington, the Speaker of the House of Commons. He accepted Pitt's resignation, and Addington became Prime Minister in March, 1801.

By now, everyone was fed up with the war. England had no allies. The navy was supreme at sea. Bonaparte's armies were the masters on land. Nobody could 'win' in the normal sense of the word. Both sides were exhausted.

So a peace was patched up at Amiens in March, 1802. England gave back all the colonies she had captured, except Ceylon and Trinidad. France gave up Southern Italy, and very little else. Nobody seriously expected the peace to last, and both sides soon broke the terms of it. Each used the breathing space to prepare for another war, which was bound to start sooner or later.

By 1803, the French were making little secret of their huge military camps all along the Channel coast. It could mean only one thing – invasion. In May, Addington's Government came out into the open and declared war, so that it could strike before the invasion fleet sailed. The naval blockades were set up again, and the old business began of finding allies. It did not seem so difficult now, because it was becoming more and more obvious that France would not be content with her present empire.

Bonaparte had spent three or four frantic years overhauling practically every department of French government – the law, commerce, finance, local administration, education – often working an eighteen-hour day, and giving his secretaries nervous breakdowns. He claimed he was upholding the ideals of the Revolution, but it was becoming increasingly difficult to believe him. The press was censored; royalists remained in exile; spies, informers, and secret police kept him in power; victory and the spoils of war kept him popular. The French soldiers who were gathering in the vast camps by the Channel were no longer seen as the liberators of Europe from royalist tyranny; they were the agents of French conquest.

The 'crusade against kings' became ridiculous in 1804, when Bonaparte crowned himself Emperor (literally – he took the crown out of the Pope's hands and placed it upon his own head). At least it simplified matters. There was no question about it now: it was France against everybody else; and there would be no peace so long as Emperor Napoleon remained master of France. The Revolution had little to do with it.

In England, Addington was defeated in the Commons. By universal consent, there could be only one man in such a crisis to take his place. In the spring of 1804, Pitt took up the burden once more, having promised not to worry the King further about Catholic Emancipation. All eyes turned across the Channel, not in lazy curiosity as in 1788, but in tense concern. With that huge, invincible army, where and when would Boney strike?

CHAPTER THREE

Old Nosey
1804–14

On 14 March, 1804, three hundred French dragoons galloped across the French border into the neutral state of Baden, in south-west Germany. They kidnapped a young Bourbon prince, the Duc d'Enghien, a member of the exiled French royal family, and whisked him back to Paris. At the castle of Vincennes he was questioned about his part in a recent plot against Bonaparte's life. Nothing could be proved against him. Not a single incriminating document could be found. In spite of that he was tried by a hasty court martial and shot.

The crime stank throughout Europe. The young prince was obviously innocent. Baden was a neutral state. The dictator of France, who claimed to wish for nothing but peace, had shown beyond any doubt that he had no regard whatever for international law. Worse, he had openly insulted both Austria and Russia. Austria was the chief power in Germany, and could not accept this interference in her sphere of influence. The Tsar, Alexander I, was related to the ruler of Baden, and enjoyed posing as the champion of small German princes. (He himself was seven-eighths German by birth.) If Bonaparte had deliberately set out to insult the two Emperors, he could hardly have made a better job of it. He later admitted, though with no sorrow, that the murder of Enghien was 'worse than a crime; it was a mistake'.

It played right into Pitt's hands. Faced with that enormous army just across the Channel, Pitt knew that he had to distract Bonaparte's attention somehow. He also knew that the only recipe for peace was the destruction of Bonaparte; and the only way to bring about that was to unite Europe against him. In short, another coalition.

The Austrians, having been thrashed twice, had not been eager for a third war, and Tsar Alexander had begun his reign as an admirer of Bonaparte. The murder of the Duc d'Enghien began to tip the scales the other way. The Tsar, moreover, had the same ambitions as his grandmother, the old Empress Catherine – to break through from the Black Sea into the Mediterranean. That meant carving up the Turkish Empire. But the recent French expeditions to Egypt and Syria had made it look as if Bonaparte had the same idea. Alexander did not want any rivals.

The Austrian court was not noted for cavalier dash or taste for adventure, but even the Hapsburgs could not go on taking insults for ever. The Baden affair had made it clear that the French had no respect for anyone in Germany. Before very long Bonaparte had calmly announced that Italy was his business too; he had himself proclaimed King of Italy in May, 1805. The Austrians reacted at last, in sheer self-defence. By the summer of that year, Pitt had his coalition – England, Austria, and Russia.

Ideally, he would have liked the alliance to be bigger. Sweden cheerfully joined, but she was a power of only the second or third rank. The big absentee was Prussia. King Frederick William was, like the Hapsburgs earlier, too overawed by Bonaparte to dare a declaration of war. Nor would he allow Russian troops to march through his lands. Finally, Spain, whose navy could have been useful, had turned against Britain. French ships were already helping themselves to all the Spanish ports and dockyards, so Pitt had decided to make the Spanish Government come out into the open by capturing the great silver convoy homeward bound from Mexico. The Madrid court had duly declared war, in December, 1804.

When 1805 opened, then, Pitt knew that he would have to make plans to deal with two enemy fleets, not one. The traditional method had been, and still was, blockade. Since the war with France had broken out again in 1803, battered British squadrons in Channel, Biscay, Atlantic, and Mediterranean had clung by their fingernails to their positions through the most appalling weather. Enduring month after month of cramped living and soaked clothes, salt pork and weevilly biscuit, grinding hardship and unspeakable boredom, they clawed their way through deluge and doldrum, burning sun and ice-laden spray, fog, frost and gale to keep the Frogs, and now the Dons too, bottled up in their harbours.

If they could not get out, they could not invade. Admiral Jervis, now First Lord of the Admiralty, gave this assurance to his fellow-members of the House of Lords: 'I do not say the French cannot come, my lords; I only say they cannot come by sea.'

Bonaparte, while he was hurling orders and abuse at his craven admirals, understood the position just as clearly. He could never push the English away from the Channel to give his invasion fleet room and time to cross. Very well – if he could not push them, he would pull them. If his chicken-hearted admirals did not want to fight the English, at least they could slip out of port and run. The English would give chase. If enough French and Spanish squadrons led the English a dance across the Atlantic, there might be a chance for his cowardly sailors to make a sudden dash back to the Channel with a united fleet, and hold it long enough to get the soldiers over. It would not matter then if the English came back or not; the damage would have been done. That was the plan.

Villeneuve, commander of the French squadron in Toulon, watched and waited. Not even the British could keep such a huge blockade totally sealed for ever; there was bound to be a chink in the door sooner or later. After a false start in January, 1805, Villeneuve tried again in March, succeeded, and set all sail for the West Indies. Similar instructions had been sent to the commanders stuck in harbour up and down the French and Spanish coast. From Brest, Rochefort, Cadiz, and Cartagena, they were to dodge the blockade, sail across the Atlantic, and rendezvous in the West Indies. Bonaparte frankly did not mind if the British did guess where they were going; they always reacted immediately to any threat of attack on their precious sugar islands in the West Indies. If they dashed off to defend Jamaica, or chased Villeneuve just in order to fight him, it would get them out of the way.

As it happened, Nelson, in command of the Mediterranean Fleet, guessed rightly, and set off in pursuit across the Atlantic, hoping to bring Villeneuve to battle on the other side. Villeneuve meanwhile waited in the Caribbean for the other squadrons to turn up as planned. He waited in vain. The ships in Cartagena and Brest had never come out of harbour; only six sail of the line had joined him from Cadiz; and the Rochefort squadron had arrived too early, waited, given up hope, and gone back without him. When Villeneuve heard from his scouting frigates that Nelson had arrived, he decided that it was time for his own squadron to be on their way.

This time Nelson guessed wrongly, and thought that the enemy might be making for the Mediterranean again, possibly to invade Naples, or Sicily, or even Egypt once more. Nelson sent fast frigates to warn their lordships at the Admiralty, and himself sailed with all speed for Cadiz and Gibraltar. Lord Barham, the new First Lord, took no chances; he put a squadron under Admiral Calder at the mouth of the Channel – just in case. It was as well he did; Calder took up his station about a hundred miles west of Finisterre in time to meet Villeneuve, who had not gone for the Mediterranean. On 22 July, there was an indecisive action at long range, after which Villeneuve gave up and put back to Ferrol in northern Spain. With the immediate crisis over, Nelson was ordered back to England.

Bonaparte was still cooling his heels with his invasion army at Boulogne when he heard the news. Furious at the failure, which he blamed entirely on his cowardly and inefficient admirals, he ordered Villeneuve out again, to face the might of the English in the mouth of the Channel. By that time, Lord Barham had reinforced the Channel Fleet, so that Admiral Cornwallis commanded a huge force of thirty-six sail of the line, an unprecedented number.

Villeneuve's ships were rotten, his supplies and equipment deficient, his men ill and demoralised. He was also outnumbered. After a token push into Biscay, he turned about on 15 August, and fled for Cadiz. Collingwood watched him into harbour, took up sentry duty once more, and sent a frigate to the Admiralty with the news that the enemy had gone to ground again.

Chafing at Boulogne, Bonaparte heard that the Austrians had declared war on him. Deciding to make the best of a bad job, and burning to take out his temper on somebody, he swung his enormous army in the opposite direction, across France and Germany – destination Vienna. The great invasion threat was over – at any rate for the moment.

However, as long as the French and Spanish Fleets remained in existence, a similar threat could revive again at any time. Nelson presented their lordships at the Admiralty with a plan for breaking the stalemate of blockade and boredom; he offered a solution, a decision. Blockade had served its purpose, he said; it was time to change it, or at least to modify it. Stand away from the mouths of their harbours; let them come out; and then stop them getting back. Bring them to battle. He proceeded to unfold a scheme not merely for defeating the enemy fleet, but for annihilating it.

Nelson was on fire during those three weeks in England. There was no stopping him. His excitement and his eager plans bowled everyone over. The Cabinet gave him a free hand both in the Mediterranean and in the Atlantic off Spain. William Pitt himself came to the door with him and saw him to his coach. Lord Barham, at the Admiralty, handed him the full list of Royal Navy officers and told him to choose anyone he wanted.

As he went about his business, his appearance stamped itself for ever on the nation's memory. The frail, weather-beaten frame, the shock of hair, the glittering stars and orders, the green eye-shade (to keep the sun off his good eye, not to hide the blind one), and the empty sleeve – he was tailor-made for legend. His fellow-admirals were not so impressed; several of them regarded him as a self-centred, strutting glory-hunter. But, in those charged weeks of late summer, it was the public image that mattered. Nelson looked like England itself – small, battered, surviving by sheer willpower, never considering defeat or surrender for a minute. In a sense, for that brief time, Nelson *was* England. He knew it, and everyone else knew it.

He impressed a young major-general who had just returned from a victorious campaign on the other side of the world, in India. Few men were harder to impress than Sir Arthur Wellesley, though Sir Arthur was not very taken with him to begin with. They met, for the only time, when they were both shown into a small waiting room across the hall from the office of Lord Castlereagh, Secretary of State for War and the

Colonies. Sir Arthur knew who Nelson was, of course; there was only one admiral in England with one arm and one eye. But Nelson did not know him, and started on a conversation that amounted to little more than showing off. Sir Arthur was baffled and embarrassed. When at last he managed to get a word in edgeways, it must have been full of his usual downright common sense, because Nelson suddenly stopped, looked at him closely, and left the room – obviously to find out whom he was talking to. When he was told that the hook-nosed young general was the man who had just won the famous Battle of Assaye and made England's power in India supreme, he came back and talked like a completely different person. Sir Arthur declared later that he could not remember having had a more interesting conversation. Nelson really was, he admitted, 'a very superior man'.

On 14 September, Nelson boarded the *Victory* at Portsmouth. The Saturday crowds were bigger than usual, and people knelt as he passed them on his way to the beach. Many were in tears. Some followed him into the water.

Almost overnight he cast a similar spell over his new captains and crews. He now had a third of the entire British Navy under his sole command, and by the time he reached Spain he had welded it into a single force whose every deckhand worshipped him. Nelson had a unique capacity to inspire not only respect and admiration, but intense affection. The officers too were ablaze with enthusiasm, for Nelson had shown them a plan not for beating the enemy fleet, but for wiping it out. He proposed to attack in two columns of ships, thereby splitting the enemy line into three sections. Before the front third of the enemy line – the van – could turn about to help the centre and rear, he hoped that his force of impact would have broken up the rest and given him time to destroy as many ships as possible in a general ding-dong battle, where English superior seamanship and gunnery would tell.

It was his way of dealing with an enemy who had greater numbers, including the three most powerful ships in the world. His captains were delighted. It went flat against all the old ideas of laying one line of ships alongside another. The plan looked, and still looks, childishly simple on paper, but it took courage and imagination to go against the dead weight of over a hundred years of tradition. It is a measure of

Nelson's magic that he was able to convince his captains that such a revolutionary idea would work.

At a time when a single mistake, one solitary deviation from the rule book, could ruin an officer's career, Nelson's captains could not wait to try it out. Nelson made sure they completely understood it, and convinced them that he had confidence in them, that he trusted them to use their own judgment to make his plan work in the way that seemed best to them at the time, and that there would be no recriminations afterwards. In all his dealings with both officers and ratings, Nelson had the trick of making them believe that he was going all out to get a decision, that it would be a clear one, and above all that it would be a victorious one.

On 21 October, 1805, off Cape Trafalgar, near Cadiz, Nelson proved his argument and got his decision. Of thirty-three enemy ships of the line, eighteen were accounted for, and the rest never fought again. He also achieved the undying glory he had chased all his life. As he paced his quarterdeck, in his full dress uniform complete with stars and orders, he was an obvious target. As the *Victory* and the French ship *Redoutable* lay locked together, a sniper from the enemy rigging hit him, and he lived just long enough to know how completely he had won.

The cheers at home were strangled by grief. Nor was that the only bad news at the end of 1805. From Europe it was heard that the Emperor had moved his Grand Army so fast that he had already defeated one Austrian general at Ulm (on the day before Trafalgar), and was marching on Vienna itself. The Prussians, annoyed at his troops marching through their territory, made noises about declaring war, but the Austrian and Russian Emperors decided to give battle without waiting for Prussia to mobilise. At the Battle of Austerlitz, on 2 December, 1805, they realised their mistake too late. Bonaparte won his greatest victory. The Russians withdrew, the Austrians signed the Peace Treaty of Pressburg, just after Christmas, and Pitt's Third Coalition lay in ruins.

It finished Pitt. He had been living on his nerves for years. Always a solitary man, he had no comforts of wife or family, of racetrack or gaming club. Apart from his bottle of port, Pitt never unwound. At the end of 1805, the blows came too thick and fast – the death of Nelson, the Austrian surrender at Ulm, the disaster at

Austerlitz, the Austrian treaty at Pressburg, the withdrawal of the Russians. Finally, his best friend, Henry Dundas, was hounded from office by his political enemies.

On 23 January, 1806, Pitt died. He was only forty-six. He had been Prime Minister nearly half his life. His fondest admirers would not claim that he was as great a war minister as his father, and for a man who did such wonders for the nation's finances, his own private affairs were in an unbelievable mess; his desk was a hopeless clutter. But year after year Pitt had carried the burden of leadership. Time and again he had seen his plans crash and his coalitions come apart; time and again he had bent and picked up the pieces. He had soldiered on through one bulletin of gloomy news after another. His French enemies recognised that he was the inspiration behind England's refusal to give up. They once went so far as to pass a solemn motion in one of their revolutionary assemblies that Pitt was 'the enemy of the human race'. It was not polite, but it showed how highly they rated him and his contribution.

In England, there was no question about his supremacy. Men were stunned. It was almost impossible to imagine British politics without him. Charles James Fox, his lifelong political enemy, burst into tears at the news. Pitt's passing left a yawning gap, which no one man could hope to fill.

As is often the case, the great man was followed by a succession of smaller, mediocre ones. For a variety of reasons, not one of them was able to keep anything like the control that Pitt had commanded. The next few years saw quarrels, both public and private, between politicians and ministers, at the very time when the country's governing classes should have been united over the war. Pitt had always stood apart from petty party squabbles. Now there was nobody with his dignity or his detachment, or, for that matter, his ability.

The immediate next Prime Minister was Lord Grenville, once a follower of Pitt, and later a colleague of Fox. Indeed Fox was the leading member of his cabinet. It says something for the desperate nature of the situation that the King was prepared to have Fox at all.

The ministry soon collapsed. Fox died in September after only eight months in office, and Grenville quarrelled with the King over the Catholic problem. He had proposed to allow loyal Catholics to hold commissions in the Army; with the war at its height, he needed officers wherever he could get them. Like Pitt before, he ran foul of the King. George would not allow any concessions whatever to Catholics. Pitt had given way in 1801, and Grenville was forced to do so in 1807. When George asked him to promise never to raise the Catholic question again, he refused, and resigned in March of that year.

The Duke of Portland became Prime Minister – or rather, technically, the First Lord of the Treasury. There was no actual office called after the Prime Minister. The leader of the Cabinet was simply the King's Chief (or Prime) Minister. He could, in theory, hold any office – Home Secretary, Foreign Secretary, Chancellor of the Exchequer, or whatever. He could even hold more than one. The ministry was named after him, because he was the leading personality in that ministry. In 1783, for instance, the Government was known as the Fox–North Coalition, though neither North nor Fox was First Lord of the Treasury (they were Secretaries of State). However, the practice gradually became fixed for the First Lord of the Treasury to be automatically Prime Minister; or, to put it another way round, the man invited by the King to become Prime Minister and to form a cabinet usually took the office of First Lord of the Treasury for himself.

Portland, then, became Prime Minister in 1807, but his cabinet did not have sufficient strength. It should have done; the personalities were there. Perceval, despite a fairly late start under Addington, was already Chancellor of the Exchequer. Two disciples of Pitt, Canning and Liverpool, both held high office, and the Secretary for War and the Colonies was Lord Castlereagh, the late Secretary for Ireland at the time of the Union. That was the trouble in a way; there were too many personalities, and Portland could not hold them all together. The war was going badly too, and Portland's health broke down in 1809.

Perceval tried next, but personal quarrels made his ministry weaker than it should have been. Lord Liverpool finally took over in 1812, and remained Prime Minister for the duration of the war, in fact until 1827 – a surprisingly long period in office for a man who, on the face of it at least, had few if any obvious gifts.

It was a lean time for Britain's governing classes. Addington (now created Lord Sidmouth) was disliked by the old supporters of Pitt, most of whom refused to serve with him. When Perceval tried to get the opposition leaders to join him in order to make a united front against the foreign enemy, both Grenville and Lord Grey turned him down. Castlereagh and Canning hated each other so much that they actually fought a duel. Both survived, but it cost both of them their jobs. There was another scandal when it came out that a Mrs Clarke, an actress 'friend' of the Duke of York, the Commander-in-Chief, had been selling Army commissions behind his back. The Duke was declared not guilty of corruption, but clearly should never have allowed any lady, 'friend' or otherwise, such knowledge of official business. He was forced to resign (and was reappointed in 1811).

Then, in 1810, King George went mad again, this time for good. The Prince of Wales took up the Regency, at first temporarily and with limited powers. The Government perhaps was cautious after the Prince's behaviour in 1788. Two things, however, soon became clear. First, the King was not going to recover. Secondly, the Prince of Wales had grown older, fatter, and slower. Besides, his great friend Fox was dead. The war still had to be fought, and the Prince, who was no fool, judged that his old cronies, the Whigs, would probably run it worse than the Tories. For all his failings, the Prince was an Englishman, and longed to lead his country to victory over France. So he gave his support to the Tory Government of Perceval, who returned the compliment by granting him full kingly powers as Prince Regent. Even so, it did not help the dignity of the crown for everyone to know that there was a lonely, long-haired lunatic locked up in Windsor Castle.

Another jolt for national security came in May, 1812, when a man called Henry Bellingham walked up to the Prime Minister in the lobby of the House of Commons and shot him. Perceval died, the only Prime Minister of England to be assassinated.

Bellingham's grudge was that his investments in Russia (he was a commercial agent) had suffered severely, owing (he said) to the neglect of the British minister in St Petersburg, and he held the entire Government responsible. Indeed, he later admitted that he had nothing personal against Perceval; he just wanted to kill a Government minister; anyone would do.

It transpired that he had been seen earlier outside the Court of

Chancery, where Lord Chancellor Eldon presided; witnesses recalled that he (Bellingham) had a hand inside the breast of his coat, as if ready to pull something out. It so happened that Eldon's case finished early, and he found he had some spare time before being required in the House of Lords. So he took off his Chancellor's robes, put on a street overcoat, and went out for a walk – right past Bellingham, who of course did not recognise him in unfamiliar garb.

Eldon reckoned that he had had a very lucky escape. He went on, therefore, whether in or out of office, to vote against nearly every proposed liberal reform for the next twenty-six years. And he was by no means the most hated man in the Cabinet.

The Government, and the ruling classes generally, were so unpopular that in some parts of the country the news of Perceval's death was received with fierce delight. When his murderer suffered the extreme, and inevitable, penalty, the public hangman was pelted by the crowd.

Perceval was not to blame for all the people's troubles, nor were the ruling classes as a whole. But governments are usually blamed for bad times, whether it is their fault or not.

Bad times there certainly were. The evil effects of the Industrial and Agricultural Revolutions were growing every year, and the war served only to make them worse. The need for more clothes and munitions for the Army and Navy had brought in more machines, which in turn was putting more cottage industries out of business. More soldiers and sailors had to be fed, which meant more enclosures, which meant more unemployment, homelessness, and misery on the land. The war was cutting off the supply of foreign corn at the very time when a rising population had greater need for it. This in turn made the country more dependent on its own corn supply, and therefore on its weather. Foreign shortage sent bread prices high, and bad harvests (of which there were several) sent them higher.

True, factory-builders and owner-farmers made a great deal of money out of the war, but they were very few compared with the hundreds of thousands who saw the value of their miserable wages getting lower and lower. They were helpless to do anything about it. They could not vote; they could not form trade unions; they could not hold protest meetings; they could not circulate pamphlets. They could not do anything that even looked like criticism of the Government; it was now against the law. Their only means of expression was violence and crime. On the land they poached; in the cities they smashed machines. If caught, they could be, and were, whipped, imprisoned, transported, or hung. It did not stop them.

The war also made their lives worse in another way, and to explain this one must go back to the year of Pitt's death, 1806. Ever since Nelson's victory at Trafalgar the previous year, it had been obvious that Bonaparte had lost command of the sea for good. Britain would never be invaded. On the other hand Bonaparte had raised himself to a position of complete mastery in Europe. At Austerlitz he had defeated the Austrians. In 1806, he annihilated the Prussian Army, and in 1807, he defeated the Russians and forced the Tsar to make peace. He was in control of the whole of Western Europe except Spain and Portugal.

The situation was a complete stalemate. Neither Britain nor France could get at the other, much less win the war. Each country therefore was forced into new methods in an effort to get a decision. Each borrowed an idea, a technique, from the other; Bonaparte took up the traditional English method of blockade, and Britain attempted to put a really sizeable army on the mainland of Europe.

First, then, Bonaparte. He could not defeat the English. Very well – he would starve them. He controlled practically the whole European coastline from the Bay of Biscay to the Baltic shores of Russia. From Berlin, in November, 1806, he issued orders that no European port would receive any ships from Britain or from her colonies. So Britain could not get her Polish and Prussian corn, or the Baltic timber vital for her shipbuilding. Nor could she sell any of the huge output from her new factories and expanding industries. That, at any rate, was the theory.

Britain replied in March, 1807, with the Orders in Council, which laid down that no ship – British, colonial, or neutral – could trade with Bonaparte's ports unless they were selling British goods or unless they had paid a customs duty and bought a licence first in British ports.

Bonaparte, tit for tat, replied again, this time from Milan, in November, 1807. He ordered quite simply that any ship which put in at a British seaport would, if subsequently caught, be confiscated.

There was a difference between the two blockades. Bonaparte was trying to stop Britain selling her industrial goods and buying food and valuable shipping supplies; Britain was trying only to *regulate* trade into France – by her customs and licences system on neutrals – and so exercise a sort of valve on the French economy.

But whatever either side had in mind, it was what actually happened that mattered. Since blockades are carried out at sea, it was control of the sea that decided the question. Britain unquestionably controlled the sea. The Dutch Navy scarcely counted any more. The French and Spanish Navies were too demoralised after Trafalgar even to think of challenging the English on the high seas again. The Portuguese were persuaded to hand over their Fleet to the British. The Danes were induced to do the same (they had rebuilt after the defeat of 1801), though it took a full-scale bombardment of Copenhagen to get the Danish King to make up his mind.

Bonaparte was restricted therefore to enforcing his decrees on land, in the seaports. He could only react to British activity. The British, at sea, could prevent things happening; Bonaparte had to be content with trying to cure troubles once they had started.

He made it worse by breaking his own rules. He needed so many supplies for his army that he was forced to take imports from Britain 'under the counter', as it were. His soldiers, for example, marched in English boots and wore English greatcoats, or so the gossips had it. Fashionable French ladies could still buy, at a price, Indian muslin.

The smugglers were doing a roaring trade. One imaginative blockade-runner tried bringing his goods into Hamburg in coffins and hearses, until a keen French customs officer became suspicious about the extremely large number of 'funerals' in the city. By mountain pass and mule train, from offshore island, by months-long detour – somehow or other a trickle of goods filtered into Europe. It was not very much, but it was enough to make fun of Bonaparte's blockade.

To be effective, the blockade – the Emperor's 'Continental System' – had to be one hundred per cent watertight. If there were only a few tiny leaks in it, it would not work. Worse still, the idea which had started as a means of making life miserable for the English ended by making life even more miserable for the French and her conquered peoples.

The British ships, by their mastery of the trade routes, could cut off most of the tropical products that kept French industry going – like silk, cotton, dyes – to say nothing of everyday foodstuffs like sugar and coffee. Their expeditionary forces could, and did, mop up any remaining French, Dutch, or Spanish colonies.

The English did suffer, for the hardships and the shortages sent prices higher than ever before – hence the bitter rage of the unemployed cotton workers who had no raw cotton to work on, or the ugly crowds outside bakers' shops hearing the new bread prices, or the gloominess of a diet without sugar. But the blockade's real victim was its creator, Bonaparte. Millions of people in Europe had once welcomed the French as liberators, as the bearers of the Great Revolution. Now they knew only hardship and shortage and high prices, French spies and customs men and secret police. The French themselves started to feel the pinch. Bonaparte may have hung Paris with battle standards and victory pennants, and filled its galleries with beautiful works of art looted from every city in Europe, but he could not put coffee or tobacco in the shops.

The Continental System also forced Bonaparte into two tragic – in the end fatal – mistakes. In an effort to make the blockade more effective, he tried to gain control of yet more European coastline. The trouble so far, apart from the chinks in the system exploited by smugglers, had been that the blockade had two open ends – Spain and Portugal in the west, Russia in the east. To Bonaparte the solution was logical: take over Spain and Portugal, and tell the Tsar to do as he was told and stop trading with Britain.

It was the logic of the vain man, of the conqueror who had always solved every problem by giving orders. The Portuguese and the Spanish refused to be taken over, and the Tsar, who was also an Emperor, refused to do as he was told. Bonaparte's pride was now stung, and his judgment suffered as a result. He invaded Spain and Portugal in 1808, and got himself and his marshals bogged down in a six-year war, which produced nothing except frustration, bitterness, and high casualties. In 1812, in an effort to teach the Tsar a lesson, he invaded Russia, and lost nearly half a million men in six months. He could blame French failures in Spain on his marshals, but in Russia he was in personal command. His defeat was clear and terrible, and could not be argued away. It took another two years to finish him off, but 1812 was the beginning of the end.

There were many other reasons for his defeat, but his vanity and his lack of understanding were powerful factors. He worked too much by logic and reason. He simply could not understand why the English – the 'nation of shopkeepers', as he rudely called them – did not give in when it was so obvious that they could not win. Nor could he see why the Spanish and Russian peasants, probably the poorest and worst-treated in Europe (except the Irish), should be prepared to die in their tens of thousands for rulers and churches that oppressed them. Baffled and enraged by the English, and later by the Spanish and the Russians, he blundered from one drastic mistake to another – all as a result of his attempt to use blockade, a weapon with which he was not familiar.

In fairness it must be said that the English too found themselves involved in a war which they had not planned. For they had, in the course of the blockade, searched many American ships, confiscated many cargoes, and pressed American sailors into the British Navy. There were mature men in the government of the young United States who had a sharp memory of the bullying of Englishmen before their War of Independence. Relations between the two nations became steadily worse. There were other reasons too, mainly concerned with quarrels over the border of Canada, but it was the high-handed attitude of the British Navy that finally stung the new American republic into a spirited defence of its honour.

By a twist of irony, both Britain and France had decided by that time that the blockade was costing more than it was worth, and had given it up. But the damage was done. The American Congress had declared war before the news reached Washington. Britain had to find troops to guard Canada and invade the USA, and ships to ferry them across the Atlantic.

However, something else had come out of the blockades, this time of benefit to Britain, and to explain that one must go back to 1806 yet again.

The stalemate had forced Bonaparte to try a British idea – blockade. It also offered the chance, in the end, for Britain to try a French one – an army in Europe.

For a few years after Pitt's death, the British Government had bumbled on with Pitt's methods, or variations of them. Two expeditions to Egypt and the Dardanelles, to try to bring pressure to bear on Turkey (there were rumours of a Franco-Turkish alliance), failed in 1806 and 1807. An even wilder scheme, to try to snatch South America by persuading the Spanish colonies there to revolt from their home government, also fizzled out in disgrace. In 1809, another task force landed on the island of Walcheren off the Belgian coast. The idea was to distract Bonaparte's attention from Austria, who had declared war that year. The Austrians were defeated (again), and the British task force, torn by fevers and disease, withered away.

Then, in 1808, Bonaparte had marched into Spain and Portugal. The King of Portugal, equally terrified of British naval power and French military might, at last made up his mind, and escaped to Brazil, giving his permission – just in time – for the British to take over the Portuguese Navy. The ships were snatched from Lisbon a few days before the French army under General Junot arrived. In Spain, King Ferdinand was deposed, and Bonaparte's eldest brother Joseph placed on the throne instead. Almost at once the population rose against the French.

Both Bonaparte brothers were taken by surprise. In other countries, such as Germany and Poland, the soldiers of the French Revolution had been welcomed as the liberators who would bring the 'Rights of Man'. In Spain and Portugal they were the hated foreigner from the very beginning. There were, it is true, some Spanish reformers who wished to bring the benefits of the Great Revolution to their country, and there were those who were prepared to support any regime – native or foreign – if they could get money or promotion out of it. But the vast majority – the poor peasant population, and most of the Army – began at once a bitter war of resistance.

The French surprise turned to shock and rage when the Spaniards actually forced a French army to surrender at Baylen in southern Spain, in July, 1808. It was the first real defeat of French soldiers since the mid-1790s, and the news jolted everyone into taking notice. Bonaparte, furious, ordered more troops to Spain and Portugal, and later went there himself. The Spanish and Portuguese, unwilling to lose the advantage of their early success, asked for military assistance from England. The

English Government, despite its poor record in sending troops abroad, gave it serious consideration.

Spain and Portugal were the last hard pockets of resistance to Bonaparte on mainland Europe. If more British troops were to be used, it was surely here. Britain since Trafalgar had enjoyed complete command of the sea. If the port of Lisbon could be kept open, there was no problem about supply; the Navy could practically guarantee it. Finally, England happened to have a young general on hand who deserved to be given a chance to show what he could do.

Sir Arthur Wellesley had not been idle during his seven years in India; it had certainly made a change from his seven years of staff work and ceremonial in Ireland before the War. He developed his habit of wide reading to make himself an expert on the country he fought in. He gained experience in the administration of captured towns, and showed very early the consideration towards civilian populations which later was to earn him much respect. He prepared and nearly led expeditions to the Philippines, Java, and Egypt – each one overtaken by events and cancelled.

In the Mahratta campaign of 1803, he displayed the dapper coolness under fire that became his trademark, and at Assaye defeated an Indian army over five times the size of his own. He came back to England, with the rank of major-general, the Order of the Bath, and a sizeable fortune. In 1807, he served on the combined Army and Navy operations that resulted in the successful hijack of the Danish Fleet. (His favourite horse was named Copenhagen, and survived the whole war, indeed living till 1836.)

A general before he was forty, saviour of a subcontinent, master of his craft – not bad going for the slowcoach of the family.

So Wellesley was sent with an army to Portugal, where he soon proved his ability by defeating the French under Junot at Vimeiro. Unfortunately, the British Government spoiled it all by sending out two more generals, who were higher in rank, and far lower in energy and ability. When the French asked for an armistice, these two, Burrard and Dalrymple, not only signed a peace treaty at Cintra, but allowed the French to evacuate their entire army and baggage. With misplaced gallantry, they also provided ships for the purpose. All Wellesley's good work was thrown away.

There was a huge outcry in England, and the Government tried to protect itself by recalling all three generals. Sir John Moore was left in command of the British troops.

While Wellesley was busy justifying his actions to a court of inquiry, Moore decided to use his army to cause as much trouble as he could to the French in Spain. He quickly understood that the further the French troops marched from France, the longer became their lines of communication and supply, and the easier it was to cut them. When they were at their longest and thinnest, he set out across Spain to do exactly that.

He was unlucky; Bonaparte himself had arrived in Spain, and turned his terrifying energy, and a hundred thousand men, on Moore. Moore had no choice but to withdraw. It was a demoralising business – the winter cold, the wet, the dismal mountains in northern Spain, troops on the run and liable to break into looting and killing the civilian population. It is greatly to Moore's credit that he held his army together till it reached Corunna, the seaport in north-west Spain, and greatly to the Navy's credit that it succeeded in evacuating four-fifths of them under the noses of the French. Moore died and was buried at Corunna (January, 1809), but the soldiers – or most of them – were saved. Moreover, he had proved that a small army, properly handled, could cause trouble out of all proportion to its size.

The British Government for once read the lesson, and within three months a fresh British military force arrived in Portugal. Its general was again Sir Arthur Wellesley. He had cleared himself of the charges against him over the Convention of Cintra, and this time he was in sole command.

He had a fearsome task in front of him. His army was hugely outnumbered by the French. The enemy, apart from their one mistake at Baylen, had enjoyed almost constant victory since 1795; their glittering marshals had proved themselves the most brilliant soldiers in the world. His own army was almost untried; he had a low opinion of its troops, and of its officers. No British expeditionary force had won a campaign in Europe for half a century. There were allies – the Spanish and Portuguese armies – but nobody knew how efficient they were. Wellesley was not hopeful. Finally, there were the *guerrilleros* – the Spanish bandits who fought from caves and woods; they too were an uncertain quantity.

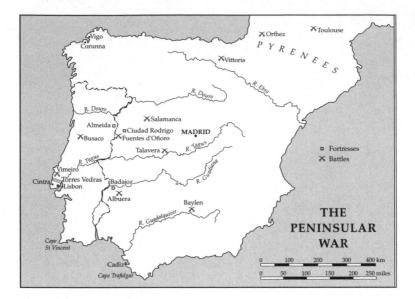

Sir Arthur set about his task with his usual thoroughness and common sense. He had already read every book on Spain and Portugal that he could lay his hands on. (He had done the same with books on India during his voyage out East.) He soon knew the country far better than the enemy did. He bullied his staff officers into producing a set of maps more accurate than anything possessed by any French marshal. He established contact with the Portuguese and Spanish regular armies, and he sent British officers into the mountains to work with the *guerrilleros*. He won the respect of the local population: he imposed savage penalties on any of his soldiers caught looting, and he actually paid, and promptly, for any food and supplies that he requisitioned. The peasants responded by giving him the neighbourhood knowledge that he needed – river currents, mountain paths for patrols, vantage points for reconnaissance, fords for crossings, local weather conditions.

The French, with their poor maps, were already at a disadvantage. Worse, the peasants hated them, and took every opportunity to put obstacles in their way. The French replied by taking hostages, by shooting them when necessary (and sometimes when not necessary) – in short by terror. The peasants in turn reacted by slitting Frenchmen's throats – drunken off-duty officers, lonely and sleepy sentries, solitary and unwary messengers. Each act of murder or revenge was answered by something worse. The *guerrilleros* added their weight to the scales against the French by hit-and-run tactics – raids on camps, burnings of stores, killings of stragglers and looters. Helped, armed, and often trained by British officers, they kept up a constant battery of pinpricks on the lumbering bodies of French armies, and so gave a new word to the language of military warfare – *guerrilla. Guerra* is the Spanish for 'war'; *guerrilla* is 'little war'; and the *guerrilleros* were the men who fought it, without mercy, for six years. To British governments and historians, the campaign in Spain and Portugal has always been the Peninsular War; to the Spanish it has always been the Great War of Independence.

To win back Spain, Wellesley had to begin with Portugal, and in May, 1809, he cleared out Marshal Soult and his army with one battle. Following up his advantage, he moved into Spain, hoping to take Madrid itself. The French met him at Talavera in July. Wellesley won the battle, and was honoured with the title of viscount by a cheering nation. He adopted the name Wellington to go with it, to avoid confusion with his elder brother Richard, who was also a member of the House of Lords.

However, he had advanced too far too fast; there were other French armies closing in on him, and the regular Spanish army let him down. He was therefore forced to pull back to Portugal, where he was closer to his supply lines from the Navy. The key to his whole position was the port of Lisbon, and to make it safe he constructed three bristling lines of defences in front of the city. British engineers and Portuguese labourers spent over a year building the famous Lines of Torres Vedras. Lisbon stood on a jutting piece of land, so each end of the Lines stretched to the sea, and was therefore guarded by the guns of the Navy. Thus the Lines could not be turned or outflanked. Once he felt sure that the French could never push him into the water, he set about his plans for the campaign proper.

He spent much more time now in planning; Talavera had taught him that. Wellesley – or rather Wellington, as he now was – was not a spectacular general, but he was a thorough one. Thorough and hardworking. He devoted hours every day to humdrum details like bread supplies and bullock wagons, tents and maps, regular accounts and camp discipline. He drove his officers hard, and soldiers appreciated it. This tireless, hook-nosed, poker-faced general seemed to be everywhere; he never missed a thing. Wellington did not draw from his men the affection that Nelson did from his sailors, but he won their trust and their respect. As the months passed, they slowly began to realise that they had a general at last who might put the French in their place. As long as 'Old Nosey' was there, they felt, everything would be all right.

The first test came in 1810, when two of Bonaparte's finest marshals, Soult and Masséna, began an all-out attack on Portugal. Wellington knew that the main lines of French advance would have to be along the three main river valleys – the Douro, the Tagus, and the Guadiana. He ordered his border fortresses – Almeida, Ciudad Rodrigo, and Badajoz – to hold up the enemy as long as they could while his Portuguese allies gathered in the harvest and completed his stores. He put the finishing touches to the Lines of Torres Vedras.

His fortresses were captured in the end, but the French were delayed. Then, as he withdrew, Wellington deliberately stripped the countryside of everything that could possibly be of use to the French. It depressed the Portuguese to see the burning and destruction, but they now trusted Wellington enough to accept it. To raise their morale, he halted on his retreat to face the French on a ridge at Busaco. He retreated again after the battle, but there were three French dead on the field for every Englishman.

Having thus tweaked the Frenchmen's noses, Wellington went to ground behind Torres Vedras, and defied Masséna to do anything about it. The French high command had had no idea that the Lines were even there, much less what to do about them. Their own lines of supply were stretched almost to breaking, and Wellington had scraped the land so bare that the French spent most of the their time that winter looking for food. They never launched one major attack. By the spring of 1811, they had lost 25,000 men, and had no choice but to turn round and march back into Spain.

Wellington now came out again, and spent the summer of 1811 trying to recapture his lost fortresses of Almeida, Ciudad Rodrigo, and

Badajoz. At the same time he had to avoid being sandwiched between any of the huge French armies that were eager to pin him down. It needed all his maps and his mountain guides and his *guerrilleros* to do it. If he got the chance, he struck at weak points when his intelligence service told him that there were fewer numbers against him. There was one bloody battle, at Fuentes d'Oñoro, but the French withdrew afterwards, and Wellington regained Almeida. There was another at Albuera, where the Portuguese Army won a good reputation for itself. Wellington had always thought more highly of the Portuguese troops than he did of the Spanish, and Albuera confirmed his opinion.

In the autumn he retreated into Portugal again, but this time the French made little effort to follow him; they had no taste for another hungry winter in front of Torres Vedras.

By the end of 1811, Wellington had captured only one fortress, but he had proved many points. First, he had shown that, with the right maps and the right information, a small army could give the run-around to an enemy ten times as big. Secondly, he had revealed serious weaknesses in the French army, chiefly in their methods of attack. Ever since the 1790s, the French leaders had fought nearly every battle in pretty much the same way – a big bombardment of guns; an infantry assault in massed columns to crash through the enemy line; and cavalry charges to cut down the survivors as they ran away. Wellington rarely fought on ground that was not of his own choosing, and there was usually a ridge behind which his men could shelter from the guns. He had now drilled his infantrymen so that their long thin lines could pour a hail of musket and rifle fire upon either side of the advancing columns, and so break them up before they made contact. And, when the French cavalry charged, the English formed a square – a bristling human fortress of bayonets that the horses would not jump at.

New tactics were no use without the discipline to make them work. Wellington more than once referred to his soldiers as 'the scum of the earth', and he did not have much patience either with his junior officers. To him they were spoilt playboys who could be trusted only to make a mess of things. But he bullied them all into becoming a fine army with a great pride in itself. He treated both colonels and corporals as if he were a sort of fierce but devoted father. He never allowed himself to show any affection for them, but he was clearly pleased with their efforts. 'Scum of the earth, enlisted for drink' they may have been when they joined up, but the Duke was quick to add, 'It really is wonderful that we should have made them the fine fellows they are.' Officers and men alike would slave away for him without question, and treasured his few words of praise.

One thing they appreciated in particular was the fact that he was not generous with his men's lives. He was constantly aware that he was outnumbered, and that his army, as he put it, was 'the last army in Europe'. He did not risk it unnecessarily in the quest for glorious victories. It is a tribute to his grip on the army that they never doubted his abilities even in retreat.

Thirdly, it was now proved beyond argument that his army could not be pushed out of Portugal. Although the Emperor continued to pour troops into the peninsula, the decision he wanted persistently eluded him. As French failures and frustration grew, the rest of Europe began to take heart. Perhaps the superman really could be beaten after all.

Wellington, however, would have been the first to admit that the success was not all due to his own gifts (though he gave himself full credit where it was due). Another talent he possessed was the ability to keep everything in proportion. He was aware, for instance, of the effect of a new exploding shell, the invention of a certain Major Shrapnel. Another new idea was the rifle. Unlike the old musket, it had the spiralled 'rifling' inside the barrel, which caused the ball, or bullet, to spin very fast on discharge; this gave greater accuracy at longer ranges. It was not invented in the Peninsular War, but it did become widely used then. Moore among others had grasped its importance. Wellington was grateful, too, for the Army reforms which had at last made it impossible for boys of twelve to be officers. Moore again, before his ill-fated Spanish command, had spent much time training a new type of light-armed, fast-moving infantryman; these men – the famous 'green jackets' – equipped with the new rifle, did splendid scouting work in Spain.

Spain, as the saying went, was 'a country where small armies are defeated and large armies starve'. The French, who had always lived off the land in the richer, more fertile countries of northern and central Europe, found food supply a constant headache in Spain. The *guerrilleros* were another. A third was the Emperor himself. Bonaparte, who had visited Spain only once, to chase Moore's army into the sea, could not understand why his marshals made such heavy weather of it. Each piece of bad news from Spain, which might take weeks to reach him, would cause him to dash off a flurry of furious orders, which would take more weeks to get back. By that time they were often hopelessly out of date. His marshals had the choice of obeying them, while knowing that they would not work, or disobeying them, and facing the Emperor's wrath if they did not produce victories. Worse, the marshals, for all their brilliance, were not easy men to work with. Indeed, their very brilliance sprang from their individualism. There was no overall French commander in Spain, and many French movements were spoiled by petty jealousies between the senior officers.

When Wellington re-entered Spain in 1812, the marshals faced yet another difficulty because the Emperor began withdrawing some crack regiments in preparation for his Grand Army's invasion of Russia. They finally lost the remaining two frontier fortresses to the English – Ciudad Rodrigo and Badajoz – though Wellington paid a terrible price in casualties, especially at Badajoz, where he momentarily lost control; his crazed survivors, drunk alike with victory and liquor, ran amok in pillage and slaughter. He had to draft in fresh troops to form hanging parties to mete out summary justice in the town square.

Then Marshal Marmont was caught unawares just south of Salamanca in July, and in forty minutes Wellington won his biggest victory so far. He rode in triumph into Madrid, and moved north to cut the main French supply line.

This time it was Wellington who overstretched his supplies. The French recovered, and there were still enough of them to force him back. He dared not face a decisive battle with the whole French army. By the winter of 1812, he was sheltering in Portugal again.

As Wellington hibernated behind Torres Vedras, enjoying his new title of earl, Europe buzzed with far more dramatic news. The Emperor's Grand Army, half a million men, had been swallowed up in Russia. Whatever the reason – battle, hunger, desertion, frostbite, pneumonia – the clear fact was that fewer than 10 per cent had survived. It was a stark, unmistakable defeat.

The whole of Europe stirred itself for one more effort. The Russian armies, having expelled the French from the soil of Mother Russia, now lumbered after them. The Prussians shook off French domination and declared war, and the Austrians followed suit. The new British Foreign Secretary, Castlereagh, provided the money as usual to pay for the armies, and made all the allies promise that they would not make a separate peace with Bonaparte. At long last, every major power realised that the old diplomatic game would no longer work; everything, absolutely everything, had to take second place to the defeat of the Corsican upstart Emperor.

In England the new Prime Minister, Lord Liverpool, was able to achieve more teamwork among ministers than the Cabinet had seen for a long time. He did little to help those suffering from enclosures or high prices or unemployment; he was not over-sympathetic to Irish Catholics; indeed reforms of any kind attracted little of his attention. But he did pursue the war effort with great determination. He backed the new allied coalition, he never wavered in his support of Wellington, and he took appropriate steps to fight the Americans, who had declared war in June, 1812.

The American war was never more than a sideshow compared with the colossal struggle against France, though the British Government was forced to find precious soldiers to fight it. What made it ridiculous was that the apparent reason for the war – the British counter-blockade and searching of American ships – had been removed; when President Madison of the USA declared war, he did not know that Lord Liverpool had already agreed to call off the blockade. Neither side succeeded in producing a really solid victory. The Americans failed in their invasion of Canada; the British had to make do with burning the American government buildings in Washington. Apart from some dashing raids by American and British ships, that was about all there was to it. Communications were so poor that a battle was fought at New Orleans after the peace treaty had been signed, because the British commander simply had not heard. He lost the battle too.

Many Americans had little heart for the war; the 'States' were far from 'United'. The British had no desire to fight another War of American Independence. Both sides signed the peace treaty with a certain amount of relief. Other causes of dispute (besides the blockade) – the boundary between the USA and Canada, fishing rights, territorial waters, and so on – were all left in the air.

Europe was what mattered in 1813 and 1814. Bonaparte continued to win battles in central Europe, but they became more and more costly. After each one he was forced to withdraw, as soldiers from Russia, Prussia, Austria, Bavaria, Sweden, and Holland joined in for the kill. His health was declining; many of his best soldiers were dead. Many more, in garrisons all over Europe, were mopped up as the allies advanced westwards.

In the peninsula, Wellington marched out of Portugal for the last time. In June, 1813, he won the decisive battle against 'King' Joseph at Vittoria, and the main French army streamed back over the Pyrenees into France.

The spring of 1814 saw armies invading France from all sides. Bonaparte performed near-miracles with boy soldiers and raw recruits, but miracles were not enough. By the end of March, allied troops were in the outskirts of Paris, and in April the Emperor formally abdicated and surrendered. In the south of France, Wellington plugged away in his methodical manner against Marshal Soult; he besieged and captured Toulouse before a messenger brought the news that the Emperor had accepted defeat.

Wellington gave a party to celebrate. At the end of the dinner he rose to propose the toast of 'Louis XVIII' – the new Bourbon ruler of France. But that was only the beginning. An excited Spanish officer proposed a toast to Wellington, the liberator of Spain – '*El Libertador de España*'. The Portuguese, the French, everybody followed – '*Liberator de Portugal!*', '*Le Libérateur de la France!*', '*Le Libérateur de l'Europe!*' The cheering was deafening for ten full minutes. Wellington at last rose and bowed. Some said afterwards that they could see tears in his eyes. He could think of nothing to say, and finally, thoroughly confused, he told the waiters to bring in the coffee. It was the only time Wellington was ever caught unprepared.

The war was over.

CHAPTER FOUR

A Wave of Gadgets

In 1798, a young clergyman called Thomas Malthus published the results of his research. Like those of many books in the eighteenth century, its title was a little long-winded: *An Essay on the Principles of Population as it affects the Future Improvement of Society.* The book drew attention to the fact that population was growing, and to the more alarming fact that it would continue to grow.

It would grow, he said, because more food was being produced. More food meant a healthier population, which meant a more fertile one, which meant more mouths to feed. In a short time the increased food supply would be swallowed up by galloping numbers, and the country would be worse off than before. The only means of regulating the rise in population were not the methods of men but those of nature – famine, plague, and war. (He also suggested that the system of public assistance to the poor served to keep more poor alive, who would breed yet more paupers, without producing any greater food supply. So poor relief would not improve the situation; it would worsen it. This theory goes a long way to explain why public attitudes to poverty were so harsh.)

The arguments of Malthus, though by no means accurate, were widely accepted. If the population really was growing as fast as he said, perhaps the country was in for a drastic food shortage. Certainly several harvests in the 1790s had been bad. Perhaps one of the dreadful natural disasters he foresaw was just around the corner, and just how many paupers were being kept alive by public charity?

Whatever the answer turned out to be, it seemed that a logical first step would be to find out exactly how big the population was. Urged on by George Rickman, a clerk in the House of Commons, the Government found time during the French War to take the first-ever census in Britain.

That was in 1801. The returns showed that the population of Great Britain was about 10,500,000, which was a considerable increase from the 5,000,000 or so at the beginning of the eighteenth century. Admittedly the earlier figure was not a very scientific estimate, but the difference in numbers was, by any standards, remarkable. If there remained any doubts about whether the population had stopped going up or not, they were removed by the figures from later censuses – 12,000,000 in 1811, 16,000,000 in 1831, 21,000,000 in 1851. By the end of the nineteenth century, the population had trebled within a hundred years. To repeat – it doubled in the eighteenth century, and it trebled *again* in the nineteenth.

Historians have, understandably, been concerned to find out why. The obvious explanation would appear to be a rise in the birth rate. But numbers would also increase because of a fall in the death rate. Or again, was the real reason not that more babies were being born, but that more survived? These babies would grow up, marry, and produce more children, more of whom would survive, and so on.

The short answer is that nobody knows. Historians are forced to guess. This is no criticism. Guesses do not have to be wild stabs with a pin into the paper. They can be intelligent and careful, based firmly on a great deal of painstaking research. Nevertheless, they are still guesses. Honest historians know that their guesses could at some future time be proved wrong. Students must remember that guesses may come near the truth without revealing the whole truth; they simply lift a corner of the veil.

Consider that population rise again. Was it really because fewer people were dying so early? Certainly the overdrinking of deadly cheap gin in the 1720s and 1730s saw many Londoners into early graves (the common advertisement – 'Drunk for a penny, dead drunk for twopence' – often proved to be not only a tempting offer but a drastic fulfilment). So when a new tax in 1751 sent up the price of gin, it is reasonable to assume that the lives of would-be drinkers were prolonged. But then again, the alternative was beer, and beer could produce alcoholism too; what else was there to drink in cities with virtually no pure tap water? Or in the country, for that matter, where a muddy, cattle-clogged stream represented the village supply?

Another guess claimed that improvements in medicine were responsible. Certainly the standards of midwifery were raised, which helped to reduce the frightening death rate of infants and of mothers in or just after childbirth. The idea of fighting infection by inoculation – injecting a small dose of the disease taken from a known victim – was pioneered early in the century. It was argued that if you injected this small amount into the human system, the body would fight it; this would give it the strength to stand up to the full impact of the disease itself. The problem was one of *judging* the amount, and there were some fatal accidents in the early days. The technique of vaccination – letting the virus from a victim of cowpox into a small cut on the patient's arm – carried the idea further. (The Latin word for 'cow' is *vacca* – hence 'vaccination'.) It is true too that Scottish doctors were far better trained than English ones.

Against this, however, must be set other equally well-documented facts. Nobody knew anything about how epidemic diseases such as cholera and typhus spread. Very few authorities accepted the idea that there was a connection between disease and dirt. Medicines, for the most part, were concoctions based on old wives' recipes, and were just as likely to be deadly as they were to be harmless. (Mother Bailey's Quieting Syrup, for instance, contained opium. It could not only 'quiet' the squalling infant; it could put him to sleep for good.) Very little was understood about drugs. Surgery was even more hit-and-miss – literally. There were no anaesthetics in general use until the 1840s, and no antiseptic precautions until the 1860s. Amputations were nightmares of rum-fuddled victims, leather straps, screams, scraping saws, and stumps dipped in liquid tar. (Small wonder that soldiers and sailors in battle dreaded the surgeon's table more than the muzzles of the enemy guns.)

Most internal operations common today were impossible; we shall never know how many people died of, say, a 'routine' complaint like appendicitis. Moreover, most of these medical services, such as they were, were available only in towns, and most of the population were country-dwellers. Perhaps this fact in turn helps to explain why the rural death rate fell faster than the urban one – not because country folk had access to these doubtful services, but because they did not.

A third line of enquiry came up with the guess about improved living standards. Better means of transport and communication brought a more regular and better-balanced food supply to the growing cities. Tea and sugar, for example, became normal items in the daily diet. Improvements in cattle- and sheep-breeding were putting more and healthier meat on the butchers' slabs. Soap was becoming more common. Cheap cotton garments, easier to wash, began to replace the heavier, smellier woollens. Coal became cheaper and easier to obtain, so less energy was spent merely fighting the cold.

If the reasons for the rise in population could be elusive, the symptoms were all too obvious. Villages and small towns in the Midlands and the North mushroomed into cities without any care or planning. There was no water supply, no refuse collection, no paving, no cleaning, no lighting. Factories, streets, and houses were dark (Pitt's window tax), overcrowded, crawling with crime, alive with rats, and running with waste and sewage. Epidemics of smallpox and cholera spread like bush fires.

Indeed one often pauses in the search for causes of the population explosion to wonder at the mere fact of it. In spite of poor medicine and hair-raising surgery; in spite of appalling conditions in the new cities; in spite of casualties from five wars in a hundred years up to 1815; in spite of considerable emigration – the extraordinary fact is that the population rose, and went on rising, and not only in England; the same thing was happening all over Europe.

Never had there been such a population explosion. Hardly surprising that it has attracted the attention of historians. They are concerned, too, not only with the causes but with the results; they feel that so huge a fact must have had a big influence on the later history of mankind generally. Some of them argue, with considerable justification, that people's lives are affected by this population explosion just as much as by battles, wars, treaties, and the daily decisions of politicians. They claim that their brands of history – social history and economic history

– are as important as political history. (There are those who claim that it is more important, that it is the only type of history worth studying. Perhaps they overstate their case. Again, it comes down to guessing, and to advocacy. How many people can they persuade that their guesses are the right ones?)

It is not easy to prove a direct, unbreakable line of cause and effect between one fact of social/economic history and another. A historian must put forward his ideas, his theories, his guesses; he should also explain the evidence on which he bases his conclusions; but he must leave the reader (and his fellow-historians) to decide whether his evidence is sound enough, and his guesses plausible enough.

There is no geometric proof that the rise in population produced modern democracy. Yet it is reasonable to suppose that ideas of government of the people, for the people, by the people, which became increasingly widespread after the American and French Revolutions, may have had something to do with the fact that there were many more of 'the people' around. It is surely more than coincidence that the late eighteenth and nineteenth centuries saw armies numbered by the hundred thousand; that they produced the idea of a 'nation under arms' – mass conscription; that they witnessed factories engaged in mass production. Napoleon could say, in 1813, 'What are a million men to me?' and mean it. Thousands, millions, masses, peoples, nations – all are words implying huge numbers. The world had never had to cope with such figures before. This probably helps to explain why it made so many mistakes, and why human suffering – in wars, in huddled cities, in epidemics – rose on such a fearful scale. It cannot be mere chance that the science of statistics makes its appearance at this time. Man had to evolve a means of finding out the size of the problem before he could hope to solve it. The first census, remember, was in 1801.

Yet more claims are made for the rise in population. It is alleged that it was this human explosion that produced two of the four revolutions of the late eighteenth century – the Agricultural Revolution and the Industrial Revolution. (The other two were the American Revolution and the French Revolution – and sheer numbers had something to do with them too.)

The phrase 'Agricultural Revolution' means something like this: the eighteenth century saw great improvements in agriculture – more land under cultivation, more intensive cultivation, better handling of crops, new crops (like clover and turnips), stronger and bigger breeds of sheep and cattle. Farming became more scientific. It also produced more surplus; that is, it now aimed to grow more things for sale in addition to what was grown for local consumption. Nobody can point to a single year to say exactly when the first change took place, but the general pattern is unmistakable: all these changes, taken together, altered British agriculture out of all recognition. They revolutionised it. Hence, therefore, the 'Agricultural Revolution'.

At roughly the same time occurred the Industrial Revolution – or, as one schoolboy put it in his essay, 'A wave of gadgets swept over England.' The inventions, however, were only a part of the Industrial Revolution. It consisted of many things: the harnessing of new forms of power – water and steam; the transfer of the process of making goods from the cottage and the family workshop to the factory; the development of huge natural resources of iron and coal; the concentration of population near these resources, in the Midlands and the North; the growth and expansion of a nationwide system of canals and, later, of railways; the good fortune by which a strong navy was on hand to protect the new worldwide trade routes by which raw materials could reach England; the collection of a huge overseas empire to which one could sell; the existence of a workable credit system; and the presence of interested upper and middle classes prepared to invest their money in any number and type of business enterprises. As with agriculture, it is not possible to point to one single feature and say with complete truth, 'There. That is the start. That is the seed from which sprang the Industrial Revolution.' What made the Industrial Revolution was not that schoolboy's 'wave of gadgets', or the factories, or the mines, or Birmingham and Manchester, or the canal craze, or railway mania, or ships, empire, gamblers, stock markets, and banks. It was the exciting fact that they were all emerging *at the same time* – these huge forces producing violent chain reactions on one another – all within the confines of a tiny offshore island off the continent of Europe.

Other countries may have possessed some of the ingredients of the mixture, but none save Britain – at that time – possessed them all.

Spain, for example, should have had the wealth to invest in new ideas; she had been digging gold and silver out of South America for hundreds of years. But she had no busy merchant classes, and she was in the white-knuckle grip of a Catholic Church that did not allow the lending of money for interest. Without investment and interest rates no business could thrive. France had a high population, good natural resources, a varied agriculture, and (the remains at any rate of) an overseas empire. But the eighteenth-century French nobility, which had most of the money (or investment capital) at its disposal, was forbidden by law to engage in trade. Moreover, religious persecution had caused many French Protestants – the Huguenots – to emigrate. Huguenots had provided most of France's craftsmen, engineers, and businessmen; they took their talents away with them, many to England. (It is interesting how governments who engage in persecutions of small groups within their countries show such singular lack of judgment in their choice of scapegoats or whipping boys. The French drove out the Huguenots; the Spaniards drove out the Moriscos; the Nazis drove out the Jews. In each case they lost some of the best brains in the state.)

Holland – another small country on the edge of Europe – came close to Britain in the number of ingredients for industrial revolution. It had a large, wealthy, energetic, and experienced middle class of merchants. It had vast knowledge of overseas trade and worldwide sea routes. It had a large fleet of merchant shipping. Its mainly Protestant population was not held back by outdated Catholic teaching on moneylending. It was on the main shipping routes of Northern Europe and close to the Atlantic, and it had a large overseas empire. But it had not enough resources of coal and iron.

Two more countries are worth considering, especially in the light of what happened later in the nineteenth century. One is Germany. There was a large population, plenty of navigable rivers for movement of goods, huge mineral resources, and an unbeatable central position. As in England there were already plenty of sizeable towns, and a tradition of small-scale industry stretching back for centuries. But Germany did not enjoy the years of peace that England did. There had been no fighting to speak of in England since the Civil War, and not much before it, right back to the Wars of the Roses. (Bonnie Prince Charlie's 'invasion' of England was a pitiful, half-cock affair, and the final battle was fought on a lonely moor in the Highlands.) England, Wales, Scotland, and Ireland had been united under one crown since 1603, and England, Wales, and Scotland under one Parliament since 1707. Germany on the other hand had been the scene of wars, campaigns, battles, sieges, and sackings since the days of Otto the Great in the tenth century. In 1760, far from being united, it was divided into more than three hundred separate states – some sizeable countries, some scarcely bigger than, say, York or Bristol and their environs.

The other country was the United States of America. More than any other state, perhaps, it had youth, energy, strength, minerals, huge rivers, vast coasts, natural harbours, enormous enthusiasm, and inventive skill. All the potential was there; the only shortage was of people.

These last two countries had disabilities that were not necessarily permanent. Germany could, conceivably, be united under one government, and all that industrial potential, intelligence, and mineral wealth could be harnessed under a single policy. The USA would, sooner or later, attract enough immigrants to open up its enormous resources of land and power. If and when these two things happened, how could a small country like England hope to match them and keep pace?

All that, however, was in the future. For the moment, it was England where the flames of human progress burned brightest – in the mines, the foundries, the mills, the factories of the Midlands and the North. The older industries of East Anglia, say, or the West Country, faltered and faded. They became old-fashioned and out of date because they stuck to methods that had served them well in the past. Under the old system, in the woollen trade for instance, all the manufacturing processes – spinning, weaving, dyeing, and so on – would be done in separate workers' cottages. A businessman – a clothier – would call at regular intervals, pick up the finished material, leave fresh wool, pay the agreed money earned, and move on. He might even own the spinning wheels and the looms, and rent them out. A pottery or furniture business might be a mere family affair with a handful of apprentices. A host of craftsmen in other trades carried on their work single-handed.

Most of these workmen used their bare hands with only simple hand tools. True, a miller might have his mill driven by the wind, and the ironmaker his bellows worked by water. But they were exceptions. By and large men and women earned as much as their muscles would allow.

Two things changed this – machines and factories. Machines meant using something besides human muscle to carry out industrial processes – in this case water power and steam power. If water or steam could be used to work one machine, it could be used to work several. It was easier to bring the machines to the water than it was to take water to the machines. So the next step was to house several machines near a convenient source of water (or steam). Hence the factory.

There had been gadgets and inventions before, but most of them had simply helped the single weaver or spinner to do his job more accurately or more easily, and it still made sense to take the gadget or invention to his house. The new machines now did the work so fast that no single-handed workman could keep up with them. Not only did they make many gadgets old-fashioned overnight; they made many work-men unnecessary. Clothiers could get less output from a dozen men than they could from one machine, and it was obviously cheaper to put the machines under one roof with a single power supply than it was to put one in each weaver's cottage. Old-style weavers and spinners saw their jobs disappearing. Those who still chased work had to leave their country cottages, and crowd into streets beside the new city factories. Men who had been able to work their own hours, in their own houses, to suit themselves, now had to stand at machines for hours that suited their employers. For the first time the clock and the timetable entered the working man's day.

Now power-driven machines meant iron; the old wooden machines could not stand up to steam, and to relentless, all-day use. More machines meant more iron. Here was another link in the chain. For it was in the eighteenth century that a new process of smelting iron was developed – with coke, instead of with charcoal (which went back to Roman times). The iron industry no longer needed to depend on charcoal – that is on wood, at a time when England's forests were shrinking from the assault of the construction and shipbuilding industries. The coke technique meant that the iron industry moved to the coalfields – South Wales, Shropshire, Staffordshire, Yorkshire. Many of the foundries were near hill ranges with swift-running streams, so water (and therefore steam) power was available to drive the furnaces. As the iron industry revived, and the demand for iron rose – for machines, for the muskets, cannon and shot needed in the wars against France – so new techniques improved the quality of the iron, and increased the speed with which it could be produced. Before long, enough iron was being produced to provide material for all the new ideas and techniques in architecture, industrial machinery, bridges, weapons, shipbuilding, and railways.

More iron meant more coal to make the coke to smelt it. Mines sank deeper and spread further. The great enemies to progress here were flooding, collapse, gas, and explosion. As with the iron industry, a breakthrough came in the eighteenth and early nineteenth centuries. Steam again came to the rescue, with pumps to remove the water. Traps and fans appeared (often operated by children of five or six) to keep air moving. A safety lamp was produced in 1815. As the iron industry benefited from coal, so no doubt the coal mines were helped by more iron props to prevent shafts and tunnels from caving in.

Here is a good example of how different ingredients of the Industrial Revolution interacted on each other. Coal produced the coke for better iron; more iron improved the strength of the mines, and assisted greater output of coal. In a similar way, railways were invented originally as a means of moving coal easily underground. Railways on the surface later helped businessmen to move faster around the countryside, but in so doing their yawning boiler furnaces brought more business and prosperity to the coalfields.

It was railways too, and canals, that provided the solution to another problem – how to move all the iron and coal that was being produced. England was not short of rivers, but they were not all navigable, and they did not all run conveniently near pit-heads and foundries. There were difficulties too with currents, sandbanks, seasonal rise and fall, and so on. With England's roads in the state they were – inadequate, to say the least – horses and carts were now hopelessly slow and inefficient.

The answer seemed to be canals. They could be made pretty straight; they could be regularly maintained without too much trouble; they would go where you wanted them to go; and they would provide cheap transport for heavy goods. Again, canals were not invented in the eighteenth century, but the years 1760–1820 saw so many constructed that it amounted to a 'canal revolution', and all without a Ministry of Waterways or a penny of Government money. All private enterprise.

At the same time, England's roads did at last get some attention. There was no Minister of Transport, and there was no national road policy; but all over the country groups of people would get together to raise money to improve a particular stretch of road. They applied to Parliament for permission to set up a tollgate at either end, where they would impose a charge on anyone passing through. A bar was lowered to stop vehicles, and a spiked gate discouraged impatient horsemen from jumping over. From this comes the name 'turnpike'. The organisers would be formed into a Trust, to use the money collected for the upkeep of the road and the tollkeeper's wages (and their own profits). As with canals, turnpike trusts increased by hundreds between 1760 and 1820, and gave employment to some great pioneers of road engineering.

Attention was now given to basic problems of foundation, camber, and drainage. Many early roads had followed the tracks of cattle as they mooched wavily from one village to the next, regardless of surface or slope; now careful planning took roads direct from town to town, often bypassing villages. Cuttings and embankments were constructed to soften gradients for sweating horses. More, and better, bridges appeared (the new iron again). A cheap and effective technique for road surfacing was developed.

A whole new service industry evolved – coaching. There had, of course, been coaches before, but the miles of new roads offered the chance of fast travel, and people took it. Coaching inns sprang up all over the country. A host of coaching trades and crafts – coach-builders, harness-makers, horse-dealers, drivers, guards, and grooms – burgeoned and flourished to handle the vastly-increased business.

In its short lifetime, coaching and everything to do with it became impressed upon the country's imagination. Just as the three decades of frontier history after the American Civil War are rooted in people's minds, immovably, as the 'Wild West', so the great mail coach has stamped itself – for ever, it seems – on the national memory. It is so tempting, and somehow so cosy, to think of a 'typical' English

Christmas (in the 'good old days') as being brought to one's door by a thundering coachload of jolly, red-faced, whiskered gentlemen in huge double-breasted overcoats – all against a background of robins, fresh snowfalls, and gleaming posthorns.

The surprise is that, as with the American West, the legend grew out of barely thirty years. By the mid-1840s, the coaches and the roads were being met by a deadly challenge – the railways. Canals began to decline too. Neither could compete with what the railways could offer. Canals were cheap, and could carry bulky goods, but they were slow, and could not guarantee a reliable timetable. Coaches were fast and punctual, but they were on the expensive side, and obviously they could not carry much in the way of bulk.

Railways could, and did, do everything. They were reliable; indeed, their punctuality led people to talk of 'railway time' when they wanted to express a passion for precision of the clock. They became cheap, especially as more lines brought more passengers. They were versatile; the powerful engines could pull enormous loads, regardless of size, bulk, weight, or fragility, and they were fast; the prospect of their speed must have been awesome and hypnotic to a human society that, since the birth of civilisation, had never travelled faster than fifteen miles an hour.

Admittedly railways were not particularly clean, quiet, or comfortable. Early coaches were open; they rattled abominably; they jolted and they swung; smoke belched from the ship-like funnel of the engine, and cinders could fall into the hair and on the clothes. But people travelled on them, especially after Queen Victoria declared that she liked them, and businessmen despatched their goods on them. Canals slid quietly into lily-capped stagnation, and the coaches with their posthorns clattered into legend, their epitaphs glowing defiantly on a million Christmas cards.

Now all these schemes – making machines, improving foundries, sinking mineshafts, building factories, setting up turnpike trusts, digging canals, buying land on which to construct railways – they all cost money. The men with the ideas and the energy did not have enough. They had to borrow it. Once again circumstances in England proved to be favourable.

These huge sums of money were needed at the very time when more was available. Admittedly there is guesswork here too, but it seems that more ordinary people were earning just that little bit over and above what they needed for food, shelter, and so on, and were in a mood to save it. If a country is peaceful, people are prepared to save; they are willing to make plans for the future. England was fighting foreign wars, but little serious political violence disturbed the general course of life at home.

Some people chose to save by putting their coins in a bag under the bed. Others, fortunately for the Industrial Revolution, decided to invest. They bought shares in foundry firms, or cotton mills, or railway companies, or whatever, and they simply sat back and waited for the annual interest to come trickling in.

Like every other feature of the Industrial Revolution, this was not new; there had been joint-stock companies selling shares for years, and firms like the East India Company and the Hudson Bay Company had built huge commercial empires. But the eighteenth century saw a boom in investing activity.

Englishmen since the days of Drake and Hawkins had always been ready to turn the odd pound or two in business abroad. The slave trade was one example. Piracy was another. Queen Elizabeth herself had invested in some of Drake's semi-piratical voyages (and was quick to claim her share of the profits). Every European war England fought had ended with the picking up of a colony or two somewhere or other – which offered chances either for selling manufactured goods to the 'natives' or for getting valuable raw materials from them, or both. Most schemes for trade abroad had been financed by investment. Englishmen were used to it.

Now, to add to the opportunities for investment in overseas trade, came no end of chances for investment in domestic business, transport, mining, industry, and communications. It was simply a case of the investment habit spreading, and it seemed to go in all directions. Ordinary shopkeepers bought mining shares; ironmasters built roads; a famous potter invested in a canal; shipping magnates would put their profits into the new ironworks; wealthy industrialists would buy land in order to become 'gentlemen', and would spend vast sums to develop their estates, often incorporating the very latest ideas in new farming techniques; dukes and earls would put some of their income from estate rents into the new railways and factories. Money like this – investment capital – flowed thick and fast.

Because there was so much money in circulation, it was cheap; that is, interest rates were low, as little as 3 or 4 per cent. This encouraged men to raise loans for their ideas, and so many businesses made money that people were prepared to invest at a low rate, feeling that their money was safe, and safe for a long period. A lot of paper money circulated too, because there was not enough gold to change hands for all these transactions. As with investment, people were prepared to accept paper currency because they had confidence in it; they knew they could pass it on to others who would accept it just as readily.

Of course, there were tragedies: some ideas did prove worthless; some pioneers did lose fortunes; some factories did fail; some banks did shut down. But the general trend was one of enormous bustle, energy, adventure, confidence, and success – which in turn bred more. Whichever way one looked at it, the overall picture was of a country where, even allowing for a growing population, more and more things were being made by fewer and fewer people. Machines were replacing muscle. Or, as the economists would put it, national productivity was rising.

On the land, away from the thumping foundries and the deafening mills, the same, in general, was happening; the country was being made more productive.

As with most other questions in social and economic history, it is not easy to be precise. Facts and figures may be hard to come by. A West Riding factory accountant, for example, may keep better records than a Dorset farmer. It is easier perhaps to follow the fortunes of millworkers whose weekly wages are regularly noted than of the poor rural families who scratched a living by poaching or begging on the edge of the village, and whose lives could pass with little comment or record at all, except perhaps a few cryptic entries in the accounts of the local Poor Rate officers. Some counties may offer better records than others. A trend that may appear obvious in the North is far from obvious in the South. Problems, say, of arable farming are not necessarily the problems of sheep farming. The historian must not jump to conclusions, though he does have an obligation to suggest some. After all, he is the one who has access to the evidence, not the reader. He does owe it to the reader to make a few guesses. He must, to a certain extent, direct the reader.

At the risk of sounding over-didactic, even trite, it is perhaps worth saying that the reader must be careful, though, with the historian who claims that he knows *all* the answers. These are the ones who write to prove something. For example, they may be convinced that the 'rich capitalists' have always 'exploited' the 'workers'. Or they are sure that 'man' has always 'progressed'. Or that all our lives are governed by some law of Fate. Or that the 'upper class' is always 'in conflict' with the 'masses'. All too often these historians do not examine all the evidence, or – worse – they hide the fact that other evidence exists. They are also guilty of twisting certain material to suit their ideas. They will interpret some facts in a particular way, and not admit that they could be interpreted in another way. They will squeeze the facts into their theory, instead of distilling their theory from the available facts – *all* the available facts.

It is true that much of this kind of historical writing comes in large, learned volumes not usually touched by students or general readers, or in minority magazines which are read only by those who already believe in what the magazines stand for. But it is often surprising how many – to put it mildly – unusual ideas can creep into school books, and stay there for a very long time. There have been textbooks in Spain, for example, which speak about the Armada campaign of 1588 without once mentioning Drake. Many Russian children were once – and for all one knows, still are – taught about the Second World War almost as if the Western Powers had nothing to do with it. There was the story of the German who came to visit England, browsed in a bookshop, and idly picked up an account of the Battle of Waterloo. He was astonished to read that the successful commander was the Duke of Wellington; he had always been taught that it had been won by the Prussians.

So – making due allowances for guesses, statistics, regional variations, and pet theories – why was English agriculture becoming more productive?

For a start, there was a lot more land being used. It was not that pioneer farmers suddenly began to open up untamed wilderness. Nor was there any big lopping of forests; most of that had been done by builders, shipwrights, and ironmasters. No. The change came from the land almost under the villagers' noses – the common and the waste.

Around most villages were areas – large or small – which were never ploughed. It might be because they were too wet or too stony, too steep or too distant. It might be because there was enough food grown on the existing farm strips; there was simply no need to extend them. This was the waste. The waste remained open – for pigs to snuffle, rabbits to breed, and children to gather kindling. Few bothered about who actually 'owned' it. Everyone just used it.

The same applied to the common. This was a patch of grazing ground on which villagers shared the right to put their sheep and cattle at various times of the year. There were local customs that had hardened into rules with the passage of the centuries. There were risks, naturally; the lazy man who did not look after his stock would be responsible for the spread of disease.

It was a similar picture on the main ploughing land – the arable land – in the village. It was usually divided into two or three great hedgeless fields, each one in turn split into strips owned or rented by different villagers. As with the common, there were traditions and customs and habits for the timing and manner of ploughing, sowing, reaping, and so on. As with the common, men were at the mercy of the laziest among them; strips overgrown with weeds could ruin the efforts on neighbours' land. If a clever farmer wanted to try a new idea, he was held back by the centuries-old habits of his fellows. A lot of land was wasted in 'balks' – boundaries between the many strips in each field. In all three types of land – arable fields, common, and waste – there was too much backwardness, too much inefficiency, too much (forgive the pun) waste. The answer came in the shape of fences, hedges, barriers – in a word, enclosures. In fairness to the old system, it must be said that it had served Britain perfectly well for several centuries, and might have gone on serving it longer, but for the fact that in the eighteenth century far more was suddenly required of it – food for a growing population, and for armies in numerous wars.

So the common, and the waste, and a lot of arable strips, were taken into enclosures. The great fields disappeared (a few remain almost as open-air museums), and the familiar compact fields of the English countryside took their place. This gave the chance for the second main set of improvements to operate.

With compact hedges to provide security from wandering stock, and insulation from the weeds of lazy farmers, pioneers could experiment with new breeding methods for cattle and sheep, with new crops, new fertilisers; they could try new rotations of crops (it exhausted the soil too fast if the same crop was grown on it each year, so farmers tried various systems of 'rotating' two or three or four different crops on two or three or four different fields). Scientifically-minded country gentlemen could test new ideas on ditching and draining. Those with a passion for machinery could tinker with gadgets to help ploughing, sowing, and threshing.

The general pattern of progress, though, was not regular. Far from it. English agriculture had almost as many exceptions as it had rules. For example, enclosures were not invented in the eighteenth century; there is evidence of some enclosure going back four or five hundred years before. By the same token, the medieval 'strip' system was by no means universal; a detailed history of eighteenth-century agriculture will reveal to the interested reader a bewildering jungle of variations, exceptions, and anomalies. Then again, just because a village's land was enclosed, it did not mean that it always became more productive. Conversely, some improvements took place in villages that had not been enclosed. A lot depended, too, on the basic quality of the soil in the area. Farmers, by nature perhaps, seem to be a little reluctant to change old methods. Ideas would take a long time to catch on, and, often, a longer time to spread.

But when all is said and done, it seems pretty clear that agriculture, in the sixty years or so after 1760, took a huge step forward. It must have done; it fed a population that doubled itself, and at a time when Britain's usual imports of grain from Eastern Europe were interrupted, if not blocked, by the French war.

To put it in its simplest possible terms, agriculture developed, and it developed for two reasons: there was a lot more of it; and it was a lot more scientific. True, it was not very mechanised; that came later, when the iron industry was able to improve its output, and when the gadget-minded Americans brought their talents to bear on the problem.

This question of iron output illustrates the connection between the Industrial and Agricultural Revolutions, and between the various parts of them. Sometimes these connections become so complicated that it is difficult to see which is the cause and which the effect. For example, did industry expand because of the demands created by several wars; or was it the expansion of industry that made it possible for a small country like Britain to fight so many wars (and win them)? Did the rise in population create a demand for a greater food output; or did the increase in a better food supply produce a healthier, and more fertile, population? Did enclosures cause unemployment, and so drive people to look for factory work in the cities; or did the prospect of regular employment in factories pull people away from the fields?

No doubt historians of economy and society will continue to debate and guess for a long time to come. However, what most of them would accept is that between, say, 1750 and the 1820s great things happened to England. In 1750, she was a second-rate power in Europe, with admittedly a powerful navy and some useful colonies. She had a reasonably healthy economy, but a small population which consisted mainly of country squires and tenants who did what their fathers had done. (The virtue they most admired was stability, solidity, a refusal to be shaken or rushed, a wariness of chasing after novelty – what they called 'bottom'. It was a fine thing to be reckoned 'a man of bottom'.) She had a promising middle class of merchants, craftsmen, and part-time gadgeteers, but no national plan or policy for improvement.

By 1820, she had doubled her population, expanded her agriculture, and revolutionised her industry to a point where it was miles ahead of every other country in the world. She had fought, often single-handed, and defeated the most powerful country in Europe. Her empire stretched across every continent except Antarctica. Her navy was unbeaten and unbeatable. Her wealth was such that she was in a position to consider abolishing protective tariffs on trade – for the simple reason that she was selling far more than she was buying. And all this, incidentally, was accomplished still without any national plan or policy.

It was the result of thousands of separate private decisions. It was achieved by the brains, the money, the drive, the gumption, of thousands of private individuals. Separate acts of Parliament would permit the enclosure of single villages; turnpike trusts did their own roadbuilding; industrialists invented and developed their own machines; railway companies did their own surveying; and so on. There was a great sense of confidence and of opportunity. There were no barriers of class or creed, birth or nation. Noblemen and squires alike dabbled in the new farming; clever clergymen brewed up important scientific experiments in their lonely rectories; many inventors were Nonconformists (debarred by law from politics and public office, they threw their ample talents and energies into business and science); the greatest railway engineer was the son of a French immigrant; a famous roadbuilder was blind; the first canal expert was said to be illiterate. The versatility was dazzling: an ironmaster could become a great reclaimer of moorland; a potter could revolutionise the techniques of marketing and salesmanship; a Scottish laboratory assistant could turn his hand to making steam engines. The prizes were equalling tempting; schoolmasters, innkeepers, draper's apprentices, barbers, could make fortunes. Anyone could do it – or so it seemed.

The Government never interfered, except to allow the many tiny laws to be passed which were necessary to make the various plans legal. It minded its own business, mainly for two reasons – one negative, one positive.

In the first place, it was not considered to be a government's responsibility. A king and his ministers were expected to keep law and order, conduct foreign affairs, wage wars, sign peace treaties – and very little else. No government had a social programme or an economic policy in the sense that they are understood today. There had been attempts from time to time to fix prices or wages, to deal with the poor, to stop certain imports or exports – but they had not been popular or particularly successful. There was not enough government machinery to make them work; reliable statistical information was scanty; and communications were so bad. (Men and horses could, and did, drown in potholes on main roads.) Englishmen, too, had a tradition stretching back to Saxon times of settling many of their affairs at village or county level. They were quick to resent anything that looked like government interference with their private lives. (Compare this with the over-centralised system in France, where there was hardly any chance for initiative at local level; decisions had to come from Paris.)

In the second place, the Government was learning a painful lesson from the American War. The colonists had revolted because they wanted to be free from the 'regulation' of their trade and industry by the home country. They were eighteenth-century Englishmen too, and, like their rivals and masters in Britain, full of energy, skill, inventiveness, and the desire to make money. London's rules were preventing them from doing this, so in the end they broke them.

Ministers in Westminster therefore began to consider that it might be a good idea to dispense with the rules altogether. Adam Smith in his *Wealth of Nations* (published, by a significant coincidence, in the very year that the Americans signed their Declaration of Independence) argued that trade and industry would prosper if all tiresome taxes and customs duties were removed. Prices would fall, sales would rise, and every 'Nation' would enhance its 'Wealth' in the new freedom that would follow.

Laissez-faire – leaving things alone – was the general attitude, if not the policy, of the Government. It must be emphasised, however, that the new ideas did not spread overnight. It was many years before England removed *all* tariffs and duties, but the process began with Pitt. In matters affecting private lives, there was certainly little attempt to interfere at all.

Governments, then, did not act to start the Industrial Revolution. They did not evolve policies to deal with the Industrial Revolution. They did little to influence the results of the Industrial Revolution – England's vast new wealth and strength. For the same reasons they did almost nothing (to begin with) to cope with the by-products of the Industrial Revolution.

These by-products – mostly unpleasant ones – were the cost, the price that Britain's people paid for their country's new prosperity. For every self-made man, there were hundreds, perhaps thousands, of poor ones, but such was the smugness and confidence of the lucky few that there was little sympathy spared for the many. If you were poor, ran the argument, it was your fault – because you were stupid, or idle, or shiftless, or criminal. All a man needed to do was buckle down, put his back into it, work, learn, save – and so prosper. It was as easy, or at any rate as straightforward, as that. The trouble with the poor was that they had no drive, no character, no determination, and so it went on.

There were in fact so many poor people that nobody seriously considered doing much about it. Poverty had always been simply 'there'. You could no more change it than you could change the weather. So why worry about it?

Respectable folk wrinkled their noses and stepped round poverty and misery as if it were some kind of gigantic cowpat; any contact would cause only further pollution. It occurred to very few that it might be possible to do anything about clearing it up. It took a long time to sink into society's conscience that the great changes in farming and industry, which had made so many fortunes, had also created the very misery that successful men found so tiresome.

Enclosures had made the land more fruitful. But countless poor families, who had scratched a living on the edge of waste and common, were forced into worse poverty. They could either stay on as paupers, and be resented by the ratepayers who kept them, or they could move to the cities, where the new factories might offer regular work. A few perhaps picked up casual employment on the improved farms (there might be a burst of labour demand in the actual planting of the hedges, but it was naturally short-term; and many men may not have wished to assist in setting up the symbols of their new misery), but the usual result of enclosures, especially enclosures for sheep farming, meant that less labour was required, not more.

The same principle applied to the machines. No single worker, however well muscled, could hope to compete with the new iron giants in the mills. The old cottage clothworkers saw their livelihoood disappearing, literally, in a puff of steam. They, too, had a grim choice – to sink or to drift.

How many actually moved to the growing cities may never be known for sure, but, even if none did, the city populations themselves were shooting up. Weekly wages, however low, offered some security. People could now marry younger, and had larger families. A lot of children became almost a necessary insurance policy; one or two would surely die, and the others could be sent to work in mill or mine to supplement the family income.

Life in cities for the poor was a desperate struggle, and usually a losing one. Because there were so many of them, employers had the whip hand over them all the time – in both senses. There was no guarantee of employment, the more so as each fresh machine made more human muscle unnecessary. There was no free handout for the unemployed – at any rate none really worth having. So men worked for the long hours and the low wages arranged by their masters; they had little choice. They sent their children and their womenfolk to work too. Infants of five and six would spend all day underground working ventilation flaps in dripping, gas-ridden mines; others barely older crawled under moving machinery to clear away dirt and debris; women millworkers would slave in stifling temperatures where cumbersome clothes could be caught in machines, and lungs could be ruined by fluff and dust.

When they went home they found their homes just as dark, smelly, and crowded. Many early streets were thrown up in a hurry by eager employers or building speculators with little concern beyond providing four walls and a roof. There was no town planning; there were no borough architects or surveyors. There was no domestic piped water. Several houses might share the same open privy. There was often no sewerage system, no street cleaning, no lighting, no refuse collection. There was no education service, no social service, no health service. As the terrible plight of these people worsened, so luckier and wealthier people tended more and more to stay away. For, added to the crowding, the filth, the gloom, and the smell, were two other horrors – crime and disease.

For these poor creatures, in their drudgery and despair, violence was often the only means of expression, and possibly their only hope of a square meal. They could not read; they could not write; they could not vote; they could not strike (thanks to Pitt's Combination Acts). They could not move either; where else would things be better? Overworked, tired, cramped, dirty, underfed, ignorant, and neglected – they fell in their thousands before the dreaded infections of smallpox, cholera, typhus, diphtheria.

It is true, there were a few dedicated doctors, a handful of public-health reformers, even one or two enlightened employers (who realised that they would get more effort out of healthy workers than out of sick ones). But they were voices in the wilderness, and they had a lonely struggle. It says a lot for their strength of will and sincerity that they plugged away for so many years. They worked among the poor; they wrote books, pamphlets, reports, newspaper articles; they badgered MPs to raise questions in the House; they quoted details of the worst scandals; they ran private court cases; they drew up petitions; they raised money for charities. They were often criticised as busybodies, disliked as troublemakers, ridiculed as dreamers, condemned as liars.

Perhaps with some truth too. They did poke their noses in; they did embarrass people with scandals; they did often overstate their case. Somehow or other they had to persuade Parliament to make new laws or abolish bad ones. Parliamentary action was the key to the problem. Owing to the rise in population, and the huge growth of cities, the problem had swollen out of all proportion. Self-help reform, do-it-yourself improvement, would no longer work. The Government was slowly, step by relentless step, forced to recognise that a particular social evil was a national problem, and that it would have to produce regulations on a national scale to deal with it.

But the tide turned very slowly. *Laissez-faire* was becoming a profitable policy in trade, which was why governments were so unwilling to give it up in other areas of activity. For years many irate gentlemen continued to complain about various social reforms interfering with the liberty of the individual. Employers fought many changes because the new regulations would cost them money (putting in windows, installing safer machines, cutting working hours, and so on). Many sincere Christians thought that the Devil made work for idle hands, and so felt that child labour was a fine thing. Much of the opposition to reforms came, infuriatingly, from the very people they were designed to help. Generations of them were so used to dirt, ignorance, deceit, and crime that they found it impossible to break the habit, and they *wanted* to keep their children working in the factories; how else could they make ends meet? Many simply did not have the energy remaining to respond to help.

Changes for the better did come, but they came only after countless struggles, delays, compromises, and frustrations. It was as if men's minds had become numbed by the enormity of it all.

Illiterate, overworked families, driven by harsh circumstance from the fresh country air to the stifling streets of a city, would not suddenly discover the knowledge, experience, or determination to find a way out towards freedom and self-respect. A whole country had to adjust itself, almost overnight – or so it seemed – to speeds of thirty, forty, fifty miles an hour, when the fastest means of land travel *since the dawn of time* had been a man on a horse. Speed of travel, speed of production, speed of distribution – everything was becoming faster. Suddenly the clock and the timetable were all-important.

It became commonplace during the twentieth century to talk of the evils of smog, factory chimneys, chemical pollution, city sprawl, noisy transport, violent crowds. These, and a host of allied troubles, are indeed bad, but society has nevertheless learned to live with them, and adjust to them. But for the men of the late eighteenth and early nineteenth centuries these things were happening – all at once – *for the first time*. Of course they staggered under the impact. Squires mourned that the peace of the countryside was being ruined by the monstrous trains; writers blamed factories and enclosures and greed for destroying the old, safe values of 'Merrie England'; poets described the blackened mills as symbols, almost temples, of the Devil. Men who were sensitive enough to see that a revolution was taking place were frightened by its hugeness and its unstoppability, just as Edmund Burke was horrified by the great storm unleashed in France at about the same time.

In France the end of the century saw an explosion of political energy; in Britain during the same period there was an equally shattering explosion of economic energy. These two forces helped to cause, or at least coincided with, the longest European war for 150 years. And Britain, the smaller of the two major contestants, won the war.

Chapter 3 set out to explain how this happened; this chapter may have helped to explain why.

CHAPTER FIVE

Boney's Picnic
1815

1815 should have been quiet. After twenty-three years of almost non-stop war, France had been defeated at last. Allied kings and generals had ridden in triumph through the streets of Paris. An elderly, fat, dull Bourbon king, Louis XVIII, had been accepted as the new ruler of France. The beaten Emperor had been removed, and placed on the island of Elba, just off the coast of Italy, where he could do no further harm – or so it was thought. Soldiers were demobilised; ships were taken out of commission and crews dumped on the dockside; thousands of refugees and prisoners looked forward to home and freedom. Ports, workshops, farms, cities, palaces – everything that had suffered in the longest war in 150 years – now struggled to return to normal. The whole of Europe, after the cheers of victory, heaved a colossal sigh of relief.

In Vienna, there was a vast, glittering international meeting – a congress. Rulers and foreign secretaries from nearly every country in Europe, large and small, were haggling to try to sort out a fair deal for all those who claimed damages as a result of the war. Bonaparte, the adventurer, had chopped and changed boundaries so much that the map of Europe had to be almost completely redrawn. Arguments became so fierce at times that it needed an effort to remember that only a few months beforehand they had all been fighting together against a common enemy.

Then in early March came the bombshell: Bonaparte had escaped from Elba and landed in France. Newspapers at first treated him as a lunatic gambler, but were soon forced to take him seriously. As he marched northwards, more and more soldiers joined him. Many had marched south in fact to arrest him, but when they caught sight of the familiar stocky figure in the grey frock coat, the emotion of old comradeship was too much for them. They forgot the miseries of defeat and death, and remembered only the dazzling victories and the glamorous processions. They were already bored with the lumbering Louis XVIII, and ashamed at his lack of energy. What a contrast to the dynamic Emperor. Officers were fed up with an inactive life on half-pay, and sickened at the posturings of the old-time aristocrats who had returned with the King – fading fops who could think only of settling old scores and putting back the clock. At the news of the Emperor's approach, these pathetic peacocks showed their true colours in undignified flight. The King, having sworn to defend Paris to the last drop of his blood, got into his coach and drove all the way to Brussels. By the end of the month the Emperor was on his throne, and Louis was taking shelter behind the coat-tails of the Allies.

Bonaparte claimed that he wanted no war, but few outside France took him at his word. With another huge sigh, this time of great weariness, Europe prepared to defeat him all over again, to crush this monster who should have been dead but who would not lie down.

By May there was an allied army ready in the Netherlands. Its commander-in-chief was Wellington, now raised by a grateful nation to the rank of duke. Many of his veterans from Spain had been sent to America, so he had to make up numbers with Belgians, Dutchmen, Germans, fresh recruits from England – anyone he could get. A Prussian army under Marshal Blücher – a fierce old pipe-puffing warrior, seventy-two years of age, who loathed Frenchmen – was marching to join them. Two more armies, Austrian and Russian, each over 100,000 strong, were rumbling through Germany towards the French frontier.

Bonaparte had to strike before his enemies could combine. The nearest were Wellington and Blücher, now in Belgium. He swung his army north on the high road to Brussels. The faster he moved, the more chance he had of defeating the English and Prussians separately. In the event there were two clashes on the same day, 16 June. At Quatre Bras, twenty miles south of Brussels, Wellington fought Marshal Ney to a standstill, and then withdrew north. Six miles away, at Ligny, the

Emperor in person defeated the Prussians. But the Prussians also drew
back in good order. Old Blücher was a good deal tougher than Bonaparte
thought. He had been unhorsed on the battlefield and trampled on by
French cavalry. He picked himself up, dosed himself with a ghastly
mixture of gin and rhubarb, and was ready for action again. Cannily, he
pulled his army back in a northerly direction, parallel to Wellington's
line of retreat. When the next battle came, he would still be near enough
to come and help. He promised Wellington that he would march as soon
as he heard the guns.

Bonaparte made the mistake of assuming that Blücher and his
Prussians had retired to the east, and on 17 June he sent over 30,000
troops under one of his marshals to look for them. Marshal Grouchy
understandably could not find them, and so Bonaparte fought his final
battle without 30,000 precious men.

Wellington meanwhile had dug himself in on a wooded ridge near
the village of Waterloo, twelve miles south of Brussels. It was typical
of the Duke that he had spotted this position some considerable time
before, and he had made a mental note that, if he should ever need a
good defensive position in front of Brussels, this was it.

As the French plodded through a steady downpour on the 17th,
Wellington checked his defences, and sprinkled batches of his regular
soldiers to stiffen the ranks of his foreign regiments. It all depended on
whether his lines could hold the massive French columns until the
Prussians arrived, and this time it was no mere marshal against him; his
enemy was the Emperor himself.

It rained cats and dogs all night. For all three armies – Wellington's,
Blücher's, and Bonaparte's – drenched and tired out after two battles
and miles of marching in two days (in Grouchy's case quite fruitless
marching; he did not find a single Prussian), it must have been a
wretched time.

In the morning – Sunday, 18 June – Bonaparte waited several hours
before launching his attack, hoping that the ground would dry out a
little. He was the one who had to make the first move. All Wellington
had to do was sit tight on his ridge and defy the French to shift him. A
draw would be as good as a win, because every day he held up
Bonaparte the Austrians and Russians were coming closer.

At last the French opened fire with their massed cannon. But the Duke had his men sheltering behind the ridge in his usual way. The French were obligingly doing what he had hoped they would do – attack in *their* usual way. Bonaparte was too impatient, or too cocky, or too ill, to bother with any fancy tactics or new tricks; the dog perhaps was now too old (at forty-five!). When the cannons ceased fire, he sent in his infantry columns, almost from force of habit. All through the afternoon the allied lines held together, and their accurate volleys of musket and rifle fire mowed down Frenchmen in hundreds. When Bonaparte ran true to form and sent in his cavalry, the English formed squares as they had done in Spain, and the French horses were as helpless as they had been in Spain.

Not that the English had it all their own way. Some of the fighting, particularly at certain strong points in the allied line, was bitter and savage. Casualties were heavy on both sides. But the Duke kept his head, and kept his grip on the battle. Smart and well groomed as ever (another of his nicknames was 'the Beau'), he rode up and down behind the lines on his famous chestnut, Copenhagen. Whenever there was a mistake to be put right or a vital decision to be taken, soldiers looked up and saw the familiar cocked hat and hook nose. The mere sight of them was worth a regiment. Nearly every member of his staff was killed or wounded, but he came through the day without a scratch.

Bonaparte on the other hand was more distant from the battle, both physically and mentally. He had started the day by thinking it was going to be easy – 'a picnic' was the word he had used. (It was another symptom of the over-confidence he had shown since the campaign had begun. When he had beaten the Prussians on the 16th, he had assumed with contempt that the beaten enemy would run back to Germany, and he had sent Grouchy after them merely to keep them moving.) Once the fighting had begun, he did not follow events so closely or seize any chances so swiftly as he had done at his great battles like Austerlitz. As the afternoon wore on, the French attacks became more and more desperate. They had to break the long red British lines before the Prussians arrived. Away to the east, Blücher chewed his pipe and chivvied his weary infantry and sweating gunners; he had promised Wellington, he said, and nobody was going to make him break his word.

By late afternoon they got there, and their guns, caked with mud up to the axles, began pounding the French right wing. Bonaparte was shaken at last out of his sluggishness into taking a gamble. He sent in his precious reserve, his finest troops – the Imperial Guard.

Again the deadly volleys crackled from the long red lines on the ridge. The mighty Guard hesitated, wavered, and broke. British fire power had proved too much. The Prussian infantry waded in from the east. The British lines at last advanced to clinch the victory, and the Prussian cavalry chased the remnants with sabres into the damp dusk.

At nine o'clock in the evening, Wellington met Blücher on the battlefield. The old Prussian gave him a bear hug by way of greeting. As he could speak no English, he used what were probably his only two words of French – '*Quelle affaire!*' 'What a business!' It was the sort of understatement the Duke himself was fond of using.

Wellington, as usual, did not give way to anything like delight. He knew how close the battle had been. He knew too how terrible were the losses; he broke down when he read the casualty lists the next morning. In a letter written the following month he wrote, 'I hope to God I have fought my last battle.' If there was any misery only slightly less wretched than losing a battle, he said, it was winning one.

But he had his wish. Bonaparte abdicated again, and surrendered to a British warship. This time there was to be no playing at emperors on the island of Elba. (If Blücher and the Prussians had had their way, they would have shot him.) Instead he was removed as far away as possible, to the lonely British island of St Helena, in the middle of the south Atlantic. There he lingered for another six years – reliving his victories, dictating his memoirs, trying to prove that he had been right all the time. His many words, both sensible and stupid, were lovingly written down by those long-suffering attendants who had followed him into exile. In 1821 he died. He was only fifty-one.

Once again the armies were demobilised, except for one which was billeted in France to make sure that there was no more resistance. Once again the politicians gathered at Vienna to decide the fate of the conquered enemy, and to fix the boundaries of the new Europe. Once again the Allies began arguing among themselves about the size of this state or that, about a frontier here or a new king there. The final treaty was not signed until 20 November, 1815.

Two very able statesmen, however, helped to make sure that this final settlement was a lasting one. One was the British Foreign Secretary, Lord Castlereagh. The other, surprisingly, was the French delegate, Talleyrand.

On the face of it, Talleyrand had an impossible task. The country he represented had for twenty years caused war, misery, and death all over Europe. Her upstart Emperor had forced his brothers onto European thrones; his customs officers had sealed seaports and ruined shops and businesses from Spain to the Baltic; his spies and secret police had made everyone afraid to look over their shoulder; his agents had looted museums and art galleries in nearly every important city on the continent. Those whom he had crushed the hardest, naturally, wanted the bitterest revenge, and though the victorious allies had plenty to argue about, they were all agreed that the French must never again be able to disturb the peace of Europe.

The question was, how was this to be done? The Allies disagreed on this too, and here Talleyrand saw his chance. Talleyrand had been many things in his time – a French nobleman, a bishop (though not a very holy one), a revolutionary, an ambassador to England. He had served as Foreign Secretary to Bonaparte, and he had also plotted against him. He had been a liar, a cheat, a taker of bribes, and a traitor. He had survived every change of French government since 1789. His quick wits and his intelligence had kept his head on his shoulders through the worst days of the guillotine terror. Even when the Emperor suspected his treachery, his life was safe, because he knew more about foreign affairs than anyone else in France, and Bonaparte needed his knowledge.

For Talleyrand was a diplomat to his fingertips – wise, experienced, and professional. He knew that, now the Emperor had gone, the old rules of the diplomatic game would be brought back again. Once the Allies had no monster to fear or suspect, they would begin to fear and suspect one another. He could then play off one power against another, and so take whatever chances came his way.

He knew, for example, that the Prussians and the English disagreed. Prussia had suffered from the French occupation for longer than any other major European power, and revenge was uppermost in her mind. Castlereagh, who spoke for England, argued that the way to secure a true peace was to be reasonable. If France were to be torn apart for mere revenge, he said, no Frenchman would rest until his country had regained the losses. There had to be a peace treaty that fair-minded Frenchmen would be prepared to accept as reasonable.

Talleyrand also understood how much everyone feared Russia, especially the English. Russia was far and away the biggest country, and at Vienna she was demanding yet more land as her reward for defeating the French monster. Tsar Alexander wanted Poland, which would take him right into central Europe; this worried Austria and Prussia, the two great powers in Germany. He also wanted to penetrate the Baltic Sea in the north, and the Black Sea and Mediterranean in the south, and this worried England; she drew her vital shipping supplies of timber from the Baltic, and she had many profitable trading interests in the area of the Black Sea and the Mediterranean.

There were innumerable other disputes, large and small – about boundaries, trading rights, freedom of access, damage compensation, diplomatic precedence, and so on. It would be a silly exaggeration to imply that Talleyrand wove his way through these minefields of complex negotiation with unerring accuracy and unswerving confidence and unbroken success; but whatever success the French did secure at Vienna was almost entirely due to his skill.

The result was that the final terms imposed on France were firm but not crippling. Her boundaries were cut back to what they had been in 1790. Louis XVIII was put on the throne, for the second time. An army of occupation was stationed in France, under the command of the Duke of Wellington – who else? France was also ordered to pay 'costs', as it were, for the war – a war indemnity. The actual sum – 700,000,000 francs – sounds enormous, but France's recovery after the war was so swift that the whole amount was paid off by 1818. It was also ordered that France should give back all the art treasures that had been looted from the rest of Europe.

That took care of the debts of the previous war. The next step was insurance, so to speak, against the next one. All around the borders of France, the Allies set up what were known as 'buffer states'. These were safeguards against France trying to break out again to terrorise Europe. In the north-east, Belgium was given to Holland, in order to form a strong barrier at the mouth of the Rivers Rhine and Scheldt. Higher up the Rhine, that is further south, certain lands were given to Prussia, the great power who hated France more than anyone. In the Alps, the country of Switzerland was secured; every power in Europe promised to respect it as neutral for ever. In the south, the states of Savoy and Genoa were given to the King of Piedmont and Sardinia, in order to stop the French reaching out into Italy. Beyond the Pyrenees, the old King of Spain, another Bourbon, was put back on his throne. France's only other boundary was the sea, and on the sea was the British Navy.

As further insurance, the four Great Powers – Britain, Austria, Prussia, and Russia – signed a Quadruple Alliance to keep the peace of Europe. At Castlereagh's suggestion, they also agreed to meet at intervals in the future to discuss any possible threats to international security.

All things considered, Talleyrand could not have hoped for much more. France was left in one piece; she had a Bourbon government which nobody feared; and she was given a fair chance to regain her pride and strength, if not her military power.

Castlereagh too could look back on his work at Vienna with some satisfaction. He had won the fair terms for France that he wanted, and he had set up some machinery for dealing with possible disturbances in the future. He could not prevent Russia keeping Poland, but, by giving Norway to Sweden, he had set up a friendly power in the Baltic. He was also lucky in that England was the only winning country that was a sea power. The other three were so concerned about Europe that they did not much mind, or care, how many islands and colonies England added to her empire. Most of them she had captured during the war, and she showed great shrewdness in choosing which ones to hang on to. Trinidad, Tobago, and St Lucia were valuable islands in the West Indies. The Cape of Good Hope was an obvious key point in the trade route to India; so was Mauritius in the Indian Ocean. Ceylon, at the foot of India, was a rich island as well as being on the next leg of the route to the Far East. Heligoland was a useful base in the North Sea. Malta, right in the middle of the Mediterranean, was at the vital crossroads in east–west and north–south trade.

The other three Great Powers – Austria, Prussia, and Russia – did not get everything they wanted, but they well understood that in the old diplomatic game one very rarely did. There was always a next time. Now that Bonaparte was gone, they could all be confident that there would be a next time.

Prussia got her hands on the Rhine, half of a German state called Saxony, and a coastal Baltic state called Pomerania. Metternich, the Chancellor of Austria, made his chief gains in southern Europe, where his government gained control of nearly the whole of northern Italy. That, too, would provide a buffer against France. Tsar Alexander made sure of Poland, and added to his empire with Finland in the north and Bessarabia in the south. He also persuaded every monarch in Europe to sign a vague agreement called the Holy Alliance, by which they promised in future to conduct their foreign policy according to the rules of true Christian brotherhood. Nobody took it seriously, to begin with. Most monarchs decided that, it if kept the Tsar quiet and made him happy, they might as well sign it. Only the Prince Regent refused, because Castlereagh dismissed the idea as so much nonsense.

The Vienna settlement lasted, and it lasted because, taking things all round, the Great Powers were reasonably satisfied with what they got out of it, and they realised that they could not get much more without the risk of war; and after twenty-three years of fighting, that was too horrible to contemplate.

Nobody took a great deal of notice of the smaller powers, such as Norway, or Belgium, or Bavaria, or Naples, or any of the dozens of tiny German states. Turkey was not even invited. But the arguments could not go on for ever; decisions had to be taken, and it was the four Great Powers that took them. Their aim was to keep France contained, give each other the best deal possible, and keep the peace. For the next forty years, by and large, they did.

There were indeed attempts to disturb the peace of Vienna, but they were for the most part unsuccessful. They did not come from the governments who had arranged the peace; they came from the people whose lives had been altered by the peace, and by the war before it.

The French Revolution had plunged Europe into war, twenty-three years of it. But it had also stated great truths – that all men were equal before the law, that a man had the right to believe what he liked, that he had a right to decide what sort of government should rule over him, and that people of one country should not be oppressed by the government of another. French soldiers and French civil servants had carried these ideas wherever the armies had marched. When the soldiers and civil servants were gone, the ideas remained.

They became dreams that inspired men all over Europe. Those twenty-three years had brought great misery and upset, but they had also given a glimpse of a great promised land of liberty and independence. When many of the stuffy old kings were restored to their thrones; when many of the old nobles came back to their estates, flaunting their airs and graces; when the old-time civil servants, corrupt and inefficient, began again their bumbling and their infuriating delays – men felt enraged and cheated. They had had an unforgettable glimpse of something so much better.

They felt there was nothing for it but to plan revolution again in their own countries, to do again what the French had done in 1789 – gain their liberty and their independence. It was this that produced two of the great forces of the nineteenth century in Europe – liberalism and nationalism. By liberalism (with a small 'l') was usually meant the movement to achieve the great rights of man – freedom of thought, freedom of speech, the right to vote, freedom of the press, equality before the law, and so on. Nationalism meant the desire of the people of any nation to achieve their unity or their independence from a foreign government.

A third force gave the first two – liberalism and nationalism – greater strength. That was population. For just as the population was rising fast in England, so it was rising at a similar rate in Europe. To put it briefly, there were more revolutionary movements of people in the nineteenth century because there were more people.

The ministers and princes who drew up the Vienna treaty were aware of liberalism and nationalism, but they were probably not familiar with detailed population statistics. Even if they had been, it would not have made them sympathetic to liberalism or nationalism. To them these two forces were not great dreams or great truths; they were disturbers of the peace. They had brought revolution and war. If not kept under tight control, they would bring revolution and war again.

Nobody could seriously argue with the rights of man, the men of Vienna would have said. (Pitt is supposed to have remarked once, 'Of course, everyone knows Tom Paine is right.') That was not the point. The point was that the new ideas were too unstable, that they led men into confusion and brought governments into ruin. Most people, they argued, were too poor, too rough, too uneducated, too violent, and maybe too stupid to be able to handle such dangerous things. It was like giving fireworks to a baby.

Nobody believed this more firmly than the Duke of Wellington. He had been born into an Irish Protestant landlord family, the sort of family that gave orders almost by instinct. He had spent a lifetime in the army, and had learned that nothing useful was achieved without discipline and command. He never had any illusions about his soldiers; he knew that order was maintained by fear of the lash and of the hangman's rope. He had spent twenty years fighting a war which had been caused by a revolution. He had, as he said, fought his last battle, and he prayed to God that no new revolutions would put power again into the hands of city mobs and gang leaders and bullies and crackpots and ambitious soldiers.

It would have been easy for him to sit back for the rest of his life and be a professional hero. He was the lion of European society wherever he went; kings and princes competed with one another to load him with honours – Duke, Field Marshal, Knight of the Garter in England; Prince of Waterloo in Holland; the Order of the Holy Ghost in France; Knight of the Black Eagle in Prussia; Knight of the Elephant in Denmark; Knight of St Andrew in Russia – the list was endless. He could have lived on the glory of Salamanca and Vittoria and Waterloo for as long as he liked.

But the Duke was rarely led astray by praise (though he was human enough to enjoy it). He had done nothing but his duty, and he continued to do his duty. He was only forty-six, and in Olympic good health. So, after his tour of duty with the Army of Occupation, he returned home, and placed his services at his monarch's disposal. Thereafter, he never feared to do anything if he thought it best for the good of his King and of his country, regardless of party or faction. For instance, when Lord Liverpool, anxious to recruit the support of the greatest soldier in Europe for the beleaguered Government, offered him the post of

Master-General of the Ordnance (a sort of Chief Gunner and Engineer to the nation), with a seat in the Cabinet, he made it crystal clear that, while he was happy thus to serve, he would not automatically follow the Tories into opposition if they lost an election. He saw his duty in service to the Crown, not in factious opposition to it.

If he claimed to be no pledged friend of the Tories, he was certainly no friend at all of liberals or radicals. If his opinions offended them – and he made no secret of them – that was just too bad. If the crowd, the people, the general public turned against him – and they did, more than once, in the next thirty-odd years – he showed them the same contempt he had shown to his drunken soldiers in Spain. It only confirmed his belief that ordinary people were fickle and stupid.

The great problem of England, as he saw it, was the danger of revolution. Lord Liverpool, the Prime Minister, and most of his Cabinet would have agreed with him. Liverpool was an honest man, and no fool. He was respected and liked by his colleagues. He was a conscientious prime minister. But he was not creative; he did not have, and did not like, new ideas. Liberalism, nationalism, radicalism, were new ideas; they disturbed the peace. Therefore they had to be discouraged.

The Home Secretary, Lord Sidmouth (Pitt's old rival when he was plain Henry Addington), had similar worries. He was responsible for law and order in a country that was groaning under a fearful load of war taxation. The new factories, with their machines which could each do the work of a dozen men, had caused unemployment. Thousands of soldiers and sailors returning from the war had no jobs either, and no pension. The crime rate was high, despite a savage system of penalties that could hang a man for stealing a loaf of bread. Bad harvests always brought high prices and riots. Machine-breakers often threatened the lives of owners as well as their machinery. It was a violent time. Wealthy men in their London houses did not put up iron railings for decoration. There was no police force; there was no government department to collect accurate figures; indeed there were few accurate figures to collect. Sidmouth had to get most of his facts from spies and informers. Such men were not by nature especially honest. If they needed more income, it was a simple matter to pretend that a noisy, beery crowd of workmen in a tavern might be plotting 'revolution';

they collected their blood money while nervous ministers and jumpy magistrates ordered the arrests and imposed their sentences of imprisonment or transportation.

Sidmouth, Liverpool, and most other ministers were old-style eighteenth-century noblemen trying to deal with problems of a type and size they had never seen before: the unemployment, the high taxes, the staggering rise in population (the 1811 census had shown a 14 per cent rise in only ten years); the new swarming cities with their crowds and their filth and their crime; the violence of men facing starvation because of machines or enclosures or high prices; the anger of Radical writers and speakers who saw all the wretchedness, and who could not make the Government do anything about it.

Yet the Government were doing their best according to their principles. Liverpool and Sidmouth and Lord Eldon (the Lord Chancellor, who sat on the Woolsack for twenty years and voted against everything) clung to their two central beliefs. One was *laissez-faire* – no government should interfere in the lives of its people any more than it had to. It was not a government's business. The other – the most important of all – was that a government's chief duty was to govern, to maintain law and order. If there were Radical meetings, they must be broken up; if there were agitators among workers, they must be silenced; if an organised group of men criticised the Government, they must be arrested in case they were plotting 'revolution'; if workers smashed machines, they must be imprisoned; if hungry farm labourers poached, they must be transported to Australia; if journalists wrote strong words against the King's ministers, their offices must be closed. There was no police force, so regular soldiers must be concentrated in handy barracks, and local magistrates must be given more and more power to arrest and punish. Over everything loomed the horrible ghost of 'revolution'. The Home Secretary was not an imaginative man; there was nothing else he could think of doing.

In fairness to him, it must be said that England did not have a revolution. Yet revolutions broke out in Italy, Spain, and Greece in 1820; in France, Belgium, Italy, Germany, and Poland in 1830; and in nearly every country in Europe in 1848. England escaped. This may have been because the many savage laws took all the fight out of

England's Radicals and would-be revolutionaries. It is equally likely that English society was more stable and more flexible than French society, and would not have had a revolution anyway. So does Sidmouth deserve any credit?

Credit or not, his way of dealing with the situation amounted to little more than holding the fort. It was a series of immediate reactions and hasty, hand-to-mouth remedies. In the last resort it was negative government rather than positive government. Sidmouth punished crime, protest meetings, agitation, and criticism. What he did not understand was that these were the *results* of the misery and anger caused by the war and by the Industrial Revolution. If there was to be any real solution to the problem, it would come only when the Government tackled the *causes* of the misery and anger – the unemployment, the high prices, the crowding and dirt and disease in the cities, the awful gloom and slavery of the factories, the hopeless poverty of many landless agricultural labourers.

That solution would come only when two things happened. First, there would have to be men in Parliament who understood the problems from first-hand experience. Second, Parliament would have to be convinced that *laissez-faire* was not enough; bad housing, diseased water, child labour, the lack of schools, the absence of medical services, appalling factory conditions – all these *were* the Government's business, because only a change in the law of the land would produce any improvement. It was no use leaving it to the kindness and hard work of individuals; the problem was too big.

As the new century moved forward, two processes grew that pushed Parliament in the right direction. Firstly, there was a movement to get new types of MPs into Parliament. The men who lived in the cities gave up hope of persuading the country gentlemen who made up Parliament to appreciate their troubles, and decided to get into Parliament themselves. If the old Parliament set barriers against them, then the first thing to do was to change Parliament. So the postwar years saw a revival of the campaign for Parliamentary reform. Only when Parliament truly represented the cities as well as the land, the workers and factory-owners as well as the country squires and the rich estate-owners, would the necessary improvements come about.

Secondly, the cities, and the problems in them, grew. And they grew so large and so fast that the Government was forced to take action. It was to reach the stage in the end where, instead of putting up more barriers in order to avoid revolution and a complete breakdown, Parliament had to remove barriers for exactly the same reason.

Historians are fond of calling this period or that an 'age of transition', which is a historian's way of saying that things were changing. It is like looking at a drop of water. To the non-scientist, a drop of water is a drop of water; to the man with the microscope, it is a dynamic world of endless variety and activity. Similarly, any period of history, to the casual reader or observer, may look pretty static; nothing much seems to have happened. The specialist historian, who looks at it through the microscope of detailed documentary evidence, finds on the contrary that a great deal is happening; so, to him, it is an 'age of transition' – between two relatively static periods (well, static to him) either side of his own special period – until other historians come along to study those. So in a sense every period is an age of transition.

Nevertheless, when one takes an overall backward glance down the centuries, some periods do seem to stand out as producing more change than others. This period is one of them. Its 'specialness' was apparent to those alive then; there was a sort of heady excitement, especially in the young, that they were living through great times.

The French Revolution had challenged rules so old and so strong and so universal that men were amazed: amazed that they had been challenged at all; amazed that the challenge had been so successful; and amazed that the changes had been so rapid. So many things went so quickly in France – kingship, the Catholic Church, social privilege, legal inequality, religious discrimination, judicial torture. If it could be done in France....

This challenge, moreover, was not confined to an attack on kings and nobles and bishops and judges; it was part of a more general process, known to historians as the Romantic Movement. The trouble with the eighteenth century, or so thought many young men growing up at the end of it, was that there were too many rules, too many conventions, too many set ways of doing things. There was no scope for being original, for being enthusiastic, for being even moderately lively.

Pondering their problem, these thinkers came to the conclusion that the solution was not so much to change the rules as to get rid of them altogether. What really mattered was instinct, emotion, novelty, spontaneity, enthusiasm, and total devotion. Freed from all constraints, they, predictably, came up with all sorts of ideas, which ranged from the truly brilliant to the idiotic; only time sorted out the true talent and genius and creativity from the silly notions and the pretentious nonsense.

They looked back, they looked forward, they looked away altogether – anywhere where they did not have to contemplate the decaying world that they thought they saw before their eyes. For instance, some decided that man had been happiest when he had lived in a 'state of nature', before being corrupted by modern greed and modern governments. (These views were usually debated charmingly behind the fans and the lace handkerchiefs in well-upholstered drawing rooms.) The almost total absence of scientific or anthropological information only enhanced the attraction of this vision. When Captain Cook brought back one or two Pacific natives from his voyages, they were at once identified as classic examples of the 'noble savage'.

Then again, some poets and writers also went back to the past, but not quite so far. All over Western Europe, there was a new interest in folklore, myth, and legend. Perhaps it was an attempt, in the age of nationalism, to find the roots of a nation's character, a nation's 'soul'. Fresh studies began in old languages – Erse in Ireland, Provençal in France, Flemish in Belgium, Tuscan in northern Italy. It is no coincidence that at this time the brothers Grimm were collecting and publishing their famous fairy tales.

Storytellers ransacked the history of their countries to find plots and characters for stories, which were told against a background of a distant semi-heroic age when there were heroes and villains and happy endings. Sir Walter Scott became a national celebrity on the strength of a stream of poems and novels from the romantic past of Scotland. The thousands who bought his books were not concerned about historical accuracy or with true-to-life drama, any more than a boy today watches John Wayne or Clint Eastwood in order to find out what the Wild West was really like.

Coming closer again to modern times, some writers used history for a more practical purpose. The great days of 'Merrie England' had been superseded, they said, by a new bleak age of dirt, of black, belching chimneys, of filthy urban sprawl. To William Blake the factories were 'dark, Satanic mills'; to William Cobbett London was a massive cyst on the face of Britain. What was needed was a return to the virtues and values of the great days of sturdy, independent yeomen, and apple cheeks and roast beef and old ale and John Bull.

Others sought freedom not in the past, but in nature, or rather in 'Nature', with a capital 'N'. There, in Nature, was to be found simplicity, and truth, and purity, and virtue – and inspiration for poetry and painting and music. Nature was the ultimate, the final truth, the constant factor that never let you down. While a great deal of precious nonsense may have come out of this, it is also true that a great poet of nature, Wordsworth, lived at this time, and also arguably Britain's greatest landscape painter, John Constable.

How much of all this output was genuine, and how much worthless? The names that find their way into the books are usually the ones who proved their value over the years, but there was quite probably a great deal of rubbish that was discarded on the way. The reputations of those who have survived are still a matter for debate.

An example of this is the work of Turner, accepted by many as England's greatest painter ever. Was his work, especially his later work, the evidence of the Romantic Movement in action – challenging conventions, breaking rules, constantly pushing frontiers of possibility ever forward into unknown wildernesses of experiment and further dimension? Or would he have done it in whatever period in which he lived? Or was he off his head? Were his later pictures a soaring of the spirit into a stratosphere of genius, or were they a wild career into an orbit of insanity?

To come back to earth again, the Romantic Movement did produce much that was lightweight, sentimental, wishy-washy, or just plain dotty. But the period also saw a remarkable outburst of talent in poetry, prose, painting, music, in fact in nearly every art form. An hour in any concert hall, a walk round any art gallery, a glance at any bookshelf will confirm this. People who make no pretence to any great artistic awareness are acquainted with names like Keats, Constable, Byron,

Beethoven, Shelley, Chopin, Wordsworth, Schubert, Mendelssohn, Scott, Schumann, Turner.

To take one more example, from a rather less dramatic, but no less necessary part of human existence, the fixed laws of women's fashions were also being cast aside. Society ladies were rebelling too against the tight restrictions of corsets. They also threw away their many layers of petticoats. For the first time in many years, ladies' figures in simple, low-cut dresses, looked something like what they really were, and not some hourglass piece of wicker-trussed sculpture. It was romanticism again – a return to Nature. Unfortunately, the British climate being what it was, the ladies could not cast off so many underclothes, and still be beautiful in nothing but cotton dresses and goosepimples. So they borrowed an idea from professional dancers, and took to wearing knickers. Not to be outdone, the gentlemen also changed their style of leg covering; knee breeches began to give way to the more fashionable trousers.

It was new, and all very daring, and of course absolutely shocking. Worse still was the latest craze in dancing – the waltz. In the old, formal dances, the steps were often complicated, and usually stately, as was only right for properly-brought-up ladies and gentlemen. In the new waltz, everyone seemed to whirl about at a most unsightly speed. What was more, the partners had to dance actually touching each other. Embracing on the dance floor – disgusting!

None of these frightful goings-on would have been allowed by the prim George III and his frowning wife. But George, sadly, was now deaf, and blind, and mad, and Queen Charlotte had virtually retired from public life. Smart society was dominated by the Prince of Wales, the Prince Regent, 'Prinny' – a nickname which, underneath a cartoon of him, neatly suggested a mixture of being fat, foppish, and spoilt – an intelligent, middle-aged playboy whom nobody took seriously.

And yet, oddly, it was the old King who takes credit for the new fashion of holidays at the seaside. He had been very fond of Weymouth, and before long middle-class families were booking rides on the new, fast coaches, and spending their holiday hours on the seafront at Worthing and Eastbourne and Margate. And it was Prinny who joined, and soon led, the fashion in his usual extravagant way, and spent a fortune building the famous Pavilion at Brighton.

Most people who could express themselves agreed that it was an exciting time to be alive; whether for good or bad reasons, things were happening. They felt this particularly about the year 1815. Perhaps it was the Battle of Waterloo. Perhaps it was the relief that the great war was over – really over. Maybe it was the pride that England was in a position of power and authority that she had never held before in Europe. Or again it may have been the sense of challenge in facing the peace and all the problems it would bring. Whatever it was, 1815 was a special year.

But it must be remembered that there were many, many more people who could not express themselves, because they could not read, write, vote, organise, or strike. They knew nothing of Scott's novels or Turner's paintings or Beethoven's symphonies. The nearest they got to a waltz was holding the horse's head for a penny as the society ladies arrived for the ball. They never saw the seaside because they could never afford the fare. They knew nothing of these things, and they cared nothing.

Life for them was a grim business of surviving. There was nothing special for them about 1815 – except that the breadwinner of the family had returned from the wars with one leg and no pension; that a son caught poaching had been packed off on a prison ship to Australia for seven years; and that the price of bread had gone up – again.

CHAPTER SIX

Prinny
1816–20

The list of difficulties and troubles facing ordinary British people during the years immediately following the Napoleonic War makes depressing reading. Most postwar periods in any country are hard times, but the sheer weight, number, and variety of woes in 1816 make the truth of this assertion crushingly painful.

One hardly knows where to begin. Life in the Army and Navy was harsh and uncertain, but many men came to look back in later years on their war service as the finest time of their lives. Yet they came home – half a million of them – with nothing but memories, scars, and a few looted trinkets in their knapsacks. No rehabilitation schemes, no help from welfare officers, no convalescent homes, no pensions – nothing. A tired, impoverished Government were simply relieved that there were now half a million men whose arrears of pay they need no longer worry about. They were able-bodied, were they not? (Well, most of them.) Had they not learned self-reliance in the defence of their country (for which everyone was grateful, naturally)? Let them return to their homes, and seek out work for themselves like everyone else. If they did not, it only confirmed the suspicion voiced by the Duke himself – that they were 'the scum of the earth, enlisted for drink'. 'Fine fellows' maybe, in uniform, but 'scum' out of it.

It was a sentiment expressed not so much out of callousness as out of ignorance. Without a Department of Employment, no Government minister had any clear idea of the causes or extent of the problem. There were no statistics to show how many workers had been laid off when factories completed their final arms contract or the rattling mills sent off their last shipment of uniform serge. Nobody kept records of how many handworkers lost their livelihood in the onslaught of the new machines which no longer depended on muscle or acquired skill. Irish immigrants poured out of smelly holds at docksides in Liverpool, Glasgow, and Bristol, in untold numbers, and snatched jobs because they were prepared to work for lower wages. Unheard and uncounted, poor tenant farmers were reduced to the status of labourer by the new enclosures, which took away their rights on the village common and waste; nothing must be allowed to stand in the way of the improving landlords, who were patriotically developing the land to grow more food for the gallant lads in the Army and Navy. By a double-edged irony, these wealthier men also faced debt when their Government contracts were cut after the war – so they laid off more men and cut the wages of the remainder.

It was a temptation for desperate men in the countryside to go to the cities, where the swelling, thudding factories and foundries surely would offer more work. The Government had no way of monitoring the amount of this migration either, or the level of frustration and failure that awaited the new arrivals. (They are in good company, because economic historians disagree to this day as to the exact nature and extent of this 'flight to the cities'.)

It was common knowledge, though, that, if life for the farm labourer on the land was hard, for the factory worker in the cities life was unspeakable. For those who were prepared to seek it out, there was plenty of available evidence – from Radical journalists, from Methodist priests, from a few dedicated doctors, and a handful of vociferous do-gooders. Wages were almost as low as those of a farm worker – except in the mines, which were something of a special case. Mills and factories were badly lit, badly ventilated, and overcrowded with unfenced machines, below which small children had to crawl to clear away the dust and fluff while the cogs were still grinding. David Livingstone, the famous missionary, who survived years of this when he was a boy, claimed that in warm weather, the atmosphere in his mill was so stifling that workers toiled away stark naked. Hours were long, welfare was non-existent, and trade unions were illegal.

When these poor creatures – men, women, and children alike – trudged back to the home that they had left in the small hours, they could hope for little respite. Houses were jerry-built, back-to-back, unheated, unlit, overcrowded, and without personal sanitation or water. Most sewage went raw into central street gutters or was carted away in little wheelbarrows from beside the front door. Either way, it went untreated, along with factory effluent, into nearby rivers, whence was drawn most of the drinking water.

Through these stinking warrens of listlessness and despair, the twin spectres of crime and disease stalked unchecked. There was no Government policy, system, or money for street cleaning, paving, or lighting, or for a public water supply. There was no medical service, no education service, no social service, no social security, and no police force – nothing.

Worst of all, perhaps, no hope. No working-class man could become an MP in order to right these wrongs; he did not fulfil the property-owning qualification. Very few working men had the right even to vote. Not one woman did. In many cases their new city did not have a Member of Parliament anyway. So long as there was nobody to represent them, there was no chance of progress.

That left self-help – solitary protest. At a time when there were usually more workers than there were jobs, dismissal was the normal method of dealing with troublemakers – those who had any energy left after a fourteen-hour day. Naturally, any offence against property met with the full array of the judicial system – a penal code under which over two hundred offences could carry the death penalty, and a man could be sent to Australia for fourteen years for being simply found, in the privacy of his own home, in possession of a net that might conceivably be used for the purposes of catching a rabbit.

This terrible slough of despond can never be adequately imagined or conveyed. Even repetition (after Chapter 4) reinforces only the inadequacy. What could these poor creatures do? They could not read; they could not write; they could not vote; they could not strike. They had nothing to bargain with. Their only weapon was numbers, and their only means of expression was violence – mindless, purely reactive, and invariably doomed to failure.

If such a body of evidence appears to constitute a crushing indictment of the government of the day, His Majesty's ministers deserve at least an explanation of their difficulties.

They may not have had the means of knowing the extent of the problem, but they at least knew that there *was* a problem. The first official census in 1801 had revealed a population of over ten million. Ministers were appalled; they had had no idea. Unfortunately they continued to have no idea of the ways in which this statistic was reflected in the social and economic evils explained above. And, even if they had, they would immediately have replied that part at least of the problem did not concern them. Moreover, a modern-style, humanitarian solution would have seemed to them a recipe for making things worse, not better.

To take the last point first. It is worth reiterating something also said in Chapter 4. For a long time, men had been increasingly, and disturbingly, aware that population was appearing to outrun the production of food. The rate of increase of the former was outdistancing that of the latter. The evidence was also plain to see that many thousands of people died before their time – of disease, malnutrition, and general lack of care. If, by some miracle, a means were to be found of keeping more of them alive – to breed further helpless paupers – that was only solving half the puzzle; it was not solving the other half – namely of how to produce more food to feed them. So the problem would not have been made easier; it would have been made immeasurably worse. The men who thought this were not evil or cruel by nature. They were hampered by lack of knowledge and by lack of confidence. Understandably, they turned away from a possible solution that, so far as they could see, would do nothing but compound the crisis.

The events of the twentieth century enabled people living through it to take in their stride huge concepts that men of 1815, and after, found very difficult to cope with – speeds of over fifteen miles an hour, armies numbered in hundreds of thousands, mass production, the political rights of people without property, freedom of conscience – because these concepts were coming upon them for the first time, and there seemed to be so many of them.

It must also be remembered that the country had just emerged from a war of survival that had lasted almost without a break for twenty-two years – England's longest war since the Middle Ages – during which she had come closer to defeat and occupation than at any time since the Spanish Armada. The country was exhausted, poverty-stricken. The National Debt had rocketed above the £250,000,000 at the end of the American War, and it now stood at an unbelievable £860,000,000, on which the interest alone accounted for half the national income. Even if the Government had heard of the concept of the Welfare State, and had had the will to introduce it, they would have lacked the funds.

To take now the second point that the ministers might have made in their own defence – namely that, to a certain extent, the problem did not concern them. This again is not as consciously callous as it may sound to a modern ear regularly attuned to calls for charity to fight world famines or the unchecked rise in population. (We cheerfully contribute one day to stop people dying, and the next to stop them being born.) It was considered quite normal for a government in 1816 to govern – that is, to maintain law and order, to defend property, to protect the realm, to conduct relations with foreign powers, to further the country's 'interests'. It did very little else, and did not expect to.

For one thing, it did not have the resources. For another it did not have at its disposal a reliable, swift system of communications by which it could influence the day-to-day lives of its people. Thirdly, and perhaps more important because it was so deeply embedded in the national subconscious that it was rarely expressed in explicit terms, there was the feeling that a government should not interfere in the private lives of its subjects. Englishmen were proud of what they liked to call their 'liberty', even if it did sometimes mean the liberty to enjoy privilege or to push someone else around. When Pitt introduced an income tax for the first time, the cry of dismay was not so much at the modest rate as against the idea of a Government busybody asking questions about a man's private finances. In 1848, in a celebrated article in *The Times* at the height of the controversy about the Government Public Health Bill of that year, the writer declared that Englishmen did not want to be legislated into health, and that they preferred to take their chance with the cholera. The failure of prohibition in the United States is a good example of the maxim that people do not take kindly to legislation for their own good. Modern controversies about drug-taking, seat belts, censorship, and the age of consent show that there is still as much life as there ever was in the debate about government and freedom.

So Lord Liverpool and his Tories clung to their philosophy of *laissez-faire*, and concentrated upon the much more immediate problem of keeping law and order – without reliable statistical information, without adequate funds, without any real speed of communication, and without a police force. Most of them had spent their formative years watching in horror as the genie of revolution had been released from the bottle in 1789, and had cast its shadow over nearly every country in Europe.

Napoleon was now gone, a fat Bourbon king reigned again in France, and monarchs had returned to most thrones in Europe from which they had been toppled by the revolutionary armies. But the ideas of democracy, the rights of man, government for and by the people, had entered into the very soil of Europe – just like the Plague – and, like the Plague, could burst forth again unless there was constant vigilance. Once again, it was not so much that the ministers were all tyrants at heart; it was the – to them – simple truth that these ideas led to revolution, and revolution led to war, and that the casualties on the way were monarchy, church, property, peace, civilised society – everything that any reasonable man held sacred.

So the 'problem' as outlined above was seen by them from a somewhat different standpoint. If desperate farm labourers set fire to hayricks, it was a threat to property; if unemployed hand-loom weavers smashed machines or demonstrated in a town square, it was a threat to public order; if a Radical journalist rejoiced in a foreign revolution, he was a potential threat to the Crown; if Nonconformist sympathisers called for the abolition of discriminatory laws against themselves, it was a threat to the Anglican Church.

It bore resemblance to a sort of siege mentality. It was certainly living from hand to mouth. Ministers seemed to be constantly exercised with the results of the problem, whereas we can now see with hindsight that they never got around to tackling the causes of it.

Perhaps they were simply not up to it. It is both accusation and defence that they have been generally regarded as men of modest abilities, although curiously Lord Liverpool, the Prime Minister, remained in office for fifteen years, the longest term for anyone since Robert Walpole in the 1720s and 1730s, and of course Pitt. (Lord Eldon, the Lord Chancellor, held office continuously for twenty.) Specialist historians may no doubt make out better cases for them and their colleagues, and the fact is indisputable that they did do what they set out to do – namely, to keep Britain safe from revolution.

Yet there is a hiatus in the succession of personalities. Pitt, Portland, and Perceval among the Tories, and Fox, Burke, and Grenville among the Whigs were all gone. Peel, Canning, Palmerston, and Huskisson had already held office but were yet to stake their place on the national stage. The Home Secretary, Lord Sidmouth (previously Henry Addington), got his name into the history books about the war for being the man who 'came in between' Pitt's two ministries. As for the Chancellor of the Exchequer, Nicholas Vansittart, it would take a specialist indeed to produce more than a sentence or two about his record. Only the Foreign Secretary, Lord Castlereagh, had a name of national significance, and, sadly, it attracted to it a great deal of the rage and contempt that should have been more justly directed at his colleagues. In his very competent discharge of the conduct of foreign affairs, he had little to do with the task of running the country.

The jeers and the catcalls did not stop at the House of Commons or Downing Street; they went right into the royal palaces. Locked away in gilded gloom at Windsor Castle, King George III, seventy-eight years old, was both deaf and blind, periodically violent, and normally insane. He drifted about lofty, lonely chambers, prodded the keys of a harpsichord, went into mourning for himself, and gnashed his gums in frustration during his few moments of transient lucidity. He was kept alive only by his robust constitution, no doubt the fruit of his lifetime regime of early rising, frugal eating, and pious, if dull, moderation.

His eldest son, George, now Prince Regent, had long since rebelled against his father's rigid discipline. A prodigious speculator, and loser, at racetrack and gaming table, he had enlarged his already scandalous debts by massive spending on his wardrobe, his pictures, his transient friends, and, latterly, on his pavilion at Brighton. George's enemies, and the gossips and cartoonists, preferred to ignore the fact that he was intelligent and had a cultivated artistic taste; they found it much more fun to relive his spurious marriage to a Catholic commoner, Mrs Fitzherbert, and to linger over the salacious details of his ill-fated legitimate marriage with Princess Caroline of Brunswick, an eccentric, unhygienic frump, at the first sight of whom George had called for a stiff whisky. He had parted from her as soon as his dynastic duty had been done and he had fathered Princess Charlotte on her. Her behaviour thereafter was enough to fill several scandal columns on her own. Many no doubt felt that they deserved each other.

George did mellow a little with middle age. He discharged his duties as Prince Regent; he sincerely believed in England's cause in the war; and he became a good Tory. Unfortunately, he had no gift for human relations and he had no flair for publicity. His father, while he reigned, had always been popular, which must have irked the son – how could such a dullard be so well liked? Unfortunately, too, the Prince also became even more pear-shaped and laughable. His very nickname – 'Prinny' – neatly encapsulated the conception of spoilt, almost childish petulance, foppishness, and lack of vigour on his part, and of insolent overfamiliarity on the part of his subjects. It pursued him, perhaps unfairly, to his grave.

Prinny in his corsets, the King in his strait-jacket, Caroline bulging in her smelly dresses – the cartoonists had a marvellous time. Their pictures were instantly and universally comprehensible; millions who could not read leered and chuckled, and bawled their vulgar derision at the royal coach. Those millions were also aware of serious political criticism, because they gathered in eager groups around those who were literate, and listened while the latest number of Cobbett's *Political Register* was read out to them.

The circulation of this weekly journal rose to over 40,000 copies, itself an impressive figure. When it is multiplied by the number of those who sat rapt at the readers' words, it is easy to appreciate how important a national figure Cobbett had become.

William Cobbett was the son of a small farmer in Farnham, Surrey. His father taught him the three Rs; thereafter he educated himself, and was very proud of the fact. He claimed that he taught himself English grammar by the simple, if arduous, device of buying a book on it and learning it off by heart. The first book to influence him, he said, was Jonathan Swift's *Tale of a Tub*. It is perhaps too fanciful to assume that he became a political satirist because the first book to shatter him was by a master of political satire. One could equally assert that it was because he had in him the makings of a political satirist that he was bewitched by Swift's mastery of the art.

Either way, he was not satisfied with his early employment as an assistant at Kew Gardens or as a legal clerk in London. He farmed intermittently with his father, dreamed of running away to sea, finally joined the Army, and was posted with his regiment to America. He married a sergeant's daughter, who was to bear him fourteen children, and to whom he was to remain devoted. At the end of his military service, he settled for a while in France, but, disturbed by the deposition and execution of King Louis, returned to America. There he found his true calling of political journalism, and started to churn out articles in his spiky, aggressive way, cheerfully proud of the number both of friends and enemies. He chose the pen name 'Peter Porcupine' as best suited to his character and writings, and in the next few years trod on as many American corns as his broad British boots could manage. He returned to England in 1800 with a reputation as a great patriot.

He founded the *Political Register* in 1802, and launched into attacks on France and the Revolution. However, he became drawn into other issues. Nobody with his contentious disposition, self-educated assurance, and sharp pen could stay out of trouble for long. He made provocative statements, and enemies in high places, as he extended his range from the conduct of the war and Government finance to rich industrialists, civil rights for Catholics, Methodism, education, and flogging in the Army. A spell in Newgate prison for sedition in no way diminished him.

He returned to the attack with fresh onslaughts on industrial working conditions, agricultural poverty, rotten boroughs, and urban sprawl. (He always referred to London as the 'Great Wen', no doubt well aware that 'wen', besides meaning an unplanned, overcrowded city, also meant a huge, fatty cyst.)

Unlike other, more genteel Radical thinkers, Cobbett was completely down to earth. He avoided complex theorising, he gave specific examples, he simplified, he coined homely comparisons, he relished the personal insult and the juicy jibe – and they loved it. His infuriated enemies rashly tried to give tit for tat by renaming the *Political Register* as the *Twopenny Trash*, but it rebounded on them. Peter Porcupine wallowed in the insult, and trumpeted their fury to the world. Thousands more copies passed from one eager calloused hand to another.

Cobbett tried to be constructive too. He put the case that sporadic outbursts of protest would achieve nothing. The power of the Establishment, and the greed of those in positions of riches and influence, were too great. No worthwhile change would come about until new laws were enacted, and new laws would not be enacted by the Parliament that had made the old ones. The first priority was to reform Parliament – to get rid of rotten boroughs, to allow all men the vote, to abolish the property qualification for MPs, to have annual general elections, and to ensure the secret ballot. If a new Parliament could be assembled under these rules, it would by definition be bound to pass the new laws required to end the human misery that afflicted ordinary men and their families.

If something were not done, and soon, said Cobbett, something terrible would happen. These reforms would prevent revolution.

The Government saw it differently. Cobbett's ideas to them were a nightmare scenario. They would not prevent revolution; they would cause it.

There had been enough evidence already, long before the end of the war. Nearly every time there was a bad harvest, there were riots about the price of bread. Napoleon's occupation of some of the areas of Eastern Europe whence England imported cheap corn made the situation worse. When the war ended, and cheap corn began once again to come in from these countries – Prussia and Poland – the situation became worse still. England's landowners complained about being undercut by foreign prices, when they were already suffering at the cutting of Government contracts to feed servicemen. They had become heavily involved in large capital investment in farming improvements; they said that ruin now stared them in the face. Unlike the millions of poor people to whom the price of a large loaf could mean 10 per cent of a whole family's weekly income, England's landowners were represented loudly in Parliament.

Farming was the 'backbone of England'; nothing must threaten the livelihood of landowners. All MPs, by definition, were landowners. Accordingly, a Corn Law was passed in 1815, which, by a regular monitoring of the prices of English and foreign corn, and the imposition of customs duties at appropriate times, ensured that the price of bread stayed artificially high. Sad, but unavoidable – the farming industry was protected, which was what mattered.

The last years of the war had also seen the first of the many industrial riots that were to plague the cities for the next forty or fifty years. The most notorious were those in Nottingham, where workers smashed the new machines. The blindness and futility of the gesture were reflected in the alleged leader of the rioters – Ned Ludd. Poor Ned could have been (nobody is sure) a sort of local simpleton who was put up to the leadership. It is doubtful whether he long enjoyed his moment of glory; it is more doubtful whether he was ever aware of his name passing into legend. Thereafter he was supposed to have gone into hiding in Sherwood Forest – strange how Sherwood seems to attract semi-mythical heroes of the downtrodden poor – whence he emerged regularly to lead further forays on to the floor of the industrial establishment. He joined Robin Hood and the Scarlet Pimpernel and Rob Roy and Captain Moonlight in the gallery of will-o'-the-wisp heroes, and gave his name to the language. Thereafter, men who engaged in industrial unrest were promptly, if often inaccurately, christened 'Luddites'.

These instances of unrest multiplied once the war was over; men no longer felt the constraint of disloyalty in the face of the threat of Bonaparte. Miners struck in Wales; the unemployed demonstrated in Birmingham; there were more food riots; Ned Ludd came out of Sherwood again.

There was no plan, pattern, or system about all this. No Monmouth miner had the faintest idea what a desperate stocking-frame knitter in Nottingham was up to, and no Hampshire labourer gazing in brief satisfaction at a burning rick had any conception of life in a Lancashire mill.

That did not stop the Government thinking that the genie of

Revolution could be stalking the land, and weaving all the threads of local misery into a massive whiplash of sedition with which to taunt, plague, bind, and ultimately strangle authority. Just as the people had expressed their local grievances in the old ways, so the Government reacted in the old ways. They had no alternative.

They fell back on legislation, local authority, and human nature. More laws were passed to restrict public meetings and muzzle the Radical press. Justices of the Peace and city magistrates were urged to be vigilant, to be ready at the drop of a hat to read the Riot Act and call out the militia. This, apart from the occasional solitary village constable, was the only force normally available to maintain order in times of public unrest. It consisted of a local landlord and his more obedient tenants, or urban businessmen and their more bored apprentices, who might leap at the chance of some occasional street scrimmages to relieve the monotony of life at office stool, trade counter, or workbench. Abnormally, there was always the regular Army, but regiments of redcoats were not always conveniently nearby.

As for human nature, Home Secretary Sidmouth played upon the profit motive. Spies and informers roamed the country, ever watchful for signs of the dreaded 'Revolution', anxious to earn their blood money. Because of the secret and unsavoury nature of their work, their activities were no doubt exaggerated; no doubt too their reports were equally exaggerated, because the temptation to 'report' signs of 'sedition' must have been very great to men who had a living to make like everyone else. More unpopular still were the *agents provocateurs*, creatures, it was alleged, of satanic cunning and fathomless evil, who infiltrated groups of protesters, urged them on to feats of political folly, and secured their arrest by a timely betrayal to the eager shopkeepers and bumptious apprentices in the militia.

Not all Radical demonstrations were hostile. The weary Blanketeers, for instance, wanted only to hand in a petition to ask the Government to help them. Armed each with a blanket to provide minimum comfort on the long planned march from Manchester to London, they were mostly arrested or turned back by the time they reached Macclesfield. One man was credited with completing the journey; he handed in his precious petition, which was ignored.

Other meetings turned nasty because of the actions of a minority of hotheads, thus giving the authorities justification for using force. A huge meeting in Spa Fields in London in November 1816 began peacefully, but a notorious Radical speaker, Henry Hunt, began at once to screw up the tension by appearing with an escort carrying a pike to which was tied the French tricolour. Having lit the touch paper, Hunt retired; at a second meeting a fortnight later, he stayed away while his minions attacked a gunsmith's shop and led the crowd towards the City. Here they were met and dispersed by forces collected by the Lord Mayor.

Government spies, with or without the authority of the Home Secretary, manufactured incidents like the Derbyshire Rising in 1817. An agent working under the name of 'Oliver' persuaded a group of workmen that two other groups (which did not exist) were about to riot and were awaiting their assistance. The workmen's leader, Jeremiah Brandreth, led his men off to attack Nottingham Castle, and they all walked into Oliver's trap. Brandreth and three others were hanged; fourteen more were transported.

By the end of 1817, the Government were breathing a little more easily. They had suspended the law of *Habeas Corpus*, which thus gave them the right to order arbitrary arrest of seditious suspects. The Radical press was in disarray; Cobbett had fled to America to escape another prison sentence. Regulations about public meetings had been tightened. The summer had been good and the harvest plentiful, so agitation was dying down.

Suddenly, on 6 November, the nation was plunged into grief by the death in childbirth of Princess Charlotte. A boisterous, galumphing girl, she was nevertheless popular; if nothing else, she was such a contrast to the mad King, to the fat, grease-painted Regent, her father, and to her vulgar mother. Now she was gone, and with her and her dead child went the hope for the future. A great chasm now yawned where the succession had stood secure. Incredibly, out of George III's family of fifteen children, not one could boast a legitimate child. Indeed, four were still unmarried. Three more were already dead.

Simultaneously, the prospect presented itself to three middle-aged royal dukes that if they found themselves a legal wife they could be the father of the heir to the throne. While it may be false to talk of an undignified rush to the pleasurable potential of the marriage bed, nevertheless their Graces wasted no time. Before the end of 1818, all three had found themselves wives, the ladies too probably being equally captivated by the prospect of mothering a future monarch of England, and prepared nobly to overlook the fading charms of their new and eager spouses. As usual, it was Germany that produced the necessary princesses; no mere commoner would do for the ruling House of Hanover. With thirty-nine separate states still extant, there was usually somebody on the market. Edward, Duke of Kent, selected Princess Victoria of Saxe-Coburg; Adolphus, Duke of Cambridge, chose Princess Augusta of Hesse-Cassel, and the eldest, William, Duke of Clarence, settled for Princess Adelaide of Saxe-Meiningen, partly because she had let it be known that she would not merely tolerate, but would welcome, the Duke's brood of ten illegitimate children.

Princess Adelaide dutifully became pregnant – three times – and miscarried on each occasion. She and her grieving William consoled themselves with their niece; the Duke and Duchess of Kent had won the royal race, and preserved the royal race, by producing a live heir – Princess Victoria.

At a time when France, with its Revolution and then its Emperor, had turned monarchs wholesale off their thrones, and when governments throughout Europe constantly feared a return of either or both, it was vital for the monarchy, and the succession, to be secure, and to be seen to be secure. It seemed the only political system that promised any sort of stability in a world that had been turned upside down for over twenty years. The delegates at the Congress of Vienna, which had been resumed as soon as Napoleon had been seen off to St Helena, could think of no better formula for peace and security than to restore former kings to the thrones they had lost.

It might be unadventurous; it might be unpopular; it might be inconsiderate and unimaginative. But it was at least legitimate. Whatever men thought of the returning kings, no one could question the legality of their rule. George, the Prince Regent, and his Foreign Secretary, Lord Castlereagh, both upheld the principle of Legitimacy, which governed the thinking of the delegates at Vienna, and which permeated the solution they offered to the confusion brought about by twenty-odd years of war.

Stability, and the containment of France – those were the overriding concerns of the Allies. So long as they remained the overriding concerns, the Allies were likely to operate in partnership. When their representatives met in 1818 at the Congress of Aix-la-Chapelle to review the international situation, they agreed once more on their policy towards France; since she was no longer considered as a threat to European peace, the army of occupation was withdrawn, and its commander, the Duke of Wellington, returned to place his talents, and his stern advice – forthright and sincere if not always welcome – at the disposal of his monarch. Final arrangements were also made about completing the payment of the war indemnity that had been laid upon the defeated enemy. Since there was now no excuse for continuing to treat France as some kind of diplomatic leper, she was formally admitted to the 'Concert of Europe' – allowed back as an equal into the 'club' of Great Powers (though the other four – Britain, Austria, Russia, and Prussia – prudently, and secretly, signed a renewal of the Quadruple Alliance, just in case).

The official recognition that France was no longer a threat to international peace created a vacuum of intent among the other powers; this vacuum was immediately filled by a welter of separate national interests and ambitions. Prussia renewed her search for ways of uniting her scattered territories, and began to cultivate plans for a customs union – a *Zollverein*, a sort of embryonic common market – between northern German states. Tsar Alexander, though still bewitched by his 'Holy Alliance' of Christian monarchs, was worldly enough to cherish traditional Russian ambitions of spreading into the Balkans towards the Mediterranean. Metternich, the Austrian Chancellor, set about tightening his hold on the remainder of Germany and on the newly-acquired Austrian lands in Italy.

All these ideas and schemes were nothing substantially new, and international affairs in Europe might have resumed their pre-Revolution path of intrigue, alliance, war, and conference, had it not been for the new forces let loose by the Revolution.

However fleeting had been the revolutionary republics of the 1790s, however transitory the enjoyment of liberation from Hapsburg or Romanov imperialism, the memory remained. All over Europe, men had been given a taste of freedom, democracy, national independence, fairness, efficiency, the career open to the talents, liberty of conscience, and a host of other dazzling novelties made possible by the Great Revolution. These gifts were dashed from their hands by the efforts of Metternich to put the clock back and pretend that the Revolution had never happened. They were not impressed by his arguments about stability or European peace; they wanted to reach out again to grasp their visions. The return of privilege, of persecution, of foreign officialdom, of delay and elderly bumbling and corruption was no longer tiresome or even oppressive; it was intolerable.

So more revolutions broke out – in Spain and Portugal, and, later in the year (1820), in Naples and Piedmont.

The question therefore arose – what was going to be done about them? If Napoleon's assaults on the thrones of Europe constituted a threat to international peace, so then did the revolts of Spanish army officers or Piedmontese partisans. Metternich had no doubts about what needed to be done – suppression, with whatever force was necessary. Moreover, suppression in the name of the Concert of Europe, the declared guardian of European peace. The Tsar was equally willing to employ his precious Holy Alliance of Christian monarchs in this righteous crusade for law and order.

Castlereagh did not agree. He could not afford to agree. Austria, Prussia, and Russia were autocratic states. Their rulers could act as they pleased, as their selfish 'interests' dictated. England was the only Power of the four that had a parliament; neither Castlereagh nor the Prince Regent was a free agent. The English Parliament was corruptly elected by a small minority of the male population, but at least it existed; and, if it turned against what he did, Castlereagh and his colleagues could be out of office. There was also a vociferous public opinion, in spite of all attempts to stifle criticism, and Castlereagh was the least popular minister in an intensely unpopular Government.

Englishmen might approve of the Concert of Europe fighting to remove the tyrant monster, Bonaparte; they would not approve of the same soldiers being used to shoot honest citizens in the streets trying to set up their own independent state or their own democratic constitution. Englishmen were proud of their system of government, and were disposed to regard all foreign monarchies (with no parliaments) with a mixture of contempt and supercilious sympathy; if news came that attempts were being made to 'improve' things, they automatically assumed that the poor benighted foreigners in question were struggling in their innocent, confused way to imitate that paragon of political systems, the British constitution. As is so often the case, what was important was not what was happening; it was what men *thought* was happening.

Castlereagh, as a matter of personal preference, had no particular sympathy with 'the people' either as a political concept or as a likeable group of human beings, but he had to go along with the professed opinions of his country. He got round the problem by maintaining that he did not approve of *joint action* to put down revolutions in other people's countries. If, however, a government wished to use force, *on its own*, to put down revolution *in or near its own territories*, that was another matter. He had no control over that, nor did he want it.

There was another consideration. Though he had no fondness for Spanish liberals or Neapolitan revolutionaries, he was also alive to the possible advantages that could arise from successful wars of independence. If the Spanish overseas colonies in South America gained freedom from their home government, it would open up vast new markets for British trade.

Castlereagh was not good at public relations, was often absent from the House of Commons, and in any case did not see why detailed questions of foreign affairs needed to be explained. His was the familiar opinion (in the Foreign Office) that such matters were understood only by professionals. Besides, he would have found it difficult to tell the truth – that he did not want Austria or Russia to use the suppression of revolutions as an excuse to extend their power; that he personally did not give a curse for liberals or revolutionaries; that he wanted to keep as many avenues open as possible for future British trade; and that he wanted complete freedom of action in case he needed to change his mind.

In his defence, Castlereagh did not suffer from a paranoia of secretiveness, nor was he any more or less cynical than other ministers of his time. Indeed, he is generally considered to have been a very good Foreign Secretary. He knew everybody, was vastly experienced, and worked extremely hard – in a Foreign Office where the entire staff numbered only twenty-eight, including two under-secretaries and a Turkish interpreter.

He was certainly more gifted than Lord Sidmouth, the Home Secretary, who could think of no other way of dealing with the revival of radical agitation in 1819 than the previous expedients of informers, magistrates, riot acts, militia, and army.

The classic illustration of this policy came in August. 1819 was another bad year – a minor trade slump, bankruptcies, falling wages, rising unemployment. The inevitable response was another burst of Radical activity – protests, demonstrations, meetings. Cobbett was managing to edit the *Political Register* all the way from America, though because of the distances involved was forced to deal only with views rather than news, so he was losing some of his sting. Nevertheless, the cumulative effect was to make the Government and the local authorities nervous, and inclined, as ever, to overreact.

Reforming groups in Manchester announced a monster meeting for 16 August, to discuss parliamentary reform. The celebrity speaker was to be Henry Hunt, 'Orator' Hunt as he had become known, veteran of Spa Fields and other similar meetings. The organisers went out of their way to avoid trouble. The event was scheduled for a Sunday; people were encouraged to wear their best clothes; they were invited to bring their wives and children; no weapons were to be carried.

They duly assembled in good order and good humour at St Peter's Fields, a well-known open space in Manchester. Local militiamen, called out by worried magistrates, joked with people in the crowd as Henry Hunt, a conspicuous figure in his famous white top hat, made his way through the banners and flags to the rostrum. Estimates of the size of the crowd vary, as they usually do on these occasions, but it was large enough for Hunt, when he got a good view of it, to become concerned about public order. If the magistrates ordered his arrest, what would happen?

He offered to give himself up at the outset, but was told to continue.

When he began to speak, the magistrates sent in the militiamen to arrest him. Probably no one will ever know the exact pattern of motivation and action from then on. Did the crowd react in anger or bafflement at the order to arrest Hunt? Did they try to prevent the arrest, or were they simply in their way protesting their disbelief? Did the militiamen promptly use force, or were they jostled into it by fear, by the press of the crowd? When the crisis came, were they still trying to arrest Hunt, or were they trying to get out and save themselves?

Whatever was happening, it seemed to the magistrates, from their vantage point, that the militiamen were disappearing in a sea of angry, noisy people. They turned to the strategic reserve they had brought into Manchester for just such an emergency – a squadron of regular cavalry. These men were ordered to charge the crowd and disperse it.

They drew their sabres, and the panic began. Amid the screams of fear and anger, and the wild tramplings, eleven people lost their lives, including two women, and one soldier dragged from his horse by the enraged victims. Four hundred more were injured. Hunt was arrested – at last – and sentenced to two and a half years' imprisonment for conspiracy to subvert the government of the realm by force and threats. Despite a roar of horrified protest (not only from Radicals), and much-publicised subscription lists in Manchester and London for the victims of the 'Manchester Massacre', the Prince Regent congratulated the magistrates on their prompt action.

Public opinion replied by dubbing the incident 'Peterloo' in mock imitation of the Duke's great victory. Lord Sidmouth and the Government riposted with a rapid sheaf of new laws designed to ensure that such uncertainty and tragedy would not occur again, and to ensure too that the Radical activity which had brought about the circumstances in Manchester would in future become impossible. The Duke, scorning the Peterloo insult as yet more predictable evidence of the common people's fickleness and lack of sense, lent his full support to these new measures, as befitted a loyal Master-General of the Ordnance, admitted only eight months before to the Cabinet.

Henceforth no meeting of more than fifty people was to be held without the express permission of the local mayor or the Lord Lieutenant of the county in question. Magistrates were empowered to search private houses for illegal arms. Heavy penalties were imposed upon anyone caught in unauthorised military drilling. Greater surveillance was to be exercised upon the publication of 'blasphemous and seditious libels'. The procedure of the law was to be speeded up in dealing with certain cases of 'misdemeanour' (magistrates were given powers to decide guilt instead of having to wait while juries were sworn in). Finally, a newspaper stamp duty was imposed on all journals and pamphlets.

Radicals and their sympathisers dubbed these the 'Six Gag Acts', and poured torrents of abuse on them and on the distant and unknowing head of Lord Castlereagh, the Foreign Secretary. Yet, given the poor communications, the constant fear of 'revolution', and the absence of a police force, Lord Sidmouth might have argued that it was difficult for him to have done much else. The acts were to be in force for only a limited period, and most reasonable opinion acknowledged that drastic times demanded drastic remedies. The events of 1820 were to show that 'revolution' was indeed very much in the air – Spain, Portugal, Piedmont, and Naples all had one, and a member of the French royal family was assassinated – and Sidmouth could also point out afterwards, by way of justification, that England once again escaped it.

Whether she escaped because of the Six Acts, or because of a slowly-improving economy is debatable. It began to look as if the country was at last beginning to recover after the bad postwar years.

The newspaper stamp duty certainly dealt a mortal blow to Cobbett's *Political Register* by putting up its price. He had returned from America in November, 1819, bringing with him the bones of Tom Paine, the great Radical philosopher of the 1780s and 1790s, the man who had incurred the official wrath of Prime Minister Pitt with his book *The Rights of Man*. One version of the story has it that Cobbett lost the bones in the Customs.

It was only the beginning of his troubles. He soon found that his declining newspaper circulation had made him bankrupt, and he had to sell his farm. He campaigned as a Radical candidate in an election, and lost. It did not improve his temper, and he spent a good deal of 1820 knee-deep in libel suits.

Cobbett's fate was a fairly good illustration of the depths to which the Radical cause had sunk by 1820, for whatever reason. From its despair came one last lunatic effort, which, by its very lunacy and savagery, ensured that no further gestures would be made. Men of all political persuasions were horrified.

It was a plot to murder the entire personnel of the Cabinet and declare a republic. Its leader, Arthur Thistlewood, a survivor of the ill-fated Spa Fields riot, had emerged from a spell in prison brooding on a vindictive revenge. The Peterloo Massacre was, to his mind, sufficient justification for what he planned. He intended to break in on the members of His Majesty's Government while they were at a dinner party at Lord Harrowby's, on 23 February, and shoot or stab them as seemed the more convenient at the time.

A Government spy infiltrated the group, and, when zero hour came, betrayed them to a posse of constables at a house in Cato Street, off the Edgware Road. Thistlewood and four of his accomplices were executed in May – the last men to be publicly beheaded. Theirs proved to be the last effort in the French Revolution blood-and-terror tradition. Radical agitation did not cease, and Government fears did not diminish, but in hindsight it can now be seen that a sort of corner had been turned. It was as if men, shown the brink of horror and anarchy, had recoiled and retreated.

It was a sort of turning point too, in another way. As already suggested, the economy, after the artifical boom in the war and the slump immediately after it, was returning to something like normal. Things were still bad, but they were no longer desperate. The year 1820 also produced something to distract the public mind in the shape of a really juicy royal scandal.

On 29 January, 1820, George III had at last passed away. Fidgety, fond of his food, and crotchety to the last; still capable, when annoyed, of uttering dark threats that he 'would have the battle-axes brought in'; he muttered one day, *apropos* of nothing in particular, 'Poor Tom's a-cold,' and died.

It seemed that nothing essential would change. Prinny, as the new King, would merely fulfil the same duties and perform the same ceremonies as he had when Prince Regent. These quiet modifications were upset when Caroline of Brunswick returned suddenly from self-imposed exile, and announced her intention of claiming her rights as Queen.

George and the Government were appalled. In the years since her separation from her husband, Caroline had pursued a sort of female rake's progress around Europe, consorting with a motley entourage of seedy Italian attendants, and providing, with her outrageous dress, personal habits, barracks language, and indecorous behaviour, enough unsavoury gossip to keep the gutter press in fits.

Understandably, George did not want to resume the royal relationship, however formal it might be. He instructed his ministers that he wished to be rid of her once and for all; Castlereagh and Wellington led the negotiators detailed to deal with her. When she refused to be bought off, royal legal advisers assured His Majesty that they could gather enough evidence of adultery to secure a divorce.

When the news got out, the nation laughed at the pot calling the kettle black. Almost overnight, despite the fact that Caroline was stupid, vulgar, loose-living, and probably unbalanced, she became a national heroine, a victim of Prinny's selfish spite, a 'wronged woman'. The Whigs in the Opposition took up her case; it was a golden chance to embarrass the Government.

The reluctant ministers, pressed by George, introduced a Bill of Pains and Penalties to deprive her of her title and dissolve her marriage, though they were painfully aware that the debates on it would shine just as unwelcome a light on the King's private life as they would on Caroline's. Throughout the turgid hours of conflicting evidence, the Opposition enjoyed itself, and the nation gloated over all the dirty royal linen being washed in public.

Wherever Caroline appeared she was cheered and hailed as a martyr to royal vindictiveness. A group of roadmenders stopped the Duke of Wellington's horse in the street, and demanded that his Grace should say 'God save the Queen'. The Duke, for all his disdain of the common man, also knew when a military position was untenable and necessitated a discreet withdrawal.

'Well, gentlemen,' he said, 'since you will have it so, God save the Queen – and may all your wives be like her.'

By implication, the Duke was voicing a truth that everyone really knew – that the Queen was impossible. The Government was forced to drop the Bill of Pains and Penalties for fear of defeat in the Commons, but it shrewdly repeated its offer to the Queen of a pension if she would stop being a nuisance. When she accepted, she ceased to be a nuisance, and at once ceased to be of any use to the Opposition. They dropped her like a hot brick.

There was a last flicker of desperate resistance when she arrived at the coronation and demanded to be admitted. She was refused. The congregation inside the Abbey shouted 'God bless the King' with a will, and the crowd outside cheered when his procession appeared. Abject failure has no allies, and Caroline's popularity vanished almost within hours.

On the same seesaw the King's rose. When he went to the theatre, there were now few cries of 'George! Where's your wife?' His Majesty could relax in public for the first time in years, and he laughed so much at the antics of the clown Grimaldi that he burst his corsets.

The orgy of perversity had spent itself; the nation had come to its senses. There was no mourning when Caroline died less than a month after the coronation – only relief.

A measure of George's hatred of her had been shown a few weeks before, when word had arrived in London that the beast, the monster, the devil Bonaparte had died on the lonely island of St Helena.

An excited aide had burst into the King's chamber.

'Wonderful news, sir, wonderful news. Your greatest enemy is dead!'

George looked up hopefully:

'Is she, by God!'

CHAPTER SEVEN

Orange Peel

1821–25

On 12 August, 1822, Robert Stewart, Viscount Castlereagh, cut his own throat with a penknife. His funeral cortège was cheered in the streets of London; his coffin was hissed by political enemies as it was carried into Westminster Abbey; and Lord Byron composed an obscene rhyme to celebrate the occasion. It is hard to imagine a more vicious outpouring of public hatred and spite. What on earth had the man done?

Served his country in public office for most of his adult life. What is more, served it with credit and success. He had been Secretary for Ireland under William Pitt; Secretary of State for War and the Colonies – twice; Leader of the House of Commons and Secretary of State for Foreign Affairs, simultaneously and continuously, for the last ten years of his life. It was largely pressure of work in the latter two posts that brought about the depression which led to his suicide. That, and the mountain of criticism, much of it ill-informed and unfair, that was heaped upon him.

As Secretary for Ireland at the time of Pitt's Act of Union, he was blamed for forging one of the great chains of Irish oppression – the abolition of the Irish Parliament – when he was only carrying out instructions from Downing Street. As Leader of the House of Commons during the very worst period of post-war depression, he was held responsible, almost single-handedly, for the savage behaviour of the worried Government, when for much of the time he was out of the country on his work as Foreign Secretary. His work abroad was misunderstood and misjudged; his devotion to the cause of the Concert of Europe –

international co-operation between the Great Powers – was suspected as being not 'English' enough; when postwar liberal revolutions broke out he was criticised for not expressing sympathy; when the Holy Alliance put them down, he was reviled for inspiring the repression.

Yet he was acknowledged by contemporaries, even enemies, to be a man of enormous ability; he knew more about foreign affairs than any English minister before Palmerston; he was on familiar terms with every crowned head and chief minister among the greater countries of Europe. No member of the Cabinet worked harder; indeed it was overwork that killed him. He was a man of honour according to his own lights; when King George III refused to grant Catholic Emancipation as part of the agreed deal after the Act of Union, he resigned along with his master, Pitt. When he became genuinely converted to the rightness of abolishing the slave trade, he worked tirelessly for it, ready to persuade, bully, blackmail, and pay hard cash in order to obtain guarantees against it from other governments. His personal bravery was not in question; he was prepared to fight a duel with his political rival, George Canning, and once appeared in person while the mob was stoning his house, calmly closing the shutters of his windows as the missiles still flew.

It was this icy calm which gave a clue to his unpopularity. He never felt the need to justify his actions. In that sense, as Leader of the House of Commons, he was the worst possible person to explain Government policy. The man who was noted for his conciliatory attitude in Europe was the most unconciliatory of politicians at home. On the rare occasions when he did set out to explain, he did not communicate well, either orally or on paper. His style was long-winded and obscure. It took him three pages to challenge Canning to the famous duel; Canning said he would rather fight the duel than read it.

Like the Duke of Wellington, Castlereagh had a contempt for the fickleness of the mob, indeed for the mob itself. It is interesting that each peer thought highly of the other, and the Duke, characteristically, stuck up for Castlereagh against the storm of vituperation that broke on all sides. Unlike the Duke, however, Castlereagh had no unshakable military reputation to fall back on, and no public personality. Stories stuck to the Duke like burrs to a blanket; Castlereagh was faceless. He was faceless, and he was silent. When he failed to answer the slanders against himself, his shyness and reserve were interpreted as contempt – which was partly true – and his silence was interpreted as guilt – which was not. It did not prevent further slanders being laid against him.

Castlereagh shares with Neville Chamberlain the fate of having been, in some keenly-felt way, 'wrong' about two of the great issues of his day. It was to cast each of them into a limbo of non-recognition that was to last half a century, in Castlereagh's case even longer. Chamberlain became for all time the man who failed to 'see through' Hitler, and he was reviled for spinelessness when he offered the thought that peace might be preferable to war. All his virtues paled into nothing when set into the glare of these two enormous 'errors' as they were perceived at the time and in the light of history; his crime was not to be evil, but to be wrong. Castlereagh, similarly, refused to make any statement about the great new force that was loose in the world – liberalism. Being an honest man, he refused to do what most politicians do with fashionable ideas – toss a few meaningless sentences in their direction as a way of showing that they are 'up with the times'. Secondly, and finally, he had a vision of Europe that did not fit the insular perspectives of his fellow countrymen. Incidentally, the Duke agreed with him there as well.

Castlereagh's career, his achievement, and his unpopularity between them mirrored a perpetual dilemma of English foreign policy – some would say the central dilemma. It stems from a simple fact of geography: England is an offshore island of Europe. No offshore island country can follow a steady foreign policy until it can make up its mind whether it is part of its nearby continent or separate from it. Does it stand aloof and risk being left behind, or does it blend in and risk losing its identity? The history of English foreign affairs is a chronicle of constant oscillation between these two poles of opinion. It explains why, so often in the sixteenth, seventeenth, and eighteenth centuries, England became involved in continental wars late and reluctantly, and it also explains why she acquired a reputation in Europe for untrustworthiness when she withdrew before the end, leaving allies high and dry.

It has given rise to endless debate as to what is Britain's 'true' role.

There are those who claim that England has never fared well when she has become part of a larger European unit – as a distant Roman province, among the first to be abandoned in the face of the barbarian invasions; as an occupied country, exploited by a minority Norman aristocracy; as a convenient source of money to the rulers of the Angevin Empire, milked by Richard the Lionheart for his precious crusade. When English rulers in the later Middle Ages tried to reverse the process by carrying war and invasion across to the continent – the Hundred Years' War – they squandered English money and manpower in random and futile pursuit of grandiose illusions.

In more modern times, the opposite school of thought would have us believe that England reached her greatest heights when she entered the European field to play a full part in events. What would have happened if England had stood by, and allowed Philip of Spain to pursue his Catholic crusade unhindered; if Marlborough had not fought his campaigns against the ambitions of Louis XIV; if Pitt had declined to renew the war against Napoleon in 1804; if England had not continued her resistance to Hitler in 1940 when, as the German High Command declared with puzzled logic, 'their military position is so helpless'?

Then again, it could be equally well maintained that in resisting these would-be masters of Europe, England was only preserving her freedom as an offshore island. It is certainly true that, for at least the last four hundred years, England has always thrown her weight into the scales against any power that showed a will to dominate the continent of Europe. She is equally wary to this day – whether that 'power' takes the form of a Nazi dictatorship or a common currency.

It is worthy of comment that so many of England's heroes – Arthur, Alfred the Great, Harold of Wessex, Hereward the Wake, Robin Hood, right through to Drake and Nelson – have won their reputation by their attempts to preserve, against outside, Continental threat, what their countrymen perceive as some kind of unique, if intangible, Englishness. On the other hand, it is true that some of England's greatest statesmen of modern times – the Duke of Marlborough, the Elder Pitt, Churchill – have won their reputation by their insistence that England had to play her part in the destiny of Europe, that England's fortunes were inextricably tied up with those of the Continent. It is to this tradition that Castlereagh belongs, and he is by no means dwarfed in such company.

It was his misfortune that his work coincided with the natural reaction of a country which had just made a titanic effort – to want to relax and withdraw. Britain moreover could afford to: it was a British general who had defeated the greatest soldier of the age; the British Navy ruled on every ocean of the globe; the Industrial Revolution had placed her in an unchallengeable lead in the economic race; her many colonies provided her with a never-ending (it seemed) supply of raw materials. There was no country on earth at whom she could not snap her fingers if she so chose. All she required of a Foreign Secretary was a constant vigilance for her 'interests'; the Concert of Europe could go to the devil, especially if it meant consorting with the damned French, or putting down liberal revolutions hand-in-glove with the devious Chancellor of Austria, or listening to mystical nonsense from a Tsar who was more than likely a bit soft in the head (his father certainly had been).

It was a double irony that Castlereagh's successor as Foreign Secretary was his old rival and fellow-survivor from the duel, George Canning; and that much of the policy that Canning was to follow had been foreshadowed by notes and memoranda left behind by Castlereagh in the dreadful clutter of his papers. Events, and Canning's actions, were to show that Castlereagh had had a better grasp of political realities than he had been given credit for while he was alive.

For the time being, however, Canning let it be known that he was going to put England's interests first, that he was not going to be led by the nose by Chancellor Metternich or by Tsar Alexander's Holy Alliance. The country responded to his 'clap hands and let's get on with it' approach. Canning had little of his predecessor's gravity. Castlereagh, by birth, training, and temperament, belonged to the eighteenth-century tradition of diplomacy – quiet, private negotiation between aristocratic, professional equals, always in search of stability and compromise. Canning saw the conduct of foreign relations more in terms of international rivalry, almost a game. He was altogether more brash and abrasive. He had a sharp wit and an even sharper tongue. He had had to fight harder than Castlereagh to reach the top; his widowed mother had been an actress, at a time when treading the boards was regarded by many as little better than walking the streets. His rivals and enemies – no doubt victims of his jibes and insults – thought he was too clever by half. Wellington certainly did not find him easy to stomach, though with his usual fairmindedness he appreciated the skill of the new Foreign Secretary. Indeed, he advised the King to offer him the job, when he might easily have had it himself.

Canning was welcome to a prime minister whose ministry had sunk to Stygian depths of unpopularity; the Government badly needed new blood. The fifteen months or so in and around 1822 saw a new broom begin to sweep through the corridors of power. Lord Liverpool survived as Prime Minister, but he brought into the Cabinet a group of men who were to inject energy, creativity, and talent into the conduct of government. Canning accepted not only the Foreign Office, but the Leadership of the House of Commons. John Robinson was to prove a much better Chancellor of the Exchequer than his predecessor Vansittart. William Huskisson (who, like Canning, had started his political career as one of Pitt's bright young men) became President of the Board of Trade and Treasurer of the Navy. Finally, Lord Sidmouth was replaced at the Home Office by Sir Robert Peel.

Liverpool was to preside over this cabinet until his paralytic stroke in 1827; his fifteen continuous years as Prime Minister have been surpassed only by Sir Robert Walpole and the Younger Pitt – a feat all the more remarkable in the light of his own relative facelessness and lack of 'star' quality. Perhaps his real contribution lay not in himself but in his ability to spot, to encourage, and to harness talent in others. Certainly the work of these men – Canning, Robinson, Huskission, and Peel – has led historians to make a clear differentiation between the Tory Ministry of 1815–22 and that of 1822–27. A new label has stuck – the 'Liberal Tories'. Whatever the word 'liberal' means in this context – and there could be several interpretations – it seems reasonable to conclude that something of sufficient significance happened during these years to have made it worthwhile to coin the phrase.

The best evidence of this comes from an examination of the work of the new Home Secretary, Sir Robert Peel. Born in 1788, the son of a self-made cotton tycoon, he enjoyed a brilliant career at Harrow and Oxford before entering politics at the age of twenty-one; his father bought him a constituency in Ireland, where there were, conveniently, only twelve voters to canvass. In 1812, he became Chief Secretary for Ireland. As the representative of the Protestant Establishment in Ireland, as the minister of a king who claimed right of succession from the man who secured the Protestant monarchy's rule in Ireland – William of Orange – he was nicknamed, inevitably, 'Orange' Peel.

In 1817 he transferred to the more fashionable seat of Oxford University, and further enhanced his reputation by his successful chairmanship of the Bullion Committee in 1819. His report convinced the Commons that it was time for the Bank of England to renew its pledge to honour all paper notes with gold on demand – which had been suspended as a wartime austerity measure by Pitt. It proved to be both a cause and a symptom of the revival of confidence, and therefore of the economy in general, after the bad post-war years.

By virtue of his education, his ability, and his large private fortune, Peel understood the way the old landed aristocracy thought; as a result of his father's career and success, he also had an awareness of some of the new forces of the Industrial Revolution. He was an aristocrat, perhaps by temperament, and a true Tory by conviction, but his family background was to give him an ability to see further round problems than his fellow-Tories.

Now that the country was beginning to revive after over twenty years of war, Peel could see that the time was ripe for a new approach to many of the nation's troubles. Nowhere was this more clear than in the sphere of internal security, for which he, as Home Secretary, was now responsible. It was no longer enough to huddle within a sort of hand-to-mouth, sudden-reaction-to-crisis, siege mentality, where each disturbance of the peace was met with flurries of frantic legislation to tighten the screws of the penal code still further. There had to be an overview; basic assumptions had to be challenged, or at least rethought.

The most difficult mental barrier to be overcome lay in the minds of his fellow-MPs, and of their colleagues (and relations), the local Justices of the Peace. To them, most offences, or at least most serious offences, were against property. Property was far more important than the individual. Property was permanent; people died. When country gentlemen puffed their pipes and passed the port and talked huffily about 'preserving their liberty', they meant their liberty to go on enjoying their property. MPs were property-owners; they could not become MPs if they were not. Nobody could vote unless he owned property, or in a few cases inhabited certain privileged property. Property meant stability, which was the greatest of all political virtues, especially after a quarter-century of revolution and war. Too much individual thought and action brought about instability, and the world was becoming far too full of individuals – particularly property-less individuals – as the regular ten-year censuses were showing. The population was climbing at an alarming rate.

It followed, therefore, that this ever-growing population must be constantly discouraged from offences against property, by ever-more-savage penalties. (God-fearing landowners declared moreover that, since the lower classes were becoming not only more numerous and more violent but more godless, it was vital to replace their fear of Hellfire with fear of the scaffold.) By the time Peel took office, the number of crimes that could be punishable by death had risen to about two hundred – anything from breaking lock gates and wounding cattle to poaching in private rivers and petty theft. The fact that juries regularly, and humanely, refused to convict (in defiance of the evidence) did not mask the scandal of the statute book.

For years, writers, thinkers, and reformers such as Bentham, Romilly, and Mackintosh had argued that the rights of the individual were just as worth protecting as the sacred cow of property. If you always hung the common man for a lamb as well as for a sheep, it was hardly surprising that he usually stole the sheep. Give him a chance, a choice, and he might think twice before committing serious crime. Peel, borrowing freely from their ideas, set about the penal code to such good effect that within a few years over a hundred death penalties had been abolished, and more than twice as many savage punishments had been made less severe. He then applied himself to legal procedure, and conducted a massive spring-clean of all the laws relating to juries. He removed nasty relics from the past: suicides were no longer to be buried at crossroads with a stake through the heart; there were to be no more Government spies. He reformed the laws on divorce.

Now reducing the fear of the rope did not mean that the crime rate would suddenly drop. Prisons would still be in demand, perhaps more so. Peel once again, with his knack of spotting good ideas and his willingness to listen, saw the value in the arguments of prison crusaders such as Elizabeth Fry and John Howard. The case for individual dignity was heard again. There was not much point in saving a man from the rope if he was still to be treated as little better than an animal in a prison.

So a stream of reforms flowed from the Home Office to improve the prisoner's lot. Jailers were to receive a salary, and no longer had to rely on what they could screw out of the prisoner or his relatives. Cleanliness and hygiene were to be improved, and magistrates were required to carry out regular inspections. Prisoners were to receive religious instruction and basic education. Separate accommodation was to be provided for women prisoners, under women warders. It is hard to know just how effective or how widespread these reforms proved to be, especially when there are regular reminders in the daily press that the last decade of the twentieth century had not yet seen the end of 'slopping out'. Nevertheless, the genuineness of Peel's concern, and the amount of effort he expended on the matter, together justify the historian's acceptance of him as a worthy prison reformer.

Peel was at least trying. He was making an attempt to get behind the trouble. He had grasped the truth that in order to civilise the population one had to civilise the penal code under which it lived. He was, however, still a long way from going even further behind the problem, in an attempt to remove the *causes* of a lot of crime – poverty, overcrowding, neglect, disease, unemployment, and so on. To tackle all that, Parliament would have to come to a much greater appreciation of the needs and rights of the individual, and it was not ready yet. Cobbett was correct; there would have to be a change in the makeup of Parliament itself before that happened.

However, Peel's changes constituted a step in the right direction. England's rulers were moving away from the past. The reforms of William Huskisson at the Board of Trade and John Robinson at the Treasury were in similar vein.

Peel's reforms were in a way an assault on one bastion of the Establishment – property. The financial changes brought about by Robinson and Huskisson were an assault on another – regulation of trade. Some of the reasons for this can be found in three great revolutions which had been or were still taking place – the French Revolution, the American Revolution, and the Industrial Revolution.

The French Revolution, with its philosophy of the Rights of Man, stated the case of the individual against that of property. The American Revolution had shown that an economic system which relied on the mother country 'regulating' (that is, restricting) the trade of her colonies was doomed to failure. The Industrial Revolution was giving birth to a class of men – the factory-owners and shippers and general *entrepreneurs* – whose main motive was making money, preferably with as little government interference as possible.

Many Whigs and Tories alike were coming to accept that, if another disgrace such as the loss of the American colonies was to be avoided, and if the country was to profit fully from the huge industrial energy that was being generated, a new system, a new approach, would have to be devised. Adam Smith, in his free-trade gospel, *The Wealth of Nations* in 1776, had shown the Way; Pitt in principle had believed the Truth of it; more and more politicians in the 1820s were beginning to see the Light. 'Regulation' would have to go; trade would have to be liberated, allowed to develop under its own steam (thanks to James Watt, literally) – in short, left alone. Ironically, it was Britain's great rival that provided the phrase to identify this new philosophy – *laissez-faire*.

Pitt had begun the process, but had been interrupted by the war. The bad years immediately after the war were the wrong time to begin radical experiments; as one Whig politician had put it in another context during the 1790s, 'One does not repair one's house during the hurricane season.' But the hurricane season was now over. Not only that; huge new opportunities for making money were now being presented, and England's businessmen had to be allowed to take the fullest advantage of them. The Spanish and Portuguese colonies in South America were engaged in struggles for independence; here were vast new markets for the purchase of raw materials and the sale of manufactured goods. The old restrictions had to go.

One of the them was to do with shipping. Far back in the middle of the seventeenth century, when the Dutch were the greatest carriers of trade in the world, the English Government had passed the Navigation

Acts, which decreed that all goods going into and out of the colonies had to be carried in English-built and English-owned ships, with a mainly English crew. There was one exception allowed: goods from European countries might be carried direct to the colonies, but only in ships of the country of origin. Furthermore, colonial goods that were earmarked for export to countries other than England had to go through English ports first, allowing a further rake-off for English merchants. It crippled the Dutch, as it was meant to do; it tied colonial shippers hand and foot, as intended; and it put a fortune in the pockets of English merchants – which was the general idea. But by the eighteenth century the Americans, in desperation, were breaking the system. The English Government told the Americans that they must obey the system – or else. The Americans replied in effect that the system was impossible, and that breaking it and accepting the consequences was preferable to trying to survive under it. When they proved their point, the time had clearly come for changing the system – if the British wanted to keep the rest of their empire together.

So Huskisson repealed the Navigation Acts – well, nearly. Henceforth, all foreign countries could trade direct with British colonies, and restrictions were lifted on trade with the rebellious Spaniards and Portuguese in South America. But trade had still to be in British ships. The die-hards in the Tory party would not let him go the whole hog.

It was the same with the tariffs.

A tariff was a customs duty, a Government tax on an item coming into the country, and in some cases going out too. So, if an item carried a tariff, it meant that the Government took a rake-off of so many per cent when it came in as an import, or went out as an export. Naturally, the handlers of this item passed on the cost of the tariff in the price to the customer. So the tariff could be used as a weapon, as a deterrent: if the Government wanted, say, to encourage the production of home-grown tobacco, it would put a tariff on imported tobacco, and so deter potential customers by its higher price.

More often, though, the Government regarded the tariff system as a means of regular income. Indeed, had always done so, certainly since early Tudor times, when customs – or tariffs – produced one-third of

Britain invented the Industrial Revolution, and rode to world supremacy on its back until other, bigger, countries invented theirs. To a nation unused to industrial sprawl and industrial pollution, these establishments must indeed have looked, as Blake said, like 'dark, Satanic mills'.

Or was it only the poets and the artists and the prophets who bemoaned the coming of industrialisation, and who emphasised the black plumes of smoke? Here there seem to have been plenty of people of all walks of life to enjoy the sheer wonder of it all, to say nothing of the regular wages and the soaring share dividends and the cheap, fast travel.

The opening of the Stockton and Darlington Railway, built by George Stephenson in 1825. Railway fever gripped the country: in 1830 there were 69 miles of track; by 1850, 5,000. The Duke was wary of trains, partly because they seemed dangerous to ladies; the Queen, on the other hand, said she was 'quite charmed' with them. Note the wide social range of the onlookers.

After the battle of Trafalgar in 1805, the legend of Britain's sea supremacy cushioned the country into complacency for the best part of a century. When Germany began building iron-clad warships in the 1890s, it was felt to be almost unfair.

There was no national education system worthy of the name until the second half of the nineteenth century. Most early schools were financed by religious charities. This one offered free teaching to 400 boys in Severn Street, Birmingham. Older children were expected to teach the less able. In a group this size, work out how much scope there was for individual tuition.

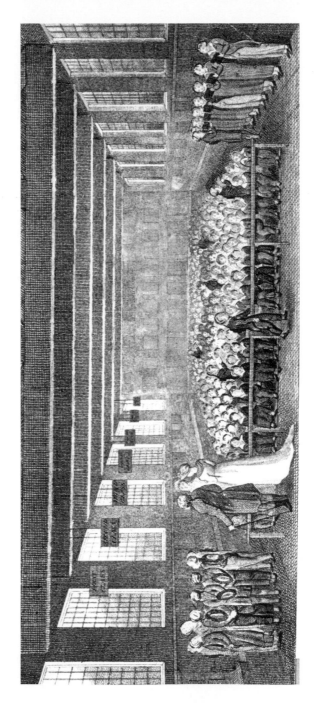

Within a decade of coming to the throne, Queen Victoria (above, seen here with Prince Albert), and her steadily-growing family, had restored to royalty its former lustre, respectability, and permanence. For once, the artist did not overstate; they looked, and were, really fond of each other. Another reason for royalty's improving fortunes was that men like the Duke served it without question all their lives. The Duke, seen here below left, is not smart simply because the artist carefully rendered the details of his uniform. Wellington was always a smart dresser; one of his nicknames was 'The Beau'. The draughtsmanship may be sadly lacking in this picture of child labour in the factories, but the sticks, the frowns, and what we would call today 'body language' nevertheless make the point.

The Great Exhibition, opened on 1 May 1851, the Duke's eighty-second birthday, drew huge crowds, who marvelled at this gigantic proof of England's vast presence as the forum and factory of the world. Here, though, no vulgar proletarian images are allowed to sully the serenity of this arcadian scene in Hyde Park. One would think that there was no such thing as a working man.

Henry VII's entire ordinary revenue. In the 1820s, the Government attitude was the same. Robinson, as Chancellor, had to balance the books, and Parliament had set its face against an income tax (discontinued after the war). So tariffs it still had to be. However, he now had a noisy lobby of merchants to listen to as well; they wanted prices kept down so that they could sell more. So he and Huskisson came up with the policy of 'tariff reform'. Tariffs were not to be abolished, but they were to come down.

The argument for tariff reform went like this. The Government had a dual responsibility – to create an income and to encourage trade. Simply putting up tariffs would bring in money, but the resulting higher prices would discourage trade. Bringing tariffs down too far, or abolishing them altogether, would stimulate trade, but would provide no Government income. But a *partial* reduction would serve both purposes. It would lower prices, and so galvanise the market; the resulting greater volume of trade would bring in more tariff income to the Treasury, even at the lower rate. To give a simple arithmetical example, the sale of 100 items of a commodity with a tariff of 5 pence on it would bring the Treasury a total of £5. If the tariff were lowered to 4 pence, the argument ran that more people would buy it, because it was cheaper. If 130 people did so, the income to the Treasury, even at the lower rate of 4 per cent, would be £5.20. So all parties would be happy – 30 extra satisfied customers, businessmen with higher sales figures, and the Treasury with a higher tariff turnover.

So the early and mid-1820s saw tariffs cut on silk, wool, cotton, linen, china, porcelain, copper, zinc, lead, iron, coffee, glass, and books. Many of the trade restrictions between England and Ireland were abolished. Commercial treaties, based on mutual tariff reduction, were negotiated with Prussia, Sweden, Denmark, Brazil, and Colombia. The policy of colonial preference began, whereby goods from colonies were allowed in at a tariff rate lower than that on goods from foreign countries.

It took a few years for Huskisson to prove his theory, but, when the trade began to flow, his case was unanswerable. Meantime, however, he and Robinson gained little credit. There was a slump at the end of 1825. It was not Huskisson's fault. The causes were wild over-speculation in South America, and the weaknesses of the English banking system, but it gave Huskisson's critics plenty of ammunition. He was not carrying the whole Tory party with him in his reforms – far from it.

His opponents could see that the logical conclusion to tariff reform (freer trade) was the removal of all tariffs – complete free trade. That meant removing the tariff on foreign corn – the repeal of the Corn Laws. If there was one sacred cow more holy than property, it was the landed interest's cherished, sacrosanct right to sell their home-grown grain on the home market at the highest price possible. If lower tariffs or – perish the thought – no tariffs at all allowed cheap Polish or Prussian corn to flood the market, it was 'the end' for the landed interest.

Industrialists, naturally, did not see it like that. To them, low tariffs on foreign corn meant cheap bread, and cheap bread meant more money in people's pockets to buy their goods. So while the landowners chewed their whiskers and wondered how far Huskisson would go, the industrialists waved their fists and declared that he was not going far enough – a familiar dilemma for reforming ministers.

Another familiar problem for Government ministers has always been the pressure group – a devoted knot of MPs or outside agitators, or both, who hammer away at the same theme month after month. Whether it was to create new legislation, or to abolish outdated or oppressive laws, these men relied on the water-on-stone method to achieve their aims.

For fourteen years Francis Place, a London tailor, toiled without remission to make trade unions legal. They had been declared illegal by Pitt's two Combination Acts of 1799 and 1800. It is true that the second act (of 1800) had mitigated the force of the first, but the general effect of the two of them had been to make all combinations of workers (or employers), for pretty well any practical purpose, criminal offences punishable by three months' imprisonment or two months' hard labour. Industrial employers were afraid of their workers, and everybody with any kind of property stake in the country was afraid of the French Revolution, so the acts were accepted without a murmur from Parliament; the first act was rushed through so fast that no workmen had time to organise a petition against it.

It did not prevent workmen from attempting to combine. Some

trades went underground – secret records, elaborate oaths, midnight meetings under hedges. Others, mainly the more affluent, such as shoemakers, coachmakers, cutlers, and compositors, tried strikes, and went to prison for their pains. The siege situation of the long war was against them; so was the awful depression after the war. Thanks to unemployment, many of them did not have working conditions to complain about.

Their cause was kept alive by the Radical tailor from Charing Cross. Francis Place was a self-made, self-educated man, which is evidence enough of his determination and thoroughness. He applied these qualities to the task he had set himself – to repeal the hated Combination Acts. He collected a huge file of information on every industrial dispute he could find news of, and used the facts therein for publicity. He dispatched a flood of letters to newspapers, winning the sympathy of several editors in the process. He visited scores of workplaces. He buttonholed, pestered, and lobbied MPs. One of them, Joseph Hume, took up his cause wholeheartedly, and between them they managed to get a Parliamentary Committee set up to examine the Combination Acts, and to hear evidence on them.

Hume got the committee packed with his friends, and Place persuaded workers to make subscriptions towards the costs of witnesses who would be called to give evidence. Nevertheless, it would have been only too easy for the deputations of the employers, with their greater funds, greater education, and greater assurance, to sway the committee to their side. Humble workmen, ushered into unfamiliar surroundings, could have ruined their case by standing tongue-tied, or by being tricked with smart questions. Place got round that by carefully selecting his witnesses, and by spending hours briefing, rehearsing, and drilling them into saying exactly what he and Hume wanted them to say.

Their next clever move was to have the Committee's brief extended to cover not only combinations of workmen, which had been opposed by many, but the emigration of artisans, which was opposed by few. That, and the skilful way in which the workmen's evidence was presented, left the Committee little option but to recommend that both acts should be repealed.

Rather than submit a report that the House of Commons should debate – and possibly amend – Hume arranged that the Committee should simply propose resolutions upon which the House should vote. Place apparently was able to alter the wording of the draft bills without any member knowing the difference, and Hume got them through a half-empty House so smoothly that the Prime Minister and Lord Chancellor both said afterwards that they did not know the bills had been passed.

The success story, unfortunately, then went awry. It was nearly ruined by the very people whom Place and Hume had been trying to help. Workmen all over the country, safe – they thought – behind the terms of the new act, put in claims for higher wages, and, when these were not forthcoming, went on strike. There were also instances of intimidation, violence, even murder. It was now the turn of the employers to press the Government to reverse the act of 1824 – to repeal the repeal. This time they wanted to go further than the original Combinations Act itself; they wanted to prohibit not only trade unions, but friendly societies, social clubs – any form of working-class association.

When a new committee was set up to investigate, it was packed by the employers, who, if they had had their way, would not have heard any witness from the workmen at all. But Place went to work again, and the committee was inundated with petitions and fresh witnesses (as well drilled as before). Every point the employers tried to make was answered by evidence from the workmen.

It did not save the trade unions from a new act, but it saved them from total extinction. The Act of 1825 allowed unions to mention wages and working hours, but not to strike, intimidate, or obstruct. Members of unions could be prosecuted for conspiracy. In effect, unions were allowed legally to exist, but very little else.

Place's pressure group had run into the well-fortified bastion of the industrial interest (which woke up to its danger just in time), and the even better-fortified bastion of the property interest. Landowners had been quite prepared to see a law that cut into the purse and privacy of the loud, free-trading businessmen who talked so loosely about repealing the Corn Laws; they reacted completely differently when private property was threatened by strikes. Private property, whoever it belonged to, must be maintained at all costs.

Similar pressure groups spent most of the eighteen-teens and eighteen-twenties running their heads against a third bastion – the Anglican Church. The law discriminated almost as much against Protestant Nonconformists – Baptists, Methodists, Presbyterians, Quakers, and so on – as it did against Roman Catholics. The Nonconformists enjoyed the questionable advantage that at least they were not suspected of plotting to further the dominion of a foreign spiritual Antichrist like the Pope. Secondly, many of them were in positions of considerable wealth and influence in business and industry; they had been barred by law from entering other forms of public life. Nevertheless, they could not vote, and they could not enter Parliament, where the bench of bishops held sway in the Lords and the Tory landed interest dominated the Commons, and Tories were – always had been – for the Established Church, Anglicanism.

Individual MPs were beginning to see that the laws against Nonconformists would have to go. Others, of a yet more liberal turn of mind, thought that, if civil rights were to be granted to Methodists, they would sooner or later have to be granted to Catholics. But the wrath of the Tory party would descend upon the head of the minister who proposed it.

Liverpool, the Prime Minister, had no policy for Government action in that direction. Peel, whatever his private feelings might have been, had his hands full with his reforms of the penal code and the legal system, and with another scheme that he was soon to unfold – his plans for a police force. Canning, the Foreign Secretary, had his dispatch box brimming with reports of revolutions. Outbreaks in Naples, Piedmont, Portugal, and Spain in 1820–1 had been succeeded by a veritable rash of them in South America, and another that had degenerated into a running war in Greece.

The revolutions in Naples and Piedmont had been put down, by Austrian forces on the orders of Chancellor Metternich, before Canning came into office, but it is unlikely that he would have done more than his predecessor, Castlereagh, to try to prevent Metternich's action. Austria was the dominant power in Italy, and Castlereagh did not challenge the right of a government to put down a revolution on its own doorstep. However, he did not go along with Metternich's philosophy of *joint* action by the Great Powers to put down revolution *anywhere*. For this reason, Castlereagh had not attended the third and fourth congresses at Troppau and Laibach, where Metternich and the Tsar had issued joint statements about the 'justice' of their declared policy. He had sent his brother only to observe, not to negotiate. The revolutions in Piedmont and Naples had been duly suppressed, by Austrian troops.

It used to be fashionable to suggest that these incidents marked the crumbling of a unique (till then) experiment in international relations – the 'Congress System'. The first congress – of Vienna – had met to secure the peace of Europe after the Napoleonic War. It was at this congress that Castlereagh had suggested periodic future meetings of the four Great Powers – Britain, Austria, Prussia, and Russia – to discuss 'common interests', and to take necessary decisions for the 'repose and prosperity of Nations, and for the maintenance of the peace of Europe'. Castlereagh wrote a formal draft, and it became Article VI of the Quadruple Alliance.

Historians in the twentieth century, often writing in the shadow of the League of Nations after 1919 or the United Nations after 1945, were tempted to read into the congresses things that were not really there. The idea grew that the five congresses – Vienna, Aix-la-Chapelle, Troppau, Laibach, and Verona – represented a first attempt at international regulation of affairs for the benefit of all, that the Great Powers were a sort of embryonic Security Council. It reached teaching syllabuses; questions on the 'Congress System' made regular appearances in examination papers.

The over-simplified view had it that the concept was the brainchild of Castlereagh, that he was, if not obsessed with it, very taken up with it – which explains why he was so often accused of putting European issues first in his conduct of foreign affairs and British issues second. Then along came Canning, who said, in effect, in his bullish way, 'Enough of this. No more kow-towing to Metternich and the Tsar and their precious congresses; henceforth we pursue a truly "British" foreign policy.' And everyone clapped – in England.

Canning, in short, reversed Castlereagh's policy, 'killed' the Congress System, and the British cheered over the grave.

Later opinion now maintains that, if indeed there was anything like a 'Congress System', all Canning did was to preside over the funeral. Castlereagh had attended only two himself, had sent his brother as mere observer to the next two, and had died two months before the last one assembled. As for international partnership and 'common interests', there had been precious little of that once the threat of France had been recognised as officially gone at the Congress of Aix-la-Chapelle.

Other commentators point out that there was no international charter, no permanent staff, no funds, no secretariat, no prescribed times for meetings – in other words that there was no such thing as a 'Congress System'. There was nothing for Canning to kill.

The more prosaic truth probably is that Castlereagh liked the idea of occasional meetings between himself and his opposite numbers, whom he knew very well. In discreet privacy, and on terms of professional intimacy, they could discuss anything important that had come up. Perhaps he hoped to continue the partnership he had helped to create for the defeat of Napoleon. When he saw that differences were beginning to open between himself and Metternich and the Tsar, he saw little point in going to further meetings where there was little chance of agreement. Travel was slow, uncomfortable, and often dangerous.

Castlereagh also saw the changing pattern of international politics with clearer eyes than his contemporaries, or many historians, gave him credit for. In a famous state paper of May, 1820, he laid down the lines along which future conduct of British foreign policy should be directed, and Canning, by and large, followed them with surprising fidelity. In different style, maybe, but in similar substance.

For example, in Spain, where the liberals had risen against their loathsome King Ferdinand, Metternich and the French King were all for sending in an army to put them down. The Tsar went further; he wanted to lead an international force to 'restore order'. Castlereagh had said that he was flatly against 'any interference in the internal affairs' of Spain. Canning agreed, and intended to make that clear at the Congress of Verona called to discuss the problem. He asked the Duke to represent England there. Theirs was not a great meeting of minds; the Duke today would have been called a Europhile, while Canning was a confirmed Eurosceptic. But the Duke was true to his creed of

Crown service, put aside his misgivings, and agreed to go, though he was not in the best of health at the time.

He was the obvious choice; like his friend Castlereagh, he knew everybody – crowned heads and all – and his military reputation gave him a lot of 'clout'. Even so, he achieved only partial success. He was able to prevent Tsar Alexander's wilder scheme; not even Metternich liked the idea of 100,000 Russians marching across Europe. But he was unable to stop a French army entering Spain and replacing Ferdinand upon his tawdry throne. The French had to camp there until 1827 to make sure that he survived. The irony did not escape observers that a Royalist French army had succeeded in Spain in a few months where the might of the Emperor had spent six years in dismal failure during the recent war. (But then they were not fighting the Duke.)

The French occupation of Spain at once threw into high relief the problem of the Spanish colonies in South America, nearly all of whom were in open revolt. Castlereagh had foreseen this too. He did not approve of assisting revolution, but now that the success of those revolutions against the Spanish Government seemed assured, he thought it realistic to give recognition to the new regimes.

Canning, with his rather more breezy style, put it slightly differently. Still smarting from the French rebuff to him in Spain, he said, 'I resolved that if France had Spain, it should not be Spain with the Indies.' He wrung a statement from the French that they had no designs on South America, and suggested joint action to the United States of America to keep out the French if they should break their word. He then proposed to recognise the new rebel countries, and stilled the doubts of fellow-Tories (who were worried about encouraging 'revolution') by pointing out that, if Britain did not seize the opportunity of South American markets, the United States would. So he got his way; the British Government formally recognised the independence of Buenos Aires, Colombia, Mexico, Bolivia, Chile, and Peru. At about the same time, President Monroe and his Secretary of State, John Quincy Adams, who were just as worried by the threat of the Russians in Alaska as by the threat of the French in South America, inserted some paragraphs into the President's annual message on the State of the Union. They let it be known that neither North nor South

America was to be regarded as a future subject 'for colonisation by any European Powers'; and that, if they were, it would constitute an 'unfriendly disposition' towards the United States. In other words, 'Hands off America'. The timing of events suggests that it was Canning's actions rather than Monroe's that proved decisive, but it was posterity that turned the President's statement into legend; the 'Monroe Doctrine' became in time a cornerstone of United States foreign policy.

Canning achieved another success in Portugal, where the revolution seemed temporarily settled by the accession to the throne of the young Queen Maria, who granted the liberals a constitution. It was one thing to accept the French invasion of Spain to put down liberalism; but a French invasion of Portugal was unthinkable. Portugal was an old ally; it gave France too much access to the Atlantic seaports; it laid open to her the Portuguese South American empire in Brazil; it would upset the balance of power. If Canning was not able to intervene in Portugal, he was certainly not going to let the French intervene, and was prepared to use the Navy to back it up.

Then affairs played into his hands. Maria's uncle, Don Miguel, a prince of right-wing leanings after Metternich's own heart, mounted an invasion of Portugal against his niece. Canning at last was able to move. He could not, according to his declared policy, intervene in the internal affairs of another country; but he could, he said, intervene to stop other people intervening. British troops were dispatched to checkmate Don Miguel and restore Maria and her liberals. Canning and the British public rejoiced, and Metternich, the Austrians, and the French had to lump it.

That left Greece. Greece was special. Everybody was an expert on Greece. The fountainhead of European civilisation; the cradle of democracy; the inspiration of all learning; the birthplace of heroes – every educated man, steeped in the Classics, knew all about Greece. At least he thought he did. What he really knew about was Ancient Greece, and he had gained his knowledge in youth, not maturity. So, when news arrived that the Greeks had started a war for independence against their overlords, the Turks, the reaction was a mixture of excitement, admiration, and nostalgia. Forgetting that the vices of the Ancient Greeks were just as great as their virtues, too many Englishmen assumed that the Greek liberation forces were peopled by Homeric heroes of prodigious bravery and deserving honour, with names like Ajax and Agamemnon.

If knowledge led them into a misconception about the Greeks, ignorance led them into a similar misconception about the Turks. Turks were vicious, corrupt, backward, treacherous, and generally pretty near the bottom of the league of 'foreigners' whom every true-blooded Englishman cheerfully despised. In any conflict between Greek and Turk, there was no question where sympathy would lie.

It was not only sentimental sympathy; it was religious loathing. Greeks were Christian; Turks were Muslim. There was a faint hangover of the old medieval hatred of the infidel. Added to that was the vague feeling that Turks were 'oriental', and therefore sunk in nameless vice and unmentionable decadence. They therefore did not deserve to succeed; it would not be fair if they did.

There were modern and practical aspects to this Graecomania. Even if Greece had not been the home of classical heroes, there would have been plenty of support from those who had applauded all the other 'liberal' revolutions since the end of the war. Even a poet like Lord Byron poured scorn on what he called 'antiquarian twaddle', but he was prepared to go out to Greece and fight for liberty; he wanted to be useful. There were also a lot of professional soldiers cooling their heels after the war; by offering their services to the Greeks, they could gain profitable employment in a noble cause – line their pockets and cosset their consciences at one and the same time. It was almost as good as the Crusades.

If it had all been as simple as liberal-minded poets and ex-Classical scholars thought it was, Canning would have had no trouble in deciding upon a course of action. Unfortunately, what he was now presented with was an early chapter in the 'Eastern Question' – a saga that was to run constantly in the programmes of the Foreign Office for the best part of a century. Indeed, with the issues of Jew and Arab, terrorist and hostage, still a running sore, it could be argued that the Eastern Question, albeit in modified form, is still with us.

Whole books have been written about the Eastern Question, and it is foolish to hope that any summary at this stage could do it justice. But it may be helpful to select just one aspect of it, in order to illustrate how difficult contemporaries found it, never mind students of history.

First, let it be made clear what part of the world is under discussion. If one stuck a compass point in a map at Constantinople, and swung the arm in a circle – radius of about six or seven hundred miles – the area so described would cover most of the territory involved in the Eastern Question as Canning was faced with it. The biggest power within that circle was the Ottoman, or Turkish Empire (so called because the Turks who established it were from a group called the Ottoman Turks). They ruled several lands in the Balkans, in south-eastern Europe – like Macedonia, Bulgaria, Rumania, Albania, Bosnia. And Greece. They also exercised a loose overlordship over Egypt, currently ruled by an adventurer of prodigious energy and resource called Mehemet Ali. (More of Mehemet later.)

The two biggest powers on the Turks' borders were the Austrian Empire of the Hapsburgs (Chancellor Metternich), and the Russian Empire of the Romanovs (Tsar Alexander, and, when he died in 1825, Nicholas). It was natural enough that these two Powers should be interested in events within the territories of their neighbour. The surprise comes when it is seen how interested Britain was; Britain was over a thousand miles away. The French also took great notice of events in this area, and they were almost as distant.

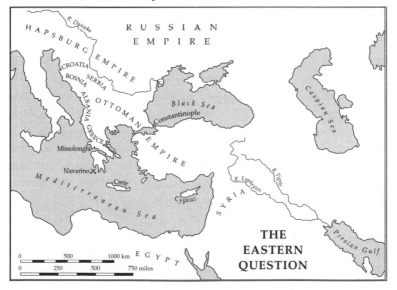

Now to the aspect of the Eastern Question under examination. A way of describing it would be to call it a sort of kaleidoscopic dimension. Every time an event shook the ingredients, they assumed a completely different pattern. One of the most infuriating features of the Eastern Question was that, whenever a crisis demanded more attention from the Powers than usual, each one of those Powers was presented with a ghastly choice of courses of action, each of which was fraught with hideous possibilities.

Take the Greek revolt. If Canning went along with strongly-expressed public sentiment (with which he privately sympathised), he would support the Greeks. However, if the Greeks won their independence, it would weaken their overlord Turkey. If Turkey became weaker, she would be easier prey for her neighbour Russia, which had been trying for years to break through the middle of the Turkish Empire and get into the Mediterranean. The nightmare threat that this presented to British trade routes there did not bear thinking about. So how could Canning square the circle – prise the Greeks away from the Turkish Empire without letting in the Russians?

In Vienna, Metternich wrestled with a similar problem. A cornerstone of Hapsburg policy for centuries had been hostility to the Ottoman Empire. The Hapsburg reputation had been built as the guardian of Christian Europe against the infidel Turk. The immediate reaction therefore should have been to support the Greeks. But, if he did, it meant that he was going against his oft-declared policy of putting down all revolutions wherever they occurred. He had kept liberalism quiet in Germany; he had sent troops to crush revolts in Piedmont and Naples; he had approved of the French quelling the revolution in Spain. How could he now favour the Greek rebels? Especially when there were numerous subject peoples in his own empire itching to do the same. Worse, if the Tsar came in on the Greek side, it would enhance Russian influence in the Balkans, and take the Russians nearer the mouth of the River Danube, which was a main artery of Austrian trade. Metternich did not want the Russians in the Balkans.

In St Petersburg, Tsar Alexander, and his ministers were also in a cleft stick. As a romantic, and as a fellow Orthodox Christian, he sympathised with the Greeks. As a political realist, he could see that if he gave active support to the Greeks, it would give him an excuse, and a noble excuse at that, for getting his foot inside the door in the Balkans. Anything that took Russian power nearer to Constantinople and the Mediterranean had to be a good idea. And yet, and yet – he, Alexander, Tsar of all the Russias, was a dictator. How could he countenance revolution? His cherished Holy Alliance had been, from its inception, dedicated in practice to the crushing of revolution wherever it had occurred.

In Paris, the French Government remembered that the mighty Napoleon had burned his fingers in that part of the world. Nevertheless, they had built up huge mercantile interests there since the war. Would they be better served by having a strong Turkey to keep the peace and impose heavy customs duties, or by having a free-for-all, with the prospect of huge profits alongside huge risks?

Foreign ministers, faced with apparently insuperable dilemmas, often wish they would simply go away. They patch up policies of wait-and-see in that hope. In this case it did not work. A crisis was precipitated by the one group who so far had figured least in all the diplomatic activity and soul-searching – the Turks themselves. When they saw that the Greeks were more than holding their own, they called in the help of Mehemet Ali, the Pasha of Egypt and Syria. Mehemet sent his son Ibrahim (one of many) with an army to southern Greece, where he proceeded to put down the revolt with most un-Turkish efficiency. Rumour had it that he intended to carry off the population into slavery. If the Powers did not do something, there might not be any Greeks left.

The early 1820s were not short of causes – the plight of the Greeks, the rights of English workmen to combine, the claims of prisoners to be treated as human beings, the need for the punishment to come somewhere near the real seriousness of the crime, civil rights for Nonconformists and Roman Catholics, the campaign for free trade. To that could be added the liberation of the Irish, the extension of the right to vote (what Cobbett was still, indefatigably, writing about), the plight of the urban poor, the even worse misery of the agricultural labourer deprived of his land and his common rights by enclosures.

Lest it be thought that this period was unique in human kindness or compassion – for each of these causes had its noisy champions – it is perhaps salutary to close by giving an account of a famous murder trial that took place in 1824. It is not so much the murder that illustrated the harshness of the times – sadly, there have been many worse, and much more recent – as the circumstances surrounding the trial and subsequent punishment.

On Friday, 24 October, 1823, William Weare, an ex-waiter and billiard sharp, returned to Hertfordshire from the Doncaster races with winnings in his pocket amounting to £2,000. He was met by John Thurtell, to whom he owed money, and driven in a chaise towards a cottage rendezvous near Elstree. The house was rented by William Probert, a bankrupt wine merchant. A second accomplice, Joseph Hunt, ex-convict, ex-tavern-keeper with a record of default on payment of bills, was to meet them and assist in Weare's murder. Thurtell had connections with the world of professional gambling, the seedier side of the licensed victualling trade, and London low-life in general. He had strong connections too with the boxing fraternity, and was on intimate terms with characters such as 'The Gasman', 'Ned Flatnose', and 'The Master of the Rolls'. Bare-knuckle boxers, professional conmen, ex-jailbirds, debtors, drink, loose women – it gives a flavour of the general level of the crime.

Probert and Hunt failed to make the rendezvous, so Thurtell carried out the murder by himself. It was particularly inept, desperate, and messy, involving shooting in the face, throat-cutting, head-bashing, and stirring the victim's brains with the barrel of the pistol. Hunt and Probert arrived in time to assist with the dumping of the body in a pond in Probert's garden. Fearful of discovery, they later dragged the body out, put it in a gig, and took it to a brook on the north side of Elstree, where they dumped it again.

The criminals were clumsy murderers and clumsy liars. There were far too many rumours of gunshots, screams, and groans in the night. Blood was found in all sorts of incriminating places. Probert's wife had seen them dragging something towards the pond. Finally, Probert turned King's Evidence. The magistrate called in two of the famous Bow Street Runners – 'Robin Redbreasts', they were called, from the bright scarlet of their waistcoats. Within a week the body was found,

Thurtell and Hunt were under arrest, and the coroner's jury had recorded a verdict of wilful murder.

So far there was nothing to distinguish this sordid, profit-motivated crime from thousands of others. What made it different was that it became the first serious crime to be subjected to 'trial by newspaper'. Even if the evidence had not been stacked against the prisoners, everything else was. Their own accomplice, Probert, had 'told all'. The judge was heard to observe that he thought it most improper to acquaint a prisoner with the evidence against him. But it was the Press and the entertainment world which, more than anyone, tried and condemned the defendants – particularly Thurtell, as he was the man who had actually done the deed.

From the start of November, prints and articles about the crime circulated freely. Newspapers made a daily meal of it, and served it up with speculative spice to a greedy public. The respected *Times* led the way. By the middle of the month, a play called *The Gamblers* – enacting the whole story – was being performed at the Surrey Theatre. The impresario had bought the actual chaise in which Weare had been driven by Thurtell, and it duly appeared on stage each night, together with the horse that had pulled it. Thurtell's lawyers managed to get it withdrawn, but it reappeared as soon as the conviction had been secured, and public necks craned once more in the light of the gas jets.

When the body of Weare was buried – at eleven o'clock at night – *The Times* devoted five and a half columns to the event, dwelling lovingly over the detail that one of the ropes broke at the crucial moment, and the coffin slipped into an upright position at the bottom of the grave. Men had to clamber into the pit to right it. The reporter concluded by suggesting that the overall effect was something which could 'hardly be surpassed'. He was wrong, and he must have scarcely believed his luck, because shortly afterwards, on an appropriately wild and stormy night, the body was exhumed in order to allow a witness to try to identify it.

Throughout November, the daily and weekly press continued to pour out a stream of anecdote, rumour, and 'revelation', with *The Times* playing a leading role – details from the early lives of the two defendants, biographies of the victim, other crimes allegedly contemplated by Thurtell. Sir Thomas Lawrence, president of the Royal Academy, wanted to gain an interview with Thurtell, for the purpose of taking a cast of his head in the interests of the science of phrenology, which claimed to be able to deduce character from the shape of the skull.

Every amateur psychologist took it upon himself to 'prove' that the defendants 'looked' like criminals. The journalist in the *London Magazine*, after duly noting voluminous details of Hunt's dress, observed that 'nothing could be weaker than his features ... destitute of the least manly expression'. Thurtell's mouth had 'a dogged appearance', his 'eyes were too small', and were 'buried deep under his protruding forehead'. Even the informer, Probert, had a face that was marked with 'deceit in every lineament', and a forehead that 'recedes villainously'. In a final sideswipe at both his education and his character, he said that 'his grammar was very nearly as bad as his heart'.

During the deliberations of the jury, scores of horses stood waiting in relays all along the road to London, to take the reporters' news. The jury took only twenty minutes to reach a verdict, and Thurtell ostentatiously took a pinch of snuff while the judge was passing sentence.

Two days later (at least the condemned man was not kept waiting) the road from London to Hertford was blocked by coaches (and expensive ones at that), many of them full of 'elegantly attired ladies' – though it was not made clear whether their elegant attire characterised their ancient breeding or their ancient profession. The reporters were as active in the crowd as the pickpockets, and *The Times* once again regaled its readers with lurid details such as the sound made by the snapping of the victim's neck.

That was not the end of it. More books, articles, and ballads were sold. The Surrey Theatre reopened with its play, *The Gamblers*. And a resourceful writer of broadsheets made a small fortune by printing one entitled *Weare Alive Again*. When deluded purchasers complained that the contents did not live up to the title, he apologised for a typographical error – no space had been left after '*We*'.

And it was still not the end. Thurtell's body was conveyed to St Bartholomew's Hospital, though not all of it got there. A finger was cut off on the way; apparently the touch of a hanged man's hand was said to be a cure for cysts. Huge crowds turned up each day to watch a famous doctor perform medical dissection on the cadaver, until the putrid state of it called a halt to the proceedings.

Hunt, the other defendant, had his sentence commuted to transportation to Australia. Probert, the informer, was hanged in 1825 for horse-stealing.

The crime had caused more sensation than any other murder up to then. What is more, it created enormous interest among all ranks of society. Men like Sir Walter Scott, the celebrity historical novelist, admitted that he went out of his way when travelling north to visit the spot where William Weare had been done to death. So many people visited Probert's cottage that his landlord, to whom Probert had fallen behind in his rent, started charging admission money. The press devoted more space to Weare's funeral than it did to the funeral of the most famous lawyer of the day, Sir Thomas Erskine.

It is debatable which feature the episode best illustrates – the harshness of human nature, the harshness of the times, or the understandable desire of people to escape from them occasionally by contemplating the misfortunes of others.

CHAPTER EIGHT

Swaggering Dan
1826–30

On 20 October, 1827, Admiral Sir Edward Codrington sank the combined Turkish and Egyptian fleets by accident. It was that rarity in British naval history – the unwanted victory. (Incidentally, it was also the last sea fight under full sail.) The King, in his Speech from the Throne at the opening of the next Parliament, referred to the incident, with masterly understatement, as 'an untoward event'. Codrington, one of Nelson's old captains and a veteran of Trafalgar, received the Order of the Bath, and the private comment from the King that it should have been a halter. There was no official celebration of the victory, and the Cabinet decided to hold an inquiry into the discretion of Codrington's behaviour. On the other hand, the King's brother, the Duke of Clarence (and heir to the throne), who had been a naval officer all his working life and was now Lord High Admiral, thought it was splendid news, and congratulated Codrington. The Tsar invested him with Russia's highest order of decoration; the Admiralty recalled him, and never employed him again.

Codrington had overdone it. Or rather, like other zealous commanders before him, he had done what many of his countrymen privately wanted him to do, without being aware how much it would embarrass the public sensibilities of the politicians.

In effect, he had saved the Greeks. The trouble was that, in so doing, he had become 'involved'. If there was one thing the Government did not want, it was to become involved in the Eastern Question. Ideally, they wanted everything to come out as they wished without having to commit themselves to any decisive action. They wanted to prise Greece away from the Turkish Empire without letting it fall under the influence – or, worse, the control – of Russia. They were prepared to see this weakening of Turkey, while at the same time hoping that Turkey would remain friendly, and remain moreover an effective barrier to Russia's expansionist plans in south-eastern Europe.

When the Greeks had made a formal request for help, Cabinet ministers were forced to come off the fence. Rejecting it was out of the question; the appeal was too urgent, too attractive, and too popular. If the rumours about Ibrahim Pasha's plans for enslaving the entire Greek population were true, action had to be now or never. If assistance were to be given, it would be one of the most welcome decisions they could take; Graecomania gripped the country. Lord Byron became a hero not for going to Greece, but for dying there. (The craze had spread across the Atlantic. New settlements on the expanding frontier of the United States were given Greek names; pretentious farmers added Greek colonnades to their farmhouses and christened their sons Homer; Ancient Greek found its rapid way into the timetables of miserable schoolboys.)

Very well – if assistance was to be provided, it was to be negative assistance. A naval squadron was dispatched to prevent reinforcements and supplies reaching Ibrahim from Turkey and Egypt. Ibrahim was to be blockaded inside the harbour of Navarino, on the south-western tip of Greece, but the squadron commander, Codrington, was not to start anything. Baffled, he applied for clarification to the British Ambassador at Constantinople, and received the quiet hint that, if all else failed, he could resort to 'cannon shot'.

Like all British naval officers at the time, he was used to action and he was used to winning; like all Englishmen, he yearned for a crack at a seedy enemy like the Turks and the Egyptians. He sailed into Navarino harbour with twenty-four ships, if not looking for trouble, certainly hoping for it. Right on cue, some undisciplined Turkish gun crew opened fire on a boat under flag of truce. Armed with his justification, Codrington went to work, and by the evening over fifty enemy ships had been sunk.

The British Government practically apologised for this 'untoward' action against an 'ancient ally', but could not prevent the Turks from turning their wrath against Russia (there had been Russian ships too under Codrington's command). The Cabinet had to sit on the sidelines during a full-scale Russo-Turkish war. When Russian forces came within 150 miles of Constantinople, British ministers suffered night-mares about the complete collapse of the Turkish Empire. They were saved from further torture by a modification of Russian foreign policy under the new Tsar, Nicholas I. The Tsar's advisers were suggesting that it might be better for Russia to interfere in the affairs of a weakened Turkey than to try to remove it altogether and face war with the Western Powers. Nevertheless, they forced humiliating terms on the Turks in the Treaty of Adrianople in 1829.

However, thanks to intense diplomatic activity, the British and the French salvaged something from the mess. They managed to secure the independence of Greece, and a promise from the Tsar that he would not interfere there. Four years later, in a final conference, the Greeks were to accept a constitutional monarchy, and Prince Otto of Bavaria agreed to become King.

That, the King and the Duke and everyone else hoped, was that. Britain had achieved two-thirds of her aims. The Greeks were free, and Russia was still a long way from the Mediterranean. Unfortunately, the Turkish Empire was seriously weakened – probably mortally. They were wrong on both counts: it was not 'that' – the Eastern Question was to raise its tiresome head several times during the rest of the century, twice at least during the Duke's lifetime; and the Turkish Empire was to rumble on for another eighty-odd years.

One of the reasons for those vague orders that Codrington received, it has been suggested, was that they had not been drafted by Canning. Canning was dead. The year 1827 had shown a remarkable casualty rate among prime ministers. In February, Lord Liverpool suffered a paralytic stroke. His successor, Canning, not a popular choice with the right wing of the party, exhausted himself by trying to keep control of foreign affairs while moving to Downing Street. He had caught rheumatic fever at the Duke of York's funeral on a bitter day in January, and never shook it off. He became unable to cope with his many enemies in Parliament. By August he was dead, after a ministry of only a hundred days. In fact, Canning's premiership had almost divided the Tories into two; his successor, Lord Goderich (formerly John Robinson, the ex-Chancellor) proved unable to hold the two together. Within months, Goderich, who had never really recovered from a breakdown following the death of a beloved daughter, was begging to be released. In January, 1828, the King had little option but to ask the foremost soldier of the age to become Prime Minister.

It did not strike Wellington as in any way inconsistent. He had a high conception of his own worth – one of his comments on the victory at Waterloo had been, 'By God! I don't think it would have been done if I had not been there' – but it was usually an accurate one. He was lionised by society and loaded with honours from every crowned head in Europe, but he was seldom led astray by conceit. He did not regard himself as any kind of military genius; nor as a famous retired soldier; nor as statesman, politician, Tory, or general celebrity. He saw himself as a servant of the British Crown and of his country.

He would do whatever his monarch asked of him. Before his famous command in Portugal in 1808, for instance, he had agreed to serve as Chief Secretary for Ireland. Then he welcomed the sudden offer to lead a military expedition to bolster the South American revolutions against Spain; for a successful young general, it certainly beat being a glorified referee between Catholic and Protestant in the land of his birth. That was cancelled at the last minute in favour of the expedition to the Peninsula.

When the war was over, he became commanding officer of the Army of Occupation in France until 1818. On his return to England, the Government felt vaguely that they ought to ensure the loyalty of the foremost soldier in Europe, so they made him Master-General of the Ordnance. They need not have worried; he would have been loyal anyway – at any rate to his country and to his principles – and to his friends. This was shown in 1822, when he was one of the few to mourn the death of Castlereagh – and publicly.

1822 saw another of the might-have-beens in Wellington's career. There was talk of his becoming Lord Lieutenant of Ireland. In the event that came to nothing too; brother Richard went instead. Arthur meanwhile accepted the commission to represent England at the

Congress of Verona, which added 'diplomat' to the growing list of his varied experience. In 1826, he was sent on a mission to St Petersburg, to sweeten the new Tsar, Nicholas I. When the old Duke of York died in 1827, he was the obvious candidate for the post of Commander-in-Chief, which he regarded as no more than his due.

He did not like Canning, however. Never had. Too smart for his own good, or anybody else's. A loose cannon in European politics; no conception of, or respect for, the concert of Europe built up so painstakingly by his late friend Castlereagh. Canning's backing of the Greeks was unwise; he, Wellington, inclined more to the traditional support of Turkey as the bastion against Russia, which was the real threat. Hence his later near-apology to the Sultan for the Battle of Navarino. He also disagreed strongly with Canning on the subject of civil rights for Roman Catholics. Canning was known to favour it; the hard core of Tories saw it as a mortal blow to the integrity of the Anglican Church, and Wellington agreed with them. He had grown up, lived, and served in Ireland, and he feared that anarchy would follow the granting of civil rights to the Catholics, who comprised three-quarters of the population. Peel, who had also served as Chief Secretary for Ireland, felt the same way.

When Canning became Prime Minister, Peel resigned from the Home Office, and Wellington resigned both as Master-General and as Commander-in-Chief. He had been prepared, at a pinch, to work *with* Canning; he was not prepared to work *under* him. The passing of Liverpool had left the Tories rudderless. First Canning, and then Goderich, had proved unable to bring a majority of the party back on to an even course. A more liberal wing, styling themselves Canningites, were swinging away from the traditional Tories like Peel, Wellington, and Eldon. It was felt that a firm hand was needed again on the tiller, and what firmer hand than that of the Duke? He now had an unshakable place in English public life. There were numerous royal dukes, but when anyone said 'the Duke', he meant only one man, and everyone knew who it was.

The Duke may have been the only choice, but he was far from being an ideal choice. He was honest, brave, and possessed of a tremendous fund of common sense; he drove himself hard, and he was never afraid of paper work. He had a soldier's simple approach to problems: he sized them up, decided upon the best course of action, and issued his orders accordingly. It annoyed him when his Cabinet colleagues did not jump to it like junior officers. He could not see the point of a party if they did not follow their leaders. He had never had much time for party politics; he had even less now. Resign by all means, but, if you stayed, you obeyed. Such was the Duke's creed.

He also lacked the politician's fondness for beating about the bush. When Huskisson, a Canningite, tendered his resignation, the Duke assumed that, being a gentleman, he meant what he said. Huskisson, who had hastily written a shamefaced letter of resignation as a sort of apology for voting against the Government on the issue of the reform of Parliament, expected that his gracious offer would be equally graciously refused. The Duke cheerfully took him at his word and let him go. The other Canningites, who included Palmerston and Melbourne, also left, and the Duke was thrown back on to the more conservative wing of the Tories. Peel therefore became Home Secretary again.

A whole plateful of hot potatoes lay before him. The first one concerned Nonconformists – Dissenters – all those members of the Protestant faith who did not accept the Anglican Established Church. The lords and bishops who returned to power with Charles II in 1660, after their defeat and exile at the end of the Civil War, took revenge on the men – nearly all Nonconformists – who had defeated and exiled them. One statute after another shackled every man and woman to support of the Established (or rather re-Established) Anglican Church. Whatever Dissenters might do in private, they would gain no public office, promotion, or advancement if they did not show public allegiance to the Church of England. As the eighteenth century advanced, however, it was gradually realised that these people were no serious threat to Church or State; they were not like Catholics, who, as every true-blooded Englishman knew, prayed daily for a return of popery and the rule of Rome. Nevertheless, the laws passed against Nonconformists in the 1660s and 1670s stuck stubbornly to the pages of the statute book, particularly two. One was the Corporation Act, which said that anyone who wanted to be a member of any corporation – that is, to share in local government – had to accept the Anglican communion. The other was the Test Act, which forced acceptance of the Anglican communion on any holder of any public office.

The authorities, and society in general, had long since learned to live with Nonconformists. Because they had been debarred officially from public service, they had turned their intellect and their energies to private enterprise, a whole world apart from treasonable plots and foreign invasions (the sorts of things that Catholics were always being suspected of). By the mid-eighteenth century, a compromise had been reached: the Test and Corporation Acts were not repealed, but Parliament passed each year an Indemnity Act, which excused Nonconformists of any offences against the two original Acts.

Many of them played a large part in the development of the Industrial Revolution, as inventors and as *entrepreneurs*. Because of their emphasis on the Christian virtue of thrift, they made money. Money gave them influence. By 1828, there was a strong body of opinion in Parliament that it was high time to call a spade a spade and wipe the Test and Corporation Acts off the statute book. The hard core of Tories still opposed this; one of the cornerstones of their party was the Established Church of England. Peel agreed with them. He had little option; he was the member for Oxford University, a stronghold of Anglican scholarship. So did the Duke, but then the Duke was an Establishment man to the core. So did Lord Chancellor Eldon, who, as advocate, judge, and minister, had regularly opposed the repeal of laws against both Dissenters and Catholics for thirty years.

Many Whigs supported repeal, either from conviction or from habitual desire to embarrass the Tory Government. What complicated the issue was that Tories from the liberal wing of the party voted with them. It is a good example of the confusion that had begun with the departure of Lord Liverpool after fifteen years of comparative stability. Canning had come and gone. Then Goderich, who had been unable to hold some of the Canningites. Now had come the Duke, who had been happy to see the back of the rest. The Duke did not believe in conciliation – if you did not agree, then you had better go. What was the point of being in a prime minister's cabinet if you were not loyal to its leader and to its beliefs?

The Duke, however, did have a higher loyalty – to carry on the

King's Government. When he saw how much support the motion for repeal had built up, he and Peel decided that it was no longer worth making it a party issue. When the Whig Lord John Russell carried a motion for the repeal of the Test and Corporation Acts, the Government accepted the inevitable, and Nonconformists thereafter enjoyed full civil rights – provided they made a declaration not to 'injure or subvert the Protestant Established Church' (which was the only consolation Lord Eldon got out of it).

Unfortunately, that was not the end of Tory troubles. Peel struck another nerve over the business of the Corn Laws.

Corn Laws were pieces of legislation passed by a Parliament of landowners to protect the pockets of landowners. Landed property was an Englishman's most precious possession. The enjoyment of profit from his property was his most precious right. One of those profits came from the sale of grain – 'corn'. The price of corn rose or fell according to the amount available, that is, according to the goodness or badness of the harvest. So a bad harvest brought low yield, and thus scarcity and high prices. It also meant that foreign corn had to be imported in order to feed the population. (England had ceased to be able to feed itself in the 1770s.) Foreign corn was cheaper. British landowners therefore feared that nobody would buy their own more expensive corn. So a Corn Law was passed in 1815 to ensure that this did not happen. No foreign corn was to be allowed into the country until scarcity had sent the price of English corn up to 80 shillings (£4) a quarter. It kept out foreign corn until the landowners had sold most of their own. Naturally, the only people displeased were the millions who found the price of bread too high.

Naturally, too, there soon appeared reformers who wanted to abolish the Corn Laws and have a free market in the hope of bringing down prices. Among these were the industrialists, who knew that cheaper bread would help to keep at bay the demand for higher wages, and who resented the way the landowners had helped to repeal the Combination Acts, which allowed trade unions to exist. Moreover, it fitted into the whole free-trade movement, which argued for complete freedom of all commercial activity without any of the old-fashioned Government 'regulation'.

Huskisson had thrown his weight against the Corn Laws. Other liberal Tories had done and were doing the same. Peel, with his family business connections, sympathised. But the power of the landed interest was too great. The most the Government could manage – the most it dared manage – was a compromise. In 1828 it produced a Sliding Scale. This enacted that when the price of English corn was high the import duty on foreign corn would be low, and when the price of English corn was low, the import duty would be high. There was a whole table of variations in between. It was not a real victory for either side, but it was a step in the 'right' direction for the free-traders, and it represented another breach in the wall of the old Tory citadel.

The third task which Peel had set himself was to cause him further unpopularity, and at the same time to ensure his immortality. This was his greatest creation – a police force. If there was one thing Englishmen had feared almost as much as a standing army, it was a police force – and for much the same reason. One of the causes of the Civil War in 1642 was Parliament's fear that Charles would turn an army loose upon them. A few years later, Oliver Cromwell really did turn an army loose upon them, and banished them. The experience passed into the national subconscious, and standing armies were ever after viewed with deep suspicion. (This fear was transported, along with the convicts and the emigrants and the refugees, to the colonies in America, where the redcoats became a symbol of oppression, and where, later, the young republic of the United States refused to keep an army in being after winning its war of survival.) Similarly, it was felt that a permanent police force could be used, or rather misused, in the same way; it was an invitation to dictatorship.

English 'gentlemen' prided themselves on their respect for the law, and on their ability to settle their own affairs at local level. Why did distant governments want to poke their noses in? Justices of the Peace and local constables had managed quite well up to now.

Well, perhaps they had – when local gossip and prying eyes were the best detectives; it would no longer suffice in the teeming, smoking, sprawling, bursting cities – of which London was the prime example.

But public prejudice died hard. A parliamentary committee in the eighteen-teens, at a time when a child could be hanged for stealing a loaf of bread and a squadron of cavalry could charge a peaceful crowd, said in its report, with barefaced hypocrisy, 'the police of a free country was to be found in rational and humane laws, in an effective and enlightened magistracy... above all in the moral habits and opinions of the people'.

Peterloo showed that there was a long way to go before England would enjoy an 'enlightened magistracy'; the Caroline Riots in 1820 suggested that the 'moral habits and opinions of the people' left a lot to be desired; and Peel's examination of the penal code proved that the laws of the land were anything but 'rational and humane'.

A police force was the logical next step to what Peel had already done. He had made the courts fit for criminals to be tried in; he had made the prisons fit for humans to be kept in; it was time to make the streets safe for citizens to be out in. Coincidentally, the Duke himself had drafted a memorandum during the Caroline Riots nine years before, advocating the formation of a police force. Peel, when he was Chief Secretary for Ireland, had started the Royal Irish Constabulary. Now he proposed to extend the same principle to the City of London.

But only in London. In 1829 it was as much as he dared do. There was suspicion enough as it was. One dark rumour, indicative of the irrational nature of much of the opposition, suggested that it was all a plot to put the Duke on the throne. Peel persisted, with a modest one thousand constables to begin with (later increased to three thousand). They were put into uniforms, they were trained, and they were paid.

After initial troubles, professionalism was vindicated. Within a decade county police forces were being set up, partly because the Metropolitan force was so successful that large sections of the criminal fraternity had migrated to the provinces. (Still no national force – again that fear of dictatorship.) Peel achieved his niche in legend, and the words 'Peeler' and 'Bobby' passed into the mythology of the language.

If Peel had known this, it might have helped to comfort him during the year 1829, when he was engulfed in a tidal wave of hatred, rage, and invective, not from the opposition, but from the members of his own party. For events now forced him to make a decisive assault upon one of the two last bastions of the party that had so far stood resolute against the force of change. The reasons for that can be summed up in the name of one gifted Irishman.

Daniel O'Connell was that rarity in Ireland – a Catholic country squire of some substance. His was one of the few Catholic families which had managed to hold on to its land. O'Connell had added to it by marrying his cousin, and by inheriting the property of two uncles. He was educated in France, and trained as a lawyer in London. By the 1820s he had a thriving legal practice in his native country. As a man of the law, he disapproved of violence and revolution; he had no time for the tradition of the Bastille and Vinegar Hill (see Chapter 2). He saw no future in plot and terror and the strategy of retaliation. On the face of it, then, he seemed the very last man to lead the Irish to liberty.

He was not even a particularly good landlord. He was content to let his estate continue as 'a model of everything that ought not to be', as one observer wryly put it. That meant that his tenants were allowed to carry on the time-honoured practice of sub-dividing their land among their inheritors. Units became smaller and smaller, and poverty deeper and deeper. Parish priests, whose income was derived from the fees of marriages and christenings and burials, did nothing to improve the situation by their encouragement of early marriage and large families. The landlords who did try to improve the situation knew that, in order to set in motion schemes for modern arable farming or sheep pasture, they had to sweep away scores of postage-stamp potato plots which represented the entire worldly wealth of whole families. Eviction condemned families often to permanent refugee status; there was no alternative accommodation, little wage labour, and next to no industry in nearby towns to provide an alternative livelihood.

The only weapon the tenant had to protect himself was the threat of violence; a timely house-burning or cattle-maiming might make a land-lord think again. It was no use going to law. The laws were Protestant; the forces of order were Protestant; the juries were Protestant; and the judges were Protestant.

There was no protection to be had from the established Church – that was Protestant too. It was also mightily endowed with huge estates, and it demanded a regular tax – the tithe – from every householder, Protestant *and Catholic*. The only comfort a Catholic tenant could usually receive from his own priest, apart from the private sacraments of confession and extreme unction, was a hasty sermon during a chilly Mass conducted under a hedge outside the village.

Crushed by the poverty of his potato plot; bullied by the rent-collector; harassed by the tithe-gatherer; hounded by the forces of order; tied hand and foot by the law – the Irish Catholic tenant evolved his own way of surviving. He ducked his head and he muttered under his breath; he told a tale without actually telling a lie; he worshipped in secret; he met his friends at night, and, fortified by liquor from their illegal still, they donned their masks and crept forth to burn barns and cut sheep's throats and leave crudely-spelt threats nailed to stable doors. When questioned by irate constables, sure they would be only too pleased to help, but unfortunately they knew nothing about anything, at all, at all.

When estate managers communicated the latest bad news to their absentee landlords in England, it confirmed 'gentlemen' in their view that the Irish were a nation of boorish, ignorant, lying, lawless, bog-swilling Papists who would bite the hand that fed them. It was more than mere prejudice on their part; Ireland, violence, and Catholicism struck deep chords of ancient communal dread. False claimants to the English throne had based themselves in Ireland on and off since the fifteenth century. King Charles, on the eve of the Civil War, had been on the point, it was believed, of bringing over the Army of Ireland to crush the noble patriots of Parliament. Foreign enemies since the days of Philip of Spain had plotted to use Ireland as a springboard for invasion. Ireland was the last refuge of the wicked Catholics, who would never be content until they had brought back the Pope and the priesthood and the mumbo-jumbo of incense and Latin chanting; superstitions such as indulgences and prostrations before statues of saints and prayers for the dead; armies of lustful monks and rabid nuns; above all the dreaded piles of firewood for the condemned heretic.

Liberal-minded men – and their numbers were mercifully growing – who thought that it was time for a different approach, and who tried to persuade Parliament to pass measures that would grant civil rights for Catholics, ran into this wall of outrage, suspicion, and fear.

It did not seem likely that a wealthy Irish landlord lawyer who abhorred violence could do much about remedying the situation. Yet it was O'Connell's feat to give the millions of poor Irish tenants a leader, a voice, a cause, a purpose, and a weapon.

For a start, he looked the part – tall, well built, handsome, with a touch of flamboyance in his dress and in his manner, and a gift for popular appeal. His nickname – 'Swaggering Dan' – fitted him like a glove. He had a keen eye, a sharp wit, and a ready tongue (he is credited with coining the nickname 'Orange' Peel when Peel was Secretary for Ireland). Above all, he had a voice – the lungs of an opera singer, and the spellbinding power of a hypnotist. Open-air meetings of thousands were the breath of life to him. Irish himself to the core, he could out-blarney all of them – and in Gaelic too if the mood took him.

To this awesome armoury of gifts, he added his wide legal experience all over Ireland, and his knowledge of English public life from his training at Lincoln's Inn.

As O'Connell saw it, the Irish were wrong to continue living in the past. There was going to be no romantic return of a Stuart Catholic king; there was going to be no miraculous elimination of the Protestant bullies who had snatched the best land in the sixteenth and seventeenth centuries. There was nothing to be gained from sitting round the peat fires and singing mournful songs about a glorious Gaelic heritage from the mists of the Dark Ages.

Nor was there any future in mindless violence: there was no overall purpose to it; it could never win; and it would serve not to loosen the grip of the Protestant Ascendancy, but to tighten it.

The practical answer was to carry the fight into England, to the House of Commons itself. That was the seat of power; it was only from the seat of power that an effective remedy would come. If Irish Catholics could win civil rights, and get into Parliament in sufficient numbers, they could work to get the hated tithe abolished, and, given time, they could gnaw away at the Act of Union, which had abolished the Irish Parliament in 1800.

With this in mind, O'Connell founded the Catholic Association in 1823. It was dedicated to those three causes – civil rights for Catholics (or Catholic Emancipation), liberating the Irish Catholic from paying tithe to the minority Anglican Church, and abolishing the Act of Union, thereby giving Ireland control over its own destiny.

Running a political organisation needed funds, and this was where O'Connell showed his genius for appeal to poor Irishmen and his skill at management. Most political clubs hitherto had been largely for men of substantial means, and had been therefore shunned by 'the people'. What O'Connell did was to convince ordinary men that political activity was within their grasp and within their pockets. He proposed to charge one penny a month. The money would be used to finance publicity, nationwide tours and meetings, petitions, and so on. Such was the trust he built up (among a nation of tenants who loathed rent) that by mid-decade the 'Catholic Rent' was bringing in hundreds of pounds a week.

That, however, was only part of it; that was the cause. The purpose was to provide the Association with a means of moving forward. Some of the rent was set aside to buy plots of land, which were worth forty shillings (£2) a year. The only concession that the Irish had won during the last hundred years had been in 1793, when Pitt had given Irish Catholics the right to vote – on the same basis as the English. That meant that the voting qualification was the same in Ireland as it was in England. In the English counties, a man could vote if he was a 'forty-shilling freeholder' – that is, if he owned land worth a rent of forty shillings a year. So, now, could an Irishman. English landowners had slept easily in their beds up to now, knowing that nine Irishmen out of ten could barely afford a new pair of shoes, never mind a plot of land worth forty shillings.

Thanks to O'Connell, they now could. The plan was simple: as the Rent came in, as much as possible would be used to buy plots of land each worth forty shillings. Irish Catholics would be installed on these plots. In time there would be enough of them to swing the vote at a Parliamentary election. If it could be done in one constituency, it could be done in others. The Irish saw that O'Connell was putting, at last, a real weapon in their hands, and one that could be used to fight the English on their own ground. The money came pouring in. By the end of the decade, the Catholic Rent was bringing in nearly £1,000 a week. O'Connell's legal mind had found a way of forging a lever that could be inserted under the English Establishment.

The Establishment woke up to the danger, and reacted in the

customary way by declaring the Catholic Association illegal. O'Connell promptly founded a new one, called it 'The New Catholic Association', and carried on as before. The authorities gave up chasing him round the houses.

The Association (the 'New' one!) in 1826 felt itself strong enough to contest an election. In Waterford, the Beresford family, which had held the seat for so long that they had come to consider it private property, was defeated by a Protestant liberal supported by O'Connell's new block of forty-shilling freeholders.

Then, in May, 1828, William Huskisson resigned. In the re-shuffle, the Duke appointed a man called Vesey-Fitzgerald as the new President of the Board of Trade. By Parliamentary custom, Vesey-Fitzgerald resigned his seat and offered himself to his constituency for re-election. His constituency was County Clare in Ireland. Vesey-Fitzgerald was a man of known liberal views; he had held the seat for some time, and he was well liked locally, even by the Catholics.

After a certain amount of hesitation, O'Connell stood against him. His lawyer's training had enabled him to spot a loophole in the Establishment's defences. The law said, as everyone knew, that a Roman Catholic could not become a member of Parliament. But there was no law that said that he could not offer himself as a candidate.

Vesey-Fitzgerald, to repeat, was a liberal-minded man who favoured Emancipation, and he was also a kindly and popular landlord. Naturally too he had the whole weight of the Protestant Ascendancy behind him. He still lost. For the five days of polling, the Catholic freeholders, egged on by timely hints from their priests, came pouring into the town of Ennis, where the election was being conducted. In a riot of shamrock and green, 2,054 votes were recorded for O'Connell against only 1,075 for Vesey-Fitzgerald.

O'Connell had tipped onto Peel's plate the hottest of all potatoes (appropriate enough, coming from Ireland). A Roman Catholic was now the elected member for County Clare, according to due process of law. O'Connell knew – Peel knew, the Duke knew, everyone knew – that, if it could be done once, it could be done scores of times. Excitement rose to fever pitch; the (New) Association gained yet more members; the Rent soared to £2,000 a week.

In the House of Commons, liberals of both parties hammered away at Emancipation. If Nonconformists had been correctly granted civil rights, why not Catholics? The argument, in logic, was unanswerable. The Duke and Peel had always opposed it, but by the end of 1828 they were forced to change their minds. Both had served as Secretary for Ireland; both understood the pressures. Both came to the conclusion that if full civil rights were not granted there would be civil war. The Duke was a soldier, and nobody defended a position more doggedly; but, as a soldier, he also appreciated the value of withdrawal when a position had become untenable. Changes of direction never troubled him in the way they did politicians; to him it was far more important that the King's Government be continued. So, when Peel offered to resign as the honourable thing to do, he overruled him, and said that it was their duty to see the Emancipation Bill through both Houses. He also needed Peel to help him break down the opposition of the King.

George IV was as loyal to his coronation oath – to uphold the Church of England – as his father had been, but fortunately he was not quite so stubborn. By the New Year, Peel and the Duke had won, though the King, in a petulant rearguard action, had insisted that the Catholic Association ('New' or otherwise) should be suppressed. The Government added two more stings to the tail of their Catholic Relief Act of April, 1829.

The positive terms of the act removed all barriers to Catholics in public life. Henceforth, only four positions were to be closed to them – Lord Lieutenant of Ireland, Lord Chancellor, Regent, and King. They were no longer required to accept Anglican communion before being allowed to serve; a simple oath of allegiance was now enough. Peel got the bill through the Commons, and the Duke saw it through the Lords, with his insistence that the only alternative was civil war. (Lord Eldon still voted against it.)

But the Government had been backed into a corner; they had no intention of allowing the same thing to happen again. O'Connell had beaten them to it by dissolving the Catholic Association, but the Act included a clause that gave the Lord Lieutenant the power to suppress any society he considered dangerous. Secondly, something had to be done to outflank O'Connell's new army of forty-shilling freeholders.

This was achieved by the simple device of raising the voting qualification by 500 per cent, to £10. It cut the Irish vote by over 85 per cent. In a final spat of smallmindedness, Parliament forced O'Connell to stand again for Clare under the new terms of the Act.

He was re-elected, but the bad grace with which the concessions had been granted, and the spiteful small print, did nothing to improve relations between English and Irish. It certainly did not make the Irish feel grateful.

It made the old guard of the Tory party furious. The Duke, because of his enormous military reputation, was unassailable. Besides, unpopularity never bothered him, and he had a lofty disregard for stupid men who could not see his common-sense point of view. Or, as one observer put it, he had a social contempt for his intellectual equals, and an intellectual contempt for his social equals. As a member of the House of Lords, the Duke could not be removed. But Peel could. A torrent of abuse descended upon his head; his action in giving civil rights to the hated Catholics became 'The Great Betrayal'; he was forced to resign his seat at Oxford University.

The backbench Tory country gentlemen saw their citadel of power crumbling further. The rot had been started by the passing of Liverpool, perhaps even earlier by the brash upstart Canning and his free-trading partner, Huskisson. Then had come another split between those who wished to accept Canning as Prime Minister and those who had refused to serve under him. He had been succeeded by the feeble, weeping Goderich, and then by a stiff-necked ex-soldier who took advice from nobody. During that time, they – the 'true' Tories – had been forced to accept the repeal of the Test and Corporation Acts, the Sliding Scale in the Corn Laws, and the sinister constables in the City of London. Now the way was open for rich Papists to buy their way into the very centre of power, and it had been achieved by those spineless members for rotten boroughs who had voted obediently as Peel and the Duke had told them to.

Suddenly, the old Tories saw a good reason for supporting the cause of Parliamentary reform, which had been dear to so many Whigs for so many years. If they could get a batch of the despised borough seats abolished, and have them redistributed to the counties, where true-blue country gentlemen held sway, it would help to stiffen their resistance to any further lunacy which their leaders might dream up. Put another way, it now seemed quite possible that the reform of Parliament, which they had opposed as a matter of instinct and blind faith for decades, could, if properly handled, turn out not to weaken their position, but strengthen it.

This issue – the reform of Parliament – touched the last ditch, the innermost keep, of the Tory fortress. The Tories had won power in the General Election of 1784, and, with one short break in 1806, had kept it ever since. It had seemed obvious that they should maintain the system that had given them that power; so for forty-five years they had consistently resisted moves by the Whigs to change it. But the 1820s had witnessed a steady weakening of their position. One leader after another had passed on – Castlereagh, Liverpool, Canning, Goderich, and now Peel. In one debate after another the old Tories' authority had been successfully challenged – free trade, corn laws, Nonconformists, police, Catholics – and by members of their own party. Rebels and turncoats, maybe, but they had called themselves Tories.

The more liberal of them – the self-styled Canningites – had since gone over to the Whigs. Now the right wing of the party – the country backbenchers – were questioning the value of continuing to defend a system that every English gentleman had once considered perfect.

Its age was certainly a splendid recommendation. Nothing had altered in it for 140 years. In a century of rapid change like the twentieth, this might be seen as a major fault; in the eighteenth and early nineteenth centuries, it was considered a prime virtue. Such was the English political system that anything which had been 'there' for a long time had a correspondingly greater chance of remaining 'there' for even longer. The more entrenched its position, the greater therefore its value. Chancellor Thurlow, who had served in Pitt's Cabinet, once said to a leading Methodist that he, Thurlow, had nothing against Methodism itself, but he preferred the Anglican Church only because it was 'established'. 'Get yourselves established,' he said, 'and I shall be for you too.'

The nature of the English Parliament had been 'established' in 1688, when the 'Glorious Revolution' had turned Catholic James II off his throne, and secured from his successor, the Dutch Protestant William

III, an assurance that he would rule in conjunction with the elected representatives of the English people – or rather of the English people who had supported him. An Act of Parliament guaranteed the validity of William's claim to the throne (no more of the Stuart 'Divine Right of Kings'), and another laid it down that there should be an election to a new Parliament at least every three years.

The rich landowners, and the wealthy gentry, who had secured this triumph of their interests, never ceased to be pleased with their success. England was their country; between them they owned most of it; and from now on it was going to be administered according to the wishes of the men they elected to Parliament (usually themselves). The King himself had given a solemn promise to that effect. Small wonder they called it the 'Glorious' Revolution. Small wonder, too, that, throughout the eighteenth century, gentlemen looked back at it with fond eyes, and saw it as the foundation of their 'liberty'. The English system, the 'constitution', was therefore perfect; it did not need changing. Anyone who said it did was a landless outsider, a rogue, a Stuart, or a Papist. If more justification should be needed, one had only to point to other countries in Europe, where England was held up as an example of 'liberty' to benighted peoples who had no parliament at all. Our system of government, said English gentlemen, was the envy of the civilised world.

However, it was not without its critics, and a modern observer would have found plenty of reasons for agreeing with them.

In theory, there were two Members of Parliament elected for each county and two for each borough. When a general election was called, the returning officer of each constituency was instructed to hold a free election, and to return the man who had received a majority of the votes cast in that constituency. A general election was held every seven years. It had been every three until 1715, when the Jacobite Rebellion – to put the Stuart James Edward on the throne – had so worried the Whig Government of George I that, in the interests of stability, they had changed the figure of three to seven. Alternatively, there could also be an election on the death of the monarch.

So far, so good. That was the theory. Strong, simple, stable, democratic, and effective. Hence, therefore – to repeat – it was 'perfect'; that was how it was presented.

The reality – the practice – was rather different. To begin with, the balance between town and country was unequal. There were 409 borough members as against only 84 county members. (It was the blind loyalty of the borough members in supporting the Duke over Ireland which had so annoyed the 'county' men, and led them to consider the possible profit to be gained in trying to reform Parliament and secure more seats for the counties.) The situation might have been justifiable if the 409 had represented a majority of the population, but they did not. It is here that the most glaring faults are shown of a system which had not been substantially changed for centuries. The fortunes of towns fluctuate over the years; some grow and some decline. Others graduate from the status of mere villages. The process had been gradual in the sixteenth and seventeenth centuries, but the eighteenth and early nineteenth had witnessed the Industrial Revolution. Cities were mushrooming in places undreamed of by the statesmen of previous ages – South Wales, the Midlands, the North, southern Scotland. Centres of population with tens of thousands of inhabitants had no member of Parliament – Sheffield, for instance, Bolton, Bradford, Birmingham, Manchester, Halifax. Conversely, boroughs with declining numbers still boasted two. The Commission of Inquiry unearthed (almost literally) boroughs which had voters in single figures, such as Gatton in Surrey, which had six. Old Sarum in Wiltshire had none at all, yet Pitt's father had sat for Old Sarum. In one notorious constituency, not only were there no voters; there was no borough – the town of Dunwich on the Suffolk coast had slipped off the edge under the water – yet there was an Honourable Member for Dunwich.

These – the Old Sarums and the Gattons – were the much-quoted cases, the shocking examples. These were the ones that were dubbed 'rotten boroughs', by the men of the time. Yet many a British statesman got his start in a rotten borough, or its variant, a pocket borough – both Pitts, Peel, Gladstone, and others.

Indeed, the greater scandal, overall, lay with these 'pocket boroughs'. These were constituencies that lay entirely within the property of a rich nobleman, and so were 'in his pocket'. Whether the population was two or two thousand, he therefore had complete control over the choice of MP. It was therefore either his son or another member of his family, or some dependent client: whoever it was, he had absolute power to dictate that member's political allegiance. Pocket boroughs were so much regarded as private property that they could be, and were, bought and sold as such.

A third variety was the 'nomination borough'. This might not be fully owned by the local magnate, but he owned enough of it, or he wielded enough local power and influence, for his right to 'nominate' the member not to be seriously questioned.

So one section of the borough system contained places where there were few if any voters; another comprised towns where there was no choice of candidate. Where there was a choice, and a respectable population, the 'system' was still clogged. In a sense, there was no 'system' at all, inasmuch as there was no uniform pattern of voting. A few boroughs allowed all adult males to participate. Others confined it to the ratepayers, or to the freemen of the borough, or to the members of the corporation. Others again said it was the right only of householders – those who 'walloped a pot' in their own hearth. Hence the famous 'potwallopers', who found their way into scores of school textbooks. And so it went on.

In the counties it was different: the vote went to any man who held the freehold title to land with a rental value of forty shillings (£2) a year – a fact of which O'Connell had recently made everyone only too well aware. Overall it has been calculated that, in 1830, about one in twenty of adult males had the vote – and of course, no woman. So much for simplicity and democracy.

However, economics now took a hand. The vote, it was agreed, was a rare commodity. Rarity at once gave it a market value. A man's vote became worth something; political managers were prepared to pay for it, so in a sense those few who did have the vote had more power than they would have had in a true democracy. Enormous sums of money changed hands during elections – in straight bribes, in entertainment costs, in hiring gangs of bully boys to 'persuade', in ensuring, one way or another, that support was placed where the rich men wanted it.

They usually had plenty of time to do it, because polling lasted several days, and was the excuse for party-going, drinking, rioting, and general shenanigans. In Ireland, deaths were not uncommon – and most of their elections were uncontested!

Finally, elections were open; there was no secret ballot. One could not swear undying support of one candidate to avoid the bully boys, and then go and vote for the other. A man mounted the hustings and said it out loud.

This was the 'constitution' which was held to be the envy of the civilised world. This was the political system under which Britain had risen to be the foremost industrial power in the world, had built the most powerful navy in the world, had amassed the biggest empire in the world, and under which she had just beaten the mightiest military dictatorship in Europe. If she had done all that with a corrupt system, what might she have done with a virtuous one?

An answer to that would probably be that it worked, corruption and all, reasonably well for most of its life, and that it should not be judged by the standards of a later age.

It was never intended to be a pure democracy. Just because Members of Parliament might speak for the people in their constituencies, it did not follow that they had to be chosen by those people. Parents spoke for their children; they were not chosen by them, yet they unquestionably had their children's interests at heart. In any case, Parliament did not represent people; it represented property. It represented 'interests' – the landed interest, the Indian interest, the sugar island interest, or whatever. Anybody who made money sooner or later bought land; it gave him an 'interest' in the country (to use the word in a slightly different way). Nobody was entitled – so the thinking ran – to have a say in the running of the country unless he physically owned a part of it. It was none of his business. To hand over a share of power to every unpropertied, illiterate oaf and yokel was to invite revolution and anarchy.

This in turn explained the open vote. The right to vote – the franchise – was not a right; it was a responsibility. The men who did have a right were the non-voters; they had a right to know how the men with the vote voted, because in a sense the voters represented them. Here was the representation.

Finally, it is a mistake for modern observers to assume that a general election was held for the purpose of changing the Government. On the contrary; it was held in order to *strengthen* the Government. No eighteenth-century government lost an election. Naturally – they had the full weight of royal favour behind them, to say nothing of the Treasury. Governments, when they were changed, were changed by the King choosing a different set of ministers.

However, the world was moving on. Just as the old system of farming could not cope with the rise in population, and the old methods in industrial production could not meet the colossal rise in demand, so the old Parliamentary system was proving unable to withstand the pressures of a new century.

There had been attempts to reform Parliament on and off for over fifty years. Pitt had tried in 1785. Numerous Whig petitions had failed, largely because of the scare created by the French Revolution. The war had necessitated a closing of ranks among the ruling classes in the interests of sheer survival and of patriotism. After the war, the Tory Government had been too obsessed with putting down any form of radicalism to consider for a moment such a ghastly prospect. But as the 1820s advanced, the movement gained momentum, fuelled periodically by slumps and bad harvests and high prices.

By 1830, it was reaching crisis point. The Whigs did not want to let in every Tom, Dick, and Harry any more than the Tories did; they owned just as much land too. But they argued that the Industrial Revolution had brought into being another form of property, another 'interest'. This interest now had to be represented. The men who ran the new industrial towns deserved to be admitted into the citadel of power; the country needed their money, and the Government needed their support. Once in, these new men would help the rulers to close the door against the Toms, Dicks, and Harrys, just as it had been closed before. There was to be no question of opening the constitution to 'democracy'. All the Whigs wanted to do was to make a last little adjustment, give a final polish to a wonderful system – to make a 'perfect' constitution even more perfect.

The Tories were not so sure, but then they were not so united. There were the genuine liberals of the party who thought that the Whigs had a point. Many of these – the Canningites – had already crossed the floor of the House to join the Opposition. Others stayed out of loyalty to old Tory principles. Many stayed because, as members for rotten and pocket boroughs, they saw their political future at risk. It was because of their stubbornness that the Tory 'county' members began to swing round to the cause of reform as a means of breaking the majority of the boroughs in the number of seats they held.

The Duke's Government stood out against it. For the Duke, the issue was stark and clear. He had spent most of his active life fighting against the results of 'democratic' experiments – the Terror, Jacobin plots, war, invasion threats, and more war. Far and away the greatest evil to afflict the world in the last forty years was the Revolution. After over twenty years of war, the cancer had been halted, and now stupid, irresponsible men wanted to give it a chance to spread again. Reform Parliament, said the Duke – tamper with the strongest and finest political system in Europe, the only one which had stood up to France – and you opened the way to revolution and anarchy.

If 1830 had not been so eventful, the Tory Government might have struggled on a while longer under the Duke's definite, if unpopular, rule. But everything that happened seemed to point only one way. In July, there was a revolution in Paris, and the Bourbon King was overthrown. Taking their cue from the French, the Belgians revolted against their Dutch overlords in August. Before the year was out, Poland had risen against their masters in Russia; Italian states had struck to free themselves from the yoke of Austria; and a rash of revolutions had broken out in Germany.

Closer to home, O'Connell, by no means content with his success in County Clare, had announced the opening of a massive new campaign to repeal the Act of Union. Closer still, the agricultural labourers of southern England, driven to despair by despicable wages and grinding poverty and savage game laws, had gone on the rampage.

In June, King George IV had died; Prinny was gone at last – totally unmourned. He was succeeded by his younger brother, the Duke of Clarence, to be crowned as William IV. The new King had no great intellectual or moral distinction, and was a thoroughly, and typically, dull Hanoverian. He had spent a worthy, if undistinguished, life in the Navy, and had fathered ten illegitimate children, all by the same woman – an actress, whom he had subsequently abandoned. At a time when royalty in England had been the inspiration of endless gossip and smutty story, and royalty in Europe was under siege or in flight from revolutionaries, William scarcely added lustre to the name of king.

In the general election that followed, the 'system' once again returned the Government, though weaker by fifty seats. The fact that losses had been so drastic was an indication of the charged atmosphere in which the election was conducted.

The Duke was still Prime Minister, but not for long. By now, the matter of Parliamentary reform superseded every other. It was no longer a question of whether or not; it was only a question of how much.

The Duke characteristically laid his cards on the table. No Tory Government of which he was Prime Minister, he said, would bring forward any measure for the reform of Parliament. Moreover, he continued, he would see it as his duty to oppose any such measure introduced by anybody else.

That brought the House down about his ears, or at any rate the House of Commons down about his hapless colleagues' ears. The Ministry finally announced its resignation in November, and the new King asked the elderly leader of the Whigs, Lord Grey, to form a government.

The battle lines were now drawn, and everyone prepared himself for a titanic struggle in the New Year. Each side had clearly stated its case, and was clearly determined to fight to the last ditch to secure its victory. In the country, an entire population, sensing the drama, held its breath. Radical campaigners, who had lobbied and agitated for decades – the Places and the Cobbetts and the O'Connells – wondered whether an aristocratic debating society like Parliament could ever produce the sort of democratic ruling body that they had in mind.

The two parties could not be further apart: the Tories said that there would be a revolution if Parliament was to be reformed; the Whigs said that there would be a revolution if it was not.

CHAPTER NINE

Finality Jack
1831–35

On 1 March, 1831, Lord John Russell rose in the House of Commons to present the Government's proposals for the Reform of Parliament. An aristocrat (third son of the Duke of Bedford), privately educated, a stalwart of the Establishment, he had nevertheless identified himself with the cause of reform since 1819. He was one of those Whigs who sensed that concession, properly timed and properly gauged, would draw the sting of Radical agitation and so avoid the ghastly prospect of revolution. It would be a final adjustment, a last touch, to the already perfect constitution. Once it had been achieved, there would be no further need of change. The Whigs would therefore have gained the credit for having made the perfect constitution even more perfect. This philosophy earned the diminutive Russell the nickname of 'Finality Jack'.

The Whigs may have seen it as a moderate measure; the Tories most emphatically did not. When Russell read out the names of all the boroughs that were to lose their seats – to be 'disfranchised' – he was greeted with laughter; he surely could not be serious. When the Tories realised that he was in earnest, their reaction was vociferous, and blended with the noisy protest of many Radicals outside Parliament, who suspected that it was some kind of Whig trick. When, however, the Radicals saw how bitterly the Tories were fighting against it, they decided that the Bill could not be all bad, and swung behind the Whigs. (This, naturally, is a simplification. Not every Radical supported the Bill; many working-class agitators had little idea what the terms were; and there was certainly no 'alliance' between Whigs and Radicals.

Indeed, the Whigs were still in the process of hanging and transporting the leaders of the Labourers' Revolt. And, as has been indicated, there were Tory country gentlemen who were not going to be sorry to see the back of some rotten boroughs.)

For the Bill – any bill – to become law, it had to pass three readings in the Commons and three in the Lords, before it went up to the King for his formal consent. Such was the fierce interest generated by this issue that every step in the passage of the Bill was watched with pinpoint urgency throughout. All three groups involved had committed everything to it. The Whigs had waged the election on it, and had declared that it was the only alternative to revolution. The Tories fought it tooth and nail, because they believed that it would *cause* revolution. The Radicals found themselves caught up in the general hopes of the nation that the Bill would reveal the Promised Land, that opening Parliament to 'democracy' would open the way to all the social reforms that city and country alike so badly needed. The excitement became self-generating; among the general population, what little knowledge there had been became clouded by fierce yearning, and the Radicals, swept along in the tide, allowed hopes to replace doubts and misgivings.

On 23 March, the Bill was given its second reading in a House fuller than anyone could remember. At three o'clock in the morning, in nail-biting tension, it passed by one vote. However, at the third reading – the 'committee' stage, when it was considered clause by clause – the Tories defeated it. Lord Grey, the Prime Minister, at once asked the King to dissolve Parliament and call another general election – which, after some hesitation and persuasion, William agreed to do.

The election was held in an atmosphere of tremendous excitement. Rarely, if ever, had there been a contest in which the issue was so single, simple, and stark. As the Whigs put it in their rallying cry, it was 'the Bill, the whole Bill, and nothing but the Bill'. The country replied with utmost clarity: the Whigs were returned with a considerably enhanced majority.

On 24 June, therefore, Lord John Russell rose to present a second Bill, not very different from the first. Because of the comfortable Whig majority, it passed all three readings, though the Tories haggled for three months in committee.

Their lordships, however, took only five days to reject it, on 8 October, by a majority of 41.

The effect on the country was shattering. After months of tension, eager interest, and suspense – the first bill passing by one vote, the general election, the new Bill, the marathon committee session – their hopes were in ruins.

Muffled bells were tolled. Two newspapers appeared in mourning. More alarmingly, riots broke out in several cities. Derby jail was sacked. Nottingham Castle was burned. Peers who had voted against the Bill were hissed and assaulted in the streets. Bishops, who had voted *en bloc* against the Bill, were singled out for special attention; several palaces suffered the flames. In Bristol the Mansion House was attacked (another casualty in the fires was Madame Tussaud's Waxworks).

Radical leaders were accused of orchestrating the violence. Whether or not the charges were unjust, the violence was clear evidence to the Duke and his die-hard Tories that revolution was just around the corner, and that the success of the Bill would bring it closer still. They felt that much more justified in their continued opposition.

The only person who could bring the House of Lords to heel was the King. He had the right to create new peers. He could therefore create enough Whig peers to swamp the Tory majority, but it meant creating over 40. William was horrified at such a figure; it would cheapen and lower the dignity of the whole House. Instead he persuaded Grey to try again with another Bill, with perhaps some modifications that might appeal to those waverers in the middle who did not wish to push the matter to extremities.

In December, 1831, Lord John Russell presented his third Bill, modified accordingly. It passed all three readings in the Commons, and went up to their lordships. It scraped past a second reading by nine votes, but in committee the Tories defeated the Government on an amendment that completely altered the Bill's complexion.

Grey now had only one card to play; he asked the King to create forty-odd new Whig peers. William refused to go beyond twenty. Grey and the entire Cabinet resigned, with some relief.

The problem was neither solved nor shelved. No Tory leader – not even the Duke – could form a government, and, while the negotiations were going on, the Commons passed a vote of confidence in Grey's ministry. In the country at large, the tension was at its height. Business life was being upset; the Radical Francis Place was advocating a run on banks to bring pressure to bear on the Duke – 'to stop the Duke, go for gold'. Liverpool Stock Exchange closed. Other leaders were suggesting a tax strike. It never rains but it pours; there were outbreaks of cholera in London and the north-east seaports. There had to be a resolution of the problem, or Whigs and Tories alike would begin to fear for the peace of the whole nation.

Grey and his Cabinet therefore were reinstated, and Grey set himself to wring out of the King a promise to create enough new Whig peers to secure the passage of the Bill through the Lords. William pointed out that it was ridiculous to try to pass a bill to abolish a batch of nomination boroughs in the Commons by means of creating a batch of nomination peers in the Lords. Grey insisted that the overriding priority was to get the Bill through, in the interests of law and order. William at last, and very reluctantly, gave way, and told Grey that he could have as many peers as he needed. He was offering the Prime Minister a blank cheque.

In the event, it did not become necessary to use it. The Duke came to the King's rescue. To preserve the King's peace of mind, and to maintain the dignity of the House of Lords (and, incidentally, to keep the Tory majority there intact), the Duke withdrew his opposition. The Tories might lose this battle, reasoned the Duke, but losing a battle was not the end of the world, as he knew better than anybody. There would be other battles, and when they came the Tory party in the Lords would still be there to fight them – with their majority still in place. When the Bill was presented for its final reading, he and most of the Tory hard-line peers left the chamber. Only twenty-two stalwarts remained to record their vote against it. The Bill received the Royal Assent on 7 June, 1832, and so became law.

By its terms, 55 old boroughs with fewer than 2,000 inhabitants lost both their seats. One, Higham Ferrers, which had only one seat, lost that too. A further 30 boroughs with two seats each, and fewer than 4,000 inhabitants, lost one of them. One oddity, Weymouth and Melcombe Regis, which had four members, lost two. That provided 143 seats for redistribution.

Of that total, 130 were split between the counties and new boroughs – 65 each. (Here, no doubt, was the Tory county interest fighting to cut back the imbalance between county and borough.) Among the boroughs, two seats were awarded to each of 22 larger new towns; 21 received one each. That left 13: 8 went to Scotland, and 5 to Ireland.

So much for the re-distribution of seats. However much the Act's critics might complain, it had made a move in the right direction. It was not so obvious in the matter of the franchise, the right to vote.

In the boroughs, all the old, peculiar, and downright eccentric qualifications were removed, and replaced by one that was simple and universal. Henceforth, a man had the vote if he was a householder of property worth at least £10 per year. In the counties, the forty-shilling freeholder remained, but there were added two more categories. Land held on a long lease of a minimum of £10 per year qualified the tenant for a vote, as did land held on a short lease of at least £50 per year. Finally, there was to be a register kept of all those entitled to vote in each constituency, and polling was to be restricted to only two successive days.

The parties and toasts and bonfires up and down the country celebrated the victory rather than the progress. When the Radicals sobered up, they began to see that the 'Great Reform Act' was a very mixed blessing.

For a start, the total number of people now eligible to vote had gone up by only about a half, from 435,000 to 652,000 – in a population of 16,000,000. Indeed, the abolition of the old franchises and new residence rules had caused about 80,000 people to *lose* the vote. Borough electorates were now mostly bigger, but they were still manageable; bribery would be more expensive, but it could still be done. And events were to show that it was still considered worthwhile. The arrival of the voting register was to give more opportunity for sharp practice in the adding (and removing) of 'qualified' names. There was no provision for a secret ballot, so the scope for intimidation remained.

More important, the Act did not recognise the rights of the individual; it merely modified the rights of property. Every qualification to vote was based on owning or renting some. A house worth £10 a year may not sound much in the twenty-first century, but it represented modest affluence in 1832; the majority of humble city houses were worth considerably less than that. Indeed the figure of £10 was chosen precisely in order to *exclude* a large number of householders.

In effect the only beneficiaries were the upper middle class, and they, having been admitted to the citadel of power, proved just as ready to repel boarders as the original garrison. The Whigs had done exactly what they had set out to do – make concessions to the rising industrial interest, cream off the head of the political opposition, and add it to the strength of the Establishment. They also claimed to have headed off a revolution.

The Tories did not see it that way at all. To the Tories it was the thin end of the wedge; what had been done once could be done again. Parliament, they said, had not seen the last of reform movements. 'I was unwilling to open a door,' said Peel, 'which I saw no prospect of being able to close.'

As for the Radicals and the people in general, it was a bitter awakening. They were the ones who had done the dangerous work of agitation that had contributed to the general sense of urgency in which the Act had been passed, and in so doing had risked the full rigour of the law, and they were the ones who had benefited the least. Their rage and frustration were to have full expression in the two decades to come.

The Whigs, naturally, were pleased, and relieved. They had reformed Parliament, and they had done it without a revolution. Lord John Russell – 'Finality Jack' – and his colleagues could now regard the problem as solved, and could turn to other pressing matters.

First was the question of education. In 1833 the Government, as a sort of sop to the educational reformers, decreed an annual grant of £20,000 for the purpose. This may seem a ridiculous figure in the twenty-first century, when the salary of one head teacher can dwarf it, but it must be set against what had gone before, and absolutely nothing had gone before.

There was no national educational system. There was no Government funding, no Government training of teachers, no inspection of standards, no subsidised building – nothing. The only Government policy was to have no policy; it was regarded as interference with the liberty of the individual to tell him whether or how he should educate his children. If they had, they would have brought down upon their heads the wrath of one religious body or another; most men (women were not expected to have views on this; they were supposed to be at home looking after the children) could not conceive the idea of teaching without its being based on religious instruction. The few Radicals who dared to suggest that teaching should be kept separate from religion were lumped with the Jews, Papists, Freemasons, atheists, and other pernicious cranks who no doubt devoured their young at the full moon. When the £20,000 finally was granted, it was shared between two religious societies, and it was to be for building purposes only.

That was not to say that there was no education at all. There was, but it was haphazard, piecemeal, stuffy, and private. Many villages had a 'Dame School', where rural mites sat at the feet of some moralising, finger-wagging old auntie who might, if she was strict, hammer in the alphabet, the catechism, and the Ten Commandments, and if she was good, basic reading and arithmetic. During the eighteenth and early nineteenth centuries the numbers grew of religious charity schools and Sunday schools, where the syllabus would be restricted by definition. Towns had independent grammar schools, which demanded modest fees and so put themselves way beyond the reach of most working people. In and around these was a kaleidoscope of varied institutions – private, public, charity, fee-paying, and free – all run by individuals according to the dictates of their character, their ability, and their pocket. And their religious beliefs. The education offered could vary from the worthless to the brilliant.

Richer families depended on governesses and private tutors, and, later, the public schools, where the curriculum was Latin and Greek, and more Latin and Greek. It was once decreed by the Lord Chancellor that it was illegal for such schools to teach other subjects. (Lord Eldon – who else?)

In the light of this, a grant of £20,000 does not seem much of a national remedy, but it was not intended to be. It was intended to shut up the agitators. It is only in hindsight that it can be seen as the first step in the long and painful way towards a national, universal, free educational system.

The Great Reform Act was also intended to shut up the agitators; only afterwards could it be seen that Peel had been right, and that it was the first in what was going to be a tiresome series. It was the same with the first education grant. Like it or not, the Government was going to be drawn, inexorably, into the business of educating its subjects.

In the same way, the year 1833 saw the first in what proved to be a long series of laws regulating the conditions in which those subjects spent their working day.

Sincere, honest, respectable, God-fearing citizens saw nothing wrong with work. It had got them, and their country, where they were; it had made the Industrial Revolution possible. No man, or woman, should be afraid of work; it was the way to bettering themselves. By the same token, there was nothing wrong with children working; it was training for the future, it was good for the character, and, as everyone knew, the Devil made work for idle hands. So education was a very questionable blessing. All teaching and no work made Jack not only a naughty boy but a rebellious boy who asked too many questions.

Most people had no idea what sort of conditions young Jack worked in; they rarely had cause to go near the big industrial cities. If they did, they would arrive on the streets hours after the factory working day had begun. Nor would they have any reason, or wish, to visit the festering slums in which young Jack lived, or the hammering, sweltering factories where he laboured upwards of twelve hours a day.

So ignorance was one obstacle that the reformers had to overcome. Lack of interest was another. Landowners, who, in spite of the new Reform Act, still made up the majority of the House of Commons, did not find factory working conditions an absorbing subject. Besides, factories were dirty, and spoiled the countryside, and factory-owners wanted to abolish the Corn Laws. It would only be worth voting for an improvement in working conditions if it put another spoke in the owners' wheels; it would serve them right for trying to depress the market in corn.

Unexpected resistance to factory reform often came from the parents themselves, who regarded their children as a necessary source of income, especially as adults were often subject to seasonal unemployment. Factory-owners liked using children because they were cheap and they were easy to push around. They were small, and were ideal for crawling under the machinery to clean it and clear the fluff; with luck it was not even necessary to turn it off.

The philosophers and the intellectuals and the moralists had their say too. A government which tried to restrict the working of factories was going against the by now sacred principle of *laissez-faire*. No businessman should be prevented from working to make a profit, so long as he was not breaking the criminal law. No worker should be denied the right to work eighteen hours a day at a mechanical loom or a stocking frame if he wished (after all, nobody was forcing him at swordpoint, so presumably it was his choice). No government should come between employer and employee in a 'free' country. And it was already agreed that leisure was bad for children. God had worked six days in the week from morning to night, so it ought to be good enough for everyone else.

Battle was joined by the reformers – high-minded Anglicans and Nonconformists, a handful of enlightened factory-owners, a knot of devoted MPs, and at least one dedicated peer, the Earl of Shaftesbury. The indefatigable William Cobbett also added his twopenn'orth: from his new vantage point as member of the reformed House of Commons he poured scorn upon the factory-owners' strident defence of the existing conditions. To listen to them, he said with heavy irony, one would suppose that the entire prosperity of the country depended upon the labour of 300,000 little girls in Lancashire.

Richard Oastler, a land agent and fiery advocate of reform, and John Fielden, a charitable factory-owner, attacked the hypocrisy of the Slavery Abolitionists, who devoted all their time to the cause of slaves in the Americas, when far worse slavery was going on under their noses. William Wilberforce, the leader of the Abolitionists, was a member for Yorkshire, where some of the worst factories lurked. 'The little white slaves of the factories,' remarked Oastler. 'What a pity,' said Fielden, 'that these ... factory children happen to be white instead of black.'

In December, 1831, Shaftesbury had brought in a Bill for reducing the working hours of adults to ten hours a day. The factory interests managed to stall it by having a committee set up to investigate the whole question of conditions in the factories. Just as the committee which investigated the trade union question owed its success to Francis Place, so the committee on factory conditions owed its success to the untiring work of another dedicated reformer, Michael Sadler, banker, Christian, and MP for Leeds.

Thanks to Sadler, the committee piled up a mountain of irrefutable evidence, and made known for the first time a sickening chronicle of exploitation, petty tyrannies, exhausting hours, poor wages, beatings, deformities, uncompensated accidents, and general horror.

The owners took shelter behind the screen of individual freedom; an adult had the right to choose whether he worked ten hours a day or more. They were prepared, being charitable Christian men, to consider the case of children, who were of course too young to know what was good for them. It was a way of diverting the attack. Shaftesbury, defeated in the House, was forced to accept the Government compromise of a Factory Act that dealt only with the working hours of children.

Henceforth, no child under the age of nine was permitted to work in a textile mill (though there was a curious exception made in the case of silk mills). Between the ages of nine and thirteen, no child was to work more than 48 hours a week, or more than 9 hours a day. From thirteen to eighteen, 'young persons' were to be employed for no more than 12 hours a day, or 69 hours a week. There was to be no more night work. The educational reformers managed to squeeze some of their ideas into the small print: the act also made provision for two hours' education to be fitted into each child's working day. Finally, inspectors were appointed to ensure that the terms of the Act were carried out.

The Act, and the working of it, are interesting reflections of what the adult world actually thought about children. Many factory owners were more concerned that these new hours for their young employees would 'ruin' them (ruin the owners, that is); they saw the shorter day – still twelve hours for a girl just turned thirteen – as suicidal generosity on their part. Parents were wary of the clauses about education; they were often more anxious about wages, and would be likely to take their children away from a mill where teaching was done well, sometimes for half a day, and pack them off to a mill where the new education clauses were sidetracked and a full working day was paid for. The educational reformers, who might be expected to have understood best of all, were oddly blind to a child's powers of resilience; they did not appear to see the difficulty in an underfed, cowed, asthmatic waif finding the energy, motivation, or self-discipline required to tackle two hours' teaching during a twelve-hour stint of grinding hardship – six days a week.

That was supposing that the Act worked perfectly – which it did not. There were two ways round the limitation of hours, for instance. Owners began to employ children in relays, so that the adults could be kept going for fourteen or sixteen hours a day. So, far from cutting the numbers of children in factories, the Act sent them up. Secondly, it was a simple matter to tamper with the clocks. When the hand approached the final hour, a glowering overseer simply pushed it back twenty minutes, swung his stick, and defied any child to come out and tell him what he was doing.

Getting round the question of age was comparatively simple. There was no register of births; children often did not know their own age. The owner had little trouble in claiming that a child 'looked' fourteen. This is one reason why, three years later, the Government began the compulsory registration of all births, marriages, and deaths.

The educational clauses were perhaps the greatest disappointment, though the most predictable one. Inspectors were supposed to arrange for the 'two hours' to be conducted at a local school, but the times rarely coincided. When they did not, the mill owner himself was required to provide facilities and opportunities, and often instructors. One inspector found a group of mites squatting in the boiler room, clutching black-grimed books, while the fireman 'taught' them in between stoking the furnace. The professionals – the two religious societies who were charged with spending the £20,000 annual grant – haggled bitterly over which precise theology should be included in the curriculum of these coal-hole academies.

The inspectors had a terrible time. There were only four of them, though the number was later raised. They were, for the most part, dedicated men who laboured long and hard to improve conditions, and to try and prevent factory-owners from flouting not only the letter but the spirit of the law.

As always, there were glowing exceptions to the common trend of grasping, brutal owners and overseers, and it must also be remembered that children were no more likely to be angels then than they are now, but the debate over factory working conditions does show a depressing general picture, only partially softened by the Factory Act of 1833.

Nevertheless, like the Great Reform Act, and the new Education Grant, it was a first. There had been factory acts before – in 1802 (sponsored by Peel's father), in 1819, 1825, and 1831 – but this was the first act with teeth, with inspectors. More were to follow in the coming decades – in a battle of wits between factory owners who found loopholes in the existing law, and inspectors and reformers who wrote fresh reports and sponsored new laws to stop them up.

The early 1830s were still hard times, but the voices of common humanity, of kindness, and of mercy were beginning to be heard, however faintly. Peel's policy of reducing the number of offences carrying the death penalty was continued: in 1832 horse-stealing, sheep-stealing, housebreaking, and coining false money ceased to be capital offences. In 1833, bull-baiting and bear-baiting were forbidden within five miles of Temple Bar in the City (a ban extended two years later to the whole country).

The year 1833 also saw the last of human slavery.

Just as the owners of some factories and mines, tucked away in remote valleys beside the vital running water and coal seams, had body-and-soul control over their employees, so the owners of the plantations in the West Indies totally possessed their slaves – work, food, housing, life, and death.

There is something about petty power, as there is about sharing out the possessions of the dead or sitting at the controls of the internal-combustion engine, that brings out the worst in otherwise reasonable people. The more complete the power, the more they can abuse it, and the greater the effrontery with which they defend what they do. For every story of cruelty in factories, there were a dozen about worse horrors on the plantations, or on the slave ships that constantly crossed the Atlantic with fresh labour to fill the gaps made by the early deaths. And the slavers had an answer for them all.

The Abolitionists kept up a constant barrage of news and scandal, which the public read with their usual mixture of shock and thrill – of captains who threw slaves overboard to lighten a damaged vessel; of Africans who tried to commit suicide by eating earth rather than board the slave ship; of the 'acceptable' (and regular) loss of a third of the 'cargo' on a transatlantic voyage due to disease and overcrowding; of the stark-naked indignity of the slave market; of beatings and rapings and maimings and lopping of limbs; of iron collars and masks; of sales that split families; of immersions of 'criminals' in vats of boiling juice.

The owners replied, with long-suffering patience, that, as the owners, they knew best what to do with their own property. Surely every Englishman had the right to the enjoyment of his own property without interference; when had such a right been challenged? Moreover, they were doing the British Empire a favour; service on the slave ships was a vital part of the training of young men for the Navy. One never knew when Britain would have a sudden need of more sailors. In pure economic terms, their contribution of sugar, tobacco, rice, cotton, and coffee was unique; the Empire and the home country could not do without them. Thanks to slave labour, they (the slave owners) could compete with foreign competition. Get rid of the slaves, and the owners would have to use wage labour, while other countries would continue with slaves; Britain's foreign rivals would then enjoy complete domination of the market because of their lower costs. It was not generally appreciated in Europe – as the owners repeatedly reminded their critics – that blacks worked better in the sun than whites, so the owners were saving possible white labourers a great deal of discomfort. And finally, to complete the picture of disinterested compassion, they were actually doing the blacks a favour as well, because, as was widely known, living conditions in Africa were far worse than they were on the plantations.

The usual devoted band of single-minded men had been keeping the cause alive for fifty years. Pitt had given his support to a motion in Parliament against the slave trade as early as the 1780s. The movement was led by Pitt's great friend, William Wilberforce, the member for Yorkshire, who gave up his life to it (and who also approved of child labour). It was opposed by the loud, rich, and powerful 'plantation interest' in Parliament, and by the silent fondness of many solid citizens for sugar, tobacco, rice, cotton, and coffee. (Wilberforce had once tried to persuade people to bring pressure to bear on the plantations by giving up sugar.) The West Indies were also a very long way away, and the slaves were, after all, only natives....

However, a growing body of high-minded churchmen, the Evangelical Christians – of whom Wilberforce was one – were slowly effecting a swing of public conscience, and were gaining more voice and influence in Parliament. The appeal to religion, to a vague sense of fairness, and to common humanity did not fall entirely upon deaf ears.

Their success came in 1807, when the slave trade was declared illegal throughout the British Empire; British subjects were forbidden to engage in it; so were any ships flying the British flag. During the peace negotiations in 1814 after the French War, Castlereagh laboured to induce his European allies to do the same. The restored Bourbon King of France agreed. Spain promised to stop it by 1820, and Portugal by 1830, both no doubt encouraged by hefty compensation awards from the British taxpayer. England's offer to use her Navy to enforce the ban brought mixed feelings from her allies; they saw in it another chance for British captains to throw their weight about all over the high seas.

Sadly, the trade continued, illegally. Wilberforce and his fellow-campaigners came to the conclusion that the only way to kill it was to kill the demand – that is, to kill the whole institution itself. If there was no more slavery on the plantations, there would be no market for fresh slaves. It is a testimony to the strength of the West Indian 'interests' in Parliament that the battle lasted another twenty-six years.

In 1833, just before Wilberforce's death, the Government abolished all slavery 'throughout the British Colonies' – though it was not as simple as it sounded. The owners demanded, and got, £20,000,000 in compensation. It represented £37.50 per slave; the average selling price of a slave at that time was £38. The scheme under which the owners were to have the ex-slaves work for them for so many years (for wages) broke down. No agency on earth could prepare thousands of slaves overnight for self-support. And the United States, naturally, did not consider itself bound by British decisions. It continued to benefit from cheap labour for another thirty years.

A great wrong had been put right; a huge festering boil had been lanced. But the healing process was to be long and painful – almost as bad in some ways as the suffering of the original boil.

The four reforms just discussed – of Parliament, of education, factories, and slavery – might be thought to indicate a remarkable level of crusading zeal in a cabinet of aristocrats, or at the very least a willingness to react to argument and evidence. But the Whigs were no more anxious than the Tories to open floodgates of reform – rather to regulate sluice gates that held back the massive weight of grievance. By timely 'bleedings' of the main body, they could ease the pressure, and so continue in power. Grey, and his successor, Melbourne, were noblemen of the old school, convinced of their God-given right to rule. They were relics of the eighteenth century, to whom the French Revolution had been the greatest shock of their lives. They might be aware of the new forces loose in the world, and they might be willing to compromise, but there was to be no question of surrender, or even of much sharing. That would be abdication of their natural responsibilities, and would open the way to anarchy. For Grey, and for Melbourne, as for the Duke and many Tories, the spectre of Revolution still stalked the unwary.

This explains why, at the height of the excitement over the general election about the reform of Parliament, Lord Melbourne, as Home Secretary, was authorising such drastic action against the poor wretches involved in the Labourers' Revolt. At the end of 1830, farm workers in nearly every county in south-east England, driven to despair by despicable wages, by savage game laws, by the loss of land and status caused by enclosures, and by the loss of employment caused by the new machines, took direct action. Their protest usually amounted to little more than rick-burning, machine-smashing, marches to the squire to demand lower rents and higher wages, and the random ducking of an unpopular gamekeeper in the local pond. By the time Melbourne and his dragoons and magistrates had finished, nine men had been hanged (including a youth of nineteen), 457 transported to Australia, and another 400-odd sent to prison. William Cobbett, now in his late sixties, but apparently just as contentious as ever, was charged with 'addressing inflammatory language to the labouring classes'.

Fortunately for Cobbett, who characteristically conducted his own defence, and used the courtroom as a pulpit from which to preach against the Government, the jury failed to agree, and Melbourne dropped the case. Within eighteen months, Cobbett was a Member of Parliament in the newly-reformed House of Commons. It was because of the intense excitement of the great struggle over the Reform Bill that the horror of those terrible punishments slipped from public consciousness. The bad news was, thankfully for the Government, buried. But the Government had not forgotten; they had no intention of being scared by the results of poverty again.

Even before the passing of the Great Reform Act was complete, they appointed a Royal Commission to investigate the whole question of poverty, and to record what steps were being taken at local level to alleviate it. (There was no national system; the last attempt to manage the problem at a national level had been during the reign of Elizabeth, nearly 250 years before.)

To their surprise, the Commissioners found not too little poor relief, but too much, and it was the usual English amateur, hand-to-mouth, do-it-yourself mish-mash. There was no overall Government supervision; there were no professional, paid civil servants because there was no system to run. It was all done at county, and above all at parish, level. Nearly two and a half centuries of being left to themselves had caused parishes to evolve a huge variety of methods for dealing with their paupers – by specially-arranged work, by free lodging, by charity in kind, by straight money payment, and by many variations on these themes – with the inevitable variety in levels of efficiency. Because of the absence of supervision, the scope for corruption and feathering of nests was mouth-watering; overseers of the poor were only human; it was more than flesh and conscience could stand.

A lot of money, therefore, which had been earmarked from local rates or tithes simply did not get through to its intended destination – the relief of the poor. But a lot more did – too much. It was found that far too many parishes allocated money to the poor and the unemployed as a matter of course, so much so that many paupers had come to look upon the relief as a rightful income. In the most flagrant cases, there was little incentive to seek paid labour when wages were so low. The situation was compounded by those ratepayers who were also employers; faced with ever-rising rate bills, these men adjusted their budgets by paying lower wages to their workers. So the men who were in regular employment saw their already meagre wages dropping further. Once again there was little incentive to offer a good week's work for a wage that dropped in places to a ridiculous 25p. a week.

It looked an impossible situation, and it showed signs, if anything, of getting worse. The lazy paupers sponged off the parish; the decent ones despaired of ever escaping the poverty trap when wages were so low. It was useless to move to another parish, because relief was available, by law, only to those born within parish boundaries. Those still in employment were bitter at the pitiful wages for the man who worked, and at the standard of living allowed to the pauper for doing nothing. The ratepayers were faced with a soaring bill, which, in national terms, had quadrupled in thirty-odd years; they felt at least entitled to protection from revolt and violence by the hands they were feeding. (Many of those involved in the Labourers' Revolt had been unemployed at the time.) The philosophers helpfully pointed out that, if healthy paupers continued to receive relief without any check, they would breed more and more paupers, until everyone in the country was poor.

The Commissioners' Report proposed to clear up this mess by new legislation, which should be based on two guiding principles. First, poor relief was no longer to be made easy; on the contrary, it was to be made extremely difficult, and anyone who in future wished to receive it had to be prepared to accept unpleasant conditions. Second, anyone who did receive poor relief on these new terms was never to be in a position of greater affluence than anyone in paid employment.

It would get rid of the spongers; it would encourage Christian thrift; it would ennoble honest labour; and it would be cheaper. The poor would not breed so much; the paid labourer would be, or should be, grateful for the guaranteed level of his wages; and the respectable property-owning ratepayer would sleep easier in his bed, with a fatter bag of gold underneath it.

The Poor Law Amendment Act became law on 14 August, 1834. It was based on a Report that only *described* poverty, without examining the reasons for it. Consequently, the Act provided only administrative machinery for coping with the results; it did not get to grips with causes. It succeeded in only a few years in replacing a state of chaos with a new regime that reassured those outside it, and reduced those inside it to misery, indignity, and despair.

The chief feature was the workhouse, which was to become one of the proverbial symbols of Victorian England. There was to be no more relief for any pauper – man, woman, or child – outside the workhouse. Anyone therefore who wished to receive it had to leave his home, belongings, everything, in order to do so. From now on he would have to be desperate to consider such a move; the workhouse was to be made deliberately unpleasant – or, as Edwin Chadwick, the co-author of the Commission's Report, put it with that stiff-necked righteousness so typical of the age, 'an uninviting place of wholesome restraint'. Chadwick went on to admit in so many words that the workhouse was to be 'the last resource of the pauper'. It was to be a place of hardship, discipline, and shame. (The idea still persisted that if you were poor it was usually your own fault.)

It turned out to be even worse than the Commissioners intended. They had envisaged separate workhouses for each class of the poor – the elderly, the able-bodied, the sick, the lunatic, the orphans, the widows – but, when it came to the building programme, the authorities applied the principle of thrift to themselves, and often put up only one per district. In practice, children were frequently thrust into the mumbling company of the senile and the imbecile, and grieving widows shivered with broken-down prostitutes. Married couples could be split, and children separated from their parents. Food provided was minimal, and the work usually repetitive, dirty, and degrading. Overseers were not selected for their powers of intelligence, imagination, or compassion.

To be fair, the Government did try. It did take responsibility. It produced a system that was intended to embrace the whole country; there was to be no more local do-it-yourself. Parishes were to be grouped into unions; unions were to build workhouses between them. Local Boards of Guardians were to be elected to run them. There were to be three paid Government Poor Law Commissioners, with a paid secretary – Edwin Chadwick, a man of fearsome dedication – to supervise the whole scheme. Between unions and commissioners there was installed a hierarchy of civil servants.

It looked good on paper. On the receiving end, it was different. In the farming counties, men resented the passing of the old parish system, where at least everyone knew everyone; nobody liked distant civil servants and soulless regulations. It did have the virtue of bringing down the rates, however, and employers could afford to raise wages a little. Good harvests in the middle 1830s also brought lower prices. And in many areas a fair number of blind eyes were turned to the continuation of relief outside the workhouse.

In the industrial regions, it was loathed. Periodic recessions and seasonal unemployment meant that men, and women, expected to be out of work for part of the year; it seemed an unfair harshness to put them in the workhouse when a few weeks later they could expect to be in receipt of a wage. The law took no notice; it was workhouse or nothing. Before long the workhouses were known as 'Bastilles'.

To the out-of-work hand-loom weaver in the West Riding, the workhouse was the fruit of the Great Reform of Parliament, for which he had turned out, marched in the streets, and risked imprisonment. He was not only betrayed by his rulers; he was now smitten by them too. Injury had been added to insult.

The Government felt reasonably pleased with what they had done. They had set up a framework of poor relief that was self-supporting; parishes paid for their own union workhouses and overseers. The machinery to run it was relatively cheap. Best of all, the poor rates were dropping most satisfactorily, so the middle classes were rescued from the prospect of bankruptcy. True, the workhouse might be a harsh place, but a man knew that before he went into it. For every man or woman who chose to go in, there were a dozen who chose to stay away, so costs were cut accordingly. And the alternative – to have continued with the old system – could have led to complete breakdown. Poverty was the parasite; respectable people were the main body of society. It would have been intolerable for the parasite to have destroyed the body.

For the same reason, nothing in the shape of workmen's combination was to be allowed to dictate to the rulers of society. When six Dorset farm workers formed a trade union, the 'Friendly Society of

Agricultural Labourers', at the end of 1833, they ran unwittingly into the full force of Government wrath and fear. The only thing that these men of Tolpuddle wanted to do was 'maintain the wages of farm servants', which was permitted by the existing trade union law of 1825. Unluckily for them, they had pledged themselves to each other in a secret initiation ceremony (understandable in the prevailing climate of opinion), and the Government legal experts dredged up a law that had been passed in 1797 to deal with the secret naval mutineers at the Nore. The honest promise of these six men became an 'illegal oath'; they were arrested in February, 1834, and sentenced to seven years' transportation – two were shipped to Tasmania, and four to Botany Bay.

Support committees, petitions, demonstrations, and marches cut no ice with Home Secretary Melbourne, though further pressure, kept up over the next two years, at last secured remission of the remainder of their sentences when the excitement had died down. They came back home in 1838. With the money raised by their support committee, five settled with small farms in Essex, and the sixth, George Loveless, returned to his native village, where his gravestone can still be seen in the churchyard.

It had been the pious hope of these six men that their little friendly society might become affiliated to a new and unique organisation which had appeared that year – the Grand National Consolidated Trades Union. If the Whig Government had reacted with such savagery against a humble club of farm workers in a tiny village, it takes only a glimmer of imagination to deduce how they might behave towards a plan to unite all working men to take over the entire economic machinery of the country.

Fortunately for the cause of peace, a head-on collision never occurred, though it was not for lack of trade union activity. In the years following the legislation of 1825, which allowed unions legally to exist, it was hardly surprising that trade unions were born, though they had to struggle to stay alive.

A union of Durham miners appeared in 1825. Lancashire cotton-spinners united in 1829, and tried to embrace all men in the trade with their Grand General Union of all the Operative Spinners of the United Kingdom. In 1830, its leader, John Doherty, launched the National

Association for the Protection of Labour. The following year saw the founding of a Metropolitan Trades Union, to bring together various union groups, clubs, and societies in London. In 1832, a federation of crafts and trades in the construction industry was set up, calling itself the Operative Builders' Union.

One after another, they were forced into liquidation, and for similar reasons. Employers would not meet their demands, and refused to employ men unless those men promised not to join a union, or to support one. Strikes led only to lock-outs; after weeks, sometimes months, of inactivity, the men were starved back to work.

Nor was it all the harshness of skinflint employers. Union treasurers ran away with union funds; sections of amalgamated unions quarrelled with each other; dispute and failure were followed by mutual recrimination among leaders; union newspapers failed for lack of experience and lack of ready cash. There was no deep financial reserve and no long-term political experience. There was no success to boost morale in the next fight. There was no political party to champion the cause.

The same fate befell the greatest experiment of all, despite the fact that it was led, not by an uneducated workman, but by a wealthy businessman with a vast fund of brilliant ideas and a fine record of success in industrial relations behind him.

Robert Owen was the son of a Welsh tradesman who was apprenticed to a draper. By the age of twenty he was manager of a factory in Manchester, and by the time he was thirty he was a partner in one of the largest mills in Scotland. He then set up factories at New Lanark that became a showpiece; he proved that humane treatment of workers led not to ruin but to prosperity.

From there he proceeded to the idea that more money still would pile up if middle men were cut out of the processes of making and selling, and that workers would perform better if they were given a chance to share in the running of the factory and its profits. He took up the theory that a worker was entitled to a price for what he made according to the amount of labour he had put into it; at present, he said, far too much of this price went into the pocket of the capitalist, who did very little work. The next step was to plan for a universal system under which the worker controlled all the stages of production – which would make the capitalist redundant. So there was no need for strikes; workers should not go against employers – they should simply go in the opposite direction. Employers then would have the choice of joining them in the great universal march towards mutually profitable production, or be left behind in limbo.

It sounded wonderful. So did the projects Owen promoted – 'union shops', 'villages of co-operation', 'labour bazaars', and so on. So too did his great design for an amalgamation of every organisation of workmen in the whole country – a 'Grand National Consolidated Trades Union' – which would control the economic machinery of society, and would thus have effective political control as well.

Working people responded, because Owen had a track record of industrial success, and of common humanity, and because the prospect was so attractive in a time of bitter hardship. They wanted to believe it. He offered to solve everything, and with no strikes or violence. Within months membership was in six figures.

Before the end of 1834, the GNCTU was in ruins. Faced with potential extinction, the capitalist class responded with understandable determination. Faced with an organisation that might claim to rival Parliament in its universality, the Government set its jaw more firmly than ever. The strike-breaking and lock-outs ate away the workers' slender funds. Prosecutions and harsh sentences discouraged many moderate followers.

The working members of the GNCTU simply ran into a will that was greater than their own. Employers and owners – self-made men, oozing confidence and ruthlessness – were not going to be impressed by airy-fairy newspaper articles and vague socialistic theory, and they were not going to be frightened by threats of general strikes. Ministers and magistrates had no hesitation in calling out the regular dragoons and the local militia to deal with crowds, peaceful or otherwise; they had been doing so since Peterloo.

Owen was not an instinctive politician; he was not a natural militant; and he had little control over the workings of the machinery he had so lovingly built. His followers ran into experience, organisation, and financial strength that were out of their league. The GNCTU was a lumbering balsa-wood giant of good intent, with no strength to withstand any strain or pressure.

By the end of 1834, the working families of Britain had every reason to feel bitter and downcast. The great hope of 1832 had turned into the 'Great Betrayal'. The new poor law had taken away familiar outdoor relief at the parish pump, and replaced it with soulless, impersonal, indoor tyranny in the workhouse. The hopes that had soared with Owen were now plunged into the despair of the lock-out and the persecution of the union member. Anyone who challenged this by simply meeting to talk about it faced prison or the convict ship. The decade that followed Place and Hume securing the repeal of the Combination Acts, far from bringing the people to any promised land, had led them to a wilderness of disunion and despair.

It had not been a good decade either for the Tory Party. Their stranglehold on politics since 1784 had been progressively shaken in the later twenties of the new century. Two attacks on Tory privilege – the Sliding Scale of corn duties and the repeal of the Test and Corporation Acts – had been successful. The death of Lord Liverpool had shown up splits in the wall which had been mere cracks in the plaster while he was alive; it had ended with the more liberal wing of the party moving over to join the Whigs. There had followed three new Tory prime ministers in quick succession. In 1829 had come another 'Great Betrayal', when Peel had changed his mind about Catholic Emancipation, and had stayed in office only to see the bill through. Finally, between 1830 and 1832, the Tories had waged a life-and-death struggle to hold back the reform of Parliament, and they had failed. Now the Duke, in lofty and lugubrious opposition, along with Lord Eldon and the remaining die-hards, waited stonily for the end. Anyone who took up the burden of rebuilding the party in the 1830s faced a daunting task.

Surprisingly, the man who did was probably hated by more Tories than anyone else in Parliament. Robert Peel had been forced to give up his seat for Oxford University as a result of his championing the Irish Catholics. He sat briefly for Westbury, then in August, 1830 gained the seat for Tamworth in Staffordshire. Tall, strong, imposing, he was a difficult man to ignore. He had a high intelligence, a huge capacity for work, and a great flair for debate. Like Pitt, he could be a trifle stiff and starchy, though friends and family testified to his warmth in an intimate circle – there was a story that he liked to tell broad jokes in Gladstone's presence, because he knew, mischievously, that they embarrassed him. He was confident in his own abilities, yet oddly sensitive about his own social position. All his life he retained a faint Lancashire accent. Perhaps his father's record as a self-made industrialist impelled him to be slightly aggressive towards the old Tory aristocrats of the party; he was going to 'show' them. At any rate, his combination of gifts made him stand out. Friends and enemies alike in the party realised that there was nobody else to touch him; if they wanted power, he was the one they would have to follow. They did, but many kept a note of 1829 in the back of their minds: if he had betrayed them once, he could do it again.

Peel was helped by two things. One was the opposing party, the Whigs. Lord Grey, the Prime Minister, was now old, and frankly tired. When his Cabinet split over the question of Ireland – whether to make further concessions to O'Connell or to impose further discipline – Grey thankfully resigned. His successor, the ex-Home Secretary, Lord Melbourne, was another of the old school of languid, yawning, eighteenth-century aristocrats. He was not particularly interested in energetic government either; he was not a bustling reformer by disposition, and on the whole preferred it when things were not happening to when they were. He is credited with a private remark that he found the premiership 'a damned bore'.

Within four months of taking office, he too was finding Ireland an embarrassment, and he had fallen out with the King, because he (Melbourne) wanted to make Lord John Russell the Leader of the House of Commons. William did not like the Whigs much, and liked Russell least of all. That suited Melbourne fine; he was almost as happy to go as the King was to invite the Tories.

The Duke, roused from contemplation of impending doom, was sent for. His attitude during and since the Great Reform Bill crisis had been soured, as he saw it, by the foolishness of his colleagues in passing it, and by the fickleness of the mob that stoned his house in support of it. Worse, his wife had died at the height of the excitement over the first bill. Theirs had not exactly been a meeting of twin souls, but he had his regrets about the impatience he had often shown towards her, and he had felt much closer to her at the end.

However, work for him was the antidote to every ill. He had plenty of interests outside politics and family. He was Lord Lieutenant of Hampshire, Constable of the Tower, Master of the Elder Brothers of Trinity House (the authority for the country's lighthouses), and Lord Warden of the Cinque Ports. He was spending a lot of time – and money – improving his house and estate at Stratfield Saye, between Basingstoke and Reading. In 1834 he became Chancellor of the University of Oxford, and found the cheering of the students a welcome change from the recent hooting of the London mob.

He came at his sovereign's call, naturally. He could do nothing about inevitable doom, but he could always do something about coming to his monarch's rescue. Once again, he put aside his personal feelings, and gave the advice that he thought was best for the country. He did not like Peel much more than he had liked Canning, but just as he had thought Canning was the best man for the Foreign Office in 1822, so now he thought Peel was the best man for Number Ten – and said so.

The trouble was that Peel was on holiday with his wife – in Rome. Wellington could easily have taken advantage of the situation. Instead he offered to be caretaker Prime Minister. There followed a sort of pantomime fortnight. While Peel was being sent for and was bouncing post-haste across Europe, the Duke was Minister for Nearly Everything. Each day he drove from ministry to ministry – Treasury, Home Office, Foreign Office, Colonial Office, and so on – conducting essential business in his customary efficient, matter-of-fact way, and holding the fort – or several forts – till Peel returned. It was against all the rules, but only a few carping Whigs grumbled. It is a measure of his huge reputation for rock-like integrity that nobody seriously doubted his motives. Wags made jokes about the Cabinet, for the first time in years, being in total agreement. He himself later liked to chuckle about his brief tenure of power as 'Dictator'. Peel took office in mid-December, 1834, and in the new year called for a general election.

Here there became apparent the other important factor in Peel's success, after the weariness of the Whigs. This was his ability to see issues on their own merits. For a man who gave his life to the Tory party, he was remarkably free from Tory prejudices – perhaps because of his family background. This honesty – this willingness at times to put country before party – enabled him to give great service to his country, but it also gave his fellow-Tories bitter reason to accuse him of betrayal.

It is given to few statesmen to build and split a major political party twice in a career. Peel helped to keep the Tories in a creative mood during the 1820s, then split them over Catholic Emancipation in 1829. In the early 1830s he began the rebuilding, until by the end of the decade he was in a position to lead his party back into office with a triumphant victory. (He was not to know that within another six years he was to split it again.)

A significant step in this rebuilding came during the general election at the beginning of 1835. The Tories won fresh seats, but not a commanding majority. However, in the address that Peel made to his constituents of Tamworth, he gave in effect an entirely new look to the Tory party.

The manifesto was not a party-political programme; it was a statement of belief rather than of intent. In it Peel displayed his ability to see problems on their own merits, his trick of seeing things as they really were. The Reform of Parliament, he said, was now an accepted fact. Neither he nor the party would seek to reverse it. Not only that; in future the Tory party would also pursue the course of reform, provided that it did not mean charging after every cause blindly – or, as he put it, 'living in a perpetual vortex of agitation'. If a reform was to be 'careful' and undertaken 'in a friendly temper', with proper respect for 'established rights' and with the intention only of reforming 'proved abuses' and 'real grievances', he and the party were all for it.

With this canny joint appeal to the desire for change, and to the yearning for normality, Peel hoped to raise support from the new upper-middle-class voters who had been born out of the Great Reform Act. He was in effect yanking the Tory party into the nineteenth century, forcing them away from the regrets of past defeats and pushing them towards fresh horizons of new victories. If it meant changing the face of the party, so be it; the body, he thought, still had plenty of life in it.

He gave the Tory party new hope and new energy. He also gave them a new name, or at any rate an alternative one: after 1835 it became increasingly common to refer to them as the 'Conservatives'.

CHAPTER TEN

The Nation's Darling
1836–40

In the summer of 1837, as he entered his last illness, King William had one comfort: he had lived long enough to see his niece, Alexandrina Victoria, come of age. At least the court, the Government, and the nation, would be spared the terrible prospect of a regency in the hands of the girl's awful mother, the Duchess of Kent. His Majesty was unable to attend the Princess's coming-of-age ball, but he was able to offer her an establishment independent of her mother – an offer which, to her mother's chagrin, was accepted.

William missed Ascot, which did not grieve him at all, and set his heart on living until 18 June – the anniversary of Waterloo – to miss which would have grieved him a great deal. He just made it, though it must have taken a colossal effort of will; at the time of his death two days afterwards, his lungs were turgid with blood, his heart valves ossified, and his liver and spleen both unnaturally enlarged.

Strength of will was a quality he appears to have shared with his niece, the new Queen. It must have taken a considerable effort to shake off the influence of a mother who had dominated every feature of her life since she had been born. This determination, coupled with a strong constitution and a somewhat self-righteous education, was to make her a formidable adversary in argument. Like her grandfather, George III, she was not especially intelligent, and did not relish intellectual pursuits for their own sake; but, like him too, her views, when once formed, were clung to with annoying obstinacy.

She was, however, fair-minded enough to admit that she lacked experience; and she desperately wanted to be a good Queen. Having no father (the Duke of Kent had died before she was a year old), she turned therefore to anyone who would offer helpful advice. At first it had been, naturally, her mother. After she had asserted her independence in that quarter, the next confidant was her uncle, Leopold of Saxe-Coburg, the husband of the late and lamented Princess Charlotte. However, it would not be seemly for the chief confidant of the Crown to be a German, as the Prime Minister gently hinted. If Her Majesty was not averse to the idea, he, Lord Melbourne, would be only too pleased to offer himself as guide to the difficult days that lay ahead. Being a constitutional monarch was a skill which had to be learnt like anything else.

Victoria was by no means averse to the idea. She liked Melbourne; he was like some kind, elderly relative who could be relied upon never to take advantage, never to bully, never to dominate. Melbourne, for his part, was flattered. He did not enjoy the cut-and-thrust of everyday politics, and became increasingly weary of the whole business of government as his old age approached. Now, just when he was searching harder than ever for an avenue of escape, there had arrived in his life someone to make his servitude pleasurable. The Prime Minister was a widower, after an unhappy marriage, and his only child had died young. The Queen filled an emotional vacuum in his life. Victoria, having once made up her mind to depend upon him, did so with a vengeance. She wrote to him daily; in their many meetings, she listened, she confided, and she followed his advice. Melbourne, nearly sixty, basked in the eager dependence of this lively, eighteen-year-old slip of a girl.

She was the best thing that could have happened to the monarchy at that time. For the last ten years of her grandfather's reign, the country had had to tolerate a King who was locked up in his own castle because he was not the master of his own mind. For the next ten years, Englishmen had had to endure a King who was fat, ungainly, graceless, old, selfish, and contemptuous of the common man. From 1830 to 1837, William IV – the bluff old sailor – had restored some of the Crown's popularity, but little of its dignity. Now, at last, Victoria provided youth, innocence, eagerness to please, energy – all in staggering contrast to the flesh folds and pop eyes and world-weariness of her three predecessors. Finally, her very sex appealed to the knight errant in her male population, and to the virtuous maiden in the female. It is true that there were sides to her character which turned out to be anything but endearing, and which did not improve with advancing age, but that was in the future. For the moment, Melbourne welcomed a relationship to his liking, and was grateful for anything that made the business of government easier.

Peel had done rather better in the election of January, 1835 than expected, thanks to the Tamworth Manifesto and his own undoubted abilities. But not well enough: he could not command an absolute majority, and he waited only for a suitable opportunity to resign. It came in April. Once again, he and the Duke, the Tory leader in the Lords, went into opposition. (The Duke, Peel's Foreign Secretary, had been in office exactly a hundred days. Canning had been Prime Minister for a hundred days. Napoleon's comeback in 1815 had lasted a hundred days. The Duke could hardly have missed the irony.)

The Whigs returned, and mustered enough strength to pass the last of their great reforms – the Municipal Corporations Act. But the Whigs – to use a metaphor that for the first time in the nation's history meant something – were running out of steam. By 1837 they were beset by troubles: there was rebellion in Canada; Ireland was still in turmoil; the Eastern Question was festering again; there was fresh radical unrest from a new group calling themselves the Chartists. Finally, the Government could not command an absolute majority, and was forced to depend upon the group of Irish MPs led by O'Connell. These men, the beneficiaries of the Emancipation Act of 1829 and the Reform of Parliament of 1832, held the balance of power, and O'Connell was determined to extract the maximum benefit from the situation. He was almost as big a headache in support as Peel and the revived Tories were in Opposition. Melbourne had neither the talent nor the stomach for the fray.

Through no great personal effort on his own part, his party had brought about important changes in the matter of the poor, the slaves, and the younger factory workers. Their reform of local government deserves to stand beside these reforms, though, as with the poor, the slaves, and the factory workers, the change was neither as complete nor as generously inspired as one might think. It sprang from a mixture of motives, it had a limited scope, and it enjoyed only a partial success. It certainly did not 'do' local government, except perhaps in the way that a hurried American tourist might 'do' London.

To be fair, the Whigs did realise that something badly needed to be done. In keeping with what was becoming a regular pattern, they set up a commission to investigate the state of affairs in the boroughs, the 'municipalities', of England and Wales. How were the towns of the realm being run? Back came the answer from the commission's Report – very oddly and irregularly indeed. Standards varied from the virtuous and the exemplary to the scandalous and the near-criminal. That perhaps was to be expected; human nature and human ability were very variable. One cure, then, was obvious: a few regular rules might produce a few more consistent standards.

However, that was not the main complaint. The chief criticisms fell under three headings – democracy (or the lack of it), law and order (or the lack of that), and corruption (of which there was no lack). It was noted by the Commissioners that far too many corporations – the governing bodies of the boroughs – were narrow little clubs of local bigwigs whose chief concern was to perpetuate their own power. Many boroughs did not have democratic elections; many more had no elections at all. So Whigs in Tory-held boroughs complained just as bitterly about lack of democracy as did Tories in Whig-held boroughs. Not to be outdone, Nonconformists castigated Anglican corporations, and Radicals denounced nearly all corporations that did not allow the ordinary citizen a vote.

The second point was becoming sharper as the century advanced and populations grew. How were these 'closed' corporations going to be able to maintain order in a fast-spreading industrial town which had ever-increasing numbers of wretched workers living in crowded slums on the edge of desperation and crime? Dragoons could not be available everywhere at the drop of a hat, and the new Peelers were only six years old in 1835 – and were available only in London.

Thirdly, many of these narrow little cliques had enjoyed for years the right of nominating the local Member of Parliament. Not only that; for years too many of them had been spreading their own bread with the corporation butter. If it was a blow at corruption to get rid of nomination boroughs in 1832, it was going to be another blow at corruption to get rid of the nominators in 1835. The second seemed to follow logically from the first.

What might strike a modern observer as the real point of importance – the provision of proper local services such as street paving, street lighting, street cleaning, refuse collection, a system of sewerage and sewage disposal, to say nothing of hospitals, schools, libraries, traffic control, and so on – did not figure so highly in the thinking of either the old corporations or the new reformers. Obviously many of these were completely lacking, and many people considered them desirable, but, once again, there was no pattern.

For example, it would be tempting to conclude that the towns with the worst record in the provision of local services were all those corrupt, undemocratic ones full of greedy, fat aldermen, while the few boroughs with a fully democratic organisation were shining examples of what a 'caring' corporation should be. Not a bit of it. True, some corrupt boroughs did have a shocking record, but so did some 'open' ones. Conversely, there were some 'closed' corporations whose record of achievement could stand beside the best in the land.

Moreover, the Municipal Corporations Act, when it reached the statute book, did not build the road to the Elysian Fields of democracy and universal amenity. Yet a modern student, raised in the traditions of the universal vote and the welfare state, would be wrong to expect a government in the 1830s to be thinking along the same lines. They simply found a situation that was bad, by the standards of the time, and they tried to improve it, by the standards of the time.

So the old corporations were swept away – over two hundred of them – and 178 new municipal corporations set up in their place. That got rid of the clutter. The new corporations were to be upon a common pattern of mayor, aldermen, and councillors. That took care of the 'hotchpotch' part of the problem. These borough officers were to be elected by all male householders who had been paying the poor rate for the previous three years. That was as far as men of 1835 could be expected to go towards democracy. To head off the financial temptations of office, it was decreed that borough funds were to be regularly checked by independent auditors. So the money that the new corporations were now empowered to raise was to be spent, it was hoped, on containing the poor, organising a police force, and enforcing local by-laws. Law and order were, as always, paramount. (It is a measure of the threat posed by the swelling borough populations that 'respectable folk' were losing their fear of police forces. Peel's Metropolitan constables were also establishing a worthy reputation. By 1839, county police forces had made their appearance.)

The Act did not mean, however, that all towns now had this new form of government; it applied only to the old boroughs which had possessed charters of incorporation. Unincorporated boroughs had to apply for new charters if they wished to be embraced by the Act's terms. If not, they continued in their limbo of bumble and corruption. Nor were the new corporations instructed to provide local amenities; they were only *empowered* to. Most amenities hitherto had been provided by people called Improvement Commissioners. These men, usually local worthies or local do-gooders, had been the only agents of progress. Their activities varied from town to town, their powers depended often upon special Acts of Parliament, and their success depended upon how much money they could persuade local residents to contribute – and asking for money was no less a thankless task then than it is now. So some of the new municipal corporations took such work away from the Improvement Commissioners and began to build their own model borough, and some were content to leave things as they were. As so often, there was no regular pattern.

Nevertheless, like the unsatisfactory Education Grant of 1833, and the piecemeal Factory Act of the same year, and the reform of Parliament itself, the Municipal Corporations Act of 1835 was a 'first'; it was, as the saying goes, a step in the right direction. The Duke, predictably, thought it a step in the wrong direction. The Reform Act had laid central government open to radicalism, republicanism, and anarchy; Melbourne's Municipal Corporations Act was going to do the same for local government.

The following year, 1836, saw one or two other useful reforms, like the setting up of the compulsory register of all births, marriages, and deaths. Henceforth at least, factory-owners would not be able to claim that they did not know the ages of their young workers. It would also provide the Government with much useful information, a commodity which had been distinctly lacking in the past. (The censuses continued, the first year of every decade.) Local authorities were made responsible for road maintenance and fire prevention. In 1840 there was a first attempt to improve the terrible lives of child chimney sweeps, and Rowland Hill introduced his famous adhesive postage stamp – the Penny Black. (Postage charges henceforth were to be paid by the sender, not the recipient.) The Government annual grant for education was raised to £30,000.

Not, on the face of it, a mad whirl of crusading legislation. But the weary Melbourne had his hands full for all that – with O'Connell, with the Chartists, with Canada, and with the Eastern Question.

O'Connell could be, and was, a nuisance to any government at the best of times, but Melbourne was not only plagued by him; he was shackled to him. The Whig ministry did not command an absolute majority any more than the Tories had in early 1835. The balance was held by the knot of Irish MPs let into the House by the 1832 Reform Act. If gentlemen had lulled themselves with the thought that O'Connell would be satisfied by achieving civil rights for Catholics and gaining entrance to the seat of power at Westminster, they were soon to be woken up; O'Connell was only just beginning. He descended upon the House with a whole quiver of demands – a tax on absentee landlords, help for Ireland's poor, reform of Irish town government, abolition of the tithe paid to the Anglican Church, the secret ballot, and (the greatest of all) the abolition of the Act of Union, which would give Ireland self-government.

With his powerful voice, his imposing figure, his black wig, his green frock coat and his broad-brimmed black hat, he made a considerable impression. Fellow-members noticed him, but few liked him, and hardly any would support his demand for repeal of the Union.

There was little point in bringing down the Whig Government in sheer annoyance and frustration, because the Tories were even less likely to repeal the Union than the Whigs. So O'Connell compromised; he struck a deal. In March, 1835, he met the Whig leaders at the London house of Lord Lichfield, and an understanding was reached. It was agreed that the question of the Union was to be put in cold storage.

O'Connell promised that he would no longer embarrass the Government with it. In return, Melbourne promised to introduce reforms concerning the poor, the tithe, and local government.

Both sides lived up to their side of the agreement (known, not surprisingly, as the Lichfield House Compact), though whether either was satisfied with the results is debatable. In 1838, poor-law reform came to Ireland in the shape of the workhouse and a universal poor rate. In effect the English system was transplanted to Ireland, with similar results. In 1838 also came the Tithe Commutation Act. At last Catholics and Presbyterians were to be relieved of paying a tax, physically, to the Anglican Church. But they were made to pay three-quarters of its value to their landlords, who passed it on to the Church. It seemed an odd compromise that should not have fooled anybody. It certainly did not fool the Tories, who regarded themselves as the chosen guardians of the Anglican Church. Lord Eldon died that year at last, aged eighty-seven. It must have been the last thing he voted against.

It did nothing to heal the bad relations between landlord and tenant, but at least the hated word 'tithe' dropped out of use; there was one fewer 'cause' to feel bitter about. Finally, in 1840, after much heated debate, and two defeats in the Lords, the Irish Municipal Corporations Act became law – again on much the same lines as the English version. The franchise was restricted, though – to the £10 householder. So once again a concession was not given with an entirely good grace.

However, the Government did seem to be making an effort in its choice of officers for the day-to-day running of Ireland. Lord Lieutenant Mulgrave, Chief Secretary Morpeth, and Under-Secretary Thomas Drummond were all sympathetic to the country's problems, especially Drummond. Indeed, Drummond made enemies in England by his declaration that 'property has its duties as well as its rights'; infuriated landlords felt that this almost amounted to going native.

Earlier in the thirties there had been attempts at educational reform in Ireland, with the setting up of National schools, which, if not compulsory, at least were free. The medium of instruction was English, but such was the desire for teaching that Irish Catholics accepted it. The cost of their knowledge was the decline of the native Irish language.

Drummond went further. He knew that the Union would not be

repealed in his lifetime, but he tried for five years to 'make the Union work'. He strove to gain the confidence of Catholic and Protestant alike. He strictly enforced obedience to the law by followers of both beliefs. He suppressed extremist societies on both sides. He refused to use troops to evict tenants. He recruited Catholics into the Royal Irish Constabulary. He put Catholics into juries and on the bench. He allowed them access to the higher ranks of the army and the civil service. He did what he could to develop internal trade, and tried, without success, to raise investment for a system of Irish railways. He offered a high judicial post to O'Connell (an ex-barrister), who declined with regret. O'Connell returned the compliment by publicly supporting him, and by throwing his enormous weight behind the campaign to keep the peace and observe the law.

It all seemed too good to be true. It did not last. By 1840 Drummond had killed himself with overwork. The election of 1841 gave the Tories an absolute majority, and reduced O'Connell's party of Repealers from forty to twelve. He was now over sixty-five, and he could not wait for another Whig government. So he switched back to his strategy of the 1820s – public agitation. The battle against the Act of Union was to be fought on the green turf of Ireland, where his old allies, the priests and the ordinary people, would flock to his magical mass meetings. (He had also been elected Lord Mayor of Dublin.)

It must be remembered also that two other bedrock problems remained besides the Union. The workhouse system may have been making an attempt to cope with Irish poverty, but it was doing nothing to ease it. Every observer agreed that to think of Irish poverty in terms of poverty in almost any other country in Europe was to miss the point completely. Ireland's paupers were in a class of their own.

Finally, there was the land. The native Irish had long memories. Irish history to them was a chronicle of systematic, Government-sponsored land larceny by generations of grasping immigrants, and no solution would be fully acceptable that did not remedy the results of this theft. Such a concession by a Parliament of English Protestant landlords was beyond man's powers of imagination in the 1830s.

So, for the most part, was concession to the demands of the Chartists. They too were asking the impossible, and they were more of a threat, because they were here, in England, in the very streets and squares of the cities.

To the question 'Who were the Chartists?' it would be easy to reply, 'The people who wanted the People's Charter made law.' To the obvious next question – 'What was the People's Charter?' – it would be equally easy, and equally obvious, to reply by enumerating the Charter's famous Six Points: the right to vote for every adult male, the secret ballot, the abolition of the property qualification for MPs, equal electoral districts, payment of MPs, and annual general elections.

With a political programme as complicated as that, it is small wonder that they failed. The average examination candidate has to frown hard to understand what it means; the chances are that the average Chartist, denied the benefits of a state education, had a pretty slender grasp of it too. He could pick up the idea of a general election every year easily enough, and joined the roar at mass meetings for the right to vote. (Nobody at that time, except a few cranks, took seriously the notion that perhaps women too might deserve to have the vote.) He would find it hard to imagine that the well-dressed gentlemen whom he saw at Westminster should ever find it necessary to have a wage, but then he would have to have it explained to him that what their leaders intended was having men like himself in Parliament. Such men did not have a private income; they would have to depend upon a wage to enable them to do their work of making new laws for their fellow-workers. Hence the next aim of the Chartists – the abolition of the property qualification. To be an MP one had to own property, landed property. At the risk of repetition, it was one of the rock-bottom beliefs of the ruling classes that nobody should have a say in the running of the country unless he physically owned part of it. This still applied merely to having the vote, never mind to being a Member of Parliament. (The Great Reform Act of 1832 had been careful to restrict the franchise mainly to 'householders' and 'forty-shilling freeholders'.) It had been part of the instincts of rule for so long that it was going to take an effort of the imagination as well as of the will to get people to understand the hugeness of this proposed change. Finally, 'equal electoral districts' – the idea that each constituency should have roughly the same number of people in it – would present problems to men who rarely moved outside their village or town, who could not read or write, who had trouble estimating hundreds, let alone thousands, and who had no idea what a constituency was.

It would be easy then to dismiss Chartism as a collection of woolly ideas put into the heads of ignorant workers who had not the faintest idea of what they really meant, much less how to achieve them; easy to sneer at their pathetic bursts of frantic energy; easy to feel no surprise at the news that they were a dismal failure.

However, an opposite view could become an equal distortion of the facts – that is, to claim that the Chartists were the self-conscious, and self-denying, forerunners and prophets of the whole socialist and labour movements. That would be to read too much into the record. They were probably no more the forerunners of the labour movement than the 1833 Education Grant was the inspiration of the modern Ministry of Education, or than the dinosaur was the ancestor of modern man. The one simply came before the other. Of course there are connections, if one looks closely enough, but there are connections between any two things if one looks closely enough, and one has a bee in one's bonnet.

So – who were the Chartists, and what did they do?

Chartism began in the middle of the 1830s. It was a reaction to the Industrial Revolution by the men who had suffered most from it – the working class. There had been a lot of money made out of the Industrial Revolution, but very little of it had come their way. The middle class had done something *with* the Industrial Revolution – made the country, and themselves, rich; Chartists were working men who wanted to do something *about* the Industrial Revolution – to remedy its evil results.

In order to achieve that, they planned to take a leaf out of O'Connell's book – to gain access to the citadel of power, Parliament. Once in, they would frame laws that would make life tolerable again for the working man. They wanted a say in making the laws that society expected them all to obey.

Working men as a rule do not turn out in large numbers for such a political programme unless they are powerfully stimulated, and energetically led. Where did the stimulus come from? What made a man become a Chartist?

It is like asking why so many people emigrated from Europe to the USA. There is a host of reasons. Historians may argue about their relative significance, and they may – and do – debate about which reasons were more powerful in different parts of the country. The ones that follow are not meant to be in any order of importance.

There were industrial reasons. Chartism arose out of the ashes of the early trade union movement. The first unions had split up or been starved out of their strikes. Owen's GNCTU had crumbled swiftly and silently into nothing, like a dried-out sandcastle. The Tolpuddle Martyrs, vomiting in the hold of their convict ships on the nine-month voyage to Tasmania and Botany Bay, were a terrifying example to other would-be unionists. Men who still wished to improve their wages and working conditions joined the Chartist movement because they saw it as a means to an end, and moreover a safe one; so far, the Government had not made it a prison offence to sign a petition.

Secondly, there were what would nowadays be called environmental reasons. The evil side-effects of the Industrial Revolution – the overcrowding, the bad housing, the terrible sanitation, the lack of hygiene, the absence of proper medical care, the crime rate, the near-endless list of miseries – were obvious to anyone who set foot in an industrial town and opened his eyes or twitched his nostrils. Local authorities were not as yet wealthy enough, experienced enough, or concerned enough to give them adequate attention. (The Municipal Corporations Act had been designed to provide local government, not local services.) As has been previously explained, industrialisation was a colossal shock, and society had to be given a chance to adjust to it; in time improvements would come. But the 1830s and 1840s were the decades when the shock was at its worst, and when the remedies had scarcely begun. Social historians have christened the period 'the Bleak Age', with good reason. Men who lived and suffered in it saw in Chartism an opportunity to try to improve the appalling conditions in which many of them were trapped by unavoidable poverty.

Thirdly there were political reasons. Much had been said about the reform of Parliament in the years around 1830. In the excitement and the suspense men had come to hope for too much from it. They were bound to be disappointed. But to disappointment had been added rage and frustration. Working men had joined the country-wide agitation, had risked dismissal from work, perhaps imprisonment. Their payment had been to be excluded from the terms of the Great Reform Act. The more affluent middle class, having gained their own political success and joined the ranks of the rulers, now turned their backs on the humbler and poorer of their supporters. They were no more willing to share power with the 'masses' than the upper class had been. So supporting the People's Charter, with its radical political programme of votes for all, working-class MPs, and so on, was a way of getting round them, of forcing them to share.

Finally, there was the new Poor Law. If the workhouse 'Bastilles' were disliked in the more agricultural south, they were loathed in the northern industrial areas. Men joined the Chartist movement in the hope that they could one day get rid of these arks of human misery.

The varied nature of these origins in a sense provides a sort of key to the whole nature of Chartism. It was not simple enough. It was altogether too much of a mixture. There were too many aims. There were too many reasons for becoming a Chartist; consequently people expected far more out of Chartism than it was equipped to give. There was moreover tremendous variety in the areas of its main support. For example, there were fewer Chartists in the very big cities (say, Manchester, Leeds, Birmingham) than one might expect, and rather more in the medium-sized towns such as Bradford and Bolton. Very new towns such as St. Helen's and Crewe had small numbers. Market towns and country villages had hardly any. The movement was originally London-based, but gradually the axis moved to the Midlands and the North.

Research has also shown that there was no such thing as a typical Chartist. Some came from declining trades, which would be expected. Some came from traditional trades, like printing and tailoring. (Francis Place, one of the founders, was a tailor, and a one-time champion of the unions.) The very poorest workers, like those in factories and mines, did not give regular support. They tended to turn out when times were bad – in times of slump and high bread prices after bad harvests. In other words, not all Chartists were Chartists all the time – which made it difficult for the leaders to keep up the pressure.

Francis Place and William Lovett, the new leaders of Radical opinion (Cobbett and 'Orator' Hunt were dead), founded the London Working Men's Association in 1836. The Birmingham Political Union appeared in 1837, led by Thomas Attwood, a banker and Radical MP. A third element emerged in the North, led by Joseph Stephens and Richard Oastler (one of the pioneers of factory reform in his spare time). Nearly all these men were either middle-class, or at the very least upper-working-class – men of some education, respectability, and means – not the sort of men, one might think, to rouse and lead large numbers of workers.

The exception was an Irishman who joined the northern group – Feargus O'Connor. O'Connor introduced a rough, coarse-grained ingredient into the mixture of Chartist leadership. Unlike the others, too, he had much greater influence over crowds. Like his fellow-Irishman O'Connell, he was blessed with the gift of the gab. However, where O'Connell always stopped short of talking violence, O'Connor let his tongue run away with him. For a while the other leaders were able to hold him in check, and allowed him to channel his energies into running the Chartist newspaper, *The Northern Star*.

So there was variety of origin; there was variety of personnel; there was variety in the areas of support; there was variety in the consistency of support; and there was variety in the leadership. Nor did it stop there. There was variety in secondary aims. Some wanted just the Charter, and nothing else. Many of the northern Chartists, understandably, wanted to abolish the Poor Law Bastilles. Attwood, the banker, wanted currency reform. O'Connor was now talking about resettling industrial workers on small plots of land to make them independent, and, when his imagination really carried him away, spoke of a colossal union of all British and Irish working men.

There was variety finally in method. Lovett and the moderate leaders of London and Birmingham believed in what they called 'moral force'; they naïvely believed that logical and fair arguments, if properly presented to enough people, would carry the day. They believed in asking nicely. O'Connor inclined to the view that those in power would not share it unless pressure were to be brought to bear; he said that, in the end, 'physical force' would become necessary. But he never spelt out exactly what he meant by this. The result was that he worried his moderate colleagues; he excited crowds without delivering any results; and he frightened the authorities, who were determined to maintain law and order at any price, no matter how fair the demands of the demonstrators.

About the only thing the Chartists agreed on was the Charter itself, and on the need to present it to Parliament in the form of a petition.

This was debated amid high excitement in a great convention which was organised at Charing Cross in February, 1839. Delegates came from all over the country, though significantly there was not one agricultural representative. Expenses were met by a 'National Rent' (a leaf being taken here out of O'Connell's book). Lovett was elected secretary, and the talking began.

There was agreement over the manner of presenting the Petition, but great disagreement over what should be done if the Petition were to be rejected. There was more talk – about a run on banks, a general strike, a refusal to pay rents and taxes, a boycott of non-Chartist businesses, a resort to arms. Meanwhile the sessions had been adjourned to Birmingham, and still they talked. Lovett and some of his colleagues were arrested for holding an illegal meeting. When the Petition was finally presented, in June, Parliament rejected it by 235 votes to 46.

Random riots broke out in Sheffield, Barnsley, and Birmingham, and there were more arrests of ringleaders. Moderate supporters were shying away from the violence hinted at in the convention, and did not want to be associated with riots in the streets. A planned 'Sacred Month' of strikes was called off, and in August the convention was dissolved.

Nobody seemed to know what to do next. The only action took place in South Wales, and it was such a disaster that it would have been better for the cause of Chartism if it had not happened at all.

On the night of 4 November, 1839, three parties of miners planned to march down from the hills outside Newport in Monmouth, capture the town, and move on to Monmouth town, where they would release from jail a Chartist leader called Henry Vincent. It was a filthy wet night, and owing to lack of communication only one party arrived. Worse, the authorities had been warned; squads of troops and special constables waited behind barricades in the Westgate Hotel in the centre of Newport. Three volleys were enough; the miners fled, leaving a dozen or so dead. The other two groups of miners, chilled and soaked with waiting, broke up when they heard the news.

Three of the leaders – Frost, Williams, and Jones – were arrested and sentenced to death (later commuted to transportation for life). Other arrests of Chartist leaders followed around the country – including that of O'Connor.

It seems unlikely that the Newport Rising was part of a planned national rebellion, though the Government's reaction might indicate that it was prepared to believe the worst. It is possible that the event was a mere incident worked up into a huge crisis by a sensation-seeking press. Worse, it could conceivably have been a Government trap – to excite the demonstrators into action that could then be presented as treason (a reversion to the bad days of the eighteen-teens and the revolt of Derbyshire miners).

Whatever it was, it meant that by the end of the decade Chartism looked dead. Its organisation was gone, its followers were scattered, and its leaders were in prison.

Melbourne could feel slightly less beleaguered than usual. Ireland for once appeared settled, thanks to Thomas Drummond's efforts and O'Connell's cooperation. The Chartists were in disarray. And Canada, he hoped, was about to be pacified.

It had come as something of a tiresome nuisance to he told that Canada was in rebellion in 1837, though no doubt observers on the spot could have told him it was in the wind. This lack of awareness on the part of the English Government seems odd in a country that towards the end of the century was to pride itself on an empire 'on which the sun never set'. When one reads of jubilees, and durbars, and 'the Queen Empress', and 'columns' being forever sent to far-flung corners of the globe to 'pacify' the 'natives', one might be forgiven for assuming that the English Government has always been 'empire-conscious', been quick to seize any opportunity to extend the areas over which it could wave the Union Jack.

Not so.

For the first half of the nineteenth century, British ministers did not rush to commit themselves to distant rule in unknown places. Rather the opposite. Perhaps their fingers still felt blistered after the American War of Independence. Perhaps, after twenty-two years of war against France, and all those expensive expeditions to capture French and Spanish and Dutch colonies, they wanted to cut back on the budget. If capturing foreign colonies had been expensive, defending and governing their own were almost as big a burden on the taxpayer. Perhaps they now felt that trade and investment were a better prospect than direct rule; there were fewer overheads. The colonies they did retain after the war – like the Cape of Good Hope, Ceylon, Mauritius, Malta, and the Ionian Islands off the coast of Greece – were retained largely for strategic reasons.

Now that the American colonies had gone, hardly any British territory around the world had a sizeable British population that was considered worth bothering about. Canada was half French; South Africa was three-quarters Dutch; Australia was nearly all criminal. What was in New Zealand was anybody's guess – it was practically off the globe. India did not count because British administrators there did not belong to the Government; they belonged to the East India Company. Everything was weeks of travel away, and most colonists were as much out of mind as they were out of sight.

So British ministers now had few regrets about having lost North America. (They were much more interested in helping South America gain its independence from Spain and Portugal; it opened up such tempting markets for British industrial goods.) They had almost forgotten about Canada, except as a convenient safety valve to absorb the pressure of poverty-stricken immigrants from Scotland and Ireland. They had abandoned the West Indian sugar planters to the anti-slavers. They regarded Australia and Tasmania as little more than open-air prisons. The only other use for the 'Empire' was as a convenient place to which the English upper classes could pack off troublesome younger members of their families. Colonies, in the first half of the nineteenth century, were a bit of a liability.

When the Canadian Rebellion broke out, the attitude of most ministers was a mixture of annoyance and conscience: they wished they did not own the wretched place, but, since they did, and there was apparently some crisis or other, one's sense of duty decreed that something had better be done about it. John Lambton, Lord Durham, had been a thorn in the side of the Government recently; Melbourne decided to kill two birds with one stone, and sent him three thousand miles away to deal with the situation. He was given wide powers, told to get on with it, and not to be a nuisance to the Cabinet.

Out of such unpromising material was created a masterpiece in the art of government.

For a start, Durham seemed ill-fitted for the part in which he had been cast. He was vain, sour-tempered, inclined to hasty judgment, and generally a bad colleague. He was unpopular in his own party for his Radical views, and generally something of a misfit.

When he finally arrived in Canada (after allowing the crisis to stew for three months before leaving England), he found not one rebellion, but two. In Quebec, the old French half of Canada (Lower Canada), the French had rebelled, under the leadership of a rabble-rouser called Louis Papineau, against the growing numbers of English newcomers. In Ontario, the 'English' half (Upper Canada), a political journalist called William Mackenzie had led the revolt of the earlier settlers against the newcomers. (The first settlers had been those American colonists who had not wanted to fight the War of Independence. After the war, in order to escape persecution, they had fled to Canada. Now that they were established and prospering, they did not wish to share wealth or position with the new, scruffier immigrants from the slums of Britain.)

So it looked like a conflict of nations in Quebec, and a clash of social classes in Ontario. However, underneath the surface lay a deeper disagreement, which was common to both provinces. It was to do with government. In both provinces there was an elected assembly, which corresponded roughly with the English House of Commons. This could pass laws and grant (or refuse) taxes. There was a legislative council (nominated by the Crown, and roughly equivalent to the House of Lords), and, at the top, a governor, who had a set of ministers to carry out his orders. These too were chosen by the English home Government.

In times of peace, trust, and partnership (if such a time ever existed), such a system might work. In times of racial tension, economic conflict, and expanding population, it was intolerable. The locally-elected assemblies had no means of getting rid of ministers they did not like or trust; ministers had no way of compelling co-operation from the assemblies, who could bring government to a halt by refusing to grant taxes. Governors, caught in the crossfire, had the alternatives of either keeping their heads down or calling out the troops and declaring martial law; one could lead to anarchy and the other could lead to rebellion.

Governors had in fact used force to put down the 1837 rebellions – and with remarkable ease. Papineau's rising lasted a month, and Mackenzie's a week. Both ran away to the United States.

Durham arrived in May, and set about his duties with his customary briskness and Radical fervour. He saw himself as the architect of a great new dominion, and was impatient with any opposition to his grand design. He soon began to make as many enemies in Canada as he had in England. When he banished some rebels to Bermuda, tales were told that reached the ears of the Cabinet. He was reprimanded for exceeding his authority. Despite much expression of support (he was one of those people who caused strong reactions, both ways), he flung in his resignation in a huff, returned to England, wrote his report – and was dead within twenty months at the early age of forty-eight.

The Durham Report has since been hailed as the blueprint for enlightened government of a colony, though doubt has been expressed as to whether he himself was fully aware of its implications when he wrote it. In the short term, he proposed that the two provinces of Ontario and Quebec should be reunited – if only to lessen the influence of the French. (Pitt's Canada Act of 1791 had separated them.)

Melbourne's Government duly put this into effect with their Canada Act of 1840. The two provinces were formally joined, and were to have a single elected assembly, with equal numbers of members from each of the old two parts. Ministers and governors were still to be appointed by the Crown, but it was now made clear to them that their posts were by no means permanent. In other words, they had to do some decent governing if they wished to keep their office. In this way, the Government absorbed the spirit of Durham's report without actually writing it into the Act.

For Durham had been at pains to stress that the old system had been inadequate. Merely having elected assemblies, he said, was not enough. That was only 'representative' government. What was needed was a system whereby the assemblies had a way of bringing pressure to bear on the ministers of the Crown; or, to put it another way, ministers in future should have to keep the confidence of the assemblies. This was 'responsible' government. 'Responsible' did not mean governing with a conscience; it meant governing with a majority of support in the assembly, as was the case in England.

Nor did it mean independence. None of the rebels had wanted to go it alone. They had called not for independence, but for genuine partnership. Durham echoed this demand in his Report: matters of foreign policy and defence were, rightly, the responsibility of the Crown. He said many other things too, in the Report's 300 pages. But the one theme that has received the most attention was this one of 'responsible' government.

Like so many prophetic utterances, it received less attention at the time than it has done since. The Canada Act said nothing about it in so many words, though, to be fair, future governors and ministers were warned, and they did bring a more willing and conciliatory attitude to their duties. If it was not responsible government by legislation, it was certainly responsible government by implication. This was seen clearly during the later governorship of Lord Elgin, from 1847 to 1854; perhaps it was not entirely a coincidence that he was Durham's son-on-law.

During the first half of the nineteenth century, various ministers distinguished themselves as being gifted in the field of finance or social reform; others proved adept at debate or respected for powers of conciliation; others again displayed a gift for foreign affairs. Nobody built his reputation for his handling of the empire.

Colonial affairs were rarely seen as exciting. Home affairs, at best, were necessary duties; at worst, drudgery. There was little doubt about it; foreign affairs was where the glamour lay. Nobody believed this more fervently than Melbourne's Foreign Secretary, Lord Palmerston. Nobody was better suited to the post.

Henry Temple, third Viscount Palmerston, was able to sit in the House of Commons because his peerage was an Irish one. He was a Government minister for forty-eight years, and an MP for fifty-eight. He served in every ministry except those of Peel and Derby between 1807 and 1865. No other minister has come near this record.

Because of his extraordinary length of service, because of the enormous number of documents associated with him, because of his colourful personality, and because of his astounding diplomatic achievements (and mishaps), legend and argument surround him.

On a superficial level, he was the supreme example of the 'gunboat' diplomat. He waded in on Britain's behalf wherever he saw fit; he scorned diplomatic language, and believed in calling a spade a spade; he suffered neither fools nor foreigners gladly; he never scrupled to use Britain's naval and industrial strength as bargaining counters; and he firmly believed that there was no international situation that could not be improved by a dose of English advice.

Not surprisingly, he made enemies, and not all of them abroad. More cautious Cabinet colleagues never knew what he was going to do next. The Queen was to become more and more annoyed at his high-handed actions, often without proper consultation beforehand. Professional diplomats were appalled at his lack of tact. One of his nicknames, coined from his abrasive nature, was 'Lord Pumicestone'.

He was also suspect in ruling circles because he was so popular with ordinary people. He had wit and swagger, passion and style. He was fond of prize-fighting and horse-racing. A ladies' man too – another nickname was 'Lord Cupid'. He made no pretence to intellectual distinction – just the plain, simple Englishman. He was John Bull, a gent, a swell, a toff. 'Pumicestone' maybe to his equals, but 'Pam' to everyone else. To employ a theatrical metaphor – where Castlereagh played out his role as Foreign Secretary in a lonely monologue to an empty house, and Canning usually played to the half-filled stalls, Pam played unashamedly to a packed gallery. And the gallery loved it.

Nor was it all show. He published more material than any of his predecessors; he expected to be kept informed by his staff, but he in turn kept Parliament exceptionally well supplied with information. Similarly, he provided the newspapers with regular bulletins, often writing articles himself under a pen name. He timed election speeches in his constituency at Tiverton so that reporters could catch the London train and so make the morning editions. If he had a colourful image, it was clearly one that he took some care to colour himself.

It indicates a shrewd brain behind the brash language and the bullish manner. Critics also found that his apparently ill-conceived remarks camouflaged a vast knowledge. He had been Secretary at War for nearly twenty years before becoming Foreign Secretary, and had an unrivalled knowledge of European affairs. He was at home in several languages; he was a tenacious opponent in diplomatic haggling; he could draft a most competent dispatch; he had an enormous capacity for work; and when he went into action on the floor of the House of Commons, he was master of his facts.

The three main problems that faced him at the Foreign Office during the 1830s were to do with Belgium, with Spain and Portugal, and with the Eastern Question.

In August, 1830 the Belgians rose in revolt against their Dutch masters. Almost overnight, Pam was faced with a potential European war. The French might intervene on behalf of the Belgians, who were their immediate neighbours and (mainly) fellow-Catholics. The Prussians and other German princes would be asked to come to the aid of the Protestant Dutch; since it was a revolution, Austria and Russia – both monarchies – would also be against the Belgians.

And the plot was thicker than that. The joint monarchy of Holland-Belgium had been expressly created at the Congress of Vienna to form a 'buffer state' against a possible revival of French military power. The Vienna settlement had already lasted for fifteen years; most European statesmen wanted it to continue. On the other hand, if the Dutch were allowed, or assisted, to put down the Belgian revolt, the French might be tempted to come in to save the Belgians. It would be an ideal way for them to fish in troubled waters in the Low Countries, and gain access to Antwerp, the centre of Channel trade at the mouth of the River Scheldt. (Pitt had gone to war in 1792 for just such a cause – to prevent France gaining control of the opposite side of the Channel in the Low Countries. Nothing must ever threaten British trade in the Channel.) The French had already carved themselves a new empire in Algeria; there was no knowing where else their ambitions lay.

Then again, the Belgians had a genuine case for independence, and Palmerston throughout his life was sympathetic to a nation's cry for freedom. If they were to be crushed now, they would probably break out again; so that was no real solution.

Pam went to work. In the bargainings, bluffs, and stake-raisings that followed, it would be an overstatement to claim that every initiative was inspired by him, and the negotiations were spread out over several years; but the general consensus of opinion seems to be that the final settlement was a triumph for him. It took all his experience, his tenacity, his capacity for hard work, his knowledge of Europe, and his toughness (he gained one success because he physically wore out his opponents by lasting longer round the conference table).

In the end he secured Belgian independence; he persuaded Austria, Prussia and Russia to accept it. He forced the Dutch to let Belgium go. He not only induced the French to back down from support of the Belgians; he also made them withdraw their candidate for the new Belgian throne and accept the choice of Leopold of Saxe-Coburg (the uncle of Victoria, the husband of the dead Charlotte). He tore up a piece of the Vienna Settlement without a European war, and he rounded it off in 1839 by persuading the Powers to guarantee Belgian neutrality for ever. In itself, not a bad decade's work.

In between chapters of this saga on the northern frontier of France, Pam was engaged in further activity on her southern frontier too – in Spain and Portugal.

Pam did not trust the French – never had done. In this perhaps he betrayed himself as a true product of the eighteenth century, when every sound Englishman regarded the French as corrupt Papist frog-eaters who were either fighting one war or plotting the next one. Although he had worked alongside the French in the Belgian crisis, he never relaxed his vigilance for a moment.

If such an attitude can be called a 'principle', then it was one of the 'principles' of Palmerston's foreign policy – always keep an eye on France. Another, more praiseworthy principle attributed to him was the one of supporting the two 'isms' of the time – liberalism and nationalism. He was always open, it was said, to an appeal from a nation that wanted to be united, that wanted to be liberated from a foreign ruler, or that wanted to be given a share in its own government. Belgium is a case in point. So were Spain and Portugal, as will be explained in a moment. Later Italy, too. However, it can also be claimed that Pam intervened in these countries in order to minimise the influence of France there, and to keep the European peace, and used the noble causes of liberalism and nationalism as a sort of righteous camouflage.

The question – 'to intervene or not to intervene?' – was one that had exercised the minds of every foreign secretary since 1815. Castlereagh and Canning, generally, did not believe in it, but were not above a little intervention in order to stop unwelcome other people intervening. Palmerston took it a little further. The main reason he intervened in Spain and Portugal was to make sure that France intervened properly. He could hardly stop her, so he had better go along with her. Between the two of them, they could head off an even worse intervention – from the eastern powers of the old Holy Alliance – Austria and Russia and Prussia.

The situations in Spain and Portugal were similar to a remarkable degree, so similar that examination candidates can be forgiven for confusing names. It was Queen Maria and wicked uncle Miguel in Portugal, and Queen Christina and wicked uncle Carlos in Spain. In both countries, young, unmarried queens were threatened by revolt from claimant uncles; in both countries the uncles were associated with the tradition of reactionary absolutism; in both countries the queens threw themselves into the arms of the progressive liberals who demanded a constitution as the price of their support. Both crises came to a head in the same year – 1833 – and both claimants were defeated only as a result of the action of France and Britain.

Pam was willing to use the Navy, if only as a counterbalance to the French use of an army. To keep the French in line, he gathered up all four countries – England, France, Spain, and Portugal – in a Quadruple Alliance, which was signed in April, 1834. Together, they expelled both Don Miguel and Don Carlos, and established constitutional monarchies (at least for the time being).

Pam was cock-a-hoop. He had kept his eye on the French; he had expelled two unwelcome potential dictators; he had secured the gratitude of majority opinion in Spain and Portugal (which would no doubt produce dividends in the shape of trade profits in the future); and he had prevented the Austrian Chancellor Metternich and the Holy

Alliance from interfering in Western Europe. In a letter of triumph to his brother, he remarked with glee, 'I should like to see Metternich's face when he reads our treaty.'

The Quadruple Alliance, though it formally bound France and England together, did little to improve relations between Palmerston and the French Government. They thought him high-handed, and he thought them untrustworthy. The twists and turns of the Eastern Question during the middle and late 1830s served only to make relations worse.

Pam had had his first taste of it in 1832, when he had helped to set up the first independent king of Greece. He did not at first see Russia as a threat, and could not make up his mind which was the better bet for stability in the Near East – the fading Sultan Mahmud of Turkey, or his over-mighty subject, Mehemet Ali, Pasha of Egypt (the father of Ibrahim, the man who had slaughtered so many Greeks in the 1820s on behalf of the Sultan).

The Turkish Empire under Mahmud II (1785–1839) was continuing the steady decline which had been visible since the seventeenth century. At the risk of over-simplicity, it was a byword for inefficiency, corruption, decadence, and backwardness (the first printing press, for example, was not set up in Constantinople until 1726 – over two and a half centuries after those in central Europe). It sprawled, it bumbled, it lagged behind, it oppressed its subjects, and it was of course non-Christian. It was regarded by Europeans with a mixture of amazement, loathing, revulsion, and contempt. But it was still there. So long as it was still there, it was a barrier to the expansion of Russia towards the Mediterranean Sea.

Such an awful possibility was regarded by every British minister as a fate worse than death for British trade. Turkey was the junction, the depot, the clearing house, the funnel for an enormous amount of trade between Europe and Asia – trade which Britain, as a sea power, regarded as vital to her interests. If a hostile power, like Russia, were to gain unlimited access to the Straits of the Dardanelles, between the Black Sea and the Aegean Sea, the way would be open for Russian warships to sweep the Mediterranean. Hence, any move by Russia in the area was seen by worried British ministers as a threat – either a shove to overturn the ramshackle Turkish Empire, or a devious burrowing underneath to make it collapse, or a plot of diabolical cunning to gain virtual control of the whole regime.

Which makes Palmerston's early lack of concern puzzling. Perhaps he overestimated the deterrent effect of the British Navy after Navarino. Perhaps he saw more staying power in the Turkish Empire than other people did. Perhaps the whole British Government was too taken up with the debate on the Reform of Parliament. Perhaps Pam was simply too busy with Belgium and Spain and Portugal. Perhaps he thought it was more important to keep the French out of Egypt. Perhaps he misread the extraordinary adventurer, Mehemet Ali.

Mehemet Ali had started his public life as an Albanian tobacco dealer, and had risen by God knows what twists and turns to become the Pasha of Egypt. Once secured in Cairo, partly by means of French support and money, he had embarked on a series of reforms and adventures which had so strengthened his power and influence that he was in effect stronger than his overlord, the Sultan Mahmud. That was why Mahmud had called upon him, and his son Ibrahim, to help put down the revolt of the Greeks. That he had failed was due not to any great fault in Ibrahim's generalship, but to the effectiveness of Codrington's gunfire at the Battle of Navarino. It had not affected Mehemet's hold on Egypt, and it had not lessened the threat he posed to the security of the Sultan's position. If he were given the right support, it was not inconceivable that he could replace the Sultan. If Mehemet were to rule in Constantinople, he could be a much more effective barrier to Russia than Mahmud.

This was how the Tsar and his advisers were thinking too. They were now pursuing the theory that there was no point in overturning the weak Sultan if he was going to be replaced by the energetic Mehemet Ali. Better to worm their way into the trust of the Sultan, and rule from within – in effect, turn the Sultan into a puppet ally.

All these musings and ponderings were brought to a sharp halt by the sudden action of the Albanian former tobacco dealer in Cairo. Mehemet Ali put in a demand to the Sultan for some reward for his help in putting down the Greek revolt. When the Sultan refused (on the not unreasonable grounds that the Greeks had gained their independence),

Mehemet invaded Turkish territory – or, rather, his son did. Ibrahim defeated the Turks, and the Sultan appealed for help.

Britain declined, for reasons suggested above. France, with money and men tied up in investments in Egypt, tended to back Mehemet. In desperation, the Sultan turned to his old enemy, Russia. Tsar Nicholas sent Russian troops, Ibrahim withdrew, and the Sultan bought off Mehemet with Syria. The immediate pressure seemed off.

Then came the bombshell. News arrived of a treaty between the Sultan and the Tsar – the Treaty of Unkiar Skelessi, of July, 1833 – by which Turkey in effect fell under the military protection of Russia. In a secret clause (which soon became common knowledge) the Turks promised to close the Straits to foreign warships whenever Russia asked. Palmerston gnashed his teeth at his mistake, and exerted every diplomatic muscle to undo the treaty, without effect. He made a mental note not to be caught napping like that again.

For five years, he badgered the Sultan to make reforms, and urged his ambassador at Constantinople to keep up the pressure. He signed a commercial treaty with Turkey. He looked with favour on the efforts of the German officer, Moltke, to modernise the Turkish Army. He let it be known, no doubt for French and Russian consumption, that in his opinion all the talk about the decay of Turkey was 'pure and unadulterated nonsense'.

It must have gone to the Sultan's head. In 1839, when Mehemet refused to pay tribute, Mahmud went to war with him. It was total disaster: the Turkish Army was defeated; the Turkish Navy deserted to Mehemet; and the Sultan died, leaving a teenage successor.

Whichever way Pam looked at this crisis, each scenario was appalling. If Mehemet went on to conquer the whole Turkish Empire, it meant that his backers, the French, were installed astride the greatest trade routes in the world, and the line to India was under threat. If the Russians came in and rescued the new young Sultan, their grip on the Turkish Empire would become stronger, with similar results. If the Turks struggled on, with or without help, it meant that the whole area was in turmoil, with similar bad effects on trade; and with the Turkish Empire weak and preoccupied in war, Russia, Austria, and France could help themselves to bits and pieces practically at will.

Something would have to be done, and done in concert with the powers involved, so as to secure the maximum guarantee that the settlement would last.

In concert, that is, with all the powers except one – France. France was on the other side. France had shown interest in Egypt ever since Napoleon's abortive expedition there in 1798. After the war, French businessmen began to invest in Eastern Mediterranean trade, to the alarm of their English counterparts. Since the French had lost so many colonies in the years up to 1815 – in Canada, India, the West Indies, for example – she was looking to Africa as a suitable site for a new colonial empire. By the 1820s she was reaching out for Algiers and was showing interest in Senegal and Madagascar. French military experts trained Mehemet's Egyptian army. Egypt had control of the Red Sea, and the Red Sea led to India. British ministers looked at the map and quailed at the awful possibilities.

So France must be kept in its place. What followed – as with the negotiations about Spain and Portugal – was not dictated exclusively by Palmerston, nor organised entirely by Palmerston; Metternich took much of the initiative too. But the results were so much in tune with what Palmerston wanted that it seems natural to give him much of the credit for it.

A joint declaration by Britain, Austria, Russia, and Prussia guaranteed the continued existence of the Turkish Empire (the First Treaty of London, July, 1840). Mehemet Ali was to give up all his conquests except Syria, which he could hold for life. If he refused, he would lose everything, including Egypt. Foreign warships were to be kept out of the narrow seas between Turkey and Europe (the 'Straits') in time of peace – which made a nonsense of Russia's much-valued Treaty of Unkiar Skelessi. (The Russians were making the best of a bad job. They had neither the funds nor the naval strength to take on the British Navy, and they did not want Mehemet Ali in control of Turkey, so they had to accept what was for them an unavoidable compromise. At least it would have the advantage of driving a wedge between England and France; it was always useful to have two of one's chief rivals at loggerheads.)

Nobody consulted France. The French Government blustered; their ally Mehemet Ali tried to bluff it out. But Palmerston and Metternich were sure of themselves by this time. A combined British and Austrian force landed in Syria, and a British fleet bombarded a Syrian port or two. Palmerston, now in top gear, wrote to the British Ambassador in Paris that if France went to war, she would 'lose her ships, colonies, and commerce... and Mehemet Ali will just be chucked into the Nile'. No doubt the Ambassador toned down Pam's message before he conveyed it to the French Government. The French chief minister, Thiers, who wanted war, was sacked, and replaced by the more peaceable Guizot.

French face was saved by an invitation to join the other four powers in a Second Treaty of London in July, 1841. In effect it repeated the terms of the first one, with the difference that it was now guaranteed by *all* the Great Powers.

Pam had good reason to be pleased. He had prevented Mehemet Ali from overturning the Turkish Empire. He had kept out the Russians, and he had kept out the French. He had proved that neither the Russians nor the French were prepared to go to war with England. He had maintained peace. And he had secured international guarantees for a settlement that fitted exactly to British interests.

His triumph came too late to save the Melbourne Ministry. Indeed, they would have been gone long ago, had it not been for an episode known, slightly suggestively, if deceptively, as 'the Bedchamber Question'.

The Whigs had been defeated in Parliament in May, 1839. The Queen had been distraught – to be separated from her 'dearest kind Lord Melbourne'. And to have a new Prime Minister who was a Tory! Worse, to have to accept Sir Robert Peel, who was such a 'cold, odd man'.

She had at first, naïvely, offered the premiership to the Duke, and, when he declined (for the second time in five years), had asked him to take the Foreign Office. Again he said no. It would have to be Sir Robert for Prime Minister, and Sir Robert would choose his own Foreign Secretary.

Peel, it was well known, did not possess Lord Melbourne's charm, and had an awkward, stiff public manner. A bit of a cold fish. O'Connell (who had coined the nickname 'Orange' Peel years before), said his smile was 'like the silver plate on a coffin'.

With the Queen determined to be noble, and Peel suffering tortures of embarrassment, negotiations did not get off to a good start. They turned suddenly worse when Peel said that he proposed to dismiss some of the Ladies of the Royal Bedchamber. The Queen had surrounded herself with Whigs since her accession. Now that the Government was Tory (and in a minority in the House), it would not do for those closest to her to be the wives of the Prime Minister's chief political enemies. Victoria, for her part, felt that such intimate appointments were not the business of the Prime Minister. Peel did not wish to bully the Queen, and in any case did not propose to dismiss *all* the Ladies.

But the Queen had seen a chance of escape. She would be brave and steadfast in the face of this 'cold, unfeeling, disagreeable man'; she would not be bullied. Nor, when she sensed Peel's difficulty, did she offer to compromise. Would she not part with even one of her Ladies? No, not one. In the meantime, she was sending breathless messages to Lord Melbourne that he was to hold himself in readiness, for he might soon 'be wanted'.

This was the sort of *impasse* that the Duke was frequently, and increasingly, called upon to resolve. He had, over the years, become a kind of universal umpire, consulted by politicians and royalty alike, both of whom treated him with unique attentiveness and deference. His politics may at times have been tiresome to many, but his motives were never questioned. He was loyal and truthful, and he had raised common sense to an art form. His advice, if not always expected or welcome, was plain, direct, relevant, and totally disinterested.

After Peel's fall in 1835, he had cheerfully accepted life without office, and looked forward to being, as he said, 'the idlest man in town'. However, the Duke's idea of idleness was not that of other men. He still led the Tory peers in the Lords, and spoke regularly. He was still the Constable of the Tower, Lord Warden of the Cinque Ports, head of Trinity House, and Chancellor of Oxford University. He sat for numerous portrait artists, and wrote to decline the importunities of many more. There was a stream of visitors – including royalty – to Walmer Castle (his seat as Lord Warden) and to his country house at Stratfield Saye.

Right into old age he maintained a fierce and frugal regimen of narrow, uncurtained beds, early rising, and simple diet. He drank little and smoked not at all. He drove, he rode, he walked. He travelled regularly between Walmer Castle, Stratfield Saye, and Apsley House (his London home). This strict discipline enabled him to recover from two minor strokes at the end of the decade (some observers thought it caused them). His deafness was a nuisance (the result of a nearby accidental detonation, followed by negligent treatment), but did not impair his energy. He still attended church even though he could not hear the sermons, because, he said, it set a good example.

Wherever he was, whatever he was doing, a summons from his sovereign brought him at once to the royal presence. Grumbling, maybe, that there was never any peace for Wellington, but it brought him.

So now, in the matter of the Ladies of the Bedchamber, he arrived, with Peel in tow, to ask, in his businesslike, brisk way, what all the fuss was about, to be told by the prim and pouting young woman in front of him, 'Oh, *he* began it, and not me.' The Duke could see that he was not going to get anywhere, and handed over to Peel. Peel failed too. Within three days, Melbourne was Prime Minister again. But only until July, 1841; in the general election, both the Whigs and O'Connell's Irishmen suffered heavy losses, and the Tories romped home.

Victoria may have been difficult and devious to some of her ministers, but to the people at large she was still the angel on the throne. She had given a further transfusion to royalty when she married Prince Albert of Saxe-Coburg in February, 1840. Everything was so perfect that the February rain and wind cleared in deference to the occasion, and brilliant sun came out to delight the huge crowds. (The sun was to shine on much of her public ceremonial. Indeed, as the numerous royal offspring began to appear with almost monotonous regularity – nine all told – it began to look as if the sun was shining again on royalty itself.)

There then occurred a very rare instance of a reversal of the old adage about bad weather: for once the sun never shone but it blazed. At the end of this decade, the English found themselves with two heroines to worship, not one.

Grace Horsley Darling was the daughter of the keeper at the Longstone Lighthouse, off the Northumberland coast at Bamburgh. On the night of 6–7 September, 1838, the steamer *Forfarshire* was wrecked in a storm on Big Harcar Rock, in the Farne Islands. Eight members of the crew and one passenger escaped in the ship's lifeboat.

The following morning, William Darling, the keeper of the Longstone, about three-quarters of a mile away, saw movement on Big Harcar Rock. As Grace's brothers were all away, it was she who helped her father to row and investigate (having first waited for the tide to turn more favourable). They found nine survivors. It took two trips to rescue everyone; Mr Darling made the second one with a crew member while Grace made preparations to care for everyone in the lighthouse living room. This she did for a further three days while another storm raged. Grace thought little of the incident, and her father gave it only half a sentence in his journal.

For over a week, the chief concerns of the local journalists were matters like the inquest on the dead, the apparent cowardice of the crew in escaping in the one lifeboat, the bad state of the ship's boiler, and the insurance money. News of Grace's exploit did not appear in the pages of *The Times* until 19 September, twelve days after the rescue. It seemed as if the writer wanted to make up for the neglect. 'Is there,' he asked the world at large, 'in the whole of history, or of fiction even, one instance of female heroism to compare for one moment with this?'

Apparently not.

A storm of adulation broke over Grace, far greater than the original storm that had done for the *Forfarshire*. She, her family, and her house, were besieged by visitors, journalists, tourists, and gossip columnists. Locks of her hair and scraps of her dress became as common, and as spurious, as fragments of the True Cross in medieval churches. Throughout the rest of the century, in a steadily increasing stream, appeared biographies, portraits, busts, prints, poems, and songs. Girls' annuals, full of accounts of 'the rescue', poured off the presses, all for the delight, and edification, of the nation's young womanhood. Grace's likeness, or an idealised approximation of it, appeared on mugs, jugs, statuettes, models of lighthouses and rowing boats, lids of biscuit tins and chocolate boxes. Silver and gold medals from humane societies were delivered to her door, and the Lords Commissioners of Her Majesty's Treasury were commanded, as a recognition of her conduct, to make payment to her, through the Paymaster of Civil Services, the sum of 'Fifty Pounds' – when she presented the 'enclosed form, upon the proper stamp for the amount'.

Some modern views suggest that her achievement was not so much one of bravery as of athleticism. She was a tough, resourceful girl who was used to helping her father when her brothers were not there. It seems unlikely that Mr Darling would have put to sea if he thought he was thereby endangering his daughter's life; and from his later statements it appears to have been sober judgement by both of them that, if they could get to Big Harcar Rock, some of those rescued could offer their own muscle to assist the journey back. It is also true that locals were heard to comment at the time that it was low water and the sea was settled – 'anybody could have done what she did'. But that could have been envy at her sudden celebrity. Finally, while Grace and her father were rowing to Big Harcar, six fishermen, alerted by warning guns from the look-out at Bamburgh Castle, set out to row five miles from North Sunderland. When they reached Big Harcar, they found that the survivors had already been taken off by the Darlings (who had rowed only three-quarters of a mile). Whatever the nature of Grace's achievement, the real truth of it soon disappeared from view.

If Victoria was heaven-sent as a blessing to English royalty, Grace was tailor-made as a source of legend. First, the name – Grace Darling. No novelist or poet could conceivably have done better. Then her obvious bravery. At least it seemed obvious to non-seafaring people, to whom waves were 'billows', and the sea was the 'foaming main'. (Whatever her detractors may say, not many girls of her age would have leaped at the prospect of rowing nearly a mile in an open boat between rocks not long after a storm.) Next, her modesty – she honestly could not see what all the fuss was about. She was an ordinary, unremarkable young woman who had done something as a matter of course, which the world chose to regard as prodigious. Fourthly, her status – she was young, and she was unmarried. The quadruple blessing – youth, modesty, virginity, and heroism – made the legend unstoppable.

Victoria was the 'Queen of the Isles', but she was overtaken in myth by the 'Maid of the Isles'. Victoria married, had children, developed bad habits, and went on being Queen – and on, and on. Grace added the coping-stone to the monument of her legend by dying, still unmarried. She was only twenty-six.

CHAPTER ELEVEN

King Hudson
1841–45

Sir Robert Peel's new Tory Cabinet in 1841 was unusual; it contained five men who had been or would be Prime Minister at one time or another, and that was besides himself. Even the most notorious man to be excluded later went into Downing Street.

The new Foreign Secretary was Lord Aberdeen, whose unwelcome task was to smooth the ruffled feelings among European allies, especially France, left by Palmerston. A new arrival to Cabinet rank in 1843 was to be William Gladstone, one of the future giants of the latter part of the century. His great rival, Disraeli (also a Tory), had hoped for office, but was disappointed. His later actions in 1846 were said by many to be activated by motives of revenge. All these men were to be Prime Minister later. So was Lord Stanley (later Lord Derby), who became Secretary for War and the Colonies. The President of the Board of Trade, the Earl of Ripon, had already been Prime Minister; he had held office as Lord Goderich during the crumbling of the Tory party at the end of the 1820s. Finally, another past prime minister was the Duke. He held no actual office, but by virtue of his experience, his record, and his colossal prestige, he was still made a member of the Cabinet.

He was seventy-two now, and increasingly deaf, but kept up a frightening schedule of public duties. He still led the Tory peers in the Lords, and stories were told of his awesome authority there, even over his Whig opponents. He received visiting foreign royalty and VIPs, including old enemies from the Peninsula like Marshal Soult. He wrote memoranda to the Government about issues of the day like Canada or

India. He actually took on fresh responsibilities, as when in 1842 he resumed his old post of Commander-in-Chief, relinquished in 1827; amazed observers noted that it gave him a fresh lease of life.

His mountainous correspondence, which he tackled in his own hand early every morning, was perpetually swollen by unhappy but hopeful letters from old soldiers who had fallen on hard times – and he always answered. The bolder ones who accosted him in the street each received a sovereign from a purse which he carried for the purpose.

He was by now a one-man national advice bureau – everyone consulted him about absolutely everything. He grumbled fearfully about the continuous demands upon his time, but it was usually no more than grumbling. He had become a white-haired, gruff great-uncle to the nation, and, like most gruff great-uncles, he quite enjoyed it (though nobody must see).

He was held in such esteem in the new Cabinet that a minister who wished to speak would rise and go and stand beside the Duke's chair, so that his Grace might the more easily hear what was being said.

However, for all the talent, and for all the Duke's huge presence, there was no question who dominated the Cabinet – Peel. Gladstone rated him the 'best man of business who was ever Prime Minister'. Sir James Graham, his Home Secretary, said they had never had a leader who was 'so truly a first Minister as he is'. He could be shy and withdrawn outside his own family circle (which was very happy), and he showed at times a flash of temper; but nobody could doubt his honesty, his loyalty to his country, and his integrity. He led by sheer ability, character, and energy. His attention to detail was legendary. He not only supervised his own departments; he also read all the despatches that came into the Foreign Office and he introduced his own budgets. (He had a lot in common with Pitt. Both built and led a revived Tory party; both were somewhat remote; both revived the nation's finances; both towered over their contemporaries in political skill; both were utterly honest; both were enormously respected; both were universally mourned when they went.)

Peel certainly needed all his energy to deal with the problems that awaited him when he entered Number Ten. Colonies in South Africa were seething with disputes among English, Dutch, and African inhabitants – made no easier by old slavers and new missionaries. There were awkward disputes in China and Afghanistan that were reflecting credit on nobody. The previous good relations with France were, thanks to Palmerston, under severe strain. Daniel O'Connell, his party shrunken by the general election, had retreated to Ireland, where he was planning another great campaign of agitation, this time directed at the Act of Union. At home, there was an economic depression, which was going to get worse during the winter of 1841–2. Unemployment was rising; so were prices. A bad harvest had pushed up the cost of a quartern loaf of bread to about a shilling, or roughly 10 per cent of a farm worker's weekly wage. The tax income of the Government was falling, and, for the past five years, the Whigs had been unable to balance the budget.

Somehow or other money had to be raised, prices brought down, and trade revived. 'We must,' wrote Peel, 'make this country a cheap country for living.' The problem was that, in order to bring down the price of imported goods, the customs duty would have to be cut; and four-fifths of the Treasury's income was derived from customs duties. Peel argued, like Huskisson in the 1820s, that, if prices came down, more people could afford to buy, so the total income from customs duties would go up, even at the lower percentage rate. There would of course be a time lag while this happened, during which the Government's income would fall, so another source of revenue would be required to tide them over.

Peel proposed to revive the income tax, at the modest rate of sevenpence in the pound (barely 3p.). It would be only for five years, he said. (No Chancellor of the Exchequer or Prime Minister has since removed it.) During the next three years, Peel abolished the customs duties on over six hundred articles, and lowered them on nearly all the remaining four hundred. Business men and industrialists benefited from cheaper imported raw materials, and ordinary people could more easily afford to put things like meat, butter, potatoes, cheese, sugar, and coffee on the family table.

That still left the most basic commodity of all – bread. No matter how much Peel wished to bring down the price of bread, he dared not tackle head-on the massive agricultural interests in Parliament, still the core of his own party. The Corn Law of 1815, introduced in order to stop cheap foreign corn coming in to undercut the home-grown variety, may have helped English growers, but it did nothing to ease the lives of poor people driven further down into misery by the constantly high price of bread. Huskisson had introduced his Sliding Scale of import duties in 1828, which lowered the import duty on foreign corn when the price of domestic corn was high (in times of bad harvest), and raised it when the price of domestic corn was low (in times of good harvest). That way, the domestic producer could feel reasonably sure of being able to sell his output, particularly when there was a lot of it.

Peel did not wish to antagonise the landed interests by removing the protection of the Corn Laws altogether; at the same time he knew that millions of poor stomachs were grumbling about the price of bread. If he had not known, the Anti-Corn Law League was telling him, and had been telling the whole nation, ever since it had been founded in 1838. Led by Richard Cobden, MP for Manchester, and John Bright, a Quaker businessman from Rochdale, the League beat relentlessly at the Corn Laws. In meetings, speeches, petitions, pamphlets, news sheets, questions in the House, and any other means at their disposal, Cobden and Bright preached the same gospel – free trade, removal of all tariffs and duties. Repeal of the Corn Laws was only a step in that direction, but, naturally, a big one. It would remove the stranglehold of the landed interests from the nation's windpipe, and it would help to hand over control of the nation's welfare to the men best equipped to bring prosperity – the businessmen and the industrialists, the 'intelligent' middle classes. The whole Anti-Corn Law movement was crystallised into one brilliant slogan – 'cheap bread'.

Peel compromised. He produced a more finely-tuned version of Huskisson's Sliding Scale. Like many compromises, it pleased neither side. The landed interests suspected Peel (the son of a Lancashire industrialist), and they had never really trusted him after his turn-about over Catholic Emancipation. And the Anti-Corn Law League did not let up for a moment. What saved the situation for the time being was three good harvests – in 1842, 1843, and 1844 – which kept down the price of bread.

The next task was to encourage business – to make commercial enterprise less dangerous. He set up courts to deal with bankruptcy, and did away with the old practice of putting men in prison for modest debt. Peel then turned his attention to banking. Too many banks had been in the habit of issuing their own banknotes, often with too little gold backing. This might have become necessary in periods of industrial expansion, when more money was needed to secure investments, to pay wages, to meet bills, or to pay the higher prices. In a time of recession, however, banks had been besieged by worried customers who wanted their gold instead, and had been forced to close – with the result that many of their customers had also gone broke.

In a great piece of legislation – the Bank Charter Act of 1844 – Peel established the Bank of England as the only place from which legal banknotes could in future be issued. He separated the note-issuing department from the pure banking department. He laid down that no more than £14,000,000 worth of paper money could be issued without gold backing. (They used Government stock instead. That is, anyone who wished to redeem the banknotes would be paid out in another piece of paper – a certificate of ownership of so much Government stock, which could be bought and sold, but which was not of course as easily negotiable as gold.) Any issue of paper money in excess of £14,000,000 had to be backed with bullion – that is, solid metal or coin, mostly gold, which had to be physically there in the bank's vaults, in case.

Peel had hoped that, by thus controlling the number of banknotes in circulation, he might curb inflation. Prices certainly did come down during his ministry, but it is more likely that they dropped because of his tariff reforms than because of his Bank Charter Act. However, it did concentrate the handling of the nation's currency in the hands of the Bank of England, and made for greater general stability.

In the short run, though, it did not control the periodic waves of wild speculation that occurred. There had been one in the mid-1820s and another in the 1830s. Companies were floated on tides of optimism and unsecured capital; when they failed, investors found themselves jointly responsible for the company's debts, not merely to the extent of their original investment, but to the very limit of their property. Modest investors could, and often did, lose everything in their company's collapse. The answer was to make investors liable to repay company debts only to the extent of their actual investment – the principle of 'limited liability'. If capitalists wanted to attract money from middle- or even working-class investors, they would have to offer some guarantee along these lines. However, in the 1840s, 'unlimited liability' was considered the 'natural' way of going about things, and the principle of limited liability did not receive the backing of law until the Joint Stock Companies Act of 1856.

Nevertheless, despite this continued weakness in the world of business, Peel's reforms put Britain back in credit; he balanced the books, and went on to make a profit. As a sign of returning confidence, he lowered the rate of interest on £250,000,000 worth of Government stock (that is, part of the National Debt – the money the Government has borrowed over the years from its own people) from 3.5 per cent to 3 per cent. This meant that the holders of that stock would henceforth receive the lower rate of interest, but such was the new confidence in the way Peel was handling affairs that they still regarded it as a sound investment. There was no rush to ask for their capital back. It saved the Treasury £1,500,000 a year.

Rising business confidence was expressed in yet another orgy of investment, this time in railways. If the prospect of making a fortune was dangled attractively enough in front of the man with money to invest, it seems there was nothing that could stop him investing it, limited liability or no limited liability.

The Duke did not hold with railways – they were not necessary. If he had his way, no lady would ever travel on one. But he used them now and then. Everybody did: they were unavoidable; they were unmissable; their impetus, like their engines, looked unstoppable. They were so new; they were so different; their impact in the early nineteenth century must have been rather like that of aeroplanes in the twentieth. The one skipped between cities as the other skipped between continents. Such power, such mastery! As the aeroplane liberated man from the support of the earth, so the train freed him from reliance on animal muscle – the horse. So completely had the horse dominated travel since the dawn of Western civilisation that, when the train came along to supersede it, man could think of no other way to describe its strength than in terms of 'horsepower'.

The principle of the railway is no more complicated than the idea of using a plank of wood to stop the wheel of a wheelbarrow sinking into mud or rubble. They had done it in quarries and mines for centuries. Wheelbarrows had evolved into trucks with four wheels. To stop wheels slipping sideways they had used ridges or flanges on the boards, or rails. The next step, to stop the flanges clogging with rubbish, was to transfer the flange from the rail to the wheel. Another natural idea was to use the 'railways' not only down in quarries and mines, but up on the surface, to move produce to the canal or the dock.

Railways might have remained like that, while stagecoaches speeded up road travel and canals linked all the main rivers to open up the entire countryside, had it not been for the invention of the steam engine. It was only a matter of time before someone came up with a steam locomotive, a vehicle that could move itself instead of merely working pumps and industrial machines. Surprisingly, it was not immediately applied to the railways. Some of the early lines had fixed engines, which pulled the 'trains' of trucks by a winch; it was quite a while before someone thought of putting the engine *on the rails*.

All this was happening in the first two decades of the nineteenth century. It was not until the 1820s that it occurred to anyone that it might be profitable to carry not only goods, but passengers.

The first lines must have been an extraordinary mish-mash. Engines did not run all the way; horses were still employed over certain stretches to pull the trucks. Railway-line companies did not own the rolling stock; haulage companies rented the line for set periods, and sometimes rented the engine too. Passengers – the very first ones – travelled in open trucks, literally. In an early, primitive attempt at safety, passengers were locked into the first closed carriages – until a fire inside caused a terrible incident.

Railways, like the improved roads and the newly-built canals, owed much to the genius, energy, and resource of gifted individuals – to none more than to George Stephenson, the son of a Tyneside colliery fireman. Stephenson, who, it is said, learned to read and write only when he was nineteen, virtually picked up railway engineering as he went along; there was nobody to teach him. He had established a huge reputation in the north of England before he was approached to build the Stockton and

Darlington Railway. Five years later he was commissioned to construct another from Liverpool to Manchester. Not only did he accomplish this, in the teeth of much local opposition, and in spite of fearsome physical obstacles; he and his son Robert won the public competition for the best railway engine with the *Rocket*. It was not the fastest, but it was the most reliable, with an average speed over the measured distance of fourteen miles an hour. (Another competitor – there were only four altogether – sprang a leak in its boiler, which was plugged with oatmeal. It seized up in a froth of black porridge.)

On 15 September, 1830, the 'Liverpool and Manchester' was formally opened, almost submerged in a sea of celebrities, which included the Duke, who was then Prime Minister, and William Huskisson, the local MP, who was recovering from a recent injury. In a sad mixture of ignorance, surprise, limping panic, and total misjudgment, Huskisson was struck by the *Rocket*, and had his thigh broken. He was whisked to hospital (by the *Rocket*), but died shortly afterwards.

This, and other accidents, did not stop railway fever gripping the country. Engines belched steam, smoke, and sparks; trains rattled, rolled, dipped, and swung. But people leaped on them. Journeys were loud, dirty, and uncomfortable, but they were adventures.

The prophets of doom were either laughed at or proved wrong. Medical experts said that the human body could not stand being rushed through the air at five times the speed of a stagecoach. (Hence the Duke's chivalrous concern for the delicate female frame.) Birds flying overhead would drop dead from the sky; cows terrified by trains would miscarry and stop giving milk; hens would stop laying; lambs would be born black because of the smoke. Experience and the march of science took care of most of that.

More active opposition came from landowners, who objected to the railways spoiling the peace of the countryside, upsetting their game preserves, and ruining their new drainage schemes by diverting watercourses to build embankments. When they discovered that railway companies, with money pouring in from eager investors, were prepared to pay almost any price for vital strips of land, some of them of no great agricultural value, many landowners mysteriously began to change their minds.

The stagecoach companies saw their fortunes fading away, literally, in a puff of smoke, but they were helpless to prevent it. Railways could do everything they could do, and do it bigger and better and faster and cheaper. A whole race of working people – drivers, guards, ostlers, grooms, coaching inn staff, harness-makers, coach-builders, horse-breeders – saw their livelihood disappearing with the coaches. Many no doubt joined the opposition; the railways needed staff too.

The canal companies had no defence either. No canal barge, with an average speed of three miles an hour, could possibly compete. Railway companies, who were no angels, hastened the process by buying up canals and leaving them to rot.

Some of the last ditches of suspicion and prejudice disappeared when Her Majesty pronounced herself 'quite charmed' with rail travel. Nothing could stop the railway companies now – except their own greed and carelessness.

In an incredibly short time, tunnels, viaducts, cuttings, embankments, junctions, and marshalling yards appeared all over the country. A terrifying breed of men – the railway navvies, whose strength and stamina were surpassed only by their thirst – changed the face of Britain with little more than sweat and muscle, pick and shovel, bucket and spade – and a little gunpowder. In 1830 there were just sixty-nine miles of track in Britain. By the end of the decade there were over five hundred. By the end of the forties there were five thousand. (By 1870, there were over fifteen thousand.)

Just as the Government was anxious to make England 'a cheap country for living', so it was also anxious to make it a cheap country for travelling. In a famous Act of Parliament in 1844, Gladstone, as President of the Board of Trade, decreed that every railway company had to run a train each way on its line, at least once a day, stopping at every station. There was a minimum speed too – twelve miles an hour; and a maximum charge – a penny a mile (an old penny). There was to be accommodation for third-class passengers, and every carriage was to have a roof. Gladstone appears to have thought of everything; he also laid it down that, if companies did not comply with these regulations, the Government could exercise an option, after twenty-one years, to nationalise them.

Though travel became cheap, building did not; one authority quoted the cost at about £40,000 a mile. That meant that a lot of money had to be raised. Companies had to paint glossy pictures of plans and profits. They must have been very successful, because money came in cascades from eager, and mostly ignorant, investors. In the mid-thirties occurred the 'little boom'; in the mid-forties came the big one – 'railway mania'. Investors large and small, not attracted by Peel's modest rate of 3 per cent on Government stock, were bewitched by the railway company prospectuses, which dangled huge dividends before them, and made little mention of practical difficulties of construction or of running costs. Few questions were asked on either side, so long as the money changed hands and hopes ran high.

It was only a matter of time before the first railway tycoon appeared, in the unlikely shape of a linen draper from York called George Hudson. He went first into banking, then into railway speculation. He began takeovers of other lines. As his property grew, he used his successes to induce more people to invest money in further projects – construction of new lines and purchase of existing ones. By the mid-forties he controlled a fifth of the nation's rail network, and was known as the 'Railway King'.

But the expansion could not go on at the same rate; sooner or later the bubble of crazy investment and woolly ambitions and unsound management had to burst. It coincided with, or was caused by, a bad trade slump, partly brought on by bad harvests in 1845 and 1846. By 1847, the USA and Europe were caught up in the first worldwide financial crisis.

Hudson had not helped matters by his odd business methods. He paid high dividends out of capital instead of out of profits. He bought shares of rival companies with the capital of others that he controlled. He was caught out robbing Peter to pay Paul, his 'kingdom' collapsed like a pack of cards, and he prudently left the country.

Another 'monarch' lost his throne at about the same time; the 1840s saw the last of Swaggering Dan, the uncrowned King of Ireland.

Because his party had been much reduced in the House of Commons by the general election of 1841, O'Connell had decided to revert to his previous strategy of public agitation. The Tory Government of 1829 had given way on Catholic Emancipation under the threat of civil war;

if O'Connell could build up enough pressure through more mass meetings, perhaps the Tory Government of the 1840s could be made to do the same on the Act of Union.

He was on home ground in every sense. He was in his beloved Ireland; he was talking to ordinary Catholics instead of doing deals with Protestant ministers in Westminster; he was in the open air and using his gifts for rousing crowds. And such crowds. At Tara, where the old High Kings of Ireland had once been crowned, it was said that a quarter of a million people came to hear him. (Even allowing for a hundred per cent exaggeration, it was a spectacular achievement for a man of sixty-eight.)

Once again the old organisation went into action. After a slow start, the 'Rent' came pouring in. The tours and the speeches drew a new generation of eager young men to support the cause of 'Repeal'. In order to embarrass the Government further, support was pointedly given to the other repeal movement, the Anti-Corn Law League. O'Connell declared that 1843 was to be 'Repeal' year. He never intended to use force, but he used forceful language. He called his mounted escorts 'repeal cavalry'; he heaped abuse and ridicule on his political enemies. One mass meeting after another roared its delight. It looked to many observers as if they were waiting, poised and tense, for their beloved Dan to give them the word.

This time Peel met him head-on. On 8 October, 1843, O'Connell planned to address another monster meeting at Clontarf, just outside Dublin. Once again the site had been chosen with care; Clontarf was the place where the greatest king of medieval Ireland, Brian Boru, had defeated the Vikings in 1014 and thus preserved the liberty of his country. Only twenty-four hours before the meeting was due to take place, the Government banned it.

O'Connell, the lawyer and man of peace, accepted the ban, and rushed out handbills to spread the news in time. There was no crowd, and no trouble. Instead of being grateful to O'Connell for using his authority to keep the peace, the Government then arrested him, charged him with criminal conspiracy, and had him condemned by a packed Protestant jury in Dublin. The verdict was later reversed on appeal to the House of Lords, but the Repeal movement had suffered a clear defeat.

O'Connell accepted the reality, and switched back yet again – to his policy of the 1830s of trying to do deals with the Whigs in Parliament. Unfortunately, he was no longer the unquestioned leader of Ireland. His defeat and his absence in prison awaiting appeal had undermined his position. His son, who tried to carry on for him, did not have his father's magic, and fell out with the younger men who had joined the movement.

This new generation – who now called themselves 'Young Ireland' – were jealous of O'Connell's magic as a mob orator. They did not like his exclusive appeal to Catholics; they wanted to speak for *all* Irishmen. They looked back to Wolfe Tone's United Irishmen of the 1790s, and they were not afraid to consider the possibility of violence. They were too young to remember the revolution of 1798 and the terrible reprisals inflicted by the army. To put it bluntly, they thought O'Connell had gone old and soft; he was past it.

Meanwhile, Peel, having defused the situation, was doing his best to meet Irish demands. There was no question of repealing the Act of Union, but he did attack the problems of land and education. He set up a commission under the Earl of Devon to enquire into the landlord-tenant relationship. It was customary in Ireland to expect a tenant, when he rented land, to put up fences, to drain ditches, and to build a house, at his own expense. He in turn expected to be allowed to stay in possession so long as he paid his rent. Too many landlords, however, claimed that they had the right to rent their land to anyone else they wished, whenever they wished. This raised the question of compensation – paying the outgoing tenant something towards his expenses in fencing, draining, and building. When the Devon Commission proposed a law to ensure this compensation, the outcry from landlords blocked it, and Peel never got the chance to try again.

He ran into similar trouble with his attempts to improve Irish education. In an attempt to win over Catholic opinion, he proposed to raise the annual grant to Maynooth College (a training college for Catholic priests) from £8,000 to £26,000. It ran into a storm of anti-Catholic feeling; opponents included Lord John Russell, the leader of the Whigs, John Bright of the Anti-Corn Law League, and a member of his own Cabinet, Gladstone, who actually resigned over it. (Gladstone was noted for his exceptionally tender conscience and his fierce principles, and was rumoured to carry a letter of resignation around in his pocket, just in case he needed it in a hurry.)

It was worse with the Queen's Colleges in 1845. In an attempt to divorce education from religious domination and thereby avoid the haggling between Catholic and Protestant, Peel set up three new colleges, at Belfast, Cork, and Galway, which were to have no religious connections at all. They were to provide no religious teaching; students could get along in their chosen field of study without any attempt to influence their beliefs. The colleges were at once denounced by both sides as 'Godless colleges' and 'dangerous to the faith and morals of the people'. But, as with Maynooth, Peel went doggedly ahead, with mixed fortunes.

So, by the end of his ministry, little of the 'Irish Question' had been answered. Catholics in theory enjoyed full civil rights, and the hated tithe had gone. But there was still an Established Anglican Church in a country that was nine-tenths Catholic. A small landlord class of foreign descent still owned most of the land. There was still no Irish Parliament.

And now there was no 'Liberator'. O'Connell's health had broken down, partly owing to his three months' imprisonment while awaiting appeal. He was now nearly seventy. His grip on the Repeal movement had slipped after Clontarf, and he had recently made himself a figure of fun by his love affair with a Protestant girl less than half his age. His few remaining appearances in the House of Commons showed him to be a pathetic shadow of his former self. He left England to make a visit to Rome in 1847, and died on the way at Genoa.

One of his early followers had been his near-namesake, Feargus O'Connor. O'Connor had been one of O'Connell's party of repealers in the 1832 reformed House of Commons, but he quarrelled with his leader and switched his energies to the Chartist Movement.

Although he was in jail until the middle of 1841, after the Chartist failures of 1839, O'Connor continued to edit the Chartist newspaper, *The Northern Star*. It helped to keep the flame of Chartism flickering. William Lovett busied himself with educational reform, hoping to build a better-informed working class who would then stand a greater chance of achieving their ambitions. It was a very long-term policy.

Too long-term for O'Connor. He fell out with Lovett and the London group. He fell out with the Birmingham group too; he had no time for Attwood's currency reform. He fell out with another group under Joseph Sturge, who had suggested co-operation with the Anti-Corn Law League. He did not trust the League; they were too middle-class for his liking. He believed the rumours that the League's desire to bring down bread prices was only a means to an end; what the industrialists supporting the League really wanted was to secure an excuse for pushing down wages. O'Connor was wary of all city men and big business; after all, it was the factories and the machines which had put so many of his followers out of work. Finally, he thought they were all too respectable, too soft, too wishy-washy; they would not push their plans to their logical conclusion.

What would the Chartists do if the Government refused the Charter a second time? Lovett and the moderates believed in the power of logical argument, of steady persuasion, of 'moral force'. O'Connor said, and wrote, that only 'physical force' would make ministers take notice.

He never quite spelt out what he meant by this phrase, but he used enough excited language to worry his moderate colleagues, and to disturb the Government. Lovett and Sturge would have nothing further to do with him; the League, some of whose members might have been willing to join an alliance under the banner of 'cheap bread and the vote for all men', were offended by his hostility and suspicion towards them. The Government, who saw in him a combination of Orator Hunt and William Cobbett, would make no concessions to a rabble-rouser.

For O'Connor, like O'Connell and Henry Hunt, had the gift of moving people. Lovett was a theorist, a book man, a desk organiser; O'Connor could talk to people, he had passion, he had magic. Perhaps, like Dan, he had the Irish blarney; perhaps he had learned from his early master. And like Cobbett, O'Connor ran an exciting and successful newspaper. For every literate reader of *The Northern Star*, there were many more who gathered round to have it read to them.

The trouble was that O'Connor was in a sense too successful; he had so excited working men, so convinced them that the Charter was their ticket to the golden future, that he had not prepared them for failure. Desperate men believed him because the only alternative was hopelessness. When, in May, 1842, the House of Commons rejected the second Chartist petition by 287–49 votes, the bottom fell out of the movement.

As in 1839, Chartism floundered. When a series of strikes swept the northern counties in response to proposed wage cuts in the depression, O'Connor did not produce a clear lead. After all his talk about physical force, he dismayed the strikers by saying that he would have nothing to do with them. Then he blamed the strikes on the Anti-Corn Law League. Then, when he saw how much support they were getting, he changed his mind, and tried to harness this energy to the Chartist cause. He and other leaders toured the strike areas and made speeches of support. He got involved in the famous 'Plug Plot' – a scheme for taking plugs out of boilers in order to cut off the source of power.

As with Hunt and Cobbett, the Government took no chances. It was a time of deep depression, great hardship, misery, and discontent. There had been two attempts on the Queen's life in 1841 (there was to be one on Peel's in 1843). Troops were called out, moved quickly on the new railways, and deployed in the trouble spots. Arrests followed. Before long, most of the Chartist leadership was behind bars again, and strike ringleaders were on their way to Australia.

Moderate middle-class support was frightened off, and the League virtually washed its hands of Chartism. Lovett quarrelled with Sturge, and the moderate side of Chartism was in ruins too. Only O'Connor remained; he had escaped imprisonment through a technical error in his indictment.

For the next few years he flung himself into a new passion – his Land Scheme. He had never liked industry. He blamed it for the misery of so many men who had recently been forced off the countryside into the awful cities. His Irish background gave him the instinct that the solution lay in the land; if working men could be given a fresh start on the land, they could escape the slavery of the mills and their grasping owners, and regain their self-confidence and prosperity as small farmers. It was another version of Cobbett's dream of re-creating the yeomen of Merrie England.

O'Connor proposed to raise money by persuading working men to invest in his Chartist Co-Operative Land Society (later renamed the

National Land Company). Shares would cost twenty-six shillings each – £1.30 – and could be paid for on the instalment plan. With the money raised, land was to be bought, and divided into plots of a few acres each. A cottage would be built, and livestock provided. These plots were then to be allocated by ballot to shareholders, who would pay rent for it to the Company. With the rent money, more land was to be bought and stocked, and so on – until every working man in the country who wished to escape the cities had won his freedom.

O'Connor produced strings of figures to 'prove' that the plan could not fail. Moreover, it did not depend for success on any new law from Parliament, or on any clash with Parliament. Working men did not have to strike or demonstrate or risk prison; at last they had the means of their own salvation in their own hands.

As with Owen's GNCTU, its attractiveness was hypnotic. Money came pouring in – over £90,000 in three years, from very poor men. There were over 70,000 shareholders. A Chartist Land Bank was set up, to hold deposits and advance loans. Five estates were actually bought and settled – one near Watford appropriately named 'O'Connorville'.

The only consolation was that the Land Scheme took longer to die than the GNCTU. No other Chartist leader would have anything to do with it. The ballot winners who were settled at O'Connorville and at others in Gloucestershire, Worcestershire, and in Oxfordshire, were urban workers with little or no experience of farming. The land they were given was often of poor quality. Local farmers said that it was difficult to make a go of it with scores of acres, never mind only four or five – and they were right.

Finally, worst of all, the finance soon fell into a hopeless mess. O'Connor had got his figures wrong in the first place, and he was no accountant. A press campaign accused him of cooking the books. He was acquitted by a Parliamentary Committee of Inquiry; indeed it was shown that he had put a lot of his own money into it. But the Company could not survive; the Inquiry showed that both it and the Land Bank were technically illegal. It was wound up in 1851, by which time most of the Chartist 'yeomen' had given up, been evicted for not paying rent, and either become landless labourers or gone back to the cities. Only O'Connorville survived for another twenty-five years under its own steam.

By contrast, another working-class movement for self-help, the Co-operative Movement, set up in Rochdale in 1844, flourished. It introduced the new idea that a member received a dividend not according to how much he had invested *in* the company, but according to how much he had bought *through* the company. There was straight investment, too. But the real reason, perhaps, for the movement's success was that, unlike Chartism or O'Connell's Repeal movement, it was not challenging the Government; it was not seeking some much-publicised, nationwide showdown as implied by the Charter.

The Anti-Corn League, too, had realised that it was much more likely to succeed if it pursued one single aim, not half a dozen like the Chartists. And they found that difficult enough, particularly when 1842, 1843, and 1844 all produced good harvests and therefore lower bread prices. Cobden was near to despair more than once.

Factory reformers, yet another pressure group prodding the consciences of the nation's rulers, also concentrated on one single idea, and they registered a success in 1844. Lord Shaftesbury's Factory Act of that year is an illuminating example of the way in which religion was both an inspiration and an obstacle to reform.

If ever a reformer was motivated by sincere religious belief, it was Shaftesbury; and it was Christian ideas of charity and mercy that moved people to be shocked and compassionate when they found out exactly what was going on in factories and mills. Hence, the 1844 act shortened the number of hours allowed in the child's working day from eight to six and a half. Young persons between thirteen and eighteen, and all women, were to be restricted to a twelve-hour day. In an attempt to anticipate sharp practice (working them in relays, to keep the men going), it was also decreed that all workers were to begin the day's shift at the same hour; and a clock was made compulsory in all places of work, visible to all. Fences were to be placed round dangerous machinery, and no machine was to be cleaned while in motion.

The fact that this represented *progress* is clear illustration of many attitudes of the time – including the belief, held by many sincere Christians, that the Devil made work for idle hands. Shaftesbury had to work like a slave himself among his fellow-MPs, many of whom prided themselves on their Christian charity, in order to get the working day of, say, a girl of thirteen *down* to twelve hours. Finally, his desire to introduce a measure of educational reform ran into religion again. Nonconformists and Anglicans haggled bitterly over which of them should have the bigger say in the religious instruction of these factory waifs during their off-duty hours in the boiler room or the cellar or the stock shed. In the end, both Shaftesbury and the Home Secretary gave up; apart from giving factory inspectors the right to inspect factory 'schools' and disqualify incompetent teachers, they could make no other educational provisions at all.

So the leaders of the Ten Hours Movement got over their disappointment, and set about yet another Parliamentary bill, which would, one day, achieve their objective of a uniform ten-hour day for all working people. The factory-owners got over their frustration about the new limitations on their actions, and told their overseers to continue their old practice of moving the hands of the clock back a few minutes when they got close to the hour. Nevertheless, whatever the new Act's limitations, it was, like the 1833 Act, a step in the right direction.

A similar pattern is evident in the matter of the mines. When the Royal Commission had made its report on conditions in 1842, the nation was appalled. People had had no idea. Mines were miles from anywhere; ignorance bred rumour, exaggeration, and myth. Mines were remote, gloomy, hellish places inhabited by remote, gloomy, hellish people.

It was not so much the conditions in which the men worked; what upset respectable opinion was the extent of child and female labour – and of course there was more worry about the lack of religious belief and the possibility of sin in a mixed-sex underground ghetto than there was about the poverty, hardship, cruelty, and danger. Nevertheless, society did have the grace to be shocked at evidence of six-year-olds working underground, of young girls carrying hundredweight sacks up towering ladders, and of women (some of them pregnant) on their hands and knees pulling coal trucks like donkeys. And once roused, society did try.

The Mines Act of that year stopped all female labour underground, and that of all children under ten. Inspectors were appointed. But the owners fought a strong rearguard action. Inspectors were allowed to report only on the condition of the workers, not on the condition of the mines; there were no restrictions at all on hours.

On the issues with which it was called upon to deal – finance, trade, the railways, Ireland, Chartism, factories, mines – Peel's Government tended to follow a policy that was typical of many nineteenth-century governments – in England, at any rate. Neither Peel nor his colleagues were particularly creative, though Peel, it was said, was a good user of other people's ideas. What made them better than others before and after was perhaps their skills and energies rather than their inventiveness. Their 'policy' – by which is meant in this context their overall attitude rather than their detailed plans – could be summed up in a phrase like 'law and order, *laissez-faire*, lower expenses, and a bit of charity in a good cause'.

Law and order was certainly the priority when it came to arresting the Chartist leaders and banning O'Connell's meeting at Clontarf. *Laissez-faire* was uppermost in Peel's method of dealing with tariffs; the Government had now come a long way from the old 'regulating' ideas of the eighteenth century, which had proved so disastrous with the American colonies. Pitt had lowered some duties. After the war Huskisson had lowered more. Peel continued the process in the 1840s. Time was to show that this was only another step towards complete free trade – the removal of tariffs altogether – which was to be accomplished by Peel's disciples in the 1850s and 1860s, notably Gladstone. Lower tariffs made England 'a cheap country for living', which was Peel's objective at the outset; Gladstone's famous 'Parliamentary train' helped to make travel cheap too. Finally, it was conscience and common charity that overcame the old idea that governments should not interfere in the private lives or business of individual citizens. Despite a loud rearguard action by factory- and mine-owners – full of righteous indignation about the sacred nature of their private business affairs – steps were taken (albeit limited ones) to make life slightly less unbearable for millions of overworked and underpaid employees.

The same approach, the same general attitude, was visible when a problem appeared in the colonies – in this case South Africa. As ministers of the country which owned South Africa, the Cabinet was responsible for basic law and order, and accepted the responsibility. At the same time, it did not wish to interfere in the private or business lives of the colonists more than was absolutely necessary – again the lesson of the American colonies was still clear in the mind. It certainly did not wish to be drawn further into yet more colonial commitment; that could only mean sending out more troops for the defence of some God-forsaken territory in the back of beyond, and laying another burden on the British taxpayer. And then again, when clear evidence of injustice, cruelty, and exploitation was set before them, Cabinet ministers felt that, in common humanity, they had to make some kind of response.

The South African problem was a clear illustration of all these themes. In the first place, the British Government did not particularly want South Africa. The Cape of Good Hope and its surrounding territory had been captured from the Dutch in 1795, because of its unbeatable strategic position on the trade route from Europe to India and the Far East. At the Congress of Vienna, Britain hung on to it, for exactly the same reason.

Ideally, she would have liked to run it like a sort of southern Gibraltar. Unfortunately, there was rather more than a rock there; there were people – far too many of them, and far too different from each other. To begin with, there were the native Africans: the Hottentots, whose tribal system was breaking up under the shock of European contact, and who survived in semi-slavery or in cattle-stealing; and the Bushmen, who were living practically in the Stone Age, who had no possessions for the white man to envy, but who were not above a bit of cattle-stealing too. Neither of these peoples was a threat to 'civilisation'; the white man's only reaction to them was to have periodic 'drives' and massacres to keep them away from their grazing grounds.

The third native people – the Zulus (of Bantu origin from central Africa) – were a different proposition altogether. Bigger, stronger, more proud and more warlike, better armed and better organised, they had, under a leader of genius, Shaka, set up shop in Natal, to the north-east of Cape Colony.

Finally, spread around the great open plains – the *veldt* – were other Bantu tribes lumped together under the name of 'Kaffir', which was originally an Arab word for 'unbeliever', that is, non-Muslim. (The Arabs were the great slave traders of Africa, and they had to call their victims something.)

Leaving aside explorers, the Europeans had first arrived in force in the shape of the Dutch, either as traders or as settlers. The word 'Boer' is derived from the Dutch word for 'farmer'. For a farmer to survive in Africa, he had to be tough, independent, and resourceful – and able to defend himself. The country was hard, wide, and open. To sustain him he had his strong, if bleak, Calvinist faith, which taught him that it was his mission to bring 'civilisation' to this benighted land and its backward people – whether they wanted it or not. The parallels with the American West, the covered wagons, and the Indians are readily seen.

Then had come French immigrants, Huguenots fleeing from Catholic persecution in France. This explains the 'French' sound of many Boer names such as de Villiers, Delarey, Marais, Joubert, and Malan. However, they were Calvinist too, so the contrast with the original Dutch was not too stark.

It was different with the arrival of English rule in 1815. It was worse with the arrival of British immigrants in the early 1820s. It was worse still with the arrival of the missionaries. And running through the whole mixture was a seasoning of people of mixed race – the Griquas (literally 'bastards') – which proved that the Boers did not carry their dislike of 'Kaffirs' so far as to keep away from their women.

The history of the next ten or twenty years can therefore almost be deduced. Boers felt cut off from their cultural roots by rule in the English language. The English immigrants complained of discrimination by the majority Dutch. Missionaries were appalled at the harsh treatment of Africans by the Boers, and preached the equality of man before Christ – which the Boers said was not only interference but faulty theology. Frontier settlers constantly ran into raiding parties or reprisals by the Kaffirs – or, worse, the Zulus – who were, after all, only fighting for their own land; and they badgered the British Government to provide protection in the shape of troops. The British Government grumbled bitterly every time settlers strayed beyond the original colony, because they knew it would only lead to trouble and expense at best; at worst, it could lead to casualties, and questions in the House about waste and mismanagement. All white groups – immigrants, Boers, and missionaries alike – fumed at the fact that the British Government six thousand miles away did not know enough, did not care enough, and did not do enough.

Four events brought matters to a head.

In 1828, the Governor of Cape Colony officially gave equal status to all free men under his jurisdiction, regardless of colour. In 1833, slavery was declared abolished throughout the British Empire. In 1834, another decree, this time from the Colonial Office, made it illegal for any European settlers to cross over to the north side of the Orange River. Finally, there were proposals to set up separate states for Griquas and Bantus, in an attempt to protect them from Boer exploitation.

No matter how noble or well-intentioned these reforms may have been, the Boers did not see them that way. Equality before the law, as far as they were concerned, went flat against biological and theological truth – Africans simply were not equal, and that was that. For the same reason, freeing the slaves would only cause trouble; and owners thought the compensation much too low. And as for restricting the movement of farmers, it was further proof of the fact that the British Government had no conception of reality; Boers depended on freedom of movement to keep themselves and their herds alive in a dry country, and their regular remedy for many problems was to move away from them – to go 'trekking', to take off further beyond the horizon. They were tough and independent; they were used to looking after themselves.

So they refused to be caught in the cleft stick which the Colonial Office had fashioned for them. They decided to 'trek' right away from the reach of the British. Between 1835 and 1837, thousands of Boers and their families, in swaying, pan-clattering convoys of covered wagons (like something straight out of a Western film), set out north and east, in what has become known as the 'Great Trek'. One group set up a Boer 'republic' north of the Orange River; another went beyond that, across the Vaal River, and set up another 'republic' – the Transvaal. A third had gone east, into Natal, where they ran into the fearsome, and fearless, regiments of the Zulus, and also into another band of British immigrants who had been set up there by the Colonial Office.

The whole original problem flared again: fights between Boer and Zulu, bitter rivalry between Boer and English settlers, and general chaos all the way along the route taken by the trekkers – outraged Kaffirs, border wars, cattle raids, reprisal and revenge, and weeping missionaries bewailing the ruination of their hard work.

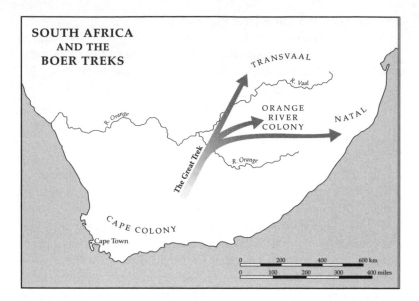

Peel's Government felt that it had no option but to declare the official occupation of Natal, which it did in 1843; order had to come first. The Boers went trekking again, and joined their brethren beyond the Orange and the Vaal. The British at first did not like the idea of the Boers getting away with it, but they could not have it both ways; if they did not want further extension of the Empire, they could hardly complain if some people simply wanted to go away from the Empire. So it was left to one of Peel's successors to recognise the two Boer republics – the Transvaal in 1852, at the Sand River Convention, and the Orange Free State in 1854, at the Bloemfontein Convention.

It was little more than a public hand-washing, and it was not effective for long. To problems of the Hottentots and Bushmen were soon to be added those of Basutos, Griquas, and Matabeles. British and Boer who remained in Cape Colony and Natal were no more friendly to each other. Missionaries were just as active. The British Government may have thought they had seen the last of the Boer trekkers, but they were mistaken. And they certainly had not seen the last of the Zulus.

If British Ministers came out of trouble in Africa with little credit, they came out with much less from a war in eastern Asia. For Britain fought a war with China in order to secure the right to engage in the (illegal) trade in opium.

Put like that, in the drugs-conscious twenty-first century, it makes the British Cabinet look like a gang of gunboat-packing Mafia bosses. Certainly it is difficult to make any trade in opium look respectable, and there were those at the time who said so – like Gladstone. However, without necessarily trying to whitewash either British ministers or British merchants, any fair account needs to be a little more detailed than that.

It was a case of the irresistible force meeting the immovable object. The Chinese Empire had enjoyed its civilisation and its economic self-sufficiency for hundreds of years; it did not need the West, and it wanted nothing from the West. Out of the blue came Englishmen, Americans, Dutch, French, Germans, and others – traders, adventurers, moneymakers, grabbers – who regarded the whole world as fair game. (The missionaries were almost as bad; it never crossed their mind that they might be interfering.)

Quite apart from the language barrier, there was a complete lack of appreciation or understanding. The newcomers were fully prepared to bargain, and could not see for the life of them why the Chinese would not negotiate like anybody else. The Chinese refused to treat as equals any 'foreign devil' who did not humble himself before their Emperor like every other subject. They would not recognise the status of any other monarch.

The best the East India Company could manage was a sort of informal toehold in the port of Canton. The official Imperial attitude in the capital, Pekin (now Peking, or Beijing), was one of contempt, but the merchants of Canton were more businesslike, and a thriving trade began in tea. The trouble was that the Chinese wanted very few goods in return, so the tea had to be paid for in silver. Before long, this was draining the coffers of the East India Company, so they hit on the idea of paying instead with opium, which grew plentifully in Bengal. Drugs were almost unknown in the West at that time, but they were widely used, and abused, in the East. The demand for opium in China became so great that fortunes were soon being made by Portuguese, Dutch, and American traders as well. Understandably, the Chinese Imperial

Government objected to their subjects becoming addicted in increasing numbers, and banned the opium trade.

It was at this time that the East India Company's monopoly of trade with China was abolished – in 1833 – and a Government agent was sent to Canton to negotiate a new commercial agreement. The Chinese simply refused to recognise either him or his government, and repeated the ban on opium. Meanwhile, the collapse of the East India Company's monopoly allowed in all sorts of less respectable operators, who traded under the counter with Chinese merchants in Canton – both sides being anxious to make a profit. Inevitably, there were broken agreements, brawls, and 'incidents'.

Then, in 1838, the Emperor sent a new man to Canton, Commissioner Lin, with instructions to root out the opium trade once and for all. To the merchants' surprise, Lin was not open to the usual bribes; when he said that the opium trade was to stop and the stocks of opium destroyed, he meant it. Elliott, the British agent, obeyed, and about £2,000,000 worth was destroyed, without compensation. Then Lin went further: he demanded the surrender of British trading ships and the trial of some sailors in Chinese courts. As before, there was no negotiation, no compromise, no sign of willingness to treat the other side as equals – 'foreign devils' had no rights.

So what had begun as a bit of drug-running on the side had escalated into a great matter of the protection of the British subject abroad and the whole principle of diplomatic negotiation between equals.

The war which followed was short and not very distinguished. Britannia still ruled the waves, and her technology was vastly superior to anything the enemy could provide. One example of the Chinese war effort may serve to illustrate: some of their guns at the harbour mouth of Canton failed to operate properly because the gunpowder had been adulterated with sand. It appeared that the gun crews, dedicated to keeping out the 'foreign devils' and their wicked opium, were themselves so addicted to the drug that they had sold some of their own gunpowder to obtain some more of it.

In a short time the Chinese were bombarded to the conference table. It was the classic example of 'gunboat' diplomacy. By the Treaty of Nanking, signed in 1842, the Chinese handed over the island of Hong

Kong to England, and allowed future trade with foreign powers to be conducted through the five ports of Amoy, Foochow, Ningpo, Shanghai – and Canton. They were also forced to pay £5,000,000 damages and compensation.

It was the sort of war in which victory was only slightly less disgraceful than defeat, though qualms of conscience in England were eased by pride in a successful deal; after all, the world had been made safer for free trade – which must make it a victory for civilisation and peace. There was not much victory, or civilisation, or peace, in the other shamefaced little cul-de-sac of colonial history in which the English Government trapped itself, at about the same time, and on the same continent.

Early in 1842, the Cabinet had to accept the unpalatable fact that their expeditionary force had been destroyed, to the last man, by the Afghans of all people. An explanation of this disaster has to take in subjects as wide-ranging as the Turkish Empire, Russian foreign policy, British imperial paranoia, and the East India Company.

As has already been explained, one of the cardinal features of Russian foreign policy has, for centuries, been the search for a warm-water seaport. The ancient Muscovy had been a landlocked state centred, naturally, on Moscow. As it grew in power, its avenues of military and commercial expansion were, equally naturally, the giant rivers – the Dvina, the Bug, the Dnieper, the Dniester, the Don, the Volga, the Ob, Yenisei, Lena, and so on. There were no roads in the tundra, the *taiga*, or the steppe. Ever since Peter the Great, the Russian Empire had spread, at varying speeds, to reach the Baltic, the Arctic, and the Bering Straits. All were vast, but all froze in winter. Another way out had to be found. That meant the Black Sea, which was reached at the expense of the Cossacks and similar semi-nomads. But it was still not enough; the real highways of trade – and the warm water – lay in the Mediterranean, and straddling the path to it was the Turkish Empire.

So Peter the Great and Catherine the Great and, more recently, Alexander I and Nicholas I had brought pressure to bear, mostly by means of war, with varying success. If it had been simply a case of Russian versus Turk, the chances are that the Russians would have got what they were after, but the plot began to thicken. The Mediterranean was also the focus of many, and valuable, trade routes belonging to the British and the French. These two peoples had their differences, God knows, but one thing they were agreed upon was that the Russians must be kept out of the Mediterranean at all costs. Hence the need to come to the rescue of the Turkish Empire whenever it was threatened – one of the salient features of the celebrated Eastern Question (see Chapters 7 and 10). Hence Palmerston's belief that all the talk about the Turkish regime being 'the sick man of Europe' was 'pure and unadulterated nonsense'.

British foreign secretaries were generally so successful, and the British Navy was so strong, that, shortly after his accession in 1825, Tsar Nicholas I told his advisers to come up with some other strategy to achieve what they wanted – the warm-water seaport.

They said, in effect, that the continued attempt to dismantle the Turkish Empire was no longer worth the candle. Even if it succeeded, it would only exchange one weak enemy for two strong ones – Britain and France. Or maybe even a third – Mehemet Ali. Far better to abandon the frontal-assault technique and settle instead for infiltration, intrigue, blackmail, and other forms of commercial skullduggery in order to milk the Turks dry of whatever resources they possessed – in short, to regard the Turks as the highway to the Mediterranean rather than as the barrier to it. Meanwhile, Russian agents should explore the possibilities of going *behind* the Turkish Empire – into the vast, largely unknown spaces (well, unknown to most Europeans) of Iraq, Iran, the Caucasus, Turkestan, Uzbekistan – and Afghanistan. (At last a connection begins to emerge.) At the risk of a clumsy pun in such a dry, land-locked area, those Russian agents might find very attractive troubled waters to fish in, and there was always the prospect (distant, but dazzling nonetheless) of tapping the riches of India and of reaching the Indian Ocean – with its permanently warm waters.

The British reacted almost as if the Russians had threatened to cross the Straits of Dover. It is true that they were not particularly interested in extending the British Empire, but they were extremely interested in hanging on to what they already had. Colonies, like clothes, suffered from fashion: in the eighteenth century the most valued overseas possessions had been the sugar islands in the West Indies (Napoleon had guessed, correctly, that, if he pretended to attack them, the British Navy would rush to defend them). By the mid-nineteenth century, far and away the most precious bauble in the imperial basket – the jewel in the crown – was India. Nothing must be allowed to threaten India. (It was Napoleon again who had provoked a violent reaction by his invasion of Egypt – was he really planning to go for India? During the long French War, the two places seem to have been of about equal importance, but, after 1815, India gradually overhauled the Caribbean.)

The irony was that the British Government did not own India, or even part of it. So-called 'British' territories in India were the property of the East India Company, and were treated as such. The Government did indeed assist with administration, defence, and general overview, but the lands were technically in the possession of a private commercial company. (It is as if a country the size of, say, Brazil, were to be run by ICI.) Nevertheless, the Government reacted as if it did own India; and it felt just as vulnerable to any threat directed, however obliquely, at its riches.

During the eighteenth century, the Company, with Government-appointed Governors and Governors-General, had waged successful wars against the French and Dutch, as well as against numerous native Indian princes (the Duke and his brother had both served there), and by about the 1820s were unquestionably the dominant power in the sub-continent. There remained a large stretch of unconquered territory to the north-west – Sind and the Punjab – over against the mountainous frontier facing Afghanistan. These two areas would have to be mopped up, of course, to tidy up the map. But the further prospect was the stark open space of Afghanistan – just about the time that the first news was coming in of Russian infiltration.

The reaction was McCarthyish in its intensity. The Company, and the British Government, were prepared to start at every hint, jump at every rumour, tremble at every possibility, of Russian penetration. Russian agents and spies were everywhere, whispering in the ears of frowning, beard-stroking amirs, building mysterious alliances, developing hideous plots, promising 'aid', placing bribes, and generally up to no good. Nothing was considered too low or too subtle or too devious for their Machiavellian minds. Thus was born the Great Game – a marathon of intrigue, espionage, and suspected double-cross that consumed the Russian and British governments, right into the twentieth century. Each side hatched unofficial schemes, sent secret missions, organised covert surveys, and generally threw money into the vast and unfamiliar spaces of Central Asia, in a constant bid to outmanoeuvre the supposed dastardly designs of the other.

In 1839, Lord Auckland, the new Governor-General, decided that a pre-emptive strike had become necessary. Wellington, who knew India, had his misgivings, but there was enough Cabinet support to give the go-ahead. Auckland's excuse for intervention was to hand – the excuse that was always to hand in a country of rival tribes and endemic war – in the form of a claimant to the throne who felt he had been hard done by. He had: he had been kicked out – two or three times – by the present ruler, Dost Mahomed, who was apparently favouring the Russians. This claimant, Shah Shuja, promised to favour the British if he were installed. The plan then was obvious – send in a column of troops, expel Dost Mahomed, put Shah Shuja back on the throne, and keep garrisons of soldiers in Kabul, Kandahar, and Jalalabad to protect his interests (and British ones too).

Which is what they did. And they stayed there for two years. During that time, the Afghans displayed their customary hatred of the foreigner – no matter which cause he was espousing; the elderly British general displayed the customary blinkered, out-of-date inefficiency of the Waterloo veteran; and the British troops displayed their customary oversexed ignorance of local taboo and religion. The British political agent was murdered. The military commander, who, after two years, was now also responsible for about 12,000 wives, children, and camp followers besides his original 4,000 troops, decided that he had no alternative but withdrawal. He negotiated an agreement with Dost Mahomed's son, Akbar Khan, for a safe conduct, all the way from Kabul to Jalalabad, near the Indian frontier.

The retreat began on 6 January, 1842, in the grip of a savage Afghan winter, along a harsh route of mountain defiles and passes, crawling with stark Afghan tribesmen with itchy trigger fingers, and firearms (*jezails*) with over four times the effective range of the English Brown Bess muskets. Discipline broke down; the women and children and some of the officers were taken as hostages (Akbar Khan

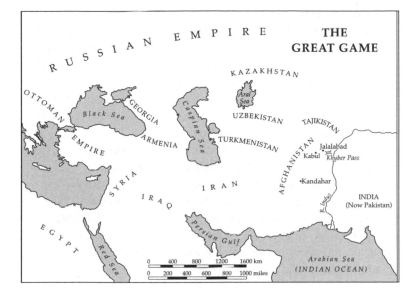

was concerned for the safety of his father, Dost Mahomed, who was in custody in India). No mercy was shown to the remaining soldiers; out of the original 4,000 or so, just one man reached safety a week later – a Dr William Brydon, an army surgeon. (Brydon must have had a charmed life; he later survived the siege of Lucknow in the Indian Mutiny.)

A relief force was sent to help the two smaller garrisons get out from Jalalabad and Kandahar, and the prisoners were rescued, so some face was saved. But Shah Shuja had by this time been killed, and there really was no reason to linger. The British left again. Dost Mahomed remounted his throne, and stayed on it for another twenty years – so much for 'instability'. In the event the Tsar did not invade – so much for the Russian threat. It had all been for nothing.

Governor-General Auckland dismissed the episode as 'a partial reverse'; Lord Palmerston, who had been Foreign Secretary when the escapade had begun, swept it under the carpet; and everyone turned with some relief to the relatively good news about the successful bullying of the Chinese in the Treaty of Nanking.

Lord Aberdeen, the new Foreign Secretary, must have hated it. Aberdeen did not share the bullish attitude of many of his countrymen. He worked for peace, and this at times made it look as if he was weak, or at any rate easily satisfied. He also worked hard to restore good relations between England and France, which had recently suffered strain thanks to Palmerston's determined action over the Eastern Question. This too was not very popular with a population that far too easily jumped to the conclusion that the villains were always the French. It was his misfortune to come immediately after Palmerston at the Foreign Office, and he did not have Palmerston's gifts for publicity and drama.

However, he was welcomed in chancelleries all around Europe; anything after Palmerston had to be an improvement. This was especially true in Paris, where the Prime Minister, Guizot, was a personal friend; they had got to know each other when Guizot had been French Ambassador in London. Between them they saved the *Entente Cordiale* (the special relationship between England and France) from two or three nasty moments during the next few years.

For example, the French conquests in Algeria disturbed the English. No actual English interests were under direct threat, and it was not easy to prove that English trade routes through the Mediterranean were vulnerable to being cut by expeditions from the North African coast. More likely it was once again the old suspicion of an old enemy; just what were the Frogs up to? (And whatever they were up to, they shouldn't be.) Guizot and Aberdeen played it down, and were able to maintain a certain amount of co-operation in the suppression of the slave trade.

When rival French and English agents in Greece intrigued against each other to gain the upper hand in relations with King Otto, again Guizot and Aberdeen conducted their own relations with tact and honesty, and a good deal of mutual trust.

A third storm in a teacup broke out in the Pacific – in Tahiti. A British Protestant missionary called Pritchard was in rivalry with some French Catholic missionaries. Each side appealed to its respective government to uphold its case. In the middle was a baffled, and half-converted, Queen of Tahiti, who appears to have altered her loyalty according to which way the political wind was blowing at the time. Faced with modern warships, she would have had little alternative.

In 1843, a local French admiral formally declared the island annexed to France. In 1844, he arrested Pritchard. Guizot and Aberdeen once again found themselves between two groups of hotheads – those gazing down the muzzles of each other's guns in the Pacific, and those Parliamentary warriors in each country who argued, from their seats in the House, that the honour of the country was at stake. In the end, mercifully, good sense prevailed. Pritchard had to leave the island, but received compensation and an apology from the French Government. Guizot gave up the annexation, but continued to maintain that Tahiti was under the 'protection' of France. For a moment, it had almost looked as if the two major powers of Western Europe were going to war about a single missionary on a single tiny island on the other side of the world.

Aberdeen's other notable contribution to good international relations concerned not an old rival, but a young newcomer to world affairs, the United States of America. The only war fought between the two countries had ended in 1814, but England's attitude to the USA had not progressed much beyond wariness and scorn of the new republic. In 1815 a commercial treaty had been signed, and in 1818 the boundary was settled between Canada and the USA – that is, the boundary between the Great Lakes and the Rockies. It was to be along the 49th parallel of latitude, and it still is – the longest undefended frontier in the world.

Other problems took longer to solve – such as the frontier in the north-east, the question of fishing and fur-trapping rights, the policing of the Great Lakes, the possible ripples of disturbance caused by the Canadian Rebellion of 1837, the unwillingness of the Americans to join in any international campaign to stamp out the slave trade, and the boundary in the far west.

President Monroe won a new respect for his country by his famous statement on foreign policy known as the 'Monroe Doctrine' in 1823. His assertion that no further colonisation or any other political incursion from Europe into America was to be tolerated has passed into the national subconscious of his people.

It was left to Aberdeen – the reasonable Aberdeen – to negotiate treaties between the two countries that settled the last of the frontier disputes. In 1842, his representative, Lord Ashburton, and the American Senator, Daniel Webster, drew up the inevitably named 'Webster-Ashburton

Treaty', which fixed the boundary between Canada and the USA in the north-east. Both Webster and Ashburton had to undergo much criticism from 'patriots' in their respective countries for having given away too much; they could not both have been right. At any rate, the treaty stood.

Feelings ran higher over the boundary beyond the Rockies. The territory was loosely named 'Oregon', and had been ruled jointly by both powers since 1818, for the simple reason that they could not think of any better arrangement. At a time when the land was practically empty, the matter had not been pressing. Now it was filling up with traders and immigrants (from about 1842, the movement among people in the, then, frontier states of Iowa, Illinois, and Missouri became known as 'Oregon fever'). American opinion wanted the word 'Oregon' to include all land up as far as Alaska, which was then owned by the Russians.

President Polk, however, had designs on California, Arizona, and Texas, which he knew would lead to war with Mexico; he had no desire for another with Britain at the same time. So when Aberdeen offered the same line – the 49th parallel – as the rest of the boundary (with a small kink in it to put Vancouver Island in Canada), he accepted. The Oregon Treaty was ratified in June 1846.

A fortnight later, Peel and Aberdeen were out of office. Events in the ten or eleven months leading up to June, 1846 had built up to dam-breaking proportions, and not even Peel's strong Tory Cabinet had been able to withstand them. Again, there is a parallel here with Pitt. Both men had so restored national finances and national confidence that they could each contemplate their achievement with pride, and look forward to yet better times.

In 1792, Pitt said in his budget speech that he could not think of another time when there was a greater likelihood of fifteen years of future peace; within a twelvemonth, England was involved in a war of survival that was to last for twenty-two years. Similarly, Peel could, in 1845, gaze with some satisfaction on a balanced budget, revived national trade, lower prices, a vigorous banking system, a sheepish Anti-Corn Law League (after three good harvests), a stricken Chartist movement, and, above all, an Ireland quieter, and shorn of the magic of O'Connell.

He, like Pitt, was undone in a twelvemonth – not by a foreign revolution, nor by a distant dictator; not by an unforeseen slump, nor by a ministerial scandal; but by the most unremarkable of adversaries – the potato.

CHAPTER TWELVE

Widow McCormack and Mr Punch
1846–51

If ever the events of five years burned themselves into the memory of a nation, the terrible tragedies of the late forties marked the Irish more deeply than the killings of Cromwell, and the persecutions of William III, and the houndings of the four Georges.

In those five years it was made clear beyond all argument that the real trouble in Ireland was not politics or religion, but the land. O'Connell had seen victory over Emancipation and the tithe and the Union only as means to an end – the end of Irish poverty.

For Ireland was poor, poor too by the standards of the time, which took into account the squalor of Sicily and the vast bleakness of Russia, where the serfs were still the personal possessions of their landlords. Those who visited Ireland and saw conditions for themselves could scarcely credit the evidence of their own eyes. They ransacked the dictionaries to find words to express their horror and revulsion. Those who had not seen for themselves often refused to believe it. Nobody, they argued from their armchairs, could be *that* poor. They could, and were, millions of them, and more each year. There was not enough land, not enough food, not enough work, and not enough money, yet the population was rising at an incredible rate. The census of 1841 had given the figure of 8,000,000 – double what it had been fifty years before. Of that figure, 180,000 families were said to have less than five acres each, 135,000 families less than an acre each, and thousands more labourers had no land at all.

True, there were some wealthy Irishmen, but they were mostly

Protestant, mostly landowners, and mostly not living in Ireland. These were the absentee landlords, whose only interest in their estates was for the rents they brought in. These rents were usually collected by middlemen, agents who squeezed more money from tenants than was really necessary in order to compensate themselves for the trouble they were taking. If a tenant could not pay his rent, he could be, and often was, evicted. His house would be pulled down ('tumbled' was the polite word), and he and his family left, literally, at the roadside.

He had, in English eyes, broken the law, or rather the legal contract with his landlord. By English law, a landlord's land was his to do with as he liked; it was as much his property as a horse or a piece of furniture. If he wished to rent out some land to a tenant for a fixed period of time, he could do so. If he wished to evict that tenant at the end of the period, he could do that too. The contract was over, and he was under no further obligation to the tenant. The tenant henceforth was trespassing; the landlord was entitled to evict that tenant, and had no need to justify his action to anybody. Furthermore, if at any time during his occupation the tenant failed to pay his rent, the landlord could evict him, and again such an action, in the landlord's view, required no justification. The contract of rent and occupancy had been broken, so it was void; out went the tenant.

The Irish did not see it in the same way. 'Ulster custom', which could be extended to the other three provinces, decreed that a tenant enjoyed certain rights over the land he rented, particularly the right to compensation for any improvements he had made during his tenancy. Since custom usually dictated that he paid for housing, drainage, and fencing out of his own pocket, the question of compensation was a regular one, and a vital one. English landlords did not recognise this: once an eviction was in force, they said, the tenant ceased to have any rights over the land he had ceased to hold.

Irish views of land rights went deeper still, into the mists of medieval history. The best land had been continually taken by English invaders and colonisers ever since the twelfth century; so far as the Irish were concerned, the English had, in fact, stolen it. All the land really belonged, in the beginning and in the end, to the Irish. So ran the Irish argument.

No court, however, would uphold it. The landlords had the money, the resources, the strength, and the law. Indeed they were the law. Irish Catholic tenants did not sit on magistrates' benches, only Protestant landlords. The police and the military forces were always called out by landlords, never by tenants. Religious prejudice made matters worse; Catholics and Protestants now reckoned they had good reasons for hating each other that had nothing to do with the world to come.

For the Irish tenant, eviction was Hell in this world. It was worse than death. There was very little industry, so there was very little wage labour; he could not earn anything much. A suspicious English Government had never encouraged Irish trade or industry in case it became a threat to English business. The Americans had been allowed to develop their own trade and industry, and look how they had repaid the mother country.

So an Irish peasant depended totally on the land, and not very much of that. Large families often made it necessary to subdivide the family's holding; it was the only wealth they possessed. If a peasant lost his land, he lost his status, his home, his house, his heritage, his dignity, his livelihood, and his food supply.

Irish families by the million depended almost completely on the potato. The surprise was that, given a regular supply, they could stay healthy on it. They could stay remarkably fertile too, as the population figures showed. But they had to have plots, however small, in order to cultivate them. (Another attraction was that the crops could be grown with very little labour.) It was because they were often deprived of them by eviction, and because they could hope for no justice from court, police, or landlord, that they turned to violence. The use of terror as a political weapon entered the Irish way of life, and has remained part of it ever since. Secret societies sprang up to protect the tenant and to ward off the landlord by calculated fright – attacks on cattle, burning of houses, manhandling of the landlord's family, in extreme cases torture and murder. The landlord's reaction was understandable, if not excusable. Discipline became tougher, penalties harsher, magistrates more savage in their sentences. And so the vicious circle was set up: each new offence was matched by fiercer reprisal.

The few good men who tried to be fair were often swept away by the tide of the problem. For instance, some landlords took an active interest in their estates and sincerely wanted to improve them, with new buildings, enclosures, schemes of drainage, and so on. But in many cases this meant eviction in order to get dirty huts and grimy squatters out of the way. The result was that the landlord who improved was often hated more than the one who stayed in England and did nothing.

By the 1840s, despite the efforts of men like Secretary Drummond, the general relationship between England and Ireland was unhealthy, to say the least. Irish Catholics were convinced that the English were a cruel breed of ignorant, arrogant, foreign, tyrannical heretics; English Protestants were equally firm in their belief that the Irish were ungrateful, lying, lazy, vicious Papists who would all be quick to slit innocent people's throats if their treacherous priests so much as dropped a word.

Then came the potato blight of 1845. There had been outbreaks before, but this was serious. The blight came again in 1846, and this time it was catastrophic. From all over Ireland came reports of whole fields of healthy green shoots turned into seas of stinking black slime almost overnight. Even potatoes hurriedly lifted from nearby fields rotted. Peasants who sighed with relief at having lifted their crop just in time opened their storehouse doors shortly afterwards to be met with heaps of oozing filth. For the warmth and dampness of the Irish climate, which favoured the growth of the potato, also offered perfect conditions in which the spores of the blight fungus could flourish. Not that that really mattered, for nobody at the time had the faintest idea of how the blight started or how it spread.

The immediate problem was not to stop the blight, but to feed the Irish. The Government at Westminster were faced with a national disaster bigger than anything since the Black Death of 1348. To their credit, they took steps to deal with the situation. It is to the credit, too, of English public opinion that huge amounts of money were collected by private charity. But the problem was too much for them; people's minds could not grasp the enormity of it. The tales of horror that poured out of Ireland were not always accepted; there was a strong view that it was just another example of the Irish gift for romantic exaggeration.

The Government clung, too, to their favourite idea of *laissez-faire*. Corn must be obtained to replace the missing potatoes, and obtained it was, quickly and efficiently, from America. But there was to be no question of Government-sponsored free hand-outs. If the Irish wanted corn, they could go to individual merchants and buy it. There must be no interference with private business. It took a long time to sink in that many Irish were too weak to make the journey to the depots, or too poor to afford the price. Those who managed both found American corn bullet-hard and difficult to grind (indeed some Irish wives had been so dependent on potatoes that they did not know *how* to grind corn). It was so hard, in fact, that some who ate it unground in their desperation, with stomachs weakened from weeks of semi-starvation, died in great pain.

What made the problem worse was that nobody ever had a chance to recover from one disaster before another struck. Not only did the potato crop fail in 1846, for the second time, but the English corn crop was poor. There was a danger of starvation in England too. This explains the extraordinary fact that at the height of the famine corn was being *exported* from Ireland to England. The landlords with the better soil commonly grew corn (some cereal crop or other), and, if they could get good prices in England, they must be allowed to do so. Nothing should interfere with an individual's right to conduct lawful business as he saw fit. The Irish peasant did not understand economic theory; all he saw was cartloads of food being taken past his hungry family under military escort, and stowed on English ships. He never understood, and he never forgot.

Tragedy was now piled on tragedy. To the horror of starvation was added that of disease. A 'dirt' disease, typhus, now began to spread fast, infecting even those healthy people who were trying to help. Bodies already weakened by starvation sank and died faster still. Those who in their hunger had taken to living on nettles, berries, roots, cabbage stalks, even rotten potatoes, died of dysentery in their thousands.

The Government, in no way put off by the failure of its corn-sales scheme, had meanwhile tried another – public works. If the Irish could not afford to buy the corn, let them earn the money with which to do so. Public works were to be organised – building piers and harbours; draining marshes; improving roads, and so on – which would give them back their dignity and the means to feed their families.

That did not work either. Far too many schemes were started without proper planning. The Irish Board of Works collapsed under the weight of all the new business; it was expected to cope with hundreds of such schemes for the whole of Ireland with a Dublin staff (admittedly enlarged later) of four. Far too many workers turned up hoping for employment, and most of those were too weak to work properly. The pay was often late.

As the end of 1846 drew near, people took some comfort from the thought that at least it rarely snowed in Ireland. The winter of 1846–7, in the event, turned out to be the longest and coldest in living memory.

Conversely, the summer of 1847 was a good one and should have produced a good harvest. It did not. Few acres were even planted; the seed potatoes from 1846 had either rotted or been eaten.

The Government was now being forced to take a greater part in dealing with the crisis, *laissez-faire* or no *laissez-faire*. It brought into action the machinery of the Poor Law. The workhouses were available, if they had not been occupied already unofficially. They soon became full to bursting. Overcrowding led to more typhus and dysentery. After a while the supply of money to run them simply dried up. Workhouses were financed by the rates; rates were paid by landlords. Landlords could not now afford rates, because rents were not coming in; rents were not coming in because tenants were either dead or crowding out the workhouse.

Workhouses started closing. Kind-hearted landlords who tried to keep them going out of their own pockets risked bankruptcy themselves. Others tried to help their tenants to save their own lives by giving them the money to buy a cheap passage on a ship. The great flight from Ireland had begun.

The Irish had always been great emigrators and fortune-hunters, but never before on the scale witnessed in the late 1840s. They begged, borrowed, or stole the money to get out, and most did not care where they went. Some committed crimes, offered themselves for arrest, and pleaded with the magistrate to transport them to the colonies. Nothing, they reasoned, could be worse than staying.

They were wrong.

Shipping swindlers took their passage money for Canada or the

United States, and packed them into unseaworthy ships which had been recently over-insured (they were known in the trade as 'coffin ships'). Rough weather, cattle-like conditions below decks, and seasickness accounted for the usual number of casualties. Many of those who had so far escaped suffering from dysentery and typhus proved to be carriers of them. Poor ship's diet, overcrowding, and dreadful sanitation spread the diseases faster than ever. If they, and the ships, completed the crossing, the next horror appeared in the immigration camps – grim attempts by the Canadian and American Governments to exercise some control over the health, numbers, and usefulness of the new flood of sickened and sickening humanity. It was the same story of weakness, poverty, disease, overcrowding, despair, and death. Those who survived all that had to find a way of getting through a Canadian winter.

Local inhabitants were little help. Residents in general regarded the Irish as poverty-stricken, diseased, quarrelsome wretches who spread filth, raised the crime rate, and lowered the standards of living in whatever area they swarmed over. Wherever they went – the USA, Canada, Wales, Liverpool, Birmingham, Glasgow – they were resented, and they were cold-shouldered. They were also deceived and swindled – over housing, rents, prices – at every turn.

The wonder is that not only did many of them stay alive; some actually lived to prosper, and, moreover, prosper enough to send money back to suffering relatives in the homeland. The Irish took their hatred of England with them, and much of the funds that supported terrorism and crime in Ireland was to come from those indestructible emigrants who 'made it' in America but who never forgot what had driven them there.

The Irish who remained at home were certainly in need of sympathy. The new year, 1848, proved to be just as dreadful as the previous three. The British Treasury refused to help the bursting workhouses. Private charity was drying up. Ireland was no longer 'news'. No country, it was felt, could go on being a disaster area for three years. As crisis followed crisis, as reports of fresh horrors poured out of Ireland, people shut their ears; they could not stand any more.

Yet the crises went on. In the spring of 1848, many survivors sold furniture, even their clothes, to get money for seed potatoes.

Superhuman efforts were made to sow a large crop. So anxious were they to make sure of a good yield that they planted potatoes on land normally used for other vegetables. Everything was gambled on a last desperate bid.

In June, the weather turned wet. In July, the blight struck again, as totally as in 1846. Dysentery and typhus continued to rage through the workhouses. In December, the European cholera epidemic reached Ireland, broke out in Belfast, and soon spread all over the country.

It failed to make headlines, because something else had happened in Ireland that did make headlines, and that turned off sympathy for Irish suffering almost as if someone had flicked a switch.

Ireland had a revolution.

Well, not exactly a revolution, but its leaders intended to have one, and the English thought they were having one; and that was enough. Englishmen who had up to now felt sorry for the Irish, and had put their hands in their pockets to prove it, felt foolish and enraged at the thought of the ungrateful savages biting the hands that were trying to feed them. It was yet further proof, if further proof were needed, that the Irish had no grace, no thanks, no trace of any decent human feelings at all.

What in fact happened was a shabby little farce.

Ever since the failure of O'Connell's Repeal Year of 1843, the 'Liberator' and his moderate Catholics had been slipping. There had grown up a newer, more vigorous group who called themselves 'Young Ireland', after a similar Italian nationalist group that had taken the title 'Young Italy'. They claimed to be more truly Irish than O'Connell's Catholics, who, they said, had been too preoccupied with religion and too much under the thumb of priests. 'Young Ireland' had Protestant members, and landlords as well, men who put Ireland first, not class or religion. Two of their leaders, Thomas Davis and John Mitchel, were Protestants. Their newspaper was called *The Nation*. They tried to unite their countrymen by an appeal to Ireland's past. (O'Connell had had no time for sentimental trips into legend and garbled history.)

They believed too that 'Repeal', as the Old Irelanders preached it, was as good as dead. It was no longer sufficient to demand a separate parliament for Ireland, or equal status for Protestants and Catholics. The famine had shown up the real trouble – land. In future, nothing would satisfy Ireland but a return of all land to the ownership of the Irish. Mere Government 'concessions' were not enough.

The chief leader of 'Young Ireland' was a Protestant landlord and ex-MP called Smith O'Brien, whose family tree positively oozed with Irish patriotism: he claimed direct descent from the fabulous Brian Boru, no less, High King of all Ireland, victor over the Vikings at Clontarf in 1014. (To grasp the hugeness of Brian Boru's reputation among Irishmen, it would be necessary to imagine a hero like Alfred the Great, Harold of Wessex, and Richard the Lionheart all rolled into one.) O'Brien and his co-leaders – Gavan Duffy, Thomas Meagher, Davis, and Mitchel – proclaimed that O'Connell's respect for the law had got the Irish nowhere. What was needed was direct action – an underground organisation of republican clubs, armed revolution – to achieve the ultimate great ideal of total independence.

O'Connell thought that 'Young Ireland', with their wild talk, would undo all his work, and he forced a split with them. Unfortunately, his health was now gone, and within a year he was dead. It was the splinter group of the Repeal movement – 'Young Ireland' – which carried on Irish agitation.

Yet they had nothing to show but the torch of hope. 'Young Ireland' had no money, no organisation, no weapons, no plans – nothing. Nothing but a widely-read newspaper and a lot of strong talk. But the Government at Westminster did not know that. They took the 'revolution' seriously, and with good reason. There had never been a year like 1848 for revolutions. In January, Palermo in Sicily; Turin in Piedmont (northern Italy now). In February, Paris. In March, Vienna and Milan. Hardly a week passed, it seemed, without disturbing news of a government in exile or a monarch in flight. Every one of Germany's 39 states had a revolution before the year was out. Elsewhere too. Brussels, Madrid, Rome, Berlin, Venice, Budapest – the list seemed never-ending.

Lord John Russell and his Cabinet colleagues were understandably wary, if not actually worried. (A Whig ministry had taken office in 1846.) At any rate they were taking no chances. Over 10,000 troops were sent to Dublin; the new Treason Felony Act (April, 1848) made 'intimidation' of Crown or Parliament punishable by transportation for fourteen years or life; in July, a bill to suspend *Habeas Corpus* flew through all its readings in both houses in two working days. (This meant that, for a set period, suspects could be arrested and held without trial.)

They were using a sledgehammer to crack a walnut. The farce was played out at Ballingarry in Tipperary on 29 July. When O'Brien at last collected enough 'rebels' to make a sizeable crowd, he found that most of them had turned up because they had expected to be fed. When they found out that he was not supplying meals, they either drifted away or stayed around simply to watch. With about a hundred or so 'rebels' left, O'Brien attacked the local police force, who had taken refuge in a nearby farmhouse. One volley from the nervous constables sufficed: the attack, and the crowd, melted away in minutes. The great revolution for the freedom of Ireland became, for all time, the Battle of Widow McCormack's cabbage garden.

O'Brien and four colleagues were sentenced to death for high treason, though this was commuted to transportation to Tasmania. Others escaped to France or America. Duffy was tried for treason five times, but no jury would convict him, and he was freed in 1849. After a short spell trying to revive *The Nation* and running a tenant protection society, he emigrated to Australia in 1855, and later rose to ministerial rank in Victoria.

Despite the ridicule and the failure, one truth survived. The centre of the problem was land. The Irish peasant must recover full ownership of his land, and any English law that fell short of that ideal was as good as dead before the ink was dry. The next half-century was going to be full of the same miseries – poverty, evictions, terror, reprisal, well-meaning laws that failed, punishments by outraged governments who felt furious at Irish ingratitude, and general Irish cussedness. Blight and famine brought their horrors again. The emigrations continued.

The 'Great Hunger' probably saw nearly 2,000,000 people into their graves, one way and another. We shall never be sure, because so many wretches crawled away to die alone, and were later tipped into nearby ditches, with no priest to honour their passing or registrar to record it. The famine achieved nothing: the Irish did not change their ways, and the English did not change their attitude. All that happened was the engraving of a bitter memory on Irish minds.

The Government must have felt grateful for deliverance as the summer of 1848 ended, because 'Young Ireland' was in fact the second possible revolution it had successfully dealt with. In April the Chartists had made their last desperate effort.

The Chartist leaders were by now out of prison again. O'Connor, though still taken up with his Land Scheme, had found time to get himself elected MP for Nottingham and to keep *The Northern Star* going. A slump in the same year produced the extra discontent to fuel a third massive effort. (All three outbursts of Chartist activity – in 1839, 1842, and 1848 – coincided with 'bad times' economically.)

Then had come the intoxicating news of the revolutions in Palermo, Turin, and, above all, Paris. Clearly, a great gesture had to be made to reflect the drama of current events. Unlike the revolutionaries on the continent, however, the Chartists were determined that theirs should be a peaceful gesture. A monster meeting would produce a procession, which would deliver to the House of Commons a monster petition demanding the six points of the People's Charter.

With governments tumbling right across Europe, with exiles already coming into England and telling the usual exaggerated stories, with 'Young Ireland' talking independence, the Government of Lord John Russell felt that it had a clear responsibility to take every precaution to ensure public order. The security of London was to be treated as a military exercise. To command such an operation there was only one possible choice: the Duke was summoned, in his eightieth year, and went about his task with his customary cool head and thoroughness. And experience; if there was one thing he knew something about, it was fortifying defensive positions.

By zero hour on 10 April, the day fixed for the monster meeting on Kennington Common, shops were shut, Government offices were barricaded, and the Royal Family had been evacuated. The telegraph system had been taken over. Gunboats patrolled the Thames. Yeomanry regiments were put on alert, and artillery detachments were deployed with a field of fire to command the bridges over the Thames – though, prudent as ever, the Duke saw no point in provoking trouble; the regular troops were to be kept out of sight. The only visible agents of law and order were to be the constables, specially sworn in for the day – 150,000 of them.

They vastly outnumbered the Chartists. O'Connor boasted that half a million would come. His own newspaper settled for 250,000. *The Times* estimated 20,000, and the Prime Minister told the Queen that he made it 12,000–15,000. The Commissioner of Metropolitan Police, Sir Richard Mayne, summoned O'Connor to meet him in a nearby public house. No attempt would be made to disperse the crowd, he told him, but no procession would be allowed to cross any of the bridges to gain access to the House of Commons. There was to be no possibility of intimidation of Parliament.

O'Connor said humbly that such a thought could not have been further from his mind. He went back and told the meeting to disperse – which it did. Not a shutter was broken, not a window smashed. (A contemporary photograph – one of the earliest – shows how respectably and formally most of the people were dressed.) A fortunate downpour of rain dampened any remaining political fervour. Relations between police and crowd were so friendly that an inspector complimented them on their good behaviour, and O'Connor proudly reported it in *The Northern Star*.

One concession on the part of the Commissioner was that the Monster Petition could be delivered to the House of Commons, and O'Connor was allowed to escort it. The huge rolls of paper were bundled into three cabs on Kennington Common. At the House, a committee was appointed to examine them.

Each roll was nine feet in circumference; the total number of signatures was supposed to be over five million. The committee reported to the House that it contained in fact only 1,975,496. (Only! Did they actually count them all?) They informed honourable members moreover that many signatures were obviously in the same handwriting; that many names were so vulgar that they dared not shock the House by mentioning them; and that many names were forgeries, since they found it difficult to believe that Sir Robert Peel, Lord John Russell, the Duke of Wellington, and Her Majesty the Queen had really been persuaded (several times, apparently) to express their support for the Charter.

Chartism was laughed out of existence. Had the House taken the trouble to examine as closely the petitions of 1839 and 1842, perhaps the same result could have been achieved earlier. The chances are that the Reform petitions of 1831 and the Anti-Corn Law petitions were just as bad, but nobody had a really good look at them either. The Chartists were unlucky, because somebody actually read what they had written; somebody actually checked their figures.

So Chartism, like 'Young Ireland', expired. There were many similarities between the two. Both O'Connor and Smith O'Brien were reacting against older and more moderate leaders who had had little success – O'Connor against Lovett, and O'Brien against O'Connell. Both believed, or said they believed, in the value of direct physical action – yet were remarkably indecisive when the crisis came. Both were inspired by the non-stop news of revolution in 1848. Both provoked excessive reaction on the part of the Government: 10,000 troops were sent to deal with O'Brien's 'revolution', and 150,000 special constables were sworn in to contain the Chartist 'revolution'. (It is easy, with hindsight, to smile at the Government's nerves. It did not look so funny in the early months of 1848, with European regimes tumbling like ninepins.) Both movements died in fiasco and were buried in shame and ridicule.

The Young Irelanders were dispersed, to prison, to the penal settlements, or to foreign countries. Ex-Chartists, however, had less to fear this time from the magistrate's bench; they had not broken the law on Kennington Common.

Some entered the reviving trade unions; others joined the temperance movement. There was no shortage of good causes – factory reform, education, public health, extending the franchise, humanitarian work of all kinds. Others – disillusioned altogether with England – emigrated, like the Irish. In the United States, the Oregon Trail to the Far West was now wide open, and American agents were advertising all over Europe for pioneer families willing to fill the cosmic spaces beyond the Mississippi. Every country which had had a failed revolution was overflowing with people anxious to forget their frustration and to seek their fortune in the great land of opportunity. The word 'fortune' soon had an even more glamorous appeal; gold was discovered in California in 1849. There were ex-Chartists, too, in the Ballarat gold rush in Australia in 1850. A few joined Garibaldi's Italian nationalist rebels. One did so well at soldiering in America that he became a general in the

Unionist army in the Civil War. Another individualist, Allan Pinkerton, also went to the United States and turned policeman – he set up the famous detective agency which helped to tame the Wild West.

At home, O'Connor tried vainly to hold Chartism together, but the tide was against him. There was no hope of any more monster meetings; petitions were now a joke. The Land Scheme was crumbling. The circulation of *The Northern Star* fell steadily. His own health was breaking down and his mind was giving way. Overwork, frustration, and heavy drinking completed the collapse. In 1852 he was certified insane; in 1854 he began to have epileptic fits; and he died in great pain in August, 1855.

He was vain, loud, crude, reckless, unstable, and unpredictable; but he possessed magic, and in his way he was sincere. Perhaps the thirty thousand working men and women who turned out in the rain for his funeral at Kensal Green Cemetery in London recognised that fact.

His dreams – the People's Charter – were realised much later. Almost every adult male had the vote by 1884; the property qualification for MPs was abolished in 1858; the re-distribution of seats in 1885 helped to equalise electoral districts; the secret ballot was introduced in 1872; and MPs received salaries as from 1911. Only annual parliaments failed to materialise.

Yet it was clear, as the honourable members chuckled over the signatures of 'Mr Punch', 'Pug Nose', and 'No Cheese', that Chartism, as a movement, had failed. And it had failed because, in spite of its apparently Radical programme, it had been trying to put the clock back, not forward. O'Connor's most devoted followers, in the North – the hand-loom weavers, and the stocking-frame knitters – had been deprived of work by the hated machines. Theirs was a protest against the new industrial system. Yet, however sad their plight, however bitter their complaint, there was no way of stopping the tide of history; they could not cancel the Industrial Revolution.

Cruelly, it was this very system that made their movement so erratic. In times of boom and fuller employment, men were less inclined to protest. In bad times, they were often too desperate; they over-protested, and got into trouble. The Chartists could not sustain a consistent political programme of agitation – unlike the Anti-Corn Law League, who plugged away at the Corn Laws year after year.

The League also showed them, if they had had eyes to see, that it was more profitable to try to tear down one piece of legislation than it was to set up six new ones; destruction is always easier than creation. The League enjoyed better leadership, more united leadership, and wealthier leadership. Chartists had different loyalties, aims, and methods according to which leader they favoured, which type of work they followed (or were dismissed from), and which part of the country they lived in.

Chartists, as a group, had little general support from society at large, little money, and little political 'clout'. They were seen by solid citizens as not quite respectable. No prominent figure pronounced himself 'converted' to Chartism. No wealthy patrons, however cranky, opened their chequebooks for them. The struggling trade unions saw little future in partnership with them; Robert Owen and the socialists did not support them; the Co-operative movement held aloof. The successful middle class, who had won entry to the citadel of power in 1832, were not willing to open it again to admit a larger group to share the profits.

Finally, the authorities, who may have shown nerves in the face of the Chartist challenge in 1848, did not show panic. Their reaction was a little over-comprehensive, but it was firm and restrained. This is all the more praiseworthy when one considers how much revolutionary activity was going on all around them in Europe during that year – and how much savage repression too. In Rome republicans were pounded into surrender with cannon; in Paris the troops mowed down citizens with rifle fire; in London O'Connor shook hands with the Metropolitan Police Commissioner in a public house, and everyone went home. It marks a significant advance on the tactics of Lord Sidmouth's Home Office when faced with the radical meetings of 1817 and 1819.

Somewhat illogically, the British Government, or at least some members of it, seemed more willing to look favourably upon the activities of the revolutionaries in continental Europe than upon those of the Radicals in Britain. The Whig Foreign Secretary, Lord Palmerston (Aberdeen's successor in 1846), had already advised some of the Italian princes to grant some reforms at once before revolution swept their regimes away. When the Italians rose to expel their Austrian overlords, and create a unified state in northern and central Italy,

Palmerston approved, and said so. None of this improved relations between England and Austria. Not that Pam would have worried overmuch. He saw support of the Italian revolution as a chance to score a point for liberalism and to win back a trick against Metternich and his Hapsburg masters for the Polish business of 1846.

The Poles were a perpetual unfortunate relative in the family of European states. Their government had been interfered with by French, German, and Russian rulers since the sixteenth century, and at the end of the eighteenth their country had been carved up and wiped off the map by Austria, Prussia, and Russia. After the Napoleonic Wars Poland had reappeared in a smaller edition, and was promptly taken over as a satellite state by Russia. In 1830 the Poles tried revolution, and failed dismally. The only piece of independent Poland left to them was the Republic of Cracow, in the far south, next to Austrian territory. To make sure that it did not inspire any other Polish revolutions, the Austrian Chancellor Metternich took it over in November 1846. Palmerston and the French chief minister, Guizot, protested, to no avail.

Part of the trouble was that Pam and Guizot did not get on well enough to take joint action, and Metternich knew it. And the reason for that went back to the affair of the Spanish Marriages earlier in the year.

Queen Isabella of Spain had reached marriageable age, and the question of finding her a suitable husband was causing concern to the rulers of France and England. One would have thought that it was purely the business of the Spanish royal family, but royal marriages, as late as the nineteenth century, could have important political implications. The royal families of France and Spain were related. King Louis Philippe of France was anxious to strengthen the relationship, and had a bachelor son conveniently available to do it, the Duke of Montpensier. Here, however, the French met the opposition of England. Ever since the seventeenth century, when Franco-Spanish royal marriages had been regularly planned, there had always been an outside chance that the same person would inherit the thrones of both countries. If this happened, one monarch could control the armed forces, resources, revenues, and overseas possessions of the two largest nations in Western Europe, and this was too big a threat to English trade to be tolerated. It would, in addition, upset the Balance of Power.

The Balance of Power was one of the guiding principles of British foreign policy: it was the notion that Britain could never allow one European country to accumulate so much power that it could *over*power any possible combination of other countries and so threaten the peace of the whole continent. It explains why she threw her weight into the scales against the Spain of Philip II, the France of Louis XIV, the Empire of Napoleon – and later the Germany of Hitler.

It explained why she spent time and effort in the 1840s to prevent a similar possible union of France and Spain.

The events that now followed, if taken out of this context, would read rather like a society gossip column; in fact the attitudes of governments, and therefore the lives of millions of people, hung upon what happened.

To begin with, Louis Philippe announced his desire to arrange a royal marriage for his son Montpensier, either with the Queen of Spain, Isabella, or with her younger sister, the Infanta, as she was officially called. England would not allow Montpensier to marry Isabella, for the usual reason that their children could possibly inherit both thrones. In 1844, a compromise had been reached between Chief Minister Guizot and his friend, Foreign Secretary Aberdeen. It was agreed that Montpensier could marry the younger sister, the Infanta, but not until Queen Isabella had been married and had produced an heir. There were two or three possible choices for Isabella's hand, among them the Duke of Seville, the Duke of Cadiz, and Prince Leopold of Coburg (who was not only the widower of George IV's lamented daughter, Charlotte, but the uncle of Queen Victoria – and, incidentally, the uncle of Victoria's husband, Prince Albert). Leopold in fact received an official offer, but rejected it because he did not have Aberdeen's or Peel's support.

Then, early in 1846, Palmerston resumed control at the Foreign Office, and once again the sharp dispatches started flying around the embassies. Guizot had trusted Aberdeen, and they had built a good relationship between their two countries – the famous *entente*. Palmerston, however, was too brisk, too outspoken, for Guizot's taste; he made the Frenchman feel uncomfortable.

In the course of one his letters Pam again mentioned Leopold of Coburg as a possible candidate for a Spanish marriage, but did *not* mention Montpensier. It looked to Guizot like another piece of high-handed interference by Palmerston. Louis Philippe felt that, as Palmerston had broken the agreement of 1844, he was free to do so as well. In the autumn of 1846, therefore, he and the Spanish Government announced the *simultaneous* weddings of Queen Isabella to the Duke of Cadiz, and of her sister, the Infanta, to the Duke of Montpensier.

Palmerston was furious. It was he who now felt that the French had gone back on *their* word. It was a shabby trick to arrange the weddings right out of the blue, and shabbier still to arrange them simultaneously, because the understanding was that Isabella should marry first and have children before the Infanta went to the altar. The shabbiest trick of all, he said, was to select as Isabella's husband the Duke of Cadiz, who was generally supposed to be incapable of fathering children. Clearly now the Infanta would produce children and Isabella not, so the Spanish throne could well pass to Montpensier's children, that is to the grandchildren of the King of France.

Trust and confidence were shattered; Guizot's work for six years was wasted. The Anglo-French *entente* lay in ruins. Yet it was largely caused by genuine misunderstanding on both sides; that, and the forceful behaviour of Palmerston, which put Guizot on the defensive. The fact remains that it need never have happened.

More ironic still, the fears and worries caused by the marriages never came to anything. The Duke of Cadiz surprised everyone by doing his dynastic duty, and Isabella duly produced a son. Montpensier, far from becoming a possible King of Spain, never became King of France either, because a revolution in 1848 turned him and his father, Louis Philippe, into political refugees, forced to seek sanctuary in – where else? – England.

It was this flurry that gave Metternich his chance in Poland, because he knew that Palmerston and Guizot no longer trusted each other enough to join forces to stop him. It was this too that explained Pam's satisfaction over events in Switzerland in 1847.

Despite its small size, Switzerland was in fact a federation like the United States, but the states were called cantons. In 1845 the Catholic cantons had left the federation and set up their own separate league (in German, *Sonderbund*). They were supported by Catholic interests in

France and Austria. The more liberal Protestant cantons, like the Northern states in the American Civil War, were trying to force them back into the union. Because of their more liberal policies, these Protestant cantons received the help of Palmerston, who mananged to keep French and Austrian influence out of Switzerland until the Protestants had won. He regarded the incident as tit for tat against Metternich for Cracow, and against Louis Philippe for the Spanish Marriages.

This was the sort of behaviour that explains Palmerston's popularity with the British public, and his unpopularity with his professional colleagues. Ordinary people liked him because he was confident and outspoken; he 'stood no nonsense'; he believed in fair play (or appeared to); he stuck up for Britain everywhere; and of course he was so often successful. Perhaps too they warmed to him for the very reason that he obviously made his stuffier colleagues uncomfortable. Now in his sixties, he was as spry, alert, vigorous, and flamboyant as ever; he brought a touch of glamour to the Foreign Office. To use a modern term, he had great box-office value.

To his colleagues, to his Prime Minister Russell, and to the Queen, he was a constant trial. He made too many quick decisions without consulting them. He was too honest and direct for a man who was supposed to be the head of the diplomatic service. The trouble was that he knew more about foreign affairs than all the rest of them put together, and even when they felt in their bones that they were right, he could always make them feel wrong by swamping them with facts and rushing them with the need for a quick decision. They were annoyed, too, by his trick of playing to the gallery. He was more popular than they were, and he knew it. How could you dismiss the most popular man in the Cabinet and still hope to win the next election?

Fellow-professionals in foreign governments found him just as exasperating. To them, it appeared as if he put British interests not simply first, but first, second, third, and last; everybody else could go to the Devil. He did not bother to wrap up awkward messages in polite language. Foreign secretaries were not supposed to call a spade a spade; Palmerston infuriated one chancellor after another by doing so, regularly.

The dispute with the Greek Government provided a good illustration of all this. Greek rulers and officials were not as efficient or as honest as they should have been by British standards, and Palmerston had already preached to them once or twice in his usual bossy way. British subjects living in Greece had more than once complained about damages or losses suffered at Greek hands. In 1847, a certain Don Pacifico claimed against the Greek Government for damage caused by a mob which had attacked his house, destroyed his possessions, and burned thousands of Portuguese bonds, worth, so he said, £27,000. His furniture alone, he declared, was worth £8,000.

It turned out that Don Pacifico was a pretty shady character, and had probably deserved everything that the mob had done to him. Most people agreed, too, that his claims for damages were wildly exaggerated. Why should the lies of a seedy Portuguese Jewish moneylender in Athens be of any interest to the British Foreign Office?

The answer lay in the trivial detail that Pacifico had once lived at Gibraltar, and so was technically a British citizen. Palmerston sailed into action, quite literally – a British naval squadron was sent to Athens to make the Greeks pay up. The French protested; the Russians were furious; the Austrians threw up their hands as if to say, 'No, not again!' At home, the Queen and Prince Albert were appalled; if this sort of behaviour went on, England soon would have no friends at all. Lord John Russell wondered, and not for the first time, who really ran the Government – he or Lord Palmerston.

The Tory Opposition felt that Pam had really overstepped himself this time, and in June, 1850 Lord Derby brought in a vote of censure in the House of Lords. It was carried by 37 votes. There followed a sensational marathon debate in the House of Commons, in which nearly every major figure in both parties spoke – Gladstone, Disraeli, Russell, Cobden, Peel (his last speech), and of course Pam himself. It was said that over 2,000 volumes of Foreign Office papers were consulted in the preparation of his speech, which lasted over four hours. He reviewed all foreign policy right back to Canning, and gave a chapter-and-verse account of his conduct of affairs since coming into the Foreign Office again in 1846.

It was a stupendous effort, and is always referred to as the *Civis Romanus sum* speech, because of its reference to the days when a Roman citizen anywhere in the Ancient Empire could claim protection from Roman law by saying '*Civis Romanus sum*' – 'I am a Roman citizen'.

Gladsone, in a later speech of equal brilliance, knocked the bottom out of several of Pam's arguments, but all his logic and eloquence were wasted; Pam's emotional appeal had been too strong. He won the debate by 46 votes. Gladstone complained bitterly that Lord Palmerston could make the House drunk on ginger beer. Public opinion, equally drunk with him, roared its approval.

It was now more difficult than ever to prise him out of office. Russell felt helpless. If my lord Palmerston were to be dismissed, he warned the Queen, he could go into opposition, bring down the Government, and come back as Prime Minister!

The Queen decided to make one more attempt to clear the air. In August, 1850, two months after the great debate, she took the trouble to set out plainly, on paper, what she expected from Lord Palmerston. She was fed up with being treated like a scatterbrained female with no head for politics. In future, she ordered, Lord Palmerston was to give her the state papers in good time, so that she could study them properly for herself; he was to tell her in advance what he proposed to do in a given situation; and, when she had agreed and signed a dispatch, he was not to alter it in any way without asking her first. She refused point-blank to be a rubber stamp.

Palmerston accepted the Queen's memorandum, said he was sorry, and promised to mend his ways. A month later he was in trouble again, this time for upsetting the long-suffering Austrians.

The Austrians had had their hands full recently, putting down revolutions in Italy, Bohemia, Hungary, and in Austria itself. By 1850, they had by and large succeeded, but their methods had in some cases made them unpopular. One of their generals, Haynau, had been unnecessarily cruel in his crushing of resistance in Italy and Hungary, so much so that he was known as 'the hyena' – in his own native Austria. Palmerston naturally had had some stern things to say about this, which had offended the Austrian Government.

Then, in September, 1850, Haynau paid a private visit to London. The press must have made his name widely known, because he was recognised when he was inspecting the brewery of Messrs Barclay and

Perkins in the City. The angry draymen did not lynch him, but they made their opinion of him unmistakable by pushing, shouting, beating him with brooms, and covering him with dirt. The Austrian Ambassador demanded an apology, which even Palmerston could not refuse. However, he made it clear by the tone of his letter that he felt no sympathy for Haynau. Worse, he sent it to the Ambassador without showing it to the Queen first. When she found out, Victoria, backed by Lord John Russell, insisted that Pam withdraw it, and send another rather less offensive note. Pam wrote a long letter to her complaining that Haynau had received no less than he had deserved. The Queen stuck to her guns, and Pam, for once, climbed down.

From now on her attitude to her Foreign Secretary was hostile, and she dropped more than one hint to Russell that he, Russell, was to 'remain firm'. Poor Russell was painfully aware that the ministry was none too strong, and probably could not survive without its most popular member. Pam, for his part, annoyed the Queen by appearing not to take her seriously; his attitude was more likely coloured by his distrust of her immediate advisers – her husband, Prince Albert; Albert's chief confidant, Baron Stockmar; and Leopold, the Queen's uncle, now King of the Belgians. They were German, and so, in Pam's book, suspect.

So Pam went on his way, unrepentant, while the Queen fumed and Russell sighed, and the gossip press chuckled behind its hand.

The weakness of the ministry was not all Russell's fault, nor was it Pam's. It stemmed from the political crisis of 1845 and 1846, which had thrown the whole party system into disarray and confusion. It ushered in a period of great fluidity in party politics, which was to last for about twenty years.

In 1782, when the events described in this book began, politics were also in a state of confusion, after the American War. Thanks to the long ministry of the Younger Pitt, they stabilised again. By the turn of the century, the terms 'Whig' and 'Tory' were pretty clearly definable. The Tories were in office, and stayed there, with one brief break in 1806–7, from 1784 until 1830. Then the Whigs, under Grey and later Melbourne, held power, with two short breaks in 1834–5 and in 1839, until 1841. In that year, Peel and his rebuilt Tory party won the general election with a handsome majority.

(A word of warning here. Because one talks of 'party politics', it must not be assumed that the two major parties behaved as do the two major parties today. As has been shown, the two names – 'Whig' and 'Tory' – meant clear things between 1784 and 1845, but the party organisation was far different then from what it is now. There was no party 'machine', no annual party congress, no party manifesto, no party 'whips' – that is, voting discipline – no party 'line'. Moving from one party to another – as men like Melbourne, Palmerston, and Huskisson did – was not seen as such a disloyal act as it would be now. That is not to say that the party system meant nothing – far from it. There were party loyalties, party issues, and party disputes, which could be just as sincere and just as deep as they are today. The background was simply different.)

Party distinctions, then, seemed fairly clear, up to and including Peel's Tory ministry of the 1840s. Peel had such a good record of achievement, and enjoyed such prestige (he had won over even that staunch Whig, the Queen), that there seemed no reason why the Tories could not go on to fresh triumphs.

Then the Great Famine began, and Peel knew that a drastic situation demanded drastic remedies. The Corn Laws would have to go. The last bastion of the old Tory landowners would have to be dismantled. The Duke added his unkind comment to the chorus of rage from Peel's hitherto silent supporters in the country constituencies: 'Rotten potatoes have done it all; they have put Peel in his damned fright.'

The Tory country gentlemen had never been completely sold on Peel (the son of a north-country industrialist). They had not liked the concessions to the Nonconformists in the repeal of the Test and Corporation Acts. They had gone along with the reform of Parliament only when it dawned on them that it might produce a reduction of the rotten boroughs and so enable them to enlarge their own influence in the House with more county seats. But the greatest blow had come three years earlier, when in 1829 Peel had told them that civil rights would have to be granted to Catholics. As Parliamentary reform had been an assault on their grip of the political life of the country, so Catholic Emancipation had been an assault on their dominance in the religious life of the country. They never truly forgave Peel for this; the event became known as 'the Great Betrayal'.

They had continued to support him in the 1830s for the simple reason that there was nobody else in sight with the remotest chance of leading the party back into power, and they had gone on supporting him for the same reason – but grimly and warily.

Now had come this second betrayal: Peel was contemplating a final assault, on their economic primacy in the country. Agriculture had always been regarded as the backbone of the nation. England was not a nation of shopkeepers, as Napoleon had once sneered; it was a nation of farmers. So said the country gentlemen. At all costs the home market in corn (cereal crops) must be preserved in a healthy state. If that meant imposing duties on the import of foreign corn in order to keep out cheap competition, so be it. If that meant a higher price for bread, that was unfortunate but unavoidable; it was a price that had to be paid.

But not by them. By all those poor people who depended on loaves of bread to stay alive. Here was the giant injustice. So said the Anti-Corn League of Richard Cobden and John Bright. England was no longer purely a nation of farmers and villagers; it was a nation too of cities and factories and businessmen and railways – and of poor city-dwellers. The landowners no longer had a right to dictate the economic policy of the country. If businessmen could live in a world of international trade and competition where tariffs were falling or disappearing, so too could the farmers; these were the new facts of economic life. Besides, the farmers were worrying to no purpose; if falling tariffs brought lower prices of industrial goods, imported foodstuffs, and raw materials, the removal of the Corn Laws would ensure a flow of cheap corn and lower bread prices. More people would be able to afford not only more bread but more of other kinds of food as well, so the farmers would sell more produce overall and thus share in the new prosperity. In short, the free-traders wanted to apply the principle to agriculture as it was being applied to everything else.

The landowners fought back, with dark hints that Cobden and the other businessmen of the 'Manchester School' were interested in cheap bread only because it would provide industrialists with an excuse to bring down wages. Certainly the agitation for the Anti-Corn Law League was a mainly middle-class affair, and terribly respectable. It is no coincidence that Chartists on occasions forcibly broke up League meetings.

The League countered with the argument that the unrestricted import of foreign corn would put money in foreigners' pockets and so allow them to buy British goods of all kinds. Trade would boom, and everyone would benefit from increased national prosperity, even the stupid landowners.

The retort from the landowners was that the country was at risk of being betrayed by a group of cloddish north-country money-grubbers who spoke in outlandish accents, who enslaved their factory hands, who had no classical education, no small talk, no polite manners, in fact no idea of how a gentleman should behave, and who thought of nothing but making money to spend on their hideous town houses.

Back into the fray came the businessmen, who declared that the future belonged to those who could make their own fortunes. Landowners were nothing but relics of a feudal past of war, privilege, and exploitation, relics who now lived on the long-term legacy of centuries of screwing rents out of poor tenants. This was regarded by landowners as evidence of a colossal class inferiority complex: the businessmen were not so much interested in cheap bread as in destroying a gracious way of life that none of them understood.

Unlike the Chartists, the Leaguers could not be starved into defeat. Their chief support came not from workers on the bread line, but from industrialists and businessmen on the free-trade bandwagon. Money constantly flowed into the League's coffers, and enabled it to maintain a campaign of relentless agitation that ran right through the first half of the 1840s. Public meetings, lectures, debates, newspapers, periodicals, pamphlets, advertisements, questions in the House – the League did not miss a trick. Quick to exploit any new idea, they took advantage of the new Penny Post to distribute their material, and their speakers jumped eagerly on to the new railway trains to cover distances unthinkable twenty years before. These travelling lecturers made shameless appeals to the emotions when they described the harrowing details of working-class suffering; they broke into tears themselves, and they called forth many more from their audiences. Cobden and Bright were no mean orators themselves.

They overdid it, of course; they also got their history wrong sometimes, and their arguments were far from foolproof. But, year by year, like water on a stone, they wore away at the opinions of thinking men. By 1844, they had won over the country's biggest manufacturer, the country's wealthiest banker, and, when the Marquis of Westminster offered to subscribe, the country's richest landowner. (Though they never converted the Duke.) The harvests of 1842, 1843, and 1844 played into their enemies' hands, by being bountiful and keeping prices low. But Cobden hung on, knowing that a bad harvest had to come sooner or later.

By the time it did, in 1845, Peel himself had been converted. For a while he shied away from the terrible implications; he knew that a move from him to repeal the Corn Laws would bring down upon his head the wrath of the Tory country gentlemen who still swayed the party. It is given to few politicians to have to split their own party once in a career; it is given to even fewer to have to do it twice. In 1829 had occurred 'the Great Betrayal', when Peel had carried Catholic Emancipation through a hostile back bench of supporters. Now he was faced with the same prospect again, and understandably he hesitated.

The dreadful news from Ireland in the autumn convinced him that he could delay no longer. People had to be fed. Country had to come before party. However, deliverance seemed at hand. For in November, Lord John Russell, the leader of the Whigs, also pronounced himself convinced by Cobden's arguments against the Corn Laws. Very well – let the Whigs do it. Peel, thankful, resigned in December, 1845.

Fifteen days later he was back in office again. Russell had been unable to form a ministry. His own conversion to free trade did not mean that he carried his whole party with him; many leading Whigs were, after all, big landowners too. Russell was forced, with equal thankfulness, to hand back the 'poisoned chalice' (Disraeli's phrase) to Peel.

For six months, on, and off, the battle raged in Parliament. Peel was accused of panic, because the crisis was not as bad as he made out; as the Duke said, Peel was in a 'damned fright'. He was also accused of treachery, of betraying the party he had laboured so long to rebuild. Peel thought he could carry the party with him by his appeal to reason and charity; he was wrong. A large chunk of it broke away, calling itself 'Protectionist' (because, naturally, it wished to 'protect' British agriculture from foreign interlopers). It was led by Disraeli and Bentinck.

Disraeli had been left out of Peel's Cabinet in 1841, and was now claiming his revenge. Similarly, a Protectionist segment also broke away from Russell's Whigs.

When the vote finally came, it cut right across party lines. Peel's own supporters – the 'Peelites' – were not numerous enough, and he had to rely on the free-trading Whigs and the Radicals. In the House of Lords, the Duke, as he had done in 1832, convinced their lordships that further opposition would lead to worse problems. Despite his disdain of free trade, and despite his scorn of Peel, Wellington was keenly conscious, as ever, of a higher duty that transcended economic creed and party loyalty – the vital necessity of continuity, constitutional harmony, and peace: government must be continued. All his life, he never forgot how fatally easy it was for a civilised country to slip into strife, terror, anarchy, and dictatorship.

He might be deaf, but he was not blind. He could see as well as anyone that the climate of opinion in the country was against them; that the Commons were against them; and the Crown was against them – both the Queen and Prince Albert were free-traders. The Duke, as always, knew when a position was untenable.

After the Repeal, the vultures gathered for Peel in the Commons. Disraeli led an uholy alliance of Protectionists, Whigs, Irish MPs, and Radicals to bring down Peel's Government on 25 June, 1846. Peel never held office again.

Like so many other quarrels, the great Corn Law debate achieved very little of what it was supposed to. Repeal did not ruin agriculture, as Peel's enemies had said it would. Indeed, the period from 1846 to the mid-1870s is often labelled in the history books as the 'Golden Age' of British farming. Repeal did not bring down bread prices, as Cobden and the League said it would, though, to be fair, prices did not rise either (and world prices did, so there was, arguably, a fall in real terms in English prices). The whole principle of Protectionism, which had finished Peel, did not outlast the decade; Disraeli announced that he too now accepted the principle of free trade (which made his hounding of Peel seem, in retrospect, little more than a personal vendetta). The truth was that free trade was now so widespread, so normal, so 'modern', so obvious, that no politician could afford to oppose it.

However, the parties remained jumbled for the next twenty years. Neither side could command a healthy majority. Gladstone and the Peelites would not work with Disraeli and the Protectionists, and neither would they go the other way and work with the Whigs – at any rate not for a dozen years or so. Russell's Whigs, then, spent a third of their time in the late forties barely holding the fort, a second third trying to clear up the appalling mess in Ireland, and a final third worrying what on earth Lord Palmerston was going to do next.

They did find time to wipe the last of the Navigation Acts off the statute book, so completing the process begun by Huskisson in the 1820s. And Lord Shaftesbury and John Fielden at last piloted their Ten Hours Bill through to become law, despite the inevitable opposition of the employers. Women and children were now limited by law to a ten-hour working day. (Not men. And these new regulations applied only to textile mills; a host of other industries – earthenware, hosiery, metal, glass, paper, lace – still worked children up to sixteen hours a day.) The country squires who had seen their precious Corn Laws dismantled by bustling free-trade factory-owners now took grim pleasure in voting to stop those same factory-owners from exploiting cheap labour for such inhumanly long hours.

In 1846 a Baths and Wash-houses Act allowed local authorities to set up public washing facilities for the poor. In 1848, a Public Health Act allowed local boards of health to be set up where 10 per cent of the local ratepayers asked for them.

Notice the word 'allowed'. In the days of the welfare state, it comes as a surprise to discover that two such apparently innocent, well-meaning, and obviously humanitarian measures as these were not to be made compulsory – only optional. A hundred and fifty years ago, people were, it seems, much quicker than they are now to resent what they saw as interference by the Government in the lives of private citizens. Factory acts interfered with an owner's rights to run his own factory as he saw fit; public health acts, if made compulsory, would interfere with a man's right to be clean or dirty as he wished. (They also put up the local rates.) So many reforms that today seem unarguable – in health, education, public service generally – began in the mid-nineteenth century as trial schemes for a limited period, then graduated to becoming optional, and only after thirty years or so were elevated to the status of becoming compulsory. And usually because of this sympathy for a private citizen's rights to do as he saw fit. To repeat a notorious example, the fact that there were terrible cholera epidemics in 1831 and 1847 did not prevent a newspaper such as *The Times* from saying that it did not wish to be bullied into health by a local board of bath-night busybodies; it preferred to take its chance with the cholera.

Two more events of 1848 – which Heaven knows had been full enough, what with revolutions, Chartists, public health problems, Widow McCormack and all – are worth recording, each worlds apart from the other. In February of that year, two German writers – Karl Marx and Friedrich Engels – collaborated to publish *The Communist Manifesto* just in time to catch most of the revolutions. And in July was born William Gilbert Grace, who for the second half of the century was to lord it over the cricket fields as the Duke in the first half had lorded it over the battlefields and drawing rooms and council chambers.

As the decade drew to a close, Russell's Government drew a grain of consolation from the condition of Ireland: it was deemed to be safe enough in 1849 for Her Majesty to make a visit there. Most Irish welcomed it as a diversion from four years of tragedy and crisis, and, though much of the visit was a succession of balls and receptions and reviews in and around Dublin, the welcome in the streets from ordinary people seemed genuine enough. One old woman shouted at Her Majesty as she stepped ashore with her children, 'Ah, Queen, dear, make one of them Prince Patrick and Ireland will die for you.' The departure, with the Queen and Albert waving from their paddle steamer to crowds packing the pier, was genuinely moving. Victoria was proud of this trip. On the occasions when one of her later prime ministers, Gladstone, lectured her on the problems of that sad country, she enjoyed pointing out to him that she had been to Ireland, and he had not.

Russell's Government drew further consolation from the Queen herself. She was now accepted as part of the constitutional furniture – all the more comforting in a decade of revolution and republicanism. With each successful pregnancy, she added interest, lustre, respectability, and above all permanence to a Royal Family which had, for nearly three decades before her arrival, laboured under a succession of pop-eyed Hanoverian monarchs who were lunatics, libertines, or buffoons.

Her husband, Albert of Saxe-Coburg, was winning respect by his earnestness, his hard work, and his desire to make a worthwhile contribution to the life of his adopted country. (The Coburgs were a truly remarkable clan. This tiny German state produced a succession of eligible princes and princesses who, within two generations, negotiated nine royal marriages, three of them with England; Victoria's mother, her uncle by marriage, and her husband were all from the same family.)

Albert had already been involved in successful national exhibitions to promote the arts and industry. It seemed a natural next step to set up an international exhibition; it was to be the first ever held, and Hyde Park was considered as the site. The inevitable grumblers warned that the Park would be desecrated by mobs and criminals, and the stands weighed down with worthless 'foreign stuff'. The Duke, whose many offices included that of Ranger of Hyde Park, was not wild about the idea, but Peel said he approved, and the Duke gave Peel credit in his usual fair-minded way. Moreover, in May, 1850, the Queen was safely delivered of her seventh child and third son, on the Duke's birthday. What else could he be called but 'Arthur'? The Duke was to be godfather too.

Then in June, shortly after the *Civis Romanus sum* debate, Peel had a fall from his horse. He broke a rib, which punctured a lung, and he died four days later. He was only sixty-two. The Queen, who had long been won over from her early bleak view of him, was grief-stricken, and the whole nation was plunged into sorrow. The tributes were as numerous as they were generous and genuine. He may have had a smile 'like the silver plate on a coffin', as O'Connell had remarked, but his many gifts were so obvious that it was impossible not to respect him.

His posthumous influence helped to swing opinion finally to Hyde Park. Then came the problem of the building to house the exhibits. It had to be big enough to include them all, and simple enough to take down again afterwards, so that the Park would not be permanently spoiled. Joseph Paxton, an ex-gardener's boy and self-taught architect, came up with the successful design. He had built a huge conservatory for the Duke of Devonshire; he proposed to extend the idea for the Exhibition. It would be quick; it would be novel; it would be light; it would be spectacular; and it would be easily removable. The public was bewitched with the idea, and excited by its daring. A workforce numbered in thousands descended upon Hyde Park to erect the girders and put in place nearly 300,000 panes of glass. *Punch* christened it 'the Crystal Palace', and the name stuck.

The public was bewitched too with the Exhibition itself, when it was finally opened. Once again, the grumblers and prophets of doom were proved wrong; the show was not ruined by drink-sodden vandals and ignorant oafs. On the contrary, throughout the summer, millions of well-behaved citizens came – on the new trains – to wander through and gaze at this gigantic proof (if proof were necessary) of England's vast presence as the forum and factory of the world. The soaring success of the Great Exhibition makes an ironic contrast to the downward plunge of the Millennium Dome from salesman's pitch to comedian's butt.

The Duke attended the opening, of course – white-haired, deaf, bowed with arthritis, arm in arm with another veteran of Waterloo, the Marquess of Anglesey, limping on his artificial leg. The Queen was much affected.

It was, again, the Duke's birthday – 1 May. He was eighty-two years old. It was a touching occasion and a touching sight, and the crowd responded with loud cheers and birthday wishes.

Gruff though he was, and averse to expressions of emotion (for this reason he had a low opinion of poets), he could not have failed to be moved by this genuine outpouring of respect and affection from his monarch and her people. He could not have failed either to take pride in the colossal achievement of the country he had served so faithfully all his life (though even here his famous common sense made him wonder what 'use' the show was going to be).

It is a fitting moment to take leave of both of them.

Suggestions for Further Reading

What follows is not a list of all the sources I have consulted. Nor is it an exhaustive or a definitive bibliography. It is what it says – suggestions to those readers who may like to take their acquaintance with the Duke and his England a little further. If they take their study further still, they will come up against exhaustive, and exhausting, bibliographies soon enough.

General Histories

J. Steven Watson, *The Reign of George III, 1760–1815* (Oxford, 1960).
E.L. Woodward, *The Age of Reform, 1815–70* (Oxford, 1960).
[These two volumes from the *Oxford History of England* provide as good a solid general account as any, and cover most themes and aspects of the period.]
Kenneth O. Morgan (Ed.) *The Oxford Illustrated History of Britain* (Oxford, 1984).
[As it says, a general, 'right-through' account, with pictures.]
Asa Briggs, *The Age of Improvement* (London, 1959).
[A sound political and social survey of England up to 1867.]
I.R. Christie, *Wars and Revolutions: Britain 1760–1815* (Edward Arnold, 1982).
[A volume from the, to me, very good series by this publisher.]
J.A.R. Marriott, *England since Waterloo* (Methuen, 15th edition, 1954).
[Old, but popular – fifteen editions, as it says. A mainstay of 'A' Level students for years. Not exactly bedside reading, but my word, it does give you a lot of facts.]

Pauline Gregg, *A Social and Economic History of Britain, 1760–1963* (Harrap, 1964).

[Like the Marriott work above, hardly a compulsive page-turner, but full of solid fact and common sense.]

R.W. Seton-Watson, *Britain in Europe, 1789–1914: a Survey of Foreign Policy* (Cambridge, 1955).

[Also old, but chock full of worthy detail. If you want to find out what happened, this, and the books above, are the places to go to. But don't expect to be hypnotised, and don't set out to read them from cover to cover, and don't be disappointed or disillusioned if you don't. They are not that sort of book.]

R. Albrecht-Carrié, *A Diplomatic History of Europe since the Congress of Vienna* (Methuen, 1966).

[What it says – a blow-by-blow account of all the international incidents during the period.]

D. Thomson, *Europe since Napoleon* (Longmans, 1957, and Pelican thereafter – many editions – still in print).

[I went to Thomson's lectures at university. He had a delightful 'lean-on-the-bar', 'have-you-ever-thought-about-it-like-this?' air about him. But his informal manner disguised a formidable learning. His written style was readable, enlightening, and provoking.]

L.C.B. Seaman, *Vienna to Versailles* (Methuen, 1955).

[I have no doubt that many of his interpretations may have been questioned in the last forty years, but like Thomson above, he makes you think.]

J. Bowle, *Politics and Opinion in the Nineteenth Century* (Cape, 1954).

[It's years now since I read it, but it sticks in the mind as knowledgeable, literate, and accessible.]

Studies in Greater Detail

Cobban, *A History of Modern France* Vols. I and II (Pelican, several editions).

[A sound general account.]

Simon Schama, *Citizens* (Viking, 1989).

[A blockbuster narrative of nearly 900 pages, composed by one of those valuable historians who can really write.]

W.C. Atkinson, *A History of Spain and Portugal* (Pelican, 1967).

[It lumps the two countries together, admittedly, but it does gives the 'feel' of the peninsula. And peninsulas are special.]

D. Mack Smith, *Italy* (Michigan Press, 1959).

[Anything on Italy or Sicily by Denis Mack Smith is worth reading.]

R. Flenley, *Modern German History* (Dent, 1968).

[I must confess to lack of expertise on modern books about nineteenth-century German history. This is the best account I know of – which may well say more about me than about the book.]

L. Kochan, *The Making of Modern Russia* (Pelican, 1970, and later).

[It's Pelican, so it won't be too overpowering. And it starts its explanations right back in the ninth century, so you really get to grips with long-term essentials.]

C.A. Macartney, *Hungary: A History* (Edinburgh University Press, 1962).

[Histories of a country like Hungary, with its impenetrable language, are not exactly thick on the ground – not those written in English, that is. So you had better grab this one while the going is good.]

Edmund Curtis, *A History of Ireland* (University Paperback, 1981, one of many editions).

[Irish history is not easy, and the task of the reader is not made any easier by the nationalist and sectarian bias, which has a regular tendency to seep in through the woodwork – in both directions, if you see what I mean.]

R.F. Foster, *Modern Ireland, 1600–1972* (Penguin, 1988).

[Nearly 700 pages of pretty solid analysis and some useful historiographical comment.]

C.M. Woodhouse, *The Greek War of Independence* (Hutchinson).

— *The Battle of Navarino* (Hodder, 1965).

[Mr. Woodhouse is a Greek expert, has lived and worked there, and, I believe, served there during the War.]

Alan Moorehead, *The Blue Nile* (Hamish Hamilton, 1962).

[Early African exploration, Napoleon in Egypt, and Mehemet Ali, and a lot more. A terrific read, but then anything by Alan Moorehead always is.]

S.E. Morison and H.S. Commager (and W.E. Leuchtenburg), *The Growth of the American Republic* 2 Vols. (Oxford University Press, 1969).

[The great 'Morison and Commager', as it once was – for years the staple diet of all students of American history. Don't be put off by its daunting size. It is written with great elegance and humanity, and should dispel the illusion that all Americans are insular innocents with no understanding of the world outside their own borders. It is also surprisingly manageable – fine testimony to the thesis that the very best are usually the most easily understandable.]

Alistair Cooke, *America* (BBC, 1973).

[A personal view, but immensely readable, as one would expect from such a prolific, pensive and provoking wordsmith. Cooke was intensely proud of the compliment paid to it by the master of American historians, the Samuel Morison above, who said, amongst other intoxicating compliments, 'I should have been proud to have written it myself.']

W. Carrington, *The British Overseas* (Cambridge University Press, 1950).

[If you want to know what was going on in any British territory anywhere in the world, at any time, this is the one you pick up. If you are a glutton for punishment, there is always the *Cambridge History of the British Empire*!]

David Chandler, *The Campaigns of Napoleon* (Weidenfeld & Nicolson, 1967).

[The definitive work, written by the senior lecturer at the Royal Military Academy at Sandhurst, and recently reprinted, incidentally, by the Folio Society.]

R.F. Delderfield, *The Retreat from Moscow* (Hodder, 1967).

[A labour of love by an author with an amateur's passion, but easy to read, as are the other two of his books that I quote lower down.]

E.J. Hobsbawm and G. Rudé, *Captain Swing* (Lawrence and Wishart, 1969).

[Captain Swing was the will-o'-the-wisp who was supposed to be behind all the incidents of rural unrest in the southern counties during the very worst time of agricultural poverty in the early nineteenth century. The book is a serious study, and creaks a little under the weight of statistics, but the sympathy for the poor is there. And you need the figures to realise the depth of misery and the savagery of punishment.]

Robert Hughes, *The Fatal Shore* (Collins Harvill, 1987).

[The Australia convict saga, massively researched – notes and bibliography take up nearly ten per cent of the book – and feelingly written – by an Australian.]

Oliver Ransford, *The Great Trek* (John Murray, 1973).

[What it says – the story of the Boers' 'great escape' from British rule.]

C. Woodham-Smith, *The Great Hunger* (Hamish Hamilton, 1962).

[A sympathetic account of the unimaginable sufferings of the Irish people during the Famine of the late 1840s.]

Karl Meyer and Shareen Brysac, *Tournament of Shadows* (Little Brown and Co., 2001).

[An account of the 'Great Game', the conflict between England and Russia for mastery in the diplomatic life of Asia during the nineteenth – and even the twentieth – centuries. Long, detailed, and engagingly written.]

G.D. Clayton, *Britain and the Eastern Question: Missolonghi to Gallipolli* (University of London Press, 1971).

[Only the first three chapters are relevant to the scope of this book, but the reader may be tempted to take the theme up to the Great War. The books in this series are usually clear and unpretentious, and contain useful date lists.]

Sir Arthur Bryant, *The Years of Endurance*

The Years of Victory

The Age of Elegance (all by Collins, several editions).

[Covering the period from 1793 to 1822. It is fashionable for 'proper' historians to decry Bryant. They love throwing around phrases like 'the most plausible of misinterpreters'. This may be sour grapes because Bryant was very popular at one time, and for all I know still is. Historians as a breed are not, as a rule, charitable to a colleague's nationwide acclaim and readership. It is true that Bryant likes to tell a good story, but so long as one realises that that is what he is doing, why not enjoy it?]

Biographies

[There are hundreds of these, as you might expect, and as any glance at the shelves of a good bookshop will prove. All I can do is mention a few that I happen to know about. They are in no particular order.]

Elizabeth Longford, *Wellington* 2 Vols. (Weidenfeld & Nicolson, 1992).
[Long and detailed, researched and thorough, and written by a family descendant.]

Christopher Hibbert, *Wellington, a Personal History* (HarperCollins, 1997).
[Hugely readable, as are all the books by this author. Try him on subjects like the Gordon Riots – *King Mob*; the Indian Mutiny – *The Great Mutiny*; the Civil War – *Cavaliers and Roundheads*; the Crimean War – *The Destruction of Lord Raglan*; medieval warfare – *Agincourt*, and so on.]

N. Gash, *Wellington Anecdotes: a Critical Survey* (University of Southampton, 1992).
[It is a matter of opinion whether you prefer your good stories to remain

good stories, or whether you like them to be run to earth, and maybe thereby crushed by the trampling of inquiry. But the process is an interesting one.]

Carola Oman, *Nelson* (Hodder & Stoughton, 1950, and several editions since).

[Nelson attracts biographers like flies, and, more recently, detractors too. It may be that his personal reputation will be cut back a bit by the latter breed of historical investigator, but the nit-pickers will have their work cut out to diminish his professional achievement. Books still pour off the presses – take your pick.]

Vincent Cronin, *Napoleon* (Collins, 1971).

[If there are regiments of books written about Nelson and Wellington, there must be whole armies of them written about Napoleon. I pick this one simply because I happen to have read it – right through – and because it shows sides of Napoleon which the more orthodox of political and military biographies do not treat fully – indeed often barely refer to. Try it and see for yourself.]

A.G. Macdonnell, *Napoleon and his Marshals* (Macmillan, 1936).

[Sentiment rules here. I first read this as an 'A' Level student, and have been fond of it ever since. I like the author's style – he wrote *England, their England*, one of the funniest books in the English language – and I responded to the drama of the rise, and often sad fall, of these great individualists, many of them lowly born. They are the classic examples of the world of success and glory that the Great Revolution opened up for anyone with the talent and energy to seize their opportunities and capitalise on them. Sad in this case that the 'world' they opened up was one of warfare and conquest, but the blood still races to read about their huge achievements.]

R.F. Delderfield, *The March of the Twenty-Six* (Hodder & Stoughton, 1962).

[Another study of Napoleon's marshals, by the enthusiast I mentioned above. A writer first and a historian second.]

R.F. Delderfield, *The Golden Millstones* (Weidenfeld & Nicolson, 1964).

[If you want proof of the fact that Napoleon was a Corsican, read this study of his brothers and sisters. Family pride and clan instinct drove him to try and make generals and monarchs out of them, and they nearly all let him down, because they were simply not up to it.]

R.G. Richardson, *Larrey: Surgeon to Napoleon's Imperial Guard* (John Murray, 1973).

[This is one of the books which have stood on my shelves for several years, and which I have always been meaning to read, because it looks as if it should be very interesting. It is written by a doctor, and is taken largely from medical sources, and it is all about the real face of war – the prospect that every soldier faces every time he goes into action. If any reader beats me to it, he or she might like to tell me what they think of it.]

L.T.C. Rolt, *George and Robert Stephenson* (Longman, 1960, Pelican, 1978).

[Written by an engineer with a gift for clear explanation. Mr. Rolt also wrote biographies of two other giants of the Industrial Revolution, Brunel and Telford.]

Philip Ziegler, *King William IV* (Collins, 1971).

[A good read, by this most versatile of biographers. While we are on royal biographies, may I add one more by Christopher Hibbert, mentioned above – on George IV – two volumes of it.]

[Finally in this biography section, for no other reason than that it is about a supremely human and entertaining man...]

Hesketh Pearson, *The Smith of Smiths* (first published in 1934, and since by the Folio Society, 1977).

[In case you don't know, the Revd Sydney Smith, 1771–1845, enjoyed the reputation of being the funniest man in London.]

Contemporary Works

[Not all such works are necessarily heavy going – try one or two of the following books. You can't beat reading what they actually said at the time to get the flavour of the period. Some of these men were professional writers too, which helps. You don't have to read from cover to cover. Now and again an image or a phrase will leap from the page, and the barrier of the years falls away. You can suddenly feel that you have shaken hands with the past.]

Tom Paine, *The Rights of Man* (Everyman edition).

[Paine stated great truths, and often in strikingly simple language. So much of what we take for granted as 'basic rights' had once to be stated and argued for. Here is Paine doing it – it required courage and honesty, and so is noble.]

Edmund Burke, *Reflections on the Revolution in France* (Oxford University Press – World's Classics).

[Burke's views were in many ways the opposite of Paine's, but he stated great truths as well, and deserves study. He too is surprisingly easy to read, and he too deserves respect because he was willing to admit the possibility that he could be wrong.]

Napoleon's *Letters* (Everyman).

[A selection of about 300 of the 60,000-odd letters that the Emperor sent during his reign, illustrating the staggering extent of his industry and of his range of interests and responsibilities.]

William Cobbett, *Rural Rides* (Everyman).

[Cobbett knew his England, and wrote about it with great fluency and fondness. As with Napoleon above, one is in awe at his energy and industry, never mind his skill.]

John Cochrane, *A Pedestrian Journey* (Folio Society, 1983).

[Cochrane was a naval officer who, in 1820, conceived the idea of walking – walking – all the way from Calais to the Kamchatka Peninsula, on the far side of Siberia, which he did. Quite apart from marvelling at the achievement, the reader gets a fascinating insight into the ups and downs of travel in the early part of the nineteenth century.]

Jane Austen, the novels. Thackeray's too.

Charles Dickens, the novels, especially *Oliver Twist* for the workhouses, and *Barnaby Rudge* for the Gordon Riots.

[Because they are so 'old' to us, we might be inclined to think of these books as 'historical' novels. But they are not. They are contemporary, written with the knowledge and sympathy and immediacy of the eyewitness. The details are 'right' because the writers were there – except for *Barnaby*, and even *Barnaby* was only a generation before Dickens was born. Which brings me to historical novels proper.]

Historical Novels

[Historians will tell you that historical novelists always get it wrong, and it is true that the indifferent performers at this craft do the cause of history a disservice because they have not done enough homework, and because they are too keen to produce drama or turn a penny, no matter what the cost. But those who have taken the trouble to master the history, and to master the craft of novelist as well, can do a lot to awaken interest and to create atmosphere. Even if they do sometimes get things wrong, they can persuade you that, in general, that was what it was like. At the very least, they start you on the road.]

C.S. Forester, the 'Hornblower' series of novels. (Michael Joseph)
[The naval war against the French.]
C.S. Forester, *The Gun* and *Death to the French*. (Penguin)
[Two sharp evocations of the hardships of the Peninsular War.]
Bernard Cornwell, the 'Sharpe' series of novels. (HarperCollins)
[The Peninsular War again.]
Alexander Kent, the 'Bolitho' series of novels. (Hutchison)
[Napoleonic Wars at sea.]
Patrick O'Brian, the 'Jack Aubrey' series of novels. (HarperCollins)
[The same.]
Walter Macken, *The Silent People* (Macmillan, 1962).
[The sufferings of the Irish.]

Index